# A GENERATION
# DIVIDED

The New Left,
the New Right,
and the 1960s

Rebecca E. Klatch

UNIVERSITY OF CALIFORNIA PRESS
Berkeley  ·  Los Angeles  ·  London

University of California Press
Berkeley and Los Angeles, California

University of California Press, Ltd.
London, England

Grateful acknowledgment is made for permission to reuse an earlier version of chapter 5, entitled "The Counterculture, the New Left, and the New Right," which appeared in *Qualitative Sociology* 17, no. 3 (1994), and is also revised and reprinted from *Cultural Politics and Social Movements,* edited by Marcy Darnovsky, Barbara Epstein, and Richard Flacks, by permission of Temple University Press, © 1995 by Temple University, All Rights Reserved.

Thanks also for use of the excerpt from *Men in Dark Times* by Hannah Arendt, translated by Richard and Clara Winston, copyright © 1968 by Hannah Arendt and renewed 1996 by Lotte Kohler, reprinted by permission of Harcourt Brace & Company, and for the excerpt from "Little Gidding" in *Four Quartets,* copyright © 1943 by T. S. Eliot and renewed 1971 by Esme Valerie Eliot; reprinted by permission of Harcourt Brace & Company.

Library of Congress Cataloging-in-Publication Data

Klatch, Rebecca E.
   A generation divided : the new left, the new right,
and the 1960s / Rebecca E. Klatch.
     p.    cm.
   Includes index.
    ISBN 0-520-21713-6 (alk. paper).—
ISBN 0-520-21714-4 (alk. paper)
     1. Conservatism—United States.   2. New Left—
United States.   I. Title.
JC573.2.U6K53   1999
320.5'0973'09045—dc21             99-23809
                                CIP

Manufactured in the United States of America
10  9  8  7  6  5  4  3  2  1

For Chuck,
who nourishes my mind, body, and soul

For the Greeks the essence of friendship consisted in discourse. They held that only the constant interchange of talk united citizens in a polis. . . . However much we are affected by the things of the world, however deeply they may stir and stimulate us, they become human for us only when we can discuss them with our fellows. . . . We humanize what is going on in the world and in ourselves only by speaking of it; and in the course of speaking of it we learn to be human.

Hannah Arendt,
*Men in Dark Times*

# CONTENTS

# ILLUSTRATIONS

# ACKNOWLEDGMENTS

I am indebted to a number of people who assisted me throughout the research and writing of this book. Foremost, of course, I am grateful to the activists who told me their stories. To each of you, many thanks for your time, energy, and candor. I hope I have remained true to your words. An additional thank-you to those activists who contributed photos for use in this book. I am also particularly grateful to Dorothy Burlage for our many conversations, all of which have been enlightening and inspiring. I was very fortunate to have the opportunity to interview Aldyn McKean and Dave Jones. Aldyn died of AIDS in 1994 and Dave passed away in 1998.

Many people have given me their insight and help along the way through discussion or written comments on parts of this manuscript. In particular, I would like to thank Bob Alford, Lisa Baldez, Kathleen Blee, Wini Breines, Clay Carson, Steve Cornell, Bill Domhoff, Dick Flacks, Kathleen Gerson, Todd Gitlin, Wally Goldfrank, Harvey Goldman, Beth Haas, Anne Hornsby, Jerry Karabel, David Karen, Paul Lichterman, Mike Macy, Doug McAdam, Katherine McClelland, Carl Oglesby, Michael Shifter, Dana Takagi, and Norma Wikler. My perspective also continues to be enriched by conversations with David Riesman. I am especially indebted to Arlene Kaplan Daniels, who offered me her sociological wisdom and support in shaping the final manuscript. The transformation of this manuscript into a book greatly benefited from the knowledge and vision of Naomi Schneider as well as the expertise and support of Sue

Heinemann, both at the University of California Press. The keen eye and proficient copyediting skills of Edith Gladstone were also essential to the production of this book.

Institutional support for this project came from a number of sources: the American Association of University Women, the Stanford Humanities Center, the Rockefeller Foundation, the American Philosophical Society, the National Endowment for the Humanities, and the University of California. In addition, I would like to thank my research assistants, Donna Hunt, Robert Bulman, Tom Reifer, and Meika Loe, and a special thanks to Judy Burton, who spent hours and hours transcribing the interview tapes. Thanks, too, to Fred Faust and Mike Macy for providing me with materials from SDS and to Chris Long for access to YAF materials.

I also am grateful to a number of people who housed me while I traveled to conduct interviews: Wendy Garen, Angela Miller, Jerry Karabel and Krista Luker, David Karen and Katherine McClelland, Todd Gitlin, Ruth Rosen, and my dear friend from the 1960s, Suzie Lerner-Cohen.

Finally, this would have been a very different book without the support and perspective provided by my family. My husband, Chuck, has sustained me in innumerable ways throughout this project and always offers the necessary balance of good humor, nurturance, and cool-headed reason. Eternal thanks for your patience with me throughout this process, for your willingness and enthusiasm at reading each draft, and for being a gourmet cook, sustaining me in the most basic of ways.

Given that the subject of this book is generations, I have faced a peculiar set of personal circumstances that parallel this subject during the research and writing of this book as I married, gave birth to two children, and faced each of my parent's deaths. Thus, this book inevitably brought me to terms with the passage of time, with entry into a different stage of life, and with the transition to parenthood. So much of what is intriguing about having children is the elusiveness of generations, the knowledge that just as our children can never truly know the world from which we came, so as parents we must accept that by virtue of history they live in a world apart. So finally, for my own children, Maurice and Olivia, I owe eternal thanks for continually renewing my perspective. I learn from you daily, in ways both mundane and sacred, truths about the cycles of generations.

# INTRODUCTION

When people think of "the sixties," they commonly associate the era with civil rights protest, with the student, antiwar, and feminist movements, and with the rise of the New Left. Yet the untold story of the 1960s is about the New Right. While thousands of youth did join protests on the left, thousands of others mobilized on the right. Many of today's conservative leaders came of age during the 1960s and became politically active during their college years through participation in Young Americans for Freedom (YAF), a youth organization founded at the estate of William F. Buckley. Ironically, YAF began in 1960, the same year as Students for a Democratic Society (SDS), one of the primary organizations of the New Left. For youth on the right, the 1960s was not simply an era of antiwar demonstrations, women's liberation, hippies, marijuana, and rock festivals. As Lee Edwards, one of the founders of YAF, recalls,

> For me, as for most young conservatives, the '60s was the decade not of John F. Kennedy but Barry M. Goldwater, not SDS but YAF, not *The New Republic* but *National Review,* not Herbert Marcuse but Russell Kirk, not Norman Mailer but Ayn Rand, not Lyndon Johnson's Great Society but Ronald Reagan's Creative Society, not a "meaningless" civil war in Vietnam but an important battle in the protracted conflict against Communism. For us, the '60s began not with a bang but with a book, *The Conscience of a Conservative* by Barry Goldwater.[1]

YAF played a key role in enlisting thousands of youth in the Gold-water campaign and into the conservative movement. As one YAF activist commented early in the 1960s,

> We want to create a training ground now on campuses for articulate and effective conservative leaders. No matter what SDS says, it's not the kids who rule the world, it's the adults, and this is foremost in our minds. We're thinking of the future, and what we're doing now won't be felt for another five years. But we're going to be felt and we're going to be felt strong.[2]

His words were prophetic. Many key leaders of the New Right, including Howard Phillips, Richard Viguerie, and Connie Marshner, were members of YAF during the 1960s. Hundreds of other YAF activists from the 1960s are in Washington today, in Congress and other government agencies, heading conservative organizations and think tanks, and serving as political consultants and leaders.[3]

This book seeks to recast the way people think about the 1960s by viewing the decade as a time of ferment for the right as well as the left. Idealistic youth from one end of the political spectrum to the other formed movements to reshape American politics. Whereas youth on the left came into ascendancy during the 1960s and early 1970s, the other wing of this generation came into prominence during the mid-1970s and 1980s and began to take over the seats of institutional power. The 1960s must be seen, then, within this larger context: not only as fostering protests on the left, but also as nurturing a new generation of leaders on the right. Much of the conservative backlash of the 1970s and 1980s was led by people of the same age as leftist activists, not the older generation.

This book is not a history of the 1960s, nor is it an organizational study of SDS and YAF.[4] Instead, it is a story about two wings of one generation: their relationships, their tensions, their compatibilities, their fates. Starting with their early upbringing, I trace the lives of seventy-four SDS and YAF activists from their political awakenings into their involvement and commitment during the 1960s, through the radicalization many activists faced as their lives changed dramatically over the course of the decade. How did these particular youth get drawn into politics? What happened to them once they became "political"? And after the 1960s ended, how did activism shape their adult lives in terms of political beliefs and commitment, work, and family?

At first glance youth on the left and the right, with their diametrically opposed views of the world, seem to have little in common. Yet there are striking parallels to their stories. Activists in both groups were serious and idealistic, deeply committed to their principles, and dedicated to creating social change. All shared a passion for politics that formed the core of their lives and became central to their identity. Even more remarkable, during the course of the 1960s overlapping interests brought together segments of the left and the right as some members of YAF and SDS discovered common bonds of ideology and action.

## THE PROBLEM OF GENERATIONS

Karl Mannheim's essay "The Problem of Generations" was the original inspiration for this study. Many years ago I read Mannheim's essay and found it intriguing. He argued that people in the same age group share a historical location in the same way that people of the same class share a social location. In Mannheim's words, their common generational location limits them to "a specific range of potential experience, [which] predispos[es] them for a certain characteristic mode of thought and experience, and a characteristic type of historically relevant action."[5] Like classes, generations represent an objective condition, regardless of whether individuals consciously recognize their commonality. What must be understood is under which conditions people of particular generations develop a subjective consciousness of their location, thereby becoming a potential force of social change.

Mannheim proposed that youth, defined as ages seventeen to twenty-five, is the decisive period during which early impressions coalesce into a "natural view of the world." For a generation to become an actuality, young people must participate in a common destiny. During depressions, wars, and other periods of rapid social change, crucial group experiences act as "crystallizing agents," binding people of the same age into "generation-units." But, Mannheim cautions, while youth encounter the same historical changes, they "work up" the material of these common experiences in different ways. Variations in social background predispose people to interpret events differently. Hence, within any generation there exist separate and even antagonistic generation-units. These polar tendencies form a dynamic relationship of tension. At the same time that they are in conflict, they are also oriented toward one another; their antagonisms are part of an ongoing conversation. And as antagonistic generation-units in an epoch interpret their world in terms of one another, we must view them in relationship to one another.

A few years after reading this essay, I thought of Mannheim's ideas while I was studying women of the New Right.[6] Much to my surprise, I discovered that many of the women on the right I interviewed during the 1980s came of age during the 1960s; they were the same generation as leftists and feminists I knew. This coincidence sparked my interest in returning to Mannheim's essay and comparing the experiences of young activists of the left and right. I began to wonder how people could have lived through the same set of dramatic events and interpreted them in such radically different ways. When I began reading the literature on the 1960s, I found that although many analysts used Mannheim's ideas to understand the 1960s generation, they paid little attention to the notion of *intra*generational conflict.

Rather, one of the main questions researchers asked in analyzing the 1960s was, Why did young people mobilize during the 1960s but not during the 1940s or 1950s? In Mannheim's terms, what historical or social conditions were the catalyzing agents by which generational unity was forged? Many analysts took up this question, pointing to important structural and historical changes to explain the emergence of generational politics. These studies are instructive in understanding the conditions that fostered youth protest of the 1960s. Of key import was the demographic impact of the postwar baby boom. The coming-of-age of the baby boom generation meant that young Americans aged 14 to 24 grew to an unprecedented population of 40 million by 1970, an increase of 52 percent from the number of youth in 1960.[7] It is not simply that there were so many more young people. Young people of this era faced a unique set of historical circumstances. For one thing, a growing number of youth encountered an unprecedented prolongation of adolescence during the period between high school and their first job or marriage.[8] Erikson calls this period a "psycho-social moratorium," a time free from the pressures and commitments of adulthood.[9]

Connected to this, the work of developmental psychologists confirms Mannheim's contention that this stage in the life cycle is a particularly fertile time for intellectual and political growth. The findings of Piaget, Kohlberg, and Erikson all indicate that youth is a crucial time period for the development of critical thinking skills, the formation of moral beliefs, and the resolution of the identity crisis, conditions necessary to the formation of political ideology.[10]

An additional factor that affected youth of the 1960s was the extension of higher education to a greater percentage of the population. Ryder argues that the long period during which individuals are embedded in age-segregated schools breaks the grip of the family and provides ample opportunity for a cohort to identify as a historical entity.[11] Further, as centers of critical thinking, colleges have a crucial role in fostering questions about the social and political policies of the times. University life also provides a built-in means of communication and a base for organizing, essential ingredients in political mobilization.[12] Other significant factors in the formation of the 1960s leftist youth protest include the effects of affluence on the development of "post-materialist" values, the significance of growing up in the nuclear age, and the spread of youth culture.[13]

Previous studies have used Mannheim's ideas to understand youth protest of the 1960s but focused only on youth of the left.[14] Yet all the factors contributing to generational unity apply also to youth on the right. In fact, there has been a tendency to neglect right-wing movements in general among most social movement scholars.[15] Fewer still systematically compare the left and right. My study is unique in charting activists from two opposing movements over time, tracing the lives and political "careers" of both left- and right-wing activists. In doing so, I explore the contexts in which activists move across ideological divides, the complicated and at times unpredictable nature of political commitment and allegiances.

In short, generations are not monolithic. As Rintala puts it, "Each generation speaks out with more than one voice."[16] Given the importance of YAF to young conservatives of the 1960s, future leaders of the New Right, we need to know how the enormous social changes of the 1960s shaped and polarized people of the same cohort, causing left- and right-wing groups to understand these events in radically different ways.

## RELATED THEMES: IDENTITY, GENDER, AND CONVERGENCE

I began this project to examine the intracohort differences between activists who joined SDS and YAF. In Mannheim's terms, I wanted to know how individuals on opposite sides of the political spectrum "worked up" their experiences of the 1960s. What were the lines of division between youth of the left and right? Besides analyzing the divisions within the 1960s generation, this book also focuses on three related themes.

### Formation of Political Identity

Fundamental to this book is the exploration of political identity. When I speak of *identity* here I am referring to an individual or personal identity that defines a person as a social actor. In answer to the question "Who am I?" it conveys a sense of "the real me." Individual identity is necessarily a social identity. It is the situated self.[17] Individuals gain a sense of identity by locating themselves within a meaningful social world and seeking recognition within this web of social relationships.[18] The base of identity is "a deep communality with others"[19] that comes through membership in a collectivity. The individual self encompasses multiple identities, which it continually reproduces through interaction with others. As Hunt, Benford, and Snow put it, identities are "interactional accomplishments."[20] A person, for example, may simultaneously identify as a woman, a young adult, an artist, a kind and sensitive, caring person, and a Democrat. Some identities become more salient than others at particular stages of life. Of particular importance here is the social construction of *political* identity, the ways that political identities shift over time and are shaped through interaction with others.

Recent discussions in social movements have highlighted the importance of political identity. But analysts often use identity only in reference to "identity politics" associated with the "new social movements,"[21] failing to recognize the essential role of identity in all movements. Or they completely fuse individual identity with "collective identity."[22] I am less concerned with the construction of the collective identity of SDS or YAF per se—the organizational ideology, goals, and tactics of these social movement organizations—than the intertwining of an individual self with a political movement. Obviously, individual political identity necessarily overlaps with the collective identity of a movement, the sense of "we-ness" of the group. Fundamental to the process of becoming an activist is incorporating this collective group identity,[23] although as we shall see this fusion of individual and group identity is rarely fixed or complete.

This book examines the micro-level processes by which individuals construct a core self that is political. It is an ethnography of political socialization over the life course. Whereas most studies of social movement participation take mobilization as a starting place, this book begins with the development of political consciousness during childhood. The people it describes are not typical everyday citizens. Rather, from an early age they interested themselves in politics. As their commitment grew, they came to define themselves through their political activism. How do people become political? How does politics become part of a core identity? These are questions I consider in chapters 2 and 3.

In exploring these questions, we see parallels across the political landscape in how activist identities develop, strengthen, or dissipate over the years. The life histories of these activists illustrate in a vivid way the social processes that contribute to the formation of the self. For activists on both the left and the right, other people—parents and other family members, neighbors and community leaders, teachers, and other role models—fostered an interest in politics and shaped the development of political beliefs.

Moreover, once people began identifying as "political," beliefs continued to evolve. Berger and Luckman state, "Identity is formed by social processes. Once crystallized, it is maintained, modified or even reshaped by social relations."[24] As activists bonded to others of similar views, peers played a particularly important role in solidifying commitment and reformulating beliefs (chapter 4). Through ongoing conversations, organizational meetings, and pamphlets and position papers, they continued to develop their ideas.

In addition, experiences during collective action also transformed belief. As we will see, for leftists and for libertarians on the right, incidents during the 1960s, such as exposure to police brutality during demonstrations, radicalized activists, reinforcing their commitment to the movement while also altering their beliefs. This process similarly occurs through interaction with others. Strauss notes,

> [T]he same kinds of incidents that precipitate the revision of identity are extremely likely to befall and to be equally significant to other persons of the same generation, occupation, and social class. This is equivalent to saying that insofar as experiences and interpretations are socially patterned, so also will be the development of personal identities.[25]

The experiences and interpretations that altered the identities of libertarians and leftists during the late 1960s led to a relabeling of the self. Many people began adopting terms such as "radical," "revolutionary," and "anarchist" to describe such changes. These terms were not merely new labels; rather, they signified a shift in identity and they located individuals within a community of shared views.

Besides studying the transformation of identity over the course of the 1960s, this book also examines how political beliefs and commitment carry over to adult lives. As adults, do activists hold the same views and values? If so, do they continue to act politically? If not, what identities or issues "compete" with politics to pull individuals away from activism? Contrary to popular assumptions, leftists did not "sell out" at the end of the 1960s, becoming bankers and businessmen, and abandoning their beliefs as the country moved from the turmoil of the 1960s to the new political climate of the late 1970s and the 1980s. While most people on both the left and the right maintained their beliefs and values as adults, among those who did change, *it was right-wing activists who moved left-ward*, not the reverse (chapters 8 and 9). There are, however, striking differences in how activists adapted to their lives as adults during the 1970s, as well as differences in the current positions and lifestyles of activists on the left and right.

### The Influences of Gender

This book also compares the experiences of women and men. Few studies consider the experiences and voices of female activists. Those that do focus on the secondary status of women within the New Left show the links between New Left women and those who formed feminist organizations of the late 1960s and 1970s.[26] In my interviews I expected to hear similar grievances about sexism in the movement. Instead, I discovered that while many SDS women did perceive inequality, a minority of them found no differences in treatment based on gender, saying they felt respected by men in the movement. Their feminism grew in reaction to women's inequality in society, not out of discontent over women's secondary status within SDS.

On the right, even fewer studies pay attention to female activists.[27] When I began this work, I wanted to know, first of all, if there were any differences in the early gender socialization of women on the right and left. Second, I wanted to know if women in YAF perceived any sexism within the organization. As with SDS women, I found a division among YAF women. While the majority denied discrimination, praising the men in YAF for their fair treatment and for welcoming them to the organization, a minority did perceive sexism within the movement and criticized men on the right. What explains why some women on the left and right perceived discrimination while others say women were treated as equals? Why did some women in both SDS and YAF readily embrace feminism while others were ambivalent or even opposed it. Chapter 6 examines these issues and identifies conditions that foster women's feminist consciousness.

### The Overlap between the Left and the Right

This book is not only about the differences between youth of the left and right. It is also about the convergence between sectors of the left and right, the values and interests that bind together the two wings of the 1960s generation. What was the common ground between YAF and SDS activists? In particular, opposition to the Vietnam War and hostility toward the state forged bonds between sectors of the left and the libertarian right during the late 1960s. In addition, the counterculture became a dividing line within *both* SDS and YAF, with some members of each organization adamantly opposed to the counterculture, while others embraced youth culture in beliefs and lifestyle (chapter 5).

By the late 1960s both YAF and SDS were torn apart by internal divisions. The 1969 national conventions of both organizations proved to be pivotal. The final explosive SDS convention in 1969 resulted in the splintering of the organization and the demise of SDS. The 1969 YAF convention erupted in intense verbal—and even physical—confrontation, primarily over the Vietnam War. When one young libertarian burned his draft card on the convention floor, the crowd turned into an angry mob and, ultimately, purged all libertarians from YAF. One libertarian faction stormed out of the meeting, denouncing "domestic fascism" and calling for resistance to the Vietnam War, legalization of marijuana, and unity with SDS.

One of the consequences of this purge of libertarians from YAF was the blossoming of an independent movement of libertarians. A multitude of newsletters and organizations flourished during the 1970s, including the Libertarian Party, which began in 1973. Some of these groups sought out those with sympathetic views on the left, trying to build a common movement. This overlap between the left and right speaks to the peculiarities of American political ideology. Specifically, an affinity for values such as individual freedom, the impulse against bureaucracy and big government, the questioning of centralized authority, and the embrace of decentralization and local control are common to both left and right. These shared concerns made possible a fragile but intriguing unity among them during the late 1960s and early 1970s (chapter 7). Further, in their post-1960s lives, libertarians resemble leftists more than traditionalists in terms of lifestyle and careers.

Analysis of the overlaps and parallels as well as the differences between left and right and between women and men leads to a more nuanced understanding of ideology and of social movements. Rather than monolithic sets of political ideologies, I argue, they are fluid, ever-changing, and responsive to social and historical context. Rather than a flat movement/countermovement relationship, the complex intersection of New Left and New Right yields unexpected results. The emergence of the libertarian movement at the end of the 1960s was a "hybrid movement," drawing from both left and right. Similarly, the feminist movement of the 1970s attracted constituencies from both YAF and SDS. In short, it is not simply conflict that characterizes the relationship of left and right, but also occasional arenas of common interest and shared activism.

## METHODS OF RESEARCH

I used two methodological approaches in this study: field research and archival research. The fieldwork includes both life histories and participant-observation.

### Life Histories

I conducted life histories with seventy-four former activists: seventeen of the thirty-four women came from YAF and the other seventeen from SDS; of the forty men, nineteen were from SDS and twenty-one from YAF.[28] Given my previous research for *Women of the New Right*, I already had numerous contacts on the right. I used these contacts, names of activists I found through archival research on YAF's history, and snowball sampling to locate YAF activists. For SDS I used both personal and professional contacts, location of activists through leftist reunions, and snowball sampling. Because my aim was to gather a diverse sample, I limited the number of names drawn from any one contact. The interviews took place from July 1989 to June 1991. Each interview lasted from one to four hours, and I interviewed some people twice. In addition, phone calls and correspondence from 1997 to 1998 brought me current information about the lives of many activists in the sample.

All people in this study were active for at least two years in SDS or YAF. Although I made a serious attempt to diversify the sample, because both organizations were primarily white, all activists I interviewed are white except for three black SDS activists and one black YAF activist. I also selected people based on the following criteria: geographic diversity of activism in varying locations across the country; position among the rank-and-file as well as leadership of SDS and YAF;[29] early involvement (activists who joined from 1960 to 1964) as well as later (those who joined from 1965 to 1968).[30] Finally, I wanted the sample to reflect the ideological diversity within each organization. The YAF activists include twenty-five traditionalists and thirteen libertarians. This sample approximates the representation of libertarians in YAF during the 1960s, estimated to be between one-quarter to one-third of YAF membership.[31] For SDS ideological diversity meant including people identified with the different factions within SDS during the late 1960s. The sample includes five Progressive Labor members or sympathizers, five Weatherman members or sympathizers, and two Revolutionary Youth Movement-II members or sympathizers. The majority of SDS interviewees were either unaffiliated with any faction during the 1969 splits (twelve activists), or were uninvolved in SDS politics by 1969 (twelve activists).

My in-depth interviews focused on four sets of issues. The first took up the demographic backgrounds of activists and their parents, parents' political and religious beliefs, family dynamics, and early political and gender socialization. The second set of issues centered on political involvement and organizational experiences as well as the development of ideology. The third set of questions focused on interpretations of key events of the 1960s, for example, the 1964 and 1968 elections; the Vietnam War; the assassinations of John F. Kennedy, Robert Kennedy, and Martin Luther King Jr.; views of the U.S. government and the counterculture. Finally, questions about activists' lives since the 1960s concerned shifts in political beliefs and commitment, as well as changes in occupation, religiosity, and lifestyle (marriage and children).

After transcribing the interviews, I spent eight months coding the nearly ten thousand pages of transcript data. I culled this rich and complex set of data in order to analyze the salient forces that explain the development of activists' political identity, looking for similarities and differences by gender and ideology both within and between organizations. Although the framing of people's lives appears smooth in this text, as if motivation and meaning are self-evident to the activists, in actuality it was only through working and reworking the data, and extracting common patterns in these subjective accounts, that I discovered the essential elements of identity formation and transformation.

These face-to-face interviews were essential to answer the types of questions posed in this study. The thrust of my research aims at analyzing the development and evolution of political ideology and the enduring impact of political commitment. Such processes are best understood through analysis of life histories. Because the individuals selected for this study are committed activists, they do not represent the general population of youth who came of age during the 1960s. They belong to the "generation of the 1960s" as Mannheim understands it: the portion of this generation that dedicated themselves to social and political change during that era. While many more youth attended occasional demonstrations or meetings, the individuals here are distinct in their sustained involvement in politics.

Furthermore, given the small sample of women and men interviewed, it would be impossible to make any conclusive statements about *all* right- or left-wing youth. Rather, this study aims more modestly at analyzing the similarities and differences that characterize activists from two of the leading organizations of the left and right. Although the findings here are suggestive of more general tendencies, any final statements about 1960s activists as a whole need to rely on a much larger representative sample.

### Participant-Observation

In addition to the interviews, I also attended three reunions of leftist activists: the twentieth reunion of the Harvard-Radcliffe Strike (April 7–8, 1989), the April 3d Movement twentieth reunion at Stanford University, a gathering of Stanford activists against the Vietnam War (May 6, 1989), and the twenty-year commemoration of the 1968 Democratic Convention in Chicago (August 27–28, 1988). I also attended the twentieth anniversary banquet of the Society for Individual Liberty, which marked the birth of an autonomous libertarian movement, held in Philadelphia (August 30, 1989), and the 1989 annual convention of the Libertarian Party in Philadelphia (August 31–September 3, 1989). These meetings were informative both in terms of framing issues of continuity and change articulated by participants as they reflected over the past twenty-five years, as well as in gathering names of activists to interview.

### Archival Materials

I also examined organizational materials of SDS and YAF. The SDS papers consist of forty reels of microfilm encompassing all the documents printed by SDS throughout its history. YAF also has extensive documents (pamphlets, correspondence, papers, etc.) at its headquarters in Washington, D.C. In addition, I was fortunate to spend a year examining collections of archival materials of both the left and the right at the Hoover Archives at Stanford University. Archival materials were useful in understanding the ideological and organizational development of SDS and YAF, as well as in finding background materials on some of the activists interviewed. Textual analysis also located common themes as well as lines of division between the left and right. Archival collections used in this research are listed in Appendix A.

### Retrospective Memory

Finally, let me comment on the validity of using retrospective memory. One common concern raised with life histories is the problem of relying on people reflecting back on their lives through the prism of the present. How do accumulated experiences over the years as well as present beliefs affect these accounts? There is a rich and well-established tradition of using life histories in sociology, a method that has been fundamental to field research from the Chicago school onward. As for research on the 1960s, numerous follow-up studies of activists on the left employ retrospective memory through oral histories.[32]

The purpose of such accounts is not a factual documentation of history. Rather, life histories are necessarily subjective processes, providing insight into how people think about important events and experiences in their lives. The focus throughout this study has been subjective interpretations of activists' lives. Its aim is to use these accounts in understanding the formation of identity and the construction of meaning in individual lives.

Memories illuminate how individuals shape and reshape their identities. As recent scholarship on memory indicates, both biologists and psychologists now envision all memory operating as a subjective construction made of multiple associations, rather than a retrieval of objective representations of the past.[33] Memory is a cognitive device by which actors seek to interpret the reality they've lived.[34] People remember a particular event or experience because it had significance for them. As Gittins states, "The very process of selection in recollection provides in itself important historical data . . . what someone remembers can be a good indicator of what has been most important to that person over time."[35] Each of us reconstructs and reinterprets our past experiences in order to make sense of our lives. This act necessarily involves placing prior experiences in a larger framework and conceptualizing patterns that were not apparent at the time. Andrews points out, "It is clear that when an individual looks back over her life, she makes connections between events and situations which she would not have had the perspective to make at the time that she lived through them."[36] In short, retrospective memory is essential to come to terms with the past, to provide a framework of interpretation. These memories give a sense of continuity, a web of meaning to individual lives. Oral history, then, is a record of perceptions, rather than a re-creation of historical events. Its value is in recovering levels of experiences and understanding perceptions. As Hareven puts it, this is precisely the great value of oral histories, rather than their limitation.[37]

Acknowledging the value of memories, we also try to make sure that oral history's content has a reliable correspondence with real events. Hence the field-worker's job is to build as many checks on validity as possible. One way to do this is to ask questions that probe particular events. In these interviews I asked about a series of historical and political events in order to prod people's memory and to place them in the past. A second way to calibrate life histories is to cross-check interview material with data gathered from other interviews. A third is to use other sources of data to check validity. This study relies not only on life histories, but also on a separate set of data based on archival research. These archival materials allowed me to closely follow the development of a number of the individuals in my sample as well as to analyze the meaning of particular events during that era. At no point did any of the experiences related here fundamentally contradict the known historical accounts of documented events of the 1960s. Further, chapters 8 and 9, which discuss activists' lives since the 1960s up to the present, indicate that these individuals are not simply rewriting history through their present views. In fact, during the past ten to fifteen years some of them have experienced shifts in perspectives, yet in the interviews they still reported the way they saw things then, not simply through the lens of their present opinions.

In short, claims that life histories are based on retrospective memory and subjective accounts are true; whether they yield valid data depends on the purposes of the research. If the aim is, as it is here, to understand and compare constructions of meaning, the use of life histories is not only a beneficial way to collect data; it is really the only means to accurately and fully understand the pathways of individual lives.

In writing this book I have had a running debate in my mind about whether or not to discuss my own involvement during the 1960s. My first impulse was not to comment at all on what I was doing during the 1960s, fearing that anything I said would immediately color the reader's perceptions, leading to assumptions about some hidden agenda or bias on my part. Yet recent commentary, particularly by feminist methodologists,[38] argues for the importance of breaking the norm of invisibility by placing the author's voice into the text. To this end I explain that I came of age at the end of the 1960s and participated in antiwar demonstrations during high school in Chicago. Later, while living in Berkeley, I joined groups affiliated with the student movement, the New Left, and the women's movement. Certainly my own beliefs have shaped the questions I've asked (and have no doubt entered into my research in ways unknown to me), but as much as possible I have tried to set aside my own assumptions in listening to the stories of activists on all sides. My interest throughout this endeavor has been to understand how people both similar and different from myself came into political consciousness and how their ideas and involvement developed and changed over the course of their lives. I leave it to the reader to decide whether I have carried out this task in a fair and even-handed manner.

Finally, let me comment on the difficulty of writing about the 1960s. It is always difficult to write about "an age" or to capture the "Zeitgeist" of an era. The sixties are particularly problematic because of the wealth of events and experiences that took place in such rapid succession and because of the abundance of commentaries that already have been written about the decade. Further, given the multitude of voices from the 1960s, trying to analyze this period from multiple vantage points has been a fearsome task. Any reading of the sixties is necessarily partial; no single portrayal can ever capture the decade in its totality. I will be content if this effort refocuses our view of the era, capturing the tensions, contradictions, and complexities of people's beliefs, and illustrating the inextricable bonds between activists of the left and the right as they tried to shape the country's future.

## THE STAGE, THE ACTORS, AND THEIR WORLDS

The structure of this book is partly chronological and partly topical. Chapter 1 sets the stage by tracing the origins of SDS and YAF and comparing the founding principles of each organization. Youth in both groups encountered parallel processes of disillusionment as their ideals of America clashed with the realities of American life during the 1950s. Chapter 2 explores the backgrounds of activists and their families, contrasting the social worlds of youth of the left and right. Not only are members of SDS and YAF from different worlds, but within YAF traditionalists and libertarians stand apart in terms of social background and upbringing. Chapter 3 analyzes the catalysts to activism: the people, experiences, and historical events that provoked youth to dedicate themselves to making social change as politics became central to their identity. Chapter 4 focuses on the continuing politicization of activists as commitment intensified. Radicalization of leftists and libertarians also led to shifts in ideology and a transformation of identity. Chapters 5 through 7 examine varying divisions that occurred within SDS and YAF during the late 1960s, creating common ground between the left and right. Chapter 5 examines how and why the counterculture divided activists within SDS and YAF; at the same time the counterculture brought the worlds of the left and right together. In particular, the use of drugs unified elements of the left and right as they became enemies of the state and shared a common impulse toward personal freedom. Chapter 6 explains the divisions within both SDS and YAF over "the woman question," over whether women were first- or second-class citizens. Despite objective evidence of male dominance in each group, there was a split among women in each group in their subjective perceptions of discrimination. I argue that these differences are due primarily to organizational factors and to the availability of a language to identify inequality. Chapter 7 examines the ideological conflicts that ripped apart SDS and YAF during the late 1960s as activists became polarized and each organization faced factionalization. At the same time, these divisions increasingly drew together sectors of the left and right through common interests and participation. Chapters 8 and 9 explore the lives of activists in the aftermath of the 1960s. Chapter 8 traces the pathways of activists during the 1970s as they emerged from the 1960s and entered adult life. Chapter 9 explores the adult lives of activists during the 1980s and 1990s, examining the ways that libertarians and leftists followed different trajectories from traditionalists in terms of occupations and lifestyle. Although politics remains central to the identity of both SDS and YAF members, as they've aged the competing interests of work and family have pulled many people away from activism. Finally, I look at the children of activists as we come full circle in the formation of political identity.

Unreferenced quotations from activists come from my own interviews. For those who chose to remain anonymous, I have used pseudonyms throughout the book to maintain continuity. The list of interviews, including both identified individuals and those with pseudonyms, is in Appendix B.

# CHAPTER ONE

# THE NEW AGE

"Let the word go forth from this time and place, to friend and foe alike, that the torch has been passed to a new generation of Americans." As President John F. Kennedy spoke of the new generation in his inaugural address of 1961, two organizations of young activists were forming. These two groups, Young Americans for Freedom (YAF) and Students for a Democratic Society (SDS), produced a generation of individuals who were to have a profound effect on the political landscape of their country. Among the multitude of leftist organizations that sprang up during the 1960s, SDS was the leading organization of the New Left. Rather than being a single-issue organization, SDS embraced a range of issues including civil rights, welfare reform, opposition to the war in Vietnam, and students' rights. While over the decade of the 1960s far fewer right-wing organizations mobilized, YAF was the most prominent student group at the conservative end of the spectrum. Like SDS, YAF was a multi-issue organization, dedicated to anticommunism and the promotion of free enterprise. During the 1960s YAF mobilized on many issues diametrically opposed to SDS: against campus demonstrators, unions, and expansion of the welfare state, and in support of the war in Vietnam. The legacy of these two groups, however, is not simply measured by the political causes they promoted. Throughout the 1960s both SDS and YAF educated thousands of youth into a larger perspective of the world, inspiring and training young people to take on leadership roles, to organize their communities, to build a movement embodying their beliefs.

Each group left behind thousands of activists who were dedicated to con-tinuing their efforts toward creating social change. How did YAF and SDS form? What were the visions and ideals of the individuals who founded these two groups? What were the lines of division as well as the parallels between these two wings of the 1960s generation?

## SEEDS FOR CHANGE

YAF was founded in the shadow of the Cold War. The launching of the Soviet sputnik in 1957 provoked President Dwight D. Eisenhower to ob-tain congressional approval to set up the National Defense Education Act. Intended to encourage young Americans to become more proficient in science, mathematics, and physics, the 1958 act instituted a program of loans to foster American advancement in fields related to technical pro-gress. Included in the act was a provision requiring all recipients of funds to sign a loyalty oath to the country. The loyalty clause immediately be-came controversial; Harvard and Yale, for example, withdrew from the loan program in protest.

In a counterresponse to opposition to the oath, in December 1959 Doug Caddy, a student at Georgetown University, and David Franke, a student at George Washington University, established the National Stu-dent Committee for a Loyalty Oath. Both were members of the Intercol-legiate Studies Institute, a scholarly group set up to disseminate conser-vative ideas;[1] both also had affiliations with Young Republicans.[2] They began to notify members of each organization, telling them about their new association. In the process, young conservatives across the country came into contact with other activists of similar views.

The network of people Franke and Caddy assembled came together in July 1960. In the aftermath of the Republican National Convention in Chicago, Caddy and Franke met with these young conservative leaders, as well as with activists from the Youth for Goldwater for Vice President campaign. Inspired by Goldwater's suggestion that conservative youth ini-tiate a national organization, the group formed a thirteen-person interim committee to discuss setting up a conference to plan such an organiza-tion, with Caddy serving as director. They arranged a meeting for Sep-tember 9–11 in Sharon, Connecticut, at the family estate of William F. Buckley.[3]

Conservative student leaders were contacted, informing them of the upcoming conference. Alan MacKay, for instance, a law student at Harvard, was circulating petitions in support of the loyalty oath at the time. He dryly comments, "The first signature we got was Attila the Hun. The second was Adolph Hitler. We were regarded as being total Neanderthals. But that encouraged me to react more." Soon Alan received an invitation to Sharon and made preparations to attend.

Meanwhile across the country in Ann Arbor early in 1960 Al Haber[4] met with other members of the Student League for Industrial Democracy to discuss plans for turning it into a new organization of leftist youth. As the youth affiliate of the League for Industrial Democracy (LID),[5] they felt a need to break with the older leadership. Believing "industrial democracy" was too narrow a term, which hampered campus organizing, they debated changing the organization's name to "Student League for Effective Democracy," "Students for Social Democracy," or "National Student Forum"; finally, the young leaders decided on "Students for a Democratic Society."[6]

One of the first events planned by SDS was a conference. Held in the spring of 1960, 150 people met to discuss "Human Rights in the North." Among those attending the conference was Bob Ross, an undergraduate at the University of Michigan. Bob was unaffiliated with the student organization but already active on campus. In the days following the lunch counter sit-ins in Greensboro, North Carolina, in February 1960, Bob joined the sympathy pickets of Woolworth's in the North supporting civil rights. At about the same time he noticed an ad in the *Michigan Daily* for the SDS conference; Bob recalls,

> Michael Harrington and James Farmer spoke, and all the early SNCC [Student Nonviolent Coordinating Committee][7] leaders. . . . A few weeks later I got a call from this guy [Haber]. . . . Basically what Haber was saying [was that] he was graduating, he was leaving Ann Arbor, going to the SDS national office . . . and would we be the chapter? And, by the way, would you come to this national meeting in New York? Yes, yes, yes. So I got involved with SDS. . . . I was not politically experienced at all but . . . he had a vision of a radical movement that made total sense to me. It had to do with young people, it had to do with action. It had centrally, by the way, to do with reason.

The first convention of SDS was held in New York in June 1960. Despite the attendance of only 29 members, lively debates focused on the

purpose of SDS, student radicalism, and civil rights. Haber was elected
president. Total membership of SDS numbered 250, organized into eight
chapters.[8]

Throughout 1960 and 1961 SDS's main activity was civil rights. As
SDS took on an activist role, Haber came up against the older leadership of the League for Industrial Democracy. LID's main interest was
maintaining SDS as an educational organization, rather than an overtly
political one, as well as keeping SDS pure of any Communist influence.
After a conflict in early 1961, during which Haber was fired by the LID
executive committee and then rehired a couple of months later,[9] SDS settled down into organizing campuses. While Haber worked in the national
office in New York, Tom Hayden became field secretary, reporting on civil
rights activities out of Atlanta. By fall 1961 SDS had twenty chapters with
a total membership of 575.[10]

After setting up a national executive committee in December (with
Haber as chair, Bob Ross as vice chair, along with a dozen others on the
committee), Haber suggested SDS should write a manifesto to convey its
view of the world and to articulate a program for SDS's future. Hayden
and a few others were given the task of drafting the manuscript. Plans
were made to hold a conference in June 1962 in Port Huron, Michigan.

### The Sharon Conference

On September 9–11, 1960, over one hundred delegates from forty-four
colleges and universities assembled in Sharon, Connecticut, at the estate
of the conservative leader William F. Buckley. Among those represented
were students from Harvard, Yale, Antioch, the University of Chicago,
Columbia, Tulane, the University of Colorado, and Hunter College.[11]
The prevailing feeling was one of excitement.

Carol Dawson had been active throughout 1959 and 1960 in Young
Republicans as well as in Youth for Nixon (for president). She attended
both the Chicago meeting that planned Sharon and the conference itself.
She recalls the hopefulness and idealism of those at Sharon. "We felt like
pioneers. It was challenging. . . . It was . . . a thrill to travel up there and
be among those people." Alan MacKay also recalls the "glamour of being amidst the likes of Bill Buckley," one of the heroes of conservative
youth.

Lee Edwards, who was working at the time as editor for the national
newspaper of the Young Republican National Federation, describes the

sense of importance at Sharon. "We very definitely had that feeling [of making history]. . . . This was something special. . . . Here we were starting this youth organization with some pretty high-powered people."

Part of the excitement came from the relief of meeting so many others with shared views. Many attending had felt ostracized for being conservative activists on campus, a sense "as usual, of swimming against the current." Thus, as Scott Stanley recalls, the meeting at Sharon evoked "a new spirit . . . a kind of gathering of the clan, like being a black in North Dakota and going to Chicago. . . . We were so glad to discover that there were other unicorns in the valley."

It was not only that those attending felt different from those on campus, but they also felt estranged from their elders in the Republican Party. As Carol Dawson puts it,

> At that time, although most of us were Republicans, the Party didn't exactly welcome us with open arms. . . . We were carrying the flag of conservatism at a time nobody really understood what that meant. A lot of people considered us to be kooks. . . . They wanted to keep their distance from us. That was one of the reasons why we felt motivated to go out and start this other group. We wanted to stay active in the Party, but we wanted to have a way to also express our views independently.

**The Sharon Statement**   One of the main orders of business at Sharon was approval of a statement of principles. Stan Evans, then editor of the *Indianapolis News*, drafted a statement during his plane ride to the conference that became known as "the Sharon Statement." After editing by David Franke and Carol Dawson, the statement was read to the group assembled. The response was a standing ovation. Alan MacKay remembers, "I think there were one or two words changed, but essentially everybody's reaction [was], 'That is just about perfect. That's exactly what we want.'"

The Sharon Statement (see Appendix C) is a one-page generalized declaration of conservative principles and values. It begins, "In this time of moral and political crisis, it is the responsibility of the youth of America to affirm certain eternal truths." Among the truths affirmed are the transcendent values of individual free will and liberty; the inextricable bond between economic and political freedom; the purpose of government as protecting freedom through preservation of internal order, national defense, and the administration of justice; the genius of the Constitution, especially the clause reserving primacy to the states; and the market economy as the single system compatible with freedom. The statement also warns of the dangers of government acting beyond its rightful functions or interfering with the work of the market. Communism is named as the single greatest threat to liberty. The statement concludes by calling for U.S. policy that stresses victory over, rather than coexistence with, the Communist menace. In short, the founding creed pronounces a faith in the free market, constitutional government, and political freedom, and a determination to support resistance to Communist expansionism.[12]

The individuals who came to Sharon were unified in their faith in economic and political liberty and in their fervent anticommunism. Reflecting on the statement, Evans says he intentionally wrote it to incorporate diverse tendencies.

> My belief was, and still is, that differing emphases within the conservative camp are aspects of a single coherent body of thought and the draft was an attempt to show this. . . . In broad terms, the statement was meant to embrace both the "traditionalist" and "libertarian" schools within the conservative community. . . . The statement assumes these emphases are interdependent and that it is impossible to have one without the other.[13]

Although those who attended were unified in their anticommunism, there were also early signs of internal disputes. Lee Edwards recalls a couple of big battles at Sharon. First, there was a battle between the traditional conservatives, who were in the majority, and the libertarians. In particular, this tension produced a "big hullabaloo" over the insertion of "God" in the statement. One clause reads, "foremost among the transcendent values is the individual's use of his God-given free will." Libertarians opposed any mention of God. A vote narrowly passed retaining the word "God" in the draft. Although this dispute was easily settled at Sharon, the differences between traditionalists and libertarians would prove to be pivotal later in the 1960s.

A second debate concerned the name of the organization. Alan MacKay was one of those advocating open acknowledgment of the conservative nature of the organization by adopting the name "Young Conservatives of America." Lee Edwards and others, fearing that they'd be "tagged with the tar of conservatism" anyway, desired a name that was less overt. MacKay recalls, "The sentiment which ultimately prevailed was that we ought to use a neutral name that wouldn't immediately set off bells like American Youth for Freedom or Young Americans for Freedom." In the end, the group decided to call itself Young Americans for Freedom. The fears expressed over naming were connected to a tension some members felt with the far right. Carol Dawson remembers the difficulty some individuals felt about including members who had allegiance to the John Birch Society. "We definitely wanted to be seen as a more responsible, credible group."[14]

Another debate took place over whether to make the maximum age of membership thirty or thirty-five. Edwards, along with several others attending Sharon, was already pushing thirty. After a fairly narrow vote, the group agreed on thirty-five as the age limit. Later the age limit was increased to thirty-nine.

Despite these issues of contention, there was an overriding sense of solidarity. Alan MacKay comments, "Resisting the Communists, resisting the liberals, supporting conservative candidates, organizing conservatives on campus—that's the sort of thing we talked about and there was general agreement. . . . There weren't many conservatives in the country and we realized that. It was therefore easy . . . to get along."

In addition to considering the Sharon Statement, discussions also centered on the organizational structure of YAF. Robert Schuchman, a law student from Yale, was elected to be national chair. Doug Caddy was elected to serve as national director. Among the eleven men elected to the original board of directors were Howard Phillips, Bill Schulz, Scott Stanley, Lee Edwards, and Carl McIntire Jr., the son of the Old Right anti-Communist crusader Rev. Carl McIntire; Carol Dawson was the sole female board member. Six men were elected to be regional representatives.[15]

YAF was set up as a nonpartisan youth group; its aims were mobilizing support among conservative youth for political candidates and legislation, and acting as a voice for conservative opinion "on key issues affecting young people." As Schuchman put it, "We believe an organized and dedicated Conservative youth can nationally affect the course of political events and help Americans attain the free society envisioned by its founders."[16] Reacting against moderate Republicanism, members of YAF were comfortable seeing themselves as a youth group of the *National Review* crowd, very willing to seek and accept the counsel and aid of this older generation of conservatives.

At the end of the conference Scott Stanley recalls the feeling of being convinced that "[w]e were the wave of the future. We arrived as a mist of raindrops and went away a great and crushing wave with lots of press notice." Returning home from the weekend, Alan MacKay remembers telling his parents he had just taken part in a conference "which would either lead to absolutely nothing or would be a historic moment in the history of the country."

## The Port Huron Convention

Over the course of June 11–15, 1962, fifty-nine people arrived in Port Huron, Michigan, with the aim of drafting a statement of principles for SDS. Most of those attending were students; many were active in the civil rights movement. Eight of the eleven chapters of SDS were represented,[17] including delegates from Swarthmore, Johns Hopkins, Oberlin, and Earlham. In addition, there were unaffiliated representatives from Harvard, Yale, Wisconsin, and Indiana.[18]

Pervasive throughout the five days of the conference was a sense of exhilaration and idealism. Barbara Haber (then Jacobs) had been active at Brandeis as treasurer of the Socialist Club and also participated in ban-the-bomb demonstrations and civil rights activities. She recalls,

> It was a tremendous amassing of political experience at Port Huron. . . . Most of the people there had been hand-recruited, a lot by Al [Haber] and Tom [Hayden], who went around the country picking elites from schools. They would go find people they . . . connected with on a gut level. It wasn't, "Do you believe in the principles of unity?" It was, "You feel good to me. I have a feeling you're very bright and you're very spirited and we see things basically the same way." So this was a hand-recruited bunch of people who really wanted to use their lives to change the world, and who loved finding each other.

Looking back on her own feelings at Port Huron, Haber comments,

> I felt it was heaven. . . . It was wonderful . . . very inspiring. The people who were there clearly were exceptional. And what we were talking about was magnificent. We were really talking about the world and about life. And the intelligence and the creativity and the sparkle and the energy and humor were just great and wonderful.

Dorothy Burlage was raised in Texas and had been an activist in the struggle against segregation since 1956 and involved with various organizations in the southern civil rights movement since 1961. Like those attending the Sharon conference, she describes a sense of history in the making.

I think we knew it was historic, but I'm not sure that we knew how historic, because I don't think anybody could have predicted how much power the movement would gather over the years. . . . I was more naive. I was from a much more conservative background, so for me all of this was much more eye-opening than for some northern kids who had come from red-diaper families or studied Marx. For them it was much more part of what they were already familiar with. For me it was all new. That made it more exciting in some ways.

Reflecting on the overall spirit at the meeting, Burlage comments, "People kept operating out of idealism and their instincts about what would create a better world. It was a rare moment in history and we were blessed to be given that opportunity."

**The Port Huron Statement**   The group approached Hayden's draft of what was to be called "the Port Huron Statement" as "a living document open to change with our times and experiences."[19] For the next few days the participants broke down into small groups, each taking a section of the statement to work on. The final document was a sixty-three-page essay outlining SDS's philosophy, values, ideals, and goals.[20]

The statement begins, "We are people of this generation, bred in at least modest comfort, housed now in universities, looking uncomfortably to the world we inherit." Racism and the Cold War, symbolized by the bomb, are named as the two essential issues that provoked people out of complacency. The document goes on to discuss the disturbing paradoxes that led to disillusion with the hypocrisy of American ideals: the paradox, for example, of belief that "all men are created equal" and the reality of "Negro life" in America.

A section on "Values," placed prominently at the beginning of the statement, asserts,

We regard *men* as infinitely precious and possessed of unfulfilled capacities for reason, freedom, and love. . . . Men have unrealized potential for self-cultivation, self-direction, self-understanding, and creativity. It is this potential that we regard as crucial and to which we appeal, not to the human potentiality for violence, unreason, and submission to authority. The goal of man and society should be human independence. . . . This kind of independence does not mean egotistic individualism—the object is not to have one's way so much as it is to have a way that is one's own. Nor do we deify man—we merely have faith in his potential.

Deploring contemporary conditions of loneliness and estrangement, the statement stresses the need for human relationships based on fraternity and honesty.

Above all, the document calls for a vision of society based on participatory democracy governed by two aims: first, that individuals participate in the decisions determining the quality and direction of their lives, and second, that society be organized to encourage independence and to provide for such common participation.[21] Condemning the apathy that blanketed American life and transformed citizens into isolated individuals without connection, the statement praises student efforts against racial injustice and against the threat of war as breaking the stranglehold of apathy.

The bulk of the statement is a critique of American society of the 1950s. The influence of C. Wright Mills is evident in the image of the American masses withdrawn and isolated from public life, as well as in the critique of American institutions.[22] The document looks at American political, economic, and military elites, analyzing the way each sector contributes to the powerlessness of the American public. In terms of the political system, the statement tracks the collapse of the two-party system and the decline of the power of Congress, especially in the area of foreign policy. With regard to the economic realm, it points to the existence of poverty amid affluence and the growing concentration of wealth in America, and in particular to the "remote control economy" that excludes people from decisions about the nature and organization of their work. Organized labor, too, comes under SDS's scrutiny as the statement describes the bureaucratization of the organized sectors while also noting the decline of union representation. The most important outcome "of the authoritarian and oligopolistic structure of economic-decision-making," however, is the military-industrial complex. Again, Mills's influence is unmistakable in the discussion of the congruence of interest among military and business elites.

A large section examines the Cold War. SDS is critical of both sides. Although the statement carefully identifies the Soviet Union as aggravating international relations, U.S. policy is its main focus. Regarding communism, the document declares that "as democrats we are in basic opposition to the communist system" and goes on to criticize the centralized bureaucracy, the absence of liberty, and the undemocratic structure of the Soviet Union. "The communist movement has failed, in every sense, to achieve its stated intention of leading a worldwide movement for human emancipation." Yet juxtaposed with this critique of communism, the statement also objects to the assumption of the expansionist, aggressive nature of the Soviet Union that the United States uses to justify its proliferation of defense as well as its intervention in other countries. Further, at one point the statement names "unreasoning anticommunism" as deteriorating the democratic spirit in America by fostering fear of membership in political organizations.

In another section of the statement SDS recognizes that anticolonial movements may result in authoritarian variants of socialism and collectivism rather than in democratic capitalism. SDS recommends that U.S. policy should aim to facilitate democracy by retaining a critical identification with such countries and helping them avoid external threats to their independence. By the end of the 1960s such ideas would undergo a radical shift.

Beyond critiquing American society, the Port Huron Statement is also a call to arms, meant to rouse youth from complacency. The aim is to provoke people out of defeatism, to replace apathy with hope, to search for truly democratic alternatives. Condemning "the eclipse of social ideals," SDS seeks a new vision. The remainder of the statement considers "what is needed" in setting forth a program of change. Included in these recommendations is a call for universal disarmament, an end to aid for corrupt anti-Communist regimes, and support for nonalignment as a route to ending the Cold War. In terms of domestic issues, the document calls for strengthening democracy through the establishment of a genuine two-party system; the creation of voluntary associations that offer avenues for true participation by citizens; the abolition of institutions that stifle dissent such as the House Un-American Activities Committee (HUAC), the Senate Internal Security Committee, and loyalty oaths on federal loans; and the allocation of resources based on social needs. The statement also emphasizes the need for decentralization of communities to counter the growth of intractable bureaucracy. Pointing to the common values and goals of the movements for peace, civil rights, civil liberties, and labor, it calls for a Democratic Party responsive to these interests. The statement wholeheartedly condemns violence as a means to social change, an issue that would be at the heart of much controversy by the end of the decade.

Finally, the Port Huron Statement establishes a *new left,* distinct from the old. Believing "the dreams of the older left were perverted by Stalinism," SDS views the university as a potential base for this New Left. Referring to its authors as "students for a democratic society" the statement concludes: "If we appear to seek the unattainable, as it has been said, then let it be known that we do so to avoid the unimaginable."

The process of working on the draft of the Port Huron Statement magnified the original feelings participants had of exhilaration. The meetings were run by Robert's Rules of Order, using an elaborate system of committees and votes, but the aim was to reach consensus. James Miller reports that barely anyone attending remembers much of the content of the discussions.[23] What they *do* recall in vivid detail is the way the process intensified bonds between people. Dorothy Burlage says,

> One of the things that made it really interesting and exciting was that there were so many people from different backgrounds . . . and that everybody got to articulate what they felt . . . and what they wanted and what they dreamed of. It was amazing. I can remember people going off trying to write pieces of it. . . . It was visionary. That's the word for it—it was truly visionary.

Yet even amidst the exhilaration, internal differences erupted during the course of the five days. From the beginning there was tension between SDS and the older generation of leftists at the convention. In particular Tom Hayden and Michael Harrington, the chief representative of LID in attendance, fiercely debated the document's anti-Communist statements. Harrington criticized the statement as being too soft on the Soviets, too hard on labor and liberals, and also questioned the placement of students in the vanguard.

These tensions exploded the first evening of the conference over the seating of Jim Hawley, a representative of the Progressive Youth Organizing Committee, a front group of the Communist Party. Hawley, a high school student, attended as a nonvoting observer rather than as an SDS member. The staunch anti-Communists, represented mainly by the older left, feared allowing a member of a centralized, secretive, Soviet-sponsored group to be affiliated with the organization. Haber and Hayden, confident that SDS could not be "taken over" by secret groups and determined not to reproduce leftist battles of the past, firmly believed the organization must remain nonsectarian.[24] In contrast to YAF's smooth relationship with and admiration for their parent organization, SDS's relationship to the Old Left was characterized by difficulty and tension.[25] The Port Huron Statement demonstrated the break SDS members were making with their elders. Attacking Stalinism, critical of organized labor, and declaring the organization itself anti anti-Communist, SDS's position broadcast its antagonism to the Old Left.

A second debate centered on the values section. The original draft contained a passage that read "We regard men as infinitely perfectible." Mary Varela, a Catholic working with Young Christian Students, objected to the wording, arguing it was wrong to emphasize human perfectibility because of the doctrine of original sin. The group debated perspectives on human nature and, partly in fear of alienating Christian radicals, changed the sentence to read "We regard men as infinitely precious."[26] Interestingly, no one objected to the sexist language of the passage, the use of "men" to encompass both men and women. The awakening to issues over women's unequal place in society would come later in the 1960s.

Despite these disputes, the tone of the meetings was one of compromise and unity. The group met as a whole to discuss section after section. The most serious revisions were made on the parts regarding anticommunism. In a concession to Harrington, the document was redrafted to disassociate the organization from the Soviet model. The group also voted to retain a clause on exclusions but changed the language to read "SDS is an organization of democrats. It is civil libertarian in its treatment of those with whom it disagrees, but clear in its opposition to any totalitarian principle as a basis for government or social organization. Advocates or apologists for such a principle are not eligible for membership."[27] The issue of exclusions eventually would be fatal to SDS; once the exclusion clause was removed, the door was open to Communist sects that eventually tore apart the organization.

The document also set up a new organizational structure: the national council (the NC). In addition to the president, vice president, and fifteen members that formed the national executive committee, the NC was to include delegates from each chapter. The NC was to meet regularly to establish policy. Finally, the statement declared SDS's autonomy from LID.[28]

After staying up all night to finalize the document, the group voted to accept the amended draft and elected Tom Hayden as president and Paul Booth as vice president. Among the other fifteen national executive committee members elected, all but five had already graduated from college and all but one had attended colleges east of the Mississippi; four were women, eleven were men.[29] Soon after the convention SDS printed 20,000 copies of the Port Huron Statement for distribution. Eventually, it became the most widely read pamphlet of the 1960s generation.[30]

At the end of Port Huron, the participants left with a cemented sense of community and a new sense of hope. Many who attended remember it as a decisive moment in their life. Reflecting on his experience at Port Huron, Tom Hayden states,

At the time, we were having a transcendent experience, the kind that happens perhaps once in a lifetime. When we saw the aurora borealis at night, or finished work at sunrise, we blessed our luck at being alive and together. We were truly in love with each other; as Casey wrote later, "it was a holy time."[31]

Todd Gitlin, too, remembers the general feeling of SDS as "falling in love with a cadre." Saying he "felt graced to be in their company," Gitlin refers to the SDS circle as "a surrogate family."[32]

## TWO WINGS OF THE SAME GENERATION

Comparing the Port Huron and Sharon Statements reveals the commonalities as well as the differences between these two wings of the 1960s generation. A parallel process of disillusionment provoked the involvement of young people at either end of the political spectrum. Communism and the Cold War played a key role in this process for each wing. However, youth of the left and right interpreted these forces in contrary ways. In Mannheim's terms, while each generation-unit was profoundly affected by these historical forces, they "worked up" their experiences differently. For YAF communism was the singular influence underlying the pronouncements of the Sharon Statement. Reflecting on the statement, Moffit argues that those attending Sharon were part of a generation born into the terrible conflict of World War II who had witnessed the "bloody assaults of a little Austrian brute," along with the birth of the atomic age, and the accompanying threat of nuclear annihilation. But above all, he argues, it was communism's coming of age and the experience of the Cold War that shaped those attending Sharon. "The early years of this generation were shadowed by the growth of a new threat— the transformation of the spectre of Communism into Soviet power."[33]

Scott Stanley also points to the impact that communism had on conservative youth.

When we first began to think about public affairs . . . it was a time in which Mao was seizing China. We'd gone through the war believing that America was invulnerable. . . . Why was there no pax Americana? We knew something was wrong. . . . Our values had been betrayed. Our dreams were being destroyed. . . . We [saw] long lines of refugees escaping from the Communists. We [saw] photographs of American kids with their arms wired behind their back, shot through the head, in ditches. . . . We believed that America was

good and great and powerful, and if America's power and good-
ness had been reduced, then some enemy must have done this. . . .
[T]he movement was visceral. We felt that the things that we loved
were being taken away.

For them, communism and the Cold War represented the loss of American status, disillusion with the belief in America as the mightiest power
on earth, juxtaposed against the reality of a rapidly expanding Soviet
empire, an empire that represented bleak totalitarianism.

This sense of values betrayed is also evident in the Port Huron Statement. The introduction asserts,

> When we were kids the United States was the wealthiest and stron-
> gest country in the world; the only one with the atom bomb, the
> least scarred by modern war, an initiator of the United Nations that
> we thought would distribute Western influence throughout the
> world. Freedom and equality for each individual, government of,
> by, and for the people—these American values we found good,
> principles by which we could live as men. . . . As we grew, however,
> our comfort was penetrated by events too troubling to dismiss.

Like YAF members, SDSers also grew up with an image of America as
just and good, as the embodiment of freedom and equality. Yet just as
youth in YAF encountered a disjuncture between their ideal image and
the reality of a weakened America, so, too, youth in SDS were provoked
by the hypocrisy they perceived between the ideal of the United States
as leader of the Free World, upholder of equality and justice, and the reality of America in the 1950s.

Again, as for youth on the right, it was the Cold War that provoked
awareness and involvement. But for the founders of SDS the shadow cast
by the Cold War did not originate in the Soviet Union. They viewed the
Soviet system as a dinosaur, an overcentralized, encrusted bureaucracy.[34]
In direct response to the Sharon Statement, Todd Gitlin commented in
an SDS article from the early 1960s: "It was the Bomb, not Communism
that lay darkly over the horizon."[35] The Cold War represented nuclear
annihilation rather than Soviet expansionism, the deterioration of civil
liberties witnessed by the McCarthy period, not the loss of American
power.

Further, the disjuncture prodding SDSers to action was as much their
recognition of racial inequality as it was the shadow of the Cold War.
Noticeably absent from the Sharon Statement but vital to the concerns

of those attending Port Huron was attention to civil rights. Central to this difference in attention toward racial discrimination is the variance in values embraced by each wing. While for YAF liberty was of supreme import, for SDS equality was of utmost concern. Thus, for YAFers the gap between ideals and reality was most blatant in the thwarting of individual freedom because of the threat of communism and expansion of the state. For those in SDS, on the other hand, the most conspicuous gap separated the ideal of universal freedom and equality from the system of racial inequality that was intransigent to change.

It is not that liberty was unimportant to those in SDS. Yet even the notion of freedom was rooted in different constructs. The Sharon Statement bases its notion of liberty, above all, on free will and individual rights. The image is of a self-reliant individual standing alone, unconstrained by outside interference. For those in SDS, freedom was necessarily bound to community. The Port Huron Statement rests its vision of humanity on independence as well as on creativity, self-understanding, and the need for connection to others. Individuals attain freedom and power only through participation in the decisions shaping their lives, only through integration with others in the public realm. Connected to this vision of community, one final difference evident in the two statements is the attention that SDS (but not YAF) directed toward quality of life issues. The Port Huron Statement contains a broad critique of American culture; activists in SDS were as conscious about the texture of human relationships as about the institutions of society. The effort to build a new society was as much concerned with new forms of personal relationships, with the needs for intimacy and creativity, with the attempt to build a "true brotherhood," as it was with demands for concrete changes in the political and economic structures of society.

This emphasis on larger quality of life issues was central to SDS's goals and was a compelling force behind some activists' involvement. Andrea Cousins, an early SDS activist, tells of how she cried when she read the Port Huron Statement because she was so happy to find a political statement that embraced who she was, a statement "about how people live and how they talk to each other and how they relate to each other." Barbara Haber says the statement was radical *because* it went beyond political issues such as redistribution of wealth to look "at the kinds of relationships that people had. . . . We were going to live our lives differently than our parents. . . . We were going to use our lives as experiments." Thus, from the beginning, SDS's goals included not only political transformation but also posed the question, Can we live in a different and better way? These quality of life or cultural issues included incorporating new values and ways of being into ongoing lifestyles, attempting new forms of personal relations. Over time these issues of lifestyle and culture would attract the attention of thousands of youth, including many libertarians from YAF.

Despite these differences between the goals and styles of the two organizations, there are striking parallels between the groups. For one thing, both expressed suspicion toward large-scale organization. Although there is a noticeable difference between SDS's preference for government intervention to solve issues of inequality and to promote social welfare and YAF's firm opposition to any government expansion of this sort, both recognized the stultifying effects of bureaucracy, of public expansion without control. The Port Huron Statement talks of "bureaucratic coagulation" and calls for experiments in decentralization, ideas compatible with the ideology of YAF. There is a common strand, then, favoring the small-scale, face-to-face interaction of local communities and neighborhood control.

Abhorring submission to authority, both groups also shared a thrust toward populism, toward removal of power from hands above and its return to those below. As Tom Hayden explains, reflecting on the Port Huron Statement,

> We were rejecting the limited concept of democracy that had come to prevail, one in which expertise, specialization and bureaucracy had come to count for more than popular will. . . . Our democratic idealism flowed from a populist root, the belief that an informed public would make "better" decisions about its own interests than anyone else.[36]

This emphasis on self-determination and self-government is also at the heart of YAF activism.

In these early years SDS even expressed limited support for free enterprise and democratic capitalism. Miller reports that the original draft of the Port Huron Statement contained a passage declaring "private enterprise is not inherently immoral or undemocratic—indeed it may at times contribute to offset elitist tendencies."[37]

These seeds of commonality would later become a basis for unity between sectors of each organization. In particular, the populist thrust toward decentralization, a common impulse against authoritarianism, and eventually a shared hostility toward the state, would offer a meeting ground for members of YAF and SDS during the late 1960s.

In fact, certain members of YAF recognized common ground with the early SDS. Stan Evans, who drafted the Sharon Statement, commented,

> The impulse behind both organizations was common libertarianism: both believed society was too regimented, government too big. There was a strong impulse toward personal freedom. Many of the SDS statements I agreed with. Most of the debates I had [with SDS] were over the best way to defend personal freedom. I believe the original impulse behind SDS was a good one. . . . To me one of the great tragedies of the New Left was that derailment of the original impulse: young people as pro-freedom and pro-fairness. . . . The intuition that "corporate liberalism" was repressive—controlling, regimenting Big Government—was a very correct intuition.[38]

After the original Port Huron Statement came out, another YAF member, Don Devine, reports he had "some crazy idea of trying to get the two groups together." The issue was taken up at a YAF board meeting but nothing ever came of it. Devine was particularly drawn to the common libertarian theme of emphasis on local government and against the massive bureaucratic state, and to the shared antiestablishment language of both groups. Still another YAF activist, Louise Lacey, said when she read the Port Huron Statement she thought "it was wonderful." She identified the common bonds as being individual responsibility and individual participation. Eventually, Louise's libertarianism led her to join organizations on the left.

Although certain members of YAF recognized common ground with SDS, all the commentary by SDS members was critical of YAF. Hayden called young conservatives "politically absurd,"[39] while another critic wrote that YAF was "virtually maniacal . . . an unthinking response . . . irrational."[40] An article analyzing the Sharon Statement specifically lambasted YAF for placing economic rights above human rights, for supporting HUAC despite its abuse of civil liberties, for advocating states' rights, and even faulted the organization for its "undemocratic structure which gives almost total power to the board of directors."[41]

Leftist animosity toward YAF must be seen in the context of McCarthyism. Although SDS was critical of communism, members were well aware of the damages done by the rampant anticommunism of the 1950s. Rather than finding common ground with YAF, they were extremely wary of an organization that supported HUAC, demanded loyalty oaths, and emphasized free enterprise while ignoring issues of civil rights.

Beyond any mutual ideological impulses, whether recognized or not,

YAF and SDS activists also had similar experiences as people speaking out during a time of general apathy. Both faced the ostracism of peers and of the larger society by the very nature of their involvement. Whereas there is general recognition of the ostracism faced by those speaking out on the left, activists in YAF too felt a sense of estrangement. YAFer Carol Dawson recalls the *New York Times* using "modifiers or descriptions about us, calling us 'self-proclaimed' or 'those hot-eyed radicals.' . . . I thought, My God, they've never met us! because we were really pretty much middle-class kids." Lee Edwards eloquently remembers the public ostracism conservative activists faced:

> My God, to be a young conservative in the sixties was to be an untouchable, a pariah, a Jew in Syria, a black in South Africa. We were scum. We were reviled. We were scorned. We were insulted. We were dismissed. So we fought back. We were able to stand up. We debated. We challenged. We flaunted back at these people who said that we were nothing.

Yet at the same time that these young activists felt a sense of alienation from the mainstream population, during the early years of the 1960s both organizations were still oriented toward mainstream politics. Despite their critiques of the system, each believed in changing society through reforming its institutions. Even the names of each group seem tame compared to what was to come in the chaos of the late 1960s. Several years passed before words like "imperialism," "revolution," or "domestic fascism" cropped up in either organization. Photos of the early activists in both groups show short-haired men, often attending demonstrations in ties and jackets, and well-groomed women, in skirts that reach below their knees.

Finally, those attending the Sharon and Port Huron conferences shared a sense of idealism, a sense of limitlessness. A headiness accompanied their age, leading them to believe that they could truly change the world. SDSer Barbara Haber put it this way,

> You could say we were arrogant. But there was something much more positive about it than arrogance. . . . We [had] an adolescent or postadolescent sense of infinity. We didn't feel limitations very much. . . . We sensed that we were on to something, that we were looking with fresh eyes at reality, and that we had some kind of spirit that was special.

Similarly, on the YAF side, Lee Edwards says,

There's a certain amount of self-confidence which came up. . . . There was a feeling in those early years of growing awareness of our power and our abilities and of the difference that we could make. . . . And, of course, we were all arrogant as hell, cocky as hell.

Clearly, youth of both the left and the right felt an inner drive as well as hope, a sense of mission accompanied by idealism, which drove them to take action for social change. The torch had indeed been passed to a new generation of Americans.

# CHAPTER TWO

# BACKGROUNDS

The young women and men who became active in SDS and YAF came from different social worlds. It is not just the contrasting demographic backgrounds of activists that explain their different orientations. The worlds in which they were raised, the values and beliefs they were taught, also played an important role in shaping their political beliefs. As Karl Mannheim argues, we learn to perceive reality, to understand and define the shapes and forms around us, through the groups to which we belong. The early impressions we learn from these groups "coalesce into a natural view of the world."[1] It is not surprising, then, to find that the natural view of the world of most activists was an extension of the world in which they grew up. Rather than breaking with their parents' beliefs, for most activists there is continuity between the generations. What are the backgrounds and family orientations that provided the basis for their political activism?

People don't just join social movements out of the blue. To understand political activism we must first examine the social circumstances and influences affecting individual belief *prior* to participation. The formation of an activist identity begins long before the first step into the political world. Whereas most studies that examine activism begin with adult lives, tracing the initial issue that provoked involvement, what social movement analysis neglects is the prior impact of family, community, and schools in planting the seeds for political beliefs and action. Long before these young people joined YAF or SDS they learned activism from parents and other family members, from community and peers, from the influence of teachers, books, and schools. The focus here and in chapter 3 is on the backgrounds and environments that shaped these individuals' understanding of the world and led them to commit themselves wholeheartedly to politics.

## SOCIAL BACKGROUNDS

Comparing the backgrounds of YAF and SDS activists, we find crucial differences in class, religion, and ethnicity, as well as important differences *within* YAF between libertarians and traditionalists. Contrary, however, to other studies that find that early and late SDS activists come from different social backgrounds, the sample here shows no marked differences between early activists (those who joined SDS from 1960 to 1964) and later activists (those who joined SDS from 1965 to 1968).[2] Although early and later activists in this study do have different outlooks and orientations (see chapters 5 and 6), these differences have more to do with the variation in experiences within SDS as a result of the drastic changes in the size and nature of the organization from the early to late 1960s than they do with differences in social background.

### Class Backgrounds

Overall, the majority of members of both SDS and YAF come from privileged backgrounds. For example, both parents of over half of all activists completed at least some amount of college. But if parents' education and occupation offer a rough measure of class standing, SDS activists tend to come from more privileged backgrounds than do YAF activists. Even though this finding parallels other studies that compare right- and left-wing activists,[3] no studies to date also compare by gender. Here we find that women in both groups come from more privileged class backgrounds than their male counterparts.

The composite portrait shows SDS women have the most highly educated fathers of all those in the sample; they were employed in middle-to upper-middle-class occupations such as engineer, professor, lawyer, high-ranking government official, and geologist. Also SDS women are unique from other activists in that the majority have mothers who were employed during their childhood.[4] In contrast, while SDS men also come from homes with both highly educated mothers and fathers, the majority of their mothers stayed at home throughout their childhood. The fathers of SDS men also have more mixed occupational backgrounds than fathers of SDS women, including jobs such as assembly-line worker, postal clerk, salesman as well as doctor, professor, and journalist.

Female activists in YAF come from solid middle-class homes with fathers who were primarily employed in white-collar and professional jobs such as marketing manager, sales supervisor, businessman, advertising executive, engineer, and doctor. Their mothers have a similar educational background to mothers of SDS women, but, in contrast, the majority stayed at home to raise their children. YAF men come from the least privileged backgrounds. Their parents are the least educated and, overall, their fathers have the lowest proportion of high-status positions. Like SDS men's fathers, YAF men's fathers were employed in a range of fields including farmer, laborer, machinist, draftsman, sales representative as well as newspaper editor, business executive, anthropologist, and computer programmer. The majority of YAF men's mothers were full-time homemakers.

Libertarians within YAF come from much more privileged backgrounds than traditionalists, in terms of both educational and occupational achievement of fathers. In short, the common characterization of conservative activists as coming from lower-middle-class backgrounds is much more true for male activists than for female activists in YAF, and is particularly true for traditionalist men. When we include women and libertarians, there are far fewer differences in class background between activists on the left and right.

### Religious Backgrounds

Another difference that distinguishes leftists, libertarians, and traditionalists is religious upbringing. SDS members are evenly split between Jews and Protestants, with only a few members who were raised as Catholics. Libertarians in YAF are overwhelmingly Protestants, with a small minority who were raised as Catholics or Jews. In contrast, over half of traditionalists are Catholics, with the remainder Protestants.[5] The importance of religious upbringing is discussed below.

### Racial and Ethnic Backgrounds

The YAF sample is entirely white except for one black activist. The SDS sample consists of thirty-three white activists and three black activists.[6] Among the white activists, the overwhelming majority of YAF members claim part or all of their heritage to be northern European. In contrast,

over half of SDS members claim part or all of their heritage to be eastern European.[7]

Whereas some analysts have argued that SDS activists suffered from
"status inconsistency" because of their family's lower ethnic status,[8] there
are no significant differences between right- and left-wing activists in family lineage. A slightly higher proportion of parents or grandparents of
SDS activists were foreign-born, but about one-third of both YAF and
SDS activists report families living in the United States since the 1700s.
The more important difference is between traditionalists and libertarians
in YAF. Libertarians are twice as likely to come from families that have
been in America since the 1700s and are much *less* likely to have parents or grandparents who are foreign-born. Also, while over half of the
traditionalists in YAF come from Irish backgrounds, less than a quarter
of libertarians do so.

In sum, the demographic backgrounds of activists show that overall
SDS members in this sample tend to come from more privileged backgrounds than YAF members, although these differences are less significant
in a comparison between all SDS members and women or libertarians in
YAF. While SDS activists tend to come from either Jewish or Protestant
homes, YAF members are predominantly Catholic or Protestant. Whereas
YAF libertarians in this study tend to be white, Anglo-Saxon Protestants
from old lineage families, traditionalists are more likely to be Irish Catholic and first- or second-generation American.

## PARENTS' BELIEFS AND VALUES

Not only do these youth come from different sociological pools. They
also were born and raised in families with contrasting values and beliefs.

### Parents' Politics

Unlike most American youth, the majority of activists of both the left
and the right were raised with a consciousness of the political world and
encouraged to "think politically." Some activists grew up with politics
as a way of life, with their parents involved in a range of activities and
organizations. SDSer Barry Skolnick, for example, grew up surrounded
by politics. His father's side of the family was divided between Communists and rabbis: "Half of them were religious Jews and the other half
were orthodox reds. They both had their dogma." His father, a radical
since age fifteen, fought in the Abraham Lincoln Brigade in Spain in 1936.

Throughout Barry's childhood his father was a Communist Party organizer; blacklisted during the McCarthy era, Barry's father went underground. His mother, too, was a lifelong activist.

Like SDS members, many YAFers also came from politically active homes. Lee Edwards describes himself as a "cradle conservative." His father, Willard Edwards, a prominent journalist for the *Chicago Tribune,* covered all the congressional hearings on Communist subversion. Lee grew up knowing such figures as Richard Nixon, Joe McCarthy, and Roy Cohn. He says, "They were in our homes and we were in their homes." His mother, too, was politically active.

Even those activists who did not have parents who were actively involved in political organizations still grew up in politically conscious homes in which strong opinions were expressed and in which ideas and events were often discussed. Many name dinner time as critical to learning about and discussing politics. SDSer Naomi Schapiro describes her parents as "liberal ex-Commies." Although her mother had been in the Communist Party at an earlier age, and her father had been involved in a Marxist Zionist youth group in Germany, by the time Naomi was born both parents were disillusioned with communism. They were no longer politically active but remained well informed: "They were very interested in politics, so we talked about it at the dinner table and talked about current events. . . . My mother was always the person that all her friends called to find out who to vote for in local politics because she'd always stay informed on all the issues." Other activists also talk about parents who withdrew from active political involvement but continued to instill an identity oriented toward the political world.

Many in YAF also spoke of parents who were politically aware although not overtly active. Maggie Kohls says her father was always interested in politics, even if his only involvement was writing letters to newspapers and to congressmen. But there were books all over the house and Maggie particularly recalls her father reading *National Review.* Most of all, she remembers discussions.

> As we ate dinner together every day . . . he always talked. My sister was six years older and they talked about the news. . . . I always thought I knew what was going on. Of course, I didn't in-depth, but what I knew I picked up mostly over dinner. I remember babbling things about Kennedy that I had no basis for, like "He's going to raise taxes" and I had no idea. . . . It was things I picked up at the table.

Clearly what she picked up at the table was a foundation for her later activism in the John Birch Society and, subsequently, in YAF.

Although several of these YAF and SDS activists who had conscious but less active parents describe their parents as "not political," in fact what emerged was a portrait of parents who held strong ideological beliefs, who remained politically aware, and who clearly imparted their views to their children. SDS activist Carol Christman, for example, describes her parents as humanistic New Deal liberals. Her father was a high-level government bureaucrat so Carol was raised in Washington surrounded by politics. As she puts it, she grew up "in a politicized atmosphere. . . . I was very well informed politically. We watched the news together every night. We talked about it." Although Carol says her parents weren't really activists, she also mentions that her parents were very involved in electoral campaigns and also became involved in civil rights through the Unitarian Church. They were particularly committed to keeping the schools open during the battle over integration. Thus—despite the opinion of Carol and other youth for whom politics became a way of life—such parents were involved citizens who thought about political issues, voted, and often were engaged in the political world. In short, such parents were *more* politically active than the average person.[9]

A minority of activists come from families in which neither organizational activity nor intense political discussions took place. Parents in these homes were basically not members of political organizations, did not hold strong ideological views, and would not get into intense political discussions with their children over dinner. Activists from such homes describe their parents as "basically nonpolitical." As one YAF activist, Harvey Hukari, recalls, "In terms of my parents contributing anything to the development of personal ideology or interest in politics, no. My father was simply of the school that you're supposed to be a good citizen and obey the laws and vote and . . . behave responsibly."

Similarly, SDS activist Bernardine Dohrn describes her parents as never talking about politics. "They went and voted because we came home from school and said, 'You have to vote.'" Although parents in these homes may have had strong values, the only concrete political activity that took place was voting, and even that was not always a priority. As we'll see in chapter 3, other adults—teachers, community leaders, or other relatives— also can play an important role in instilling an activist identity.

Overall, however, not only were most parents of activists politically involved, but the clear majority of young women and men who joined

SDS and YAF fell on the same side of the political divide as their parents. Activists in YAF had parents who ranged from being old-style conservative Democrats (typically, later switching to the Republican Party), to conservative Republicans, to being members of the John Birch Society, while parents of SDS activists tended to be New Deal anti-Communists, liberal Democrats, to those identifying as socialists or Communists.

In fact, approximately one-third of these SDS activists are "red-diaper babies": their parents at some point were members of the Communist Party or were sympathizers, socialists, or strongly identified with the left. However, by the time many of these red-diaper babies were growing up, many of their parents had redefined themselves politically, identifying as liberal Democrats or liberal anti-Communists or may even have become nonpolitical.[10] As for YAF activists, just under one-half of the sample were "cradle conservatives," defined as having been raised with one or both parents who were conservative Republicans—supporters of Joseph McCarthy, for example—as opposed to parents who were moderate or more mainstream Republicans.[11]

This continuity of belief that characterizes the majority of activists confirms previous studies that examine the lineage of political ideology from parents to children.[12] Rather than a rejection of the older generation, the involvement of the majority of activists of both the left and the right represents an *extension of parental beliefs*. Flacks's comment that the great majority of leftist student activists were "attempting to fulfill and renew the political traditions of their families"[13] could just as well apply to those on the right. Whereas the younger generation may have been critical of parental beliefs, as witnessed by the Port Huron statement's critique of liberalism, few youth actually crossed over to the opposite ideological camp.

Crossovers    Yet a minority of activists *are* "crossovers," individuals who ended up on the opposite side of the political fence from their parents. SDSers were more likely to be crossovers than YAF members. For the most part, these crossover SDS activists come from families with active Republican backgrounds. Their parents range from plain old "dyed-in-the-wool Republicans" to "right-wing ideologues." Cindy Decker, whose mother was involved with the John Birch Society, describes her parents by saying, "My mom and my stepdad were very conservative Republicans. . . . When I went to see John F. Kennedy when I was a senior in high school . . . my stepfather didn't speak to me for three days because I went to see 'that Commie pinko red.'" In fact, many of these

parents of crossovers were not just conservative believers but were actively involved in conservative politics, including parents who were speech-
writers for conservative Republican candidates, campaign workers and
fund-raisers for the Republican Party, or officers in local Republican
organizations.

What distinguishes the crossovers from other members of SDS? The
majority of crossovers were raised Protestant. No Jews fell into this category, which is not surprising, given the higher proportion of Jewish parents with liberal-left orientations. Second, crossovers were more likely
to be female. In fact, all three of the women in this study who later became members of the Weatherman faction of SDS were crossovers. What
this points to is the unique position of SDS women as defiers of traditional gender roles, having in this case made a significant leap from their
parents' political beliefs. Most crossovers also came from the Midwest,
which has a tradition of populism that allows for a politics of the left as
well as the right (and two crossover activists later identified as libertarian, an ideology that draws from both the left and the right). Like those
who were raised with parents who were politically uninvolved, these
crossovers found other adults such as teachers and community leaders
who served as critical role models, provoking them to think about politics and the world in a new way.

## Parents' Values

For SDS and YAF activists the values and philosophies they were taught
by their parents became a solid foundation for their own political involvement. Particularly striking is the contrasting milieus in which those
on the right and left were raised. In discussing the lessons and values their
parents taught them, youth in SDS and YAF reflect the fact that they grew
up in separate worlds.

YAF Parents' Values    For those in YAF, one core value taught by parents
that activists repeatedly mentioned was *anticommunism*. Maggie Kohls
says she absorbed anticommunism, along with "patriotism and God and
country," from her father. He taught her that communism was "the worst
thing in the world" and that "McCarthy was a good guy." Maggie recalls being nine and reading her father's magazines that were filled with
pictures of tortured bodies in Lithuania and Estonia. Many others in YAF
remembered parents teaching them about the evils of communism or
preaching about how Stalin was worse than Hitler.

Connected to this anticommunism was a general *suspicion of big government*. Mary Fisk reflects on her father's beliefs.

> The basic issue [was] the need to restrict the power of the government, the need to keep the government out of the lives of people. He was against the income tax . . . because it was the government taking your paycheck . . . to redistribute income. . . . It was the government deciding you should have less and this person should have more. . . . He hated FDR passionately. . . . He was against any kind of socialism—the Keynesian economics that were big in the Depression.

Several other YAF activists discussed how their parents despised FDR because of the programs he introduced that expanded government. Marick Payton remembers his father getting involved in their community to stop the construction of a dam; the big dam "represented big government and . . . was seen by conservatives as a leftist liberal FDR kind of intrusion in the people's private businesses and private lives."

Along with distrust of government many YAF parents also conveyed a sense of antipathy toward the welfare state. They opposed seeing government as a way to solve problems. The fear was not just of collectivism in government but extended to *suspicion of any kind of concentration of power*. In Mitch Petry's family, for example, this fear of power translated into antiunion attitudes. Opposition to unions was rooted in a "deep-seated antagonism toward monopoly of power without any recourse . . . without any competition."

This suspicion of collectivism and power is intricately bound to belief in the *sanctity of the individual*. The underlying fear is that any form of collective organization infringes on individual freedom. Emmy Lewis speaks of the values held dear by her parents.

> My mother and father both shared very deep and passionate commitment to and love of the whole idea [of] the principles of freedom, of individual worth. That it is the individual, not the state, that is the important thing in life. . . .
>
> The motivating factor [for their political involvement]—and this was what they instilled in me—was the passionate love for . . . America because of what it represents, that it is the embodiment of what Man can achieve when there is individual liberty *with* responsibility. . . . It was never just strictly a sort of chauvinistic, nationalistic attitude. It's that America is an embodiment of . . . the highest principles . . . and values.

Like her parents, she adds, she believes that the collectivist way, where the state is supreme over the individual, diminishes the human spirit, robbing it of motivation and self-esteem.

Though critical of government getting out of hand—that is, becoming collectivist—YAFers were also brought up with a deep sense of patriotism, a love for America, and were taught to respect the leaders of the land. Belief in the work ethic, honesty, patriotism, and faith in God and country were central values instilled in youth on the right.

**SDS Parents' Values**    The world in which SDS youth were raised contrasts sharply with the world of YAFers. Rather than anticommunism being a key influence, the most common value SDS parents conveyed was the importance of *civil rights and antiracism*. Many SDSers recalled their parents speaking out against racial discrimination. Both of Bob Ross's parents believed in civil rights, but his mother was particularly "dedicated to a naive and beautiful idea of racial equality." In fact, Bob only recalls being hit by his mother one time. He remembers the incident, which occurred right before he went away to summer camp:

> It was an integrated summer camp . . . one of those "red" camps. . . . We went to an integrated public school, but from segregated neighborhoods. . . . So I had a kind of natural racism. . . . My naturalistic setting told me that black people were violent and dumb. And sometimes didn't smell too nice either. . . . So I was worried. . . . I was going to be twelve or thirteen and there would be dances [at camp]. "What would I have to do if I had to dance with a black girl, mom?" And this blow came [and] knocked me silly. . . . It was very effective. I was not injured, but boy, was I told something important is under discussion here.

Even those with parents who were not very politically involved had similar experiences. Steve Kessler, for instance, reports that his mother forbid the use of the word "nigger" because "anybody who'd do that could speak against you as being Jewish."

For some SDSers another lesson learned was to be *suspicious of the powerful*. John Brown Childs says that although his parents did not train him in any overt political thought, they did teach him a "very healthy distrust of things big," including big government and big business. John comments,

> In many ways I didn't grow up in an environment that extolled capitalism, that extolled the wonders of government. It really was a

"watch out for it" kind of environment . . . this sense [of] . . . wariness of the powerful, whatever that position might be—certainly, no great love of the leaders of the land.

Even though this distrust of big government in some ways echoes concerns expressed by YAF parents, the extension of this questioning to political leaders, and to capitalism itself, is contrary to the values learned in YAF homes. Further, such distrust does not translate into antipathy toward the welfare state or a stance against unions. Instead, parents of SDSers were more likely to convey *antagonism toward big business*. Fred Faust remembers his father sitting in the living room denouncing the big, rich companies when they closed a plant or did something "to screw the workers," complaining, "These big companies always act that way."

In contrast to their YAF counterparts, SDSers also learned about the *importance of labor unions*. Phil Hutchings tells the story of meeting Senator Robert Taft when he was eight years old. Shaking hands with the senator, he remarked to his father, "'Daddy, Senator Taft's hands are so smooth.' My father looked at me and said, 'That's because he's never done a day's work in his life!' It was my father who basically taught me about labor unions and why it was important to honor strikes and not cross picket lines."

Another core value taught to SDS youth was a *rejection of materialism* and the accumulation of goods. Some activists expressed the philosophy they learned as being *antiwealth*. Andrea Cousins reflects on the lessons instilled by her father, the author Norman Cousins.

He liked Tolstoy and the idea of living simply and that it was bad to have so much . . . [the] idea about giving things away and not keeping things. . . . I remember my father once when we were very young saying what an ugly word "mine" was, not supposed to say "mine"; and I felt very self-conscious about starting sentences with "I." There was this whole thing about not being self-centered, think of people who are less fortunate than yourself. [It] was like dropping a heavy wet blanket over one of us if you were feeling bad. . . . There was a lot of guilt for having things.

This misgiving about the use of "I" is the antithesis of the concern expressed by some YAF parents for the protection, above all, of the "I," of the individual.

The general suspicion of wealth is also tied to a *concern over poverty*, over those without resources, a value not emphasized by YAF parents.

Michael Kazin says one of the lessons he learned from his mother was "this feeling that politics should be to help those who don't have very much." Finally, some SDSers also recall the *antimilitary* values taught to them by their parents. Again, these values stand in direct opposition to the pro-defense stands taken by many YAF parents.

Although SDS and YAF youth grew up in dissimilar environments and were taught different—and even opposing—values and beliefs by their parents, the majority of youth on both sides were given similar messages on the importance of being active, of making one's opinions known, and of making change. YAF activist Carol Dawson summarizes the lessons she learned from her parents: "I'd say duty to country, commitment to family values, honesty and giving an honest day's work for your pay . . . obeying the laws, but still with an attitude that you can change things if you don't like the way they are."

This encouragement of activism was even more pronounced in the upbringing of SDS activists. One of the few black SDS members, Derek Barron, states,

> I felt from the earliest part of my youth that my family believed that you had a responsibility to stand up and speak out if something was wrong and to do something about changing it; that that's an attitude that my grandfather had, my mother had, my uncle had. . . . It was brought into its sharpest focus for me because I lived in the South, because I grew up in a segregated community.

For many youth at both ends of the political spectrum, then, speaking up and becoming active was encouraged as a respected and essential responsibility. Faith in politics and commitment to changing the world were instilled and eventually became central to the identity of youth on both the left and the right.

## RELIGIOUS UPBRINGING

For a substantial number of activists in both SDS and YAF religion also played a significant role in shaping the development of their political beliefs during their youth, albeit in different ways.

### Traditionalists' Religious Upbringing

Among YAF activists, traditionalists were much more likely than libertarians to come from homes in which religious belief and practice was an important part of their upbringing. Many traditionalists grew up in devoutly religious homes, going to church regularly and attending parochial schools. Although Connie Marshner says her family was not devout in practice, "preferring the order and hierarchy of Catholicism more than the gospel," her mother remained very Catholic because "it was a cultural thing." During her teenage years Connie's act of adolescent rebellion was to regularly attend mass, since her mother never went to mass, preferring to rest on Sundays. As Connie dutifully went off to church each week, she was teased by her family as being "high and holy," nicknamed "St. Connie." Typically, for many of the traditionalists adolescence did not bring about a requestioning of faith. Rather, as with Connie, religious belief survived and at times grew even stronger during these years.

Another traditionalist, Fran Griffin, says that her passion for politics started out with a passion for religion. She points to the importance of religion within her family. Each year at the beginning of December Fran's family went together to a novena at her local parish that lasted for nine days. Fran's father always carried a rosary with him and would say the rosary on his way to work. Her mother said her rosary every night. Fran says, "There was a real fervency about it." In discussing how religion formed the basis of her politics, Fran also recalls the reaction she had to the liberal changes brought on by Vatican II: "In college I got really turned off by a lot of the teachers who were very, very liberal. . . . It made me even more conservative because I didn't agree with them." Other traditionalists as well spoke of the opposition they and their families felt to Vatican II.

Especially for Catholics, anticommunism was an integral part of religious teachings. Several traditionalists mention specific prayers in parochial schools made for the people of Hungary during the Hungarian revolution or numerous discussions of the atrocities committed by Communists in the Ukraine against cardinals, bishops, and priests in the aftermath of World War II. Don Devine, who was sent to a Catholic boarding school from first through eighth grade, says that it was this religious training, more than his family, which contributed to his devout anticommunism.

> What made me an anti-Communist was these schools [that] served as way stations for missionaries, mainly from China, who were tossed out of their country. It's probably their stories of what happened to them that most turned me into an anti-Communist.

Other traditionalists as well speak of the anticommunism they learned in the church as being a key motive for their activism. In particular, they associated communism with godless atheism and the suppression of the church.

More generally, those raised in devout homes say their religious upbringing provided a value system that served as a framework for their politics. Mary Fisk was raised in a Catholic home and attended parochial schools throughout her youth. She sees a natural connection between her religious upbringing and her political beliefs.

> Being Catholic means you believe in orthodoxy. You accept things as some absolute truths. It's not just being God-oriented, but it's accepting that some things are always right and some things are always wrong. . . . That translates very easily into conservatism. . . . By virtue of your belief in God you believe that the individual person has a dignity and a worth that no one can take away.

For Jay Parker the clash between his religious values and the practices of the leaders of the Black Baptist Church was key to his political involvement. He grew up very active in Sunday school, very serious about religion, virtually memorizing the Bible, and even dreaming at times of becoming a minister. But as he came to know members of the Black Baptist Church, Jay became disillusioned.

> I could never reconcile how Adam Clayton Powell, with this large congregation [as the pastor of the Abyssinian Baptist Church in New York], could be in Washington, D.C. [while he was a member of Congress]. . . . How could he be in two places at one time? . . . How [could he] visit the sick members of the church?. . . Then you'd read about his escapades, the women and all that, down in Bimini, and that sort of thing . . .

Jay was further disturbed to find out about the political connections of church leaders, for instance, their ties to the Federal Council of Churches, the predecessor of the National Council of Churches, a liberal organization. Provoked to research the issue, Jay found out that the leadership of the Lutheran, Episcopalian, Methodist, and Presbyterian churches were also involved in political causes. "I discovered they were not only not serving as the shepherds in the flock, but that they were also heavily involved in politics. . . . That was the ultimate cause of [my] walking away because they were all liberal Democrats and just the opposite of what I believed." Jay began looking around for conservative leaders. This was the beginning of his political journey.

## Libertarians' Religious Upbringing

The religious backgrounds of traditionalists clearly depart from those of libertarian activists. Whereas many libertarians also grew up in religious homes, regularly attending church services, only one grew up in a devout family, attending parochial schools. Several grew up with little religious training, attending church infrequently or not at all. Further, any influence of religion on libertarians' political beliefs derived mainly from their *rejection* of religion.

There is a striking similarity to the stories told by many libertarians about their questioning of belief. After seeking out religion as they grew up, typically at some point during their adolescence these activists were struck by inconsistencies in religious belief that eventually led them away from the church. For example, as a young boy Gus DiZerega attended church classes to be confirmed as an Episcopalian. During high school he also briefly got involved with a fundamentalist group. But Gus soon became dissatisfied because, as he put it, "I was logical to a fault." During this time he began writing to a Bible correspondence school and recalls asking, "If there were only two of each animal on the ark, then what did the meat eaters eat while they were floating around out there?" He got back a letter saying that before the flood there were no carnivores.

> I remember thinking Yeah, saber-toothed tigers dug potato tubers with those things! So I didn't believe in it, but by that time a lot of why I stayed in it was fear of what would happen to me if I left it, in terms of what God would do. . . . But finally when Goldwater was nominated I decided that even if it cost me my soul, it was a chance to help serve the country. So I got involved in the campaign and stopped going to those people and felt guilty about it for probably six years afterward.

Sharon Presley, on the other hand, was brought up by her mother to be indifferent to religion. After someone gave Sharon a Bible to read as a child, she decided to go to a Presbyterian church that she attended from the sixth grade through high school. Like Gus, she tried to reconcile rationality with religious belief. She comments,

> In retrospect the reason I got involved in [the church] was . . . I was looking for a philosophy to make sense of the world. . . . But at some point [religion] stopped making sense to me. I remember very clearly what it was that began to bother me. I said, "Okay, religion says that God is love. But then these religions are also saying that

if you aren't a Christian, you're going to hell." I thought, What about all those people in Asia? Perfectly innocent people who haven't done anything wrong go to hell just because they were in the wrong place at the wrong time? This doesn't make any sense. . . . So I started drifting away.

By the time Sharon read Ayn Rand, her attitude toward religion was Why bother? Other libertarians, too, report an eventual rejection of belief. For many, this process was accompanied by identification as an atheist.

### SDS Members' Religious Upbringing

SDS activists resemble libertarians in YAF in that most did *not* grow up in devout homes, surrounded by religious belief. In fact, only four activists came from devoutly religious homes.[14] The majority of SDS activists grew up in families in which they had little or no religious training.

Further, in sharp contrast to most YAF parents, a substantial number of SDS parents were skeptical of religion and of religious institutions. For instance, Jane Adams grew up in the rural Midwest. While her parents were active in the Unitarian Church, as a child Jane decided to attend the local country church with her neighbors. She remembers how she'd have to learn a Bible verse every Sunday and how, as her father drove her to church each week, she would be memorizing it. "And he'd always debunk it. He grew up in the northern Baptist Church and became a free thinker quite early, lost his religion, and has spent a fair amount of intellectual activity around being irreligious." Others say their parents drifted away from religion because of the contradictions of reconciling the evils of the world with belief in God.

Among the nearly half of SDS activists who were Jewish, about half were raised in reform temples in which they typically attended services, either sporadically or regularly, and, if they were male, were usually bar mitzvahed. The other half of Jewish SDSers were raised with only a secular identity as Jews, with parents who were nonbelievers. These youth did not belong to any temple or receive any religious education. In fact, some parents were devout in their renunciation of religion. For instance, when Andrea Cousins was asked whether her parents were religious, she replied, "The answer is no, they were not religious, but the answer is yes, they were very religious! . . . They're religious in the sense that they really are ardent about what they think is right. They're very religious in their antireligiousness."

Included among these secular Jewish SDSers are red-diaper babies who had Communist or socialist parents. Although many of them grew up in Jewish neighborhoods, for these youth Judaism was associated with devotion to leftist doctrine. Bob Ross, who is proud of being a third-generation secular Jew, notes, "It wasn't until I was married at the early age of twenty-two that I discovered Jewish families without socialists or Communists in them. I thought it came with the territory." Clearly, the values and beliefs central to the homes of these SDSers are diametrically opposed to the fervent anticommunism at the center of many devout traditionalist YAFers' homes.

Yet despite the nonreligiosity of many Jewish SDSers, virtually all identified *culturally* with Judaism. Michael Kazin, for example, was brought up by his atheist mother in an antireligious environment. Michael did not go to Hebrew school nor was he bar mitzvahed. He used to go to a Presbyterian church for Christmas to sing Christmas carols and made a point of going to school on Yom Kippur. Yet most of Michael's friends as well as his parents' friends were Jewish. Thus, he retained a strong cultural identification with Judaism. He says he "grew up believing that he was a person whose home team was the Jews."

Beyond the wariness of parents toward religious belief, what is striking is how many of the SDSers themselves—including those from diverse religious faiths—expressed a skepticism about religion from an early age. For some of these youth, their doubts clearly derived from their parents. Helen Garvy, for example, was raised without any religious upbringing.

> I remember when I was eight or nine asking some kid what God was. He tried to explain that there was somebody; he pointed up to the sky. I remember looking up there, This is crazy. That kid believes that? (laughs). So much for religion! I wasn't going to believe something as foolish as that.

At one point Helen talked to her parents about religion; they said what was important about religion was ethics and that was what they wanted to teach her. Helen said that made sense to her.

But for other SDSers their distrust of religion departed from parental belief. Jeanne Friedman grew up in an Orthodox Jewish home and yet early on she became a skeptic. "I got thrown out of Hebrew school for asking too many questions. . . . I got this rabbi very nervous. . . . They would never have thrown a boy out of Hebrew school for asking too many questions. Any boy who asked too many questions would become treasured. . . . I was just a pain in the neck." If Jeanne had been encouraged, perhaps she would have become the star pupil. Instead Jeanne became increasingly more secular in her orientation. While she continued to obey the customs of her parents' home, such as keeping kosher and not shopping on Saturdays, her lack of belief led her away from these practices and eventually eroded her family's commitment as well.

This questioning of religious belief is similar to that of the libertarians in YAF. Like libertarians, many SDSers went through a process of disillusionment during their childhood and adolescence. Like Gus DiZerega and Sharon Presley, SDSer John Maher tried out different religions when he was a boy. John was brought up without any religious affiliation. His father was nominally Catholic and his mother was raised in both the Episcopalian and Quaker traditions. During his childhood John decided to attend different churches to see which seemed right. At age seven he stopped going to the Catholic Church because "they were sort of hellfire against Protestants and I had a Protestant mother." Similarly, he became disillusioned with the Episcopal Church. "I tended to ask questions and I can remember being in Episcopal Sunday school at the end of the war [WW II] and hearing this woman talk about how Jesus protected all the little children. I thought, This Jesus of hers is really not on the job so much." So John and a friend decided to investigate other possibilities. After systematically trying to find the perfect religion, including interviewing a rabbi and a Greek orthodox minister, they gave up, concluding all religions were limited.

Like libertarians, some SDS youth also decided they were atheists. As a boy Jim Shoch hated going to Sunday school at his reform Jewish temple. He says, "I remember . . . in kindergarten . . . playing at Terry Weinstein's house and I told her . . . I didn't believe in God. She ran off to tell her mother. She was just shocked. . . . I was always very rational and secular. It just never made sense. Where was He or She? Where was God working its will in the world?"

Three SDSers actually *did* become libertarians by the 1970s. Their stories of their drift away from religion directly parallel the libertarians in YAF. Like other libertarians, for Doug Knox it was the clash between rationality and faith that led to his disenchantment. Raised Presbyterian, as a child Doug was a believer. "I thought prayers would be efficacious and there was a God out there." But during his childhood Doug began reading about Clarence Darrow and the Scopes trial. Curious about Darrow's agnosticism, Doug read his autobiography, which "had a big impact on me because it . . . forcefully raised the problem of evil which . . .

had a big effect in undermining my religious beliefs." Doug was further disillusioned when his grandfather died under dramatic circumstances, during which time Doug fervently prayed to save him. Because his efforts proved useless, Doug concluded that prayer was not efficacious after all. By the time he was a freshman in high school, Doug was a confirmed atheist.

Given this lesser religiosity and tendency toward disbelief among SDSers, what is surprising is that many activists still identify religion, and religious values, as an important catalyst to their activism.[15] Thus, like many from YAF, religion was influential in the political development of these youth. In particular, the *values* transmitted through religion formed an *ethical framework* that provided a basis for their involvement.

The few SDSers who were raised Catholic say their religious upbringing played a clear part in their activism. One of them, Lynn Dykstra, discusses the importance of the Catholic Church.

> Where I got my value system actually came from the Catholic school and the Church where love of God, and devotion to duty, and loving everyone, and trying not to be angry, and not to kill, and all those kind of values were very loudly taught at my school. . . . I accepted those. I've always thought that was where the background came from for me to get involved in politics.

Lynn also points out that the ecumenical movement in the church in the early 1960s represented a time of openness and tolerance, which was also very appealing to her. Unlike YAFers who rejected the changes ushered in by Vatican II, for Lynn these changes were compelling, signifying a rejection of rigid dogma. Lynn says it was only when the church "began digging its feet in and not wanting to support some of the things that were right but illegal, like civil rights," that she began to turn away from the church.

Many of the Jewish SDSers, whether they were raised in a religious environment or not, also mentioned the values they learned as Jews as being important to the development of their politics. For instance, Naomi Schapiro grew up with a strong cultural identity as a Jew that, she says, influenced her politics.

> At the time I was growing up there was a tremendous left-wing Jewish culture in New York. A lot of people had been in labor unions. . . . My mother was very poor growing up. A lot of her cousins were in the Communist Party. . . . Being Jewish was being

concerned with injustice. . . . The rabbi in our temple was very involved in civil rights activities and had gotten arrested in some big
demonstration which he never let us forget. So I think there was a
very liberal sense connected with being Jewish.

Among those who were raised in a religious household, Judaism was
associated with having a sense of obligation to others, particularly to
"people who were suffering," or meant "you were supposed to care about
justice and civil rights," or Judaism was simply identified with "equality and justice and decency and democracy."

In addition, the particular impact of the Holocaust and personal exposure to anti-Semitism also shaped the political consciousness of Jewish SDSers. The majority of Jewish SDSers mentioned the Holocaust as
fundamental both to their sense of Jewish identity and to the development of their political values. One-quarter of SDS activists mentioned
relatives who were harmed or killed by Nazis. Two SDSers were raised
in communities that included many Holocaust survivors. One of them,
Vivian Rothstein, wasn't raised very religiously; she only went to temple for High Holidays. But she clearly identified as a Jew "because of
the whole experience my family had been through." Her mother was a
refugee from Germany. Vivian says, "[I] grew up in a community of
people who had either been in the camps or lost most of their family in
camps. So I felt removed from American society a little bit, which . . .
helped in later . . . being critical of the society."

Another SDSer, Norm Daniels, also lost many of his relatives in concentration camps. He comments, "I've always remembered linking in
my own mind what happened to blacks to what had happened to Jews."
Thus, in a variety of ways—by creating a feeling of estrangement, through
linkage to others' oppression, or by symbolizing ultimate evil—the experience of the Holocaust helped form the basis of motivation for these activists' own political participation.

Besides the Holocaust, personal experiences with anti-Semitism also
were formative to an activist identity. Some say that direct experiences
with anti-Semitism created the sense of being a social outcast, providing
a stance outside the mainstream that corresponded to the role of an activist. Many Jewish SDSers also recognized the commonality between
anti-Semitism and racism. Dave Strauss relayed various incidents of anti-
Semitism he experienced as a youth, from being excluded from social
events in high school, to being restricted from a fraternity as a student

at the University of Michigan. Dave says these experiences "certainly helped me understand what the black movement was about."

Beyond the values and experiences that religious identification provided, the other way that religion affected political involvement was simply by introducing young people to individuals and groups that provided an entry into political life. Some activists met people who were socially conscious and politically involved through religious institutions, opening the door to activism. For other SDSers religious leaders became important as role models. Steve Kessler says the rabbi in the reform synagogue his family belonged to played a key role in the development of his own politics. "He'd been involved in the grape boycott and he went to Selma, Alabama, and almost got trampled by horses . . . so he's disabled. It was really quite courageous of him." This rabbi was an inspiration to Steve in provoking his activism.

In short, religion and religious values were important factors that shaped the political consciousness of both left- and right-wing youth, giving them an ethical framework for their developing beliefs. But the content of that framework varied. For those from devout homes in YAF, relation to God, religious devotion, and moral absolutism provided a framework by which to judge right and wrong in the political world. For those SDS youth who were affected by religion, it was moral obligation to others and fighting injustice and inequality that prevailed. Further, SDS activists point to indirect ways, too, that religion affected their political ideology—through experiences with anti-Semitism, through the lessons of the Holocaust, and through rabbis and other religious figures who were supportive and acted as role models of political participation.

Clearly, what is essential to both groups is not simply religion per se, but religion as it is embedded in a larger context. We must know how religious upbringing relates to parents' values and political beliefs, to a larger community and culture in which an individual lives, in order to understand how religious values fit within one frame or another. Thus, for many traditionalist Catholic youth the values of the church, particularly anticommunism, coincided with their parents' political values, reinforcing belief, just as for many SDS youth religious values that emphasized injustice and responsibility to others reinforced the political and ethical values instilled in them by their parents.

Finally, what is equally important in shaping the political ideology of some members of both SDS and YAF is the *rejection of religion*. Thus, many SDS youth followed paths resembling those of libertarian YAF members in eventually rejecting religious practice and embracing a secular, atheistic worldview.

## CONCLUSION

The conditions into which we are born, the families in which we are raised, the values and beliefs that surround us, all are a taken-for-granted part of childhood. As Berger and Luckmann put it, "Every individual is born into an objective social structure within which he encounters the significant others who are in charge of his socialization. These significant others are imposed on him. Their definitions of his situation are posited for him as objective reality."[16] We inherit definitions of the world, ways of seeing, which become the basis for a "natural view of the world." Our identities are first formed through these primary attachments.

What is apparent in comparing these women and men of the left and right is the stark differences in their social background and political and religious orientations. Not only are the youth of SDS and YAF from different worlds, but even within YAF, traditionalists and libertarians stand apart. These vast differences in background and orientation of youth of the left and right predisposed each of them to react to the social changes of the 1960s in contrasting ways.

Although the differences between activists are apparent, what is also striking in the biographies of these activists is that despite these differences, most youth from both left and right shared the experience of being raised in atypical homes compared to others of their age. Their parents were politically aware and, to one degree or another, engaged and involved in the world. Further, most parents consciously encouraged their daughters and sons to be vocal and active in the political world. Thus, for the majority of these youth their parents provided them with the framework and motivation that gave shape to their identity as activists. In addition to parents, other significant people, as well as critical formative experiences, shaped the contours of political identity. These other elements are the subject of chapter 3.

# CHAPTER THREE

# THE MAKING OF AN ACTIVIST

The young women and men who joined SDS and YAF did not just grow up in families with parents who were committed to politics. Specific catalysts during their childhood sparked their involvement in the political world—people who inspired them to think in new ways, personal experiences that crystallized belief, as well as larger forces such as the civil rights movement, the 1964 Goldwater campaign, and the Vietnam War that marked their generation. In particular, activists' stories identify five critical sources of politicization: relatives and other important adults; the political climate of their communities; formative childhood experiences; high school experiences, including the influences of teachers, books, and school activities; and historical and political events. These five factors combined in varying ways to transform individual lives and to shape an activist identity.

## PEOPLE AS CATALYSTS

Besides the key role that parents play in shaping the beliefs and values of youth, for many future members of SDS and YAF, other individuals— relatives, family friends, community people—also served as role models during childhood and adolescence, inspiring early thoughts about the political world. Numerous SDS activists, for instance, discussed relatives other than parents who were influential during their growing-up years. Although few YAF members mentioned relatives, one who *did,* Kitty

Smith, relays the lessons she learned from her father's stepmother, a devout anti-Communist. Kitty's grandmother gave her pre–World War I geography books and told her,

> Now I want you to learn these. I want you to study these countries because they're going to come back. The Russians have taken over; this is now the Union of Soviet Socialist Republic so the map looks wrong to you. . . . After World War I they came under Soviet domination, but they don't want to be.

From this Kitty learned to identify Latvia, Estonia, and Lithuania and carried away a clear sense of the dangers of communism.

Terry Koch, an SDS member, also names his grandmother as influential, but the lessons she taught him are profoundly different from those Kitty learned. When Terry was six, his grandmother insisted he stay home with her during the McCarthy hearings. He recalls, "My grandmother put it in terms of right and wrong, good and evil." Those speaking out against McCarthy, she said, were "the true Americans." Terry's grandmother also told him stories about a boy she had known whose family had disowned him because of his politics. The boy ended up becoming a member of the Abraham Lincoln Brigade, sacrificing his life fighting in the Spanish civil war. Clearly, Kitty and Terry learned diametrically opposed lessons about communism and the "enemy out there."

Other SDS activists were influenced as much by the lifestyle as the politics of their relatives. This pattern applies particularly to *crossovers,* the minority of activists who ended up on the other side of the political fence from their parents. For example, throughout his childhood Rory Ellinger was drawn to his bohemian aunt and his uncle, a nationally recognized labor leader and organizer in the Socialist Party. They were key because they and their lifestyle represented a departure from Rory's Republican parents. Rory's aunt and uncle openly avowed socialism, lived together without the sanction of legal marriage, and freely used alcohol, a lifestyle not common in Webster Groves, Missouri, where Rory grew up.

This sense of being exposed to a new way, the opening of horizons, seems to be central to the stories told by crossovers in SDS. Another crossover, Beth Oglesby, says her two aunts inspired her by their "generosity of spirit and compassion for people." In contrast to her Republican mother, who was fearful and conservative, Beth says one of her aunts "opened me up to a lot of stuff. . . . By the time I was grown up, I . . . associated that kind of fearfulness and rigidity with [being] Republican."

For other activists on both the left and the right, people outside the family introduced them to a new world. Occasionally such people inadvertently led these youth on an unexpected path. For instance, Cindy Decker, yet another crossover, followed an unusual path to SDS. As a girl Cindy met a woman, Sunny, through her mother's involvement with the John Birch Society. Sunny "took me under her wing . . . and was almost like a second mother to me." Cindy would go over to Sunny's house every day and help her with political tasks such as stuffing envelopes. Most important, when Cindy was a teenager, Sunny found a sponsor for Cindy to attend the Freedom School in Colorado Springs. The experiences Cindy had there radically changed her, exposing her to libertarian ideas, atheism, anarchism, and eventually led her to the left.

More commonly, there was a continuity between the people who acted as mentors and the politics these young people adopted. During his youth Alan MacKay, a YAFer, became close to a good friend of his father's. This man was very conservative and active in town politics. Through him Alan was introduced to a prominent and well-connected conservative leader who, in turn, introduced Alan to many other conservatives. Alan says, "There's no question that both of these men affected my thinking. They reinforced what my parents and teachers had been telling me." Both men were delighted when Alan was invited to attend the Sharon conference, the founding meeting of YAF.

### COMMUNITY AS CATALYST

While some activists identify individuals as catalysts to their thinking, others discuss the influence of their community. Being embedded in a neighborhood with shared political views also contributed to the formation of beliefs. Jeanne Friedman, an SDS member, grew up in a "Bronx Democratic working-class community." She says that every kid in the Bronx worked on the Adlai Stevenson campaign the summer before the 1952 election.

> You [didn't] even know that there was somebody else running because in the Bronx at that time you wouldn't have seen an Eisenhower sign. Never. That's just what all the kids did. You all went down to the local Democratic headquarters and you stuffed envelopes and stuck things on doors. . . . It was a very activist culture. . . . You were born a Democrat. There was no choice involved. . . . It was like being born Jewish. There were certain things you had to do. You had to be interested in politics and . . . you had to regard the unions as the absolute savior of the working class.

Many YAFers, on the other hand, were embedded in communities of conservatism. Marick Payton grew up in Kansas; he describes the "midwestern common folk conservatism" of his community:

There was a paranoia and I certainly did share that. There was not merely the fear of an internal Communist revolution, but a great distrust of the federal government, and a great threat that the federal government would launch a sort of socialist welfare state. FDR was seen as the great bogeyman.

Similarly, Harvey Hukari recalls the conservative Republican enclave in San Diego where he was raised, in the heart of Goldwater country, and says the conservative climate in southern California "might be the single greatest contributing factor" to the development of his beliefs. Clearly, activists at either end of the political spectrum not only came from varying backgrounds but also grew up in dissimilar climates that encouraged contrasting values and beliefs. They were embedded in entirely different social worlds, raised with contrary assumptions about the world.

## EXPERIENCES AS CATALYST

In discussing their childhood and adolescence, many activists also relay specific experiences that instigated the process of "becoming political." For SDS members the majority of these memories concern a dawning awareness of race and class inequality.

Vivian Rothstein remembers one particular experience as her "first real political experience." While attending Hollywood High School Vivian fell in with a liberal intellectual crowd of students. One summer Vivian got a job working for a friend's father. This friend, who saw himself as "very liberal," was about to go to Reed College, while Vivian, who came from a more modest background, was going to Berkeley. Vivian's job that summer was working at her friend's father's collection company that used bogus contracts to collect debts from black and Latino families.

All summer these poor minority families would come in scared to death that their homes and their cars would be repossessed. And I knew that . . . the two men running this business weren't even lawyers . . . and that these contracts weren't even—. You know, you'd go, you'd sign, you'd buy some meat and then it turned out you'd signed for a $3,000 freezer and four years' worth of frozen meat. . . . Then these contracts are sold to collection companies who make the profits. It was an unbelievable experience for me seeing these two Jewish liberals who were sending their son to Reed doing this to blacks and Latinos.

This process of disillusion with liberalism pushed Vivian leftward. Another SDSer, Helen Garvy, became aware of inequality during junior high school through a close friendship with a black girl. Helen's political awareness grew as Helen learned about the conditions of her friend's life, for example, how her school used textbooks rejected from all the other schools and had the worst teachers. Helen comments, "I was privileged a lot in my life to get to see the world from other people's perspectives. It really tempered a lot of my outlook. . . . So I understood what segregation was about. . . . I understood all the stuff that SDS believed, which was why SDS was appealing to me."

Some members of both SDS and YAF were politicized through travel, being exposed to situations different from their own. YAFer Fran Griffin, for instance, traveled all over the world with her parents, starting with visiting Cuba when she was seven years old. She says traveling made her "understand how much better off we have it here." Seeing Russia and Czechoslovakia also made her aware of the horrors of communism. "When you travel you really can see . . . the freedoms we have. . . . So it really did help shape my beliefs to have that exposure to all these different cultures."

In contrast, SDSer Terry Koch remembers a trip he took with his family when he was twelve.

We were driving around the country and one of the things my parents did besides go to the Grand Canyon was they said, "We're going to drive through the Navajo reservation. We're going to see how these people were treated." . . . My brother had a hamburger that he hadn't finished. We were near a house and there was a dog running around. My mother said, "Okay, give the hamburger to the dog." That's one thing I was brought up with was you never waste food . . . that was a sin. . . . So my brother threw this hamburger out of the car to this dog and the kids came running up because they were hungry. That's something my brother and I have never forgotten.

While Fran took away the lesson of anticommunism, cherishing the freedom of the United States in contrast to Eastern Europe, Terry was struck by the harsh reality of inequality in his own country.

Other activists recall critical experiences of their parents speaking up and taking on the school system. Members of SDS and YAF recount parallel tales. One of the object lessons of SDSer John Brown Childs's upbringing was witnessing his parents stand up to school officials. As one of the few black students attending a predominantly white high school, John was automatically placed in the industrial arts, noncollege prep courses. Each semester his parents would march to school and demand that John be moved. Their efforts proved successful.

In a similar fashion YAFer Emmy Lewis witnessed her parents taking on the school board and winning, albeit on different grounds. Throughout her childhood Emmy's parents were voracious readers and particularly kept up with the latest educational theories. Her parents were outraged when they discovered that the superintendent of Emmy's elementary school was a "progressive Deweyite." They saw the new methods of teaching being instituted in the schools as a serious threat to the integrity of public education. Her mother, particularly incensed, composed a letter to the editor of the local newspaper. In response to this letter, Emmy's parents were flooded with phone calls. "I will never forget it as a magnificent testament of grass roots activism. . . . It was a woman responding to her intelligence and her commitment, challenging the then progressive educational dogma that was being fed to the schoolchildren." Emmy's mother called a meeting and organized; eventually the entire schoolboard was replaced with traditionalist advocates. In both cases John and Emmy were given the message that one could fight the larger structures of society and win. Although the basis of involvement radically differed, the images of successful activism became a part of John's and Emmy's consciousness.

Given the politicized environments in which activists grew up, combined with these catalyzing experiences, it is not surprising that some activists on both the left and the right already showed an interest in politics during childhood. Even at age five YAFer Lynn Bouchey recalls he was advocating nuclear war against the Soviet Union. By eight he was driving around his neighborhood on his bicycle passing out campaign literature and bumper stickers. When President Harry S. Truman fired General Douglas MacArthur, he circulated a petition among his classmates, calling for Truman's impeachment.

Similarly, some future members of SDS also became engaged in politics at an early age. Michael Kazin says he always saw himself "as something of a radical." In junior high school he recalls winning a speech contest with his talk arguing for the abolition of the House Un-American

Activities Committee. Whereas these activists were already cognizant of politics by the time they reached grade school, many others first became politically conscious during high school.

## HIGH SCHOOL AS CATALYST

For activists on both the left and the right high school stands out as a particularly important time for the formation of an activist identity. Through inspiring teachers, exposure to new ideas in books, and involvement in extracurricular activities, many youth were spurred to think and act politically.

### Teachers

Teachers often became catalysts for activism, introducing students to new ideas or inspiring them to think in new ways. YAFer Dave Walter remembers a particular high school government teacher who influenced him by teaching about the evils of communism. In contrast, SDSer Bernardine Dohrn learned a different lesson from her high school government teacher. She vividly recalls the challenges he posed to her thinking.

> He did this test the first day of class where he asked us . . . "What percentage of the world is black?" . . . "What percentage of the world is Christian?," a whole series of questions. Essentially what he got us to do in a perfect pattern was to project the world out from our white suburb as looking like us. . . . Then he was ruthless at saying what a bunch of ignorant fools we were, it was time for us to learn about the world. I remember loving it and being completely shocked.

The challenges provoked a long process of questioning, stimulating Bernardine to find out much more about the world beyond Milwaukee.

Some activists were inspired by teachers who held opposing ideological views from their own. Jeanne Friedman, the SDSer who grew up in a Bronx Democratic neighborhood, says the first Republican she ever met was a junior high school teacher. Whenever he returned Jeanne's schoolwork, he slipped in pictures of Eisenhower. Jeanne recalls,

> I hated Eisenhower. Without knowing, of course, anything about him. . . . I would put pictures of Stevenson in my folders. The teacher was wonderful. . . . We just used to fight all the time. . . .

What he was trying to get across is that you can't dislike someone when you know nothing about them. . . . He wanted me to study hard and learn more. . . . I started doing a lot more reading. . . . From that time on, I fixed that what I was going to do with my life was get into . . . political science.

In a few cases teachers stood as negative examples. Typically the encounter involved students from a conservative upbringing and liberal teachers. Gus DiZerega faced this situation in the eighth grade in Wichita, Kansas:

My homeroom teacher gave the entire class a diatribe about the John Birch Society—how they didn't believe in democracy and that sort of thing. Up until then I wanted to be a forest ranger or an architect. As I walked home . . . full of indignation that such people could exist, I asked my mother, "Do you know any Birchers?" She said, "Why, yes.". . . She said something to the effect of "You're getting a little too much left-wing propaganda in school."

Gus's mother began bringing him to meetings of conservative groups. Before long he became a committed conservative. Within a few years Gus joined a group of conservative students in high school and they eventually formed a chapter of YAF.

Other activists remember high school teachers who inspired their thinking by introducing them to particular authors. SDSer Steve Kessler was encouraged by his high school history teacher to read William Appleton Williams. At the same time his drama teacher introduced him to Bertolt Brecht, whom he also found inspiring.

## Books

In fact, many activists on the right or the left mention the importance of reading as an essential ingredient to the development of their beliefs. Books, too, led to new ideas and opened horizons. As YAFer Allen Brandstater put it, "More than most kids my age, I became a real political zealot and I attribute a lot of that to reading." Authors (and books) named as particularly influential for SDS members include existentialist writers, such as Albert Camus and Jean-Paul Sartre, as well as John Steinbeck, Ernest Hemingway, Thomas Wolfe, Alan Watts, Allen Ginsberg's *Howl,* and Michael Harrington's *The Other America.* Authors and works of particular importance to YAF members include economists Friedrich Hayek,

Ludwig von Mises, and Milton Friedman, Henry Hazlitt, Albert Jay Nock, Whittaker Chambers, Russell Kirk, Frank Meyer, Barry Goldwater, Richard Weaver's *The Mainspring of Human Progress,* Phyllis Schlafly's *A Choice, Not an Echo,* Mark Twain, and Henry Thoreau as well as the conservative magazines *National Review* and *Human Events.* John Dos Passos and Ayn Rand were named by some members of both SDS and YAF as being influential.

Some youth were introduced to these readings through their parents. Many parents of YAF members, for instance, received *National Review* and *Human Events* at home. YAFer Mary Fisk's father, a fervent anti-Communist, wasn't politically active but read a lot and discussed issues with her: "My father followed [William F.] Buckley's career and read his books. We got *National Review* and when each issue of *National Review* came, it was like the [high] point of the week." When Mary entered high school, she, too, began reading *National Review.* Given Mary's exposure to conservative ideas throughout her childhood, YAF's principles resonated with her. She comments, "When I heard YAF's message, it was one I could identify with."

One of the books that affected a number of YAFers during their youth was the best-selling autobiography by Whittaker Chambers, *Witness.* The book's main message was the importance of the struggle against atheistic communism. Jáime Ryskind says, "My mother really felt that there were two books in Western civilization. One was the Bible and the other was Whittaker Chambers's *Witness.*" Jáime's mother quoted these two books interchangeably to prove any point.

Other youth from the left and right discovered influential books and authors on their own or were introduced to them through friends. Many activists say they felt welcome relief in finding someone else with shared views. SDSer John Brown Childs says reading became "my liberation." Growing up as one of the few black children in a small town in Massachusetts, John felt marginal from an early age. He had friends but was well aware of his differences from those around him. Thus, books became his haven. "As a marginalized person, I read a lot. That was my escape. I'd read history books for the fun of it. I read a lot of sociology in the eighth grade. This is how I got out of the context in which I was in. . . . I was able to go off into other worlds through books." John started reading books about the history of African civilization that countered the racism he faced at school. His reading laid a conceptual groundwork that helped him carve out a valuable, positive sense of himself.

For Jay Parker, one of the few black members of YAF, reading was key to his development. Jay grew up in a poor family in Philadelphia. Although as a young child he had to wear shoes with holes in them, he was well aware of the wealthy families living on the Main Line, conscious that "there was a better life somewhere."

During his youth Jay was particularly influenced by two black columnists he read regularly in the *Pittsburgh Courier*, S. B. Fuller and George Schuyler. He recalls,

> You had very strong freedom of the individual [in] editorials and commentary in the newspaper at that time. That impressed me, the urging of blacks to own their businesses. . . . [That] blacks shouldn't work for other people; they should work for themselves. That's the road to independence. . . . That influenced me a lot. I knew somebody was really . . . advocating this—what I felt all along . . . [that] I used to resist what my mother would tell me.

George Schuyler became Jay's hero. Schuyler's columns encouraged Jay to think about the importance of being economically independent, of not relying on outside help, of controlling his own destiny.

For both John and Jay reading was fundamental to understanding their position as black people. Whereas John drew a sense of identity and connection from understanding his African roots and from analyzing society, Jay derived belief in the importance of individual self-reliance from his reading. It is not surprising that John is currently an anthropologist while Jay is an entrepreneur.

What is clear is that books and ideas played a key role in helping these youth think through issues, in confirming the direction of their beliefs, in instigating their commitment to politics. For some future members of SDS and YAF reading provided a framework by which they could interpret thoughts and experiences in their lives. SDSer Carl Oglesby says books helped him frame his own embryonic ideas.

> [Reading] meant that these little thoughts that flitted across my mind—thoughts of criticism, thoughts of exception-taking, thoughts of doubting—and which my normal response was to discard, suddenly started becoming very precious to me because I saw . . . the legitimacy of my own critique in reading [other's] critique. I had the innermost parts of my[self] being confirmed.

The development of Doug Knox's thought, and his shift toward the New Left, also came about primarily through books. "The thing that's most influenced me is my reading. There's just no question about it. I am a cerebral intellectual. . . . I had a tendency . . . to try to seek out the best argument on both sides of a question." When Doug was in grammar school he used to go to the Communist Party bookstore in San Francisco and then to the John Birch Society bookstore. He would buy books at both places, trying to persuade the sellers that he didn't have a lot of money and asking if they could make a special deal so he could buy more to read.

During high school Doug was particularly influenced by Camus's *The Rebel*, Ayn Rand's *The Fountainhead*, and Hayek's *The Road to Serfdom*. All of these led him in the direction of libertarianism. Although Doug was pro-Goldwater at the time, he was greatly affected by a paired set of articles he read in *Playboy* during high school by Barry Goldwater and Norman Mailer focusing on the ideal government. He was persuaded by one of Mailer's arguments to Goldwater that questioned how Goldwater could believe in individual liberty and then endorse a military budget that created a garrison state. This article influenced Doug in a more radical libertarian direction that was compatible with the New Left. In fact, Doug eventually ended up joining SDS.

Youth on the right consistently named three particular sources as fundamental to their development: William F. Buckley's *National Review,* Barry Goldwater's *Conscience of a Conservative,* and Ayn Rand. Several YAF members say *National Review* actually instigated their involvement in politics. Maggie Kohls recalls reading *National Review* during high school and bursting into tears thinking, This is wonderful! I didn't know there was anybody who agreed with me.

Other YAFers point to Goldwater's *Conscience of a Conservative* as instrumental to their activism. Allen Brandstater says the reason he got into politics was through Barry Goldwater. He was given a copy of the book during high school. Allen says, "I read through that and was underlining things and I thought, This is the savior of Western civilization." Other YAFers also point to Goldwater's book as crystallizing belief, as a kind of manifesto.

But for libertarian YAFers it was, above all, Ayn Rand who was most significant. Many libertarians say Rand taught them how to conceptualize, to put ideas in a larger framework. Sharon Presley says she was "totally apolitical" until at nineteen a friend recommended she read Rand's *Atlas Shrugged*.

It was like, "Oh, my God, what a revelation!" . . . I read the book; it came along at just the right time. . . . What she did for me was get me thinking about . . . things in those kinds of philosophical terms that I never had . . . before. I can see that in my trek through various religious stuff that that's what I wanted. But it wasn't until Rand that I had some kind of explicitly articulated theory or set of principles that made sense to me. . . . So that was a major, major influence on my life.

Shortly after reading Rand, Sharon began attending objectivist lectures in San Francisco and meeting other like-minded people. Besides libertarian YAFers, two SDS activists who became libertarians also say Rand was influential to the formation of their political beliefs.

### School Activities

Besides books and teachers, involvement at school also initiated youth into politics. By the time they reached high school, many of these young people were already active citizens in their schools, participating in high school events and activities. There is a striking similarity to the future SDS and YAF members' types of activities. About half of each group reported involvement in at least one of the following extracurricular activities: debate, student government, and editing or writing for school newspapers. Such experiences exposed them to a wide range of issues as well as teaching them skills useful to their later activism.

Those people who were active in debate unanimously commented on the ways this experience contributed to their political education by teaching them how to research issues and showing them new political perspectives. Others point to the ways that debate taught them to be intellectually rigorous, a valuable asset for their later involvement with SDS or YAF. Carl Oglesby got drawn into debate club as a sophomore. The debate question that year was universal military conscription. He comments,

I learned about issues. I learned about how arguments are structured. . . . You're trained to think, What's the other guy gonna say? What am I going to say against this point that I just made when I'm on the other side of the question? . . . Debate is excellent training for political analysis. . . . It equips you to look at issues unemotionally and to look as a matter of course for the flaws in your argument.

Because of his oratory abilities and his leadership qualities, Carl was elected president of his high school. Later he would assume the presidency of SDS.

Similarly, YAFers who were involved in debate point to its significance. YAFer Mary Fisk, who was president of her student council, also says she learned concrete skills from debate. "Debating got me into the idea of being able to argue for your beliefs. One of the issues—I can't believe—was 'Is nuclear war survivable?' I was saying, Yes . . . making the case for surviving nuclear war. . . . It got me used to arguing for certain points of view."

Student government was another activity that proved to be formative. Those participating in student government gained experience speaking, negotiating, and learning leadership skills. A few SDS members recall how they extended their roles in student government beyond traditional expectations. Michael Kazin, for instance, remembers running for student body president in high school with a platform calling for students to have a vote in *all* decisions made in the school. In reaction to this early call for "participatory democracy," his opponent ran a poster showing Nikita Khrushchev on one side, Fidel Castro on the other side, and Michael in the center shaking hands with both men. In later years Michael became the president of Harvard SDS.

Involvement with school newspapers also sharpened political perspectives and inspired commitment. YAFer Marilyn Bradley, who says she was a proselytizer from junior high school on, wrote a column in high school with her best friend, Clara. In the column Marilyn represented the right-wing perspective and Clara the left-wing view. "We did the column together and so there was this sense of engagement and passion." Some SDSers recall writing articles and editorials for their school paper on topics that were unpopular at the time. Dorothy Burlage wrote an article about the ostracism faced by the Spanish-speaking kids in her high school. Sue Jhirad's articles against nuclear power were considered "radical" for the time.

Work on student papers also provided concrete skills useful in later years. SDSer John Brown Childs, along with some friends, started their own newspaper in high school, a satirical paper that "rejected the norms." That experience, and the skills John learned in working the Linotype machine, led him eventually to work on an underground newspaper during college.

In short, through their involvement in high school activities many future members of SDS and YAF not only learned skills that were useful to their later activism, but also began to identify themselves as political beings. Although many analysts have argued that activists acquire resources and learn skills through their participation in social movements that are then transferred to subsequent political causes,[1] what is clear is that most of these youth acquired skills that *preceded* their involvement with SDS/YAF or any other social movement organization. High school activities provided a training ground for future activist careers.

### First Steps of Political Action

In addition to taking part in traditional school activities, by high school most youth on both left and right were showing signs of political awakening, taking their first steps in the political world. Although these initial ventures into politics did not involve joining an organization or sustained commitment to a cause, they were nonetheless important as they instilled a sense of efficacy and confidence. Some youth took these first steps in encounters with school officials. SDSer Barbara Haber recalls one particular incident of civil disobedience during high school. Barbara decided to ignore the school rule that dictated to all younger students the duty to rise when the seniors marched in at school assemblies.

> I thought this was disgusting. So I organized a bunch of my friends not to do it, just to sit down, stay seated. . . . This was really *the* moment in my life. Teachers came around and they pressured everybody into standing up. One by one I saw my friends give in and they stood up. I was the only one left. . . . I remember this moment very clearly, where if I stood up, I would lose something forever. But I didn't. I sat.

Barbara's action gave her a sense of power and the knowledge that she could effectively resist injustice.

A similar feistiness is evidenced in an experience relayed by YAFer Kathy Rothschild. Kathy insisted on wearing her Goldwater button to her parochial high school. The principal at the school demanded she take it off, arguing it wasn't part of the uniform. Kathy responded, "We're going to have to vote in a couple of years. We should be informed. I'm showing who I am for." One of the teachers confiscated her button. When Kathy went home that night, her father "hit the ceiling," called the principal, and demanded that unless the button was returned and Kathy was allowed to wear it, he'd pull her out of the school:

> So I got my button back and I wore it. And I told everybody who was for Johnson, "Wear the button. Let's be involved." Eventually

> I finally convinced them that we should have a debate. So we got . . .
> somebody to represent Goldwater and somebody to represent
> Johnson. . . . Then we took a straw vote. . . . It was like twenty-
> two votes for Goldwater and four hundred for Johnson.

Despite being outnumbered, Kathy learned an important lesson in standing up for what she believed in and organizing others.

For other future activists these early ventures concerned larger political issues that would become fundamental to their later involvement.
Some SDS members, for instance, had experiences that led them to stand
up for civil rights. Even if these experiences didn't involve joining organizations, they were first steps in becoming involved in a larger cause.
Jane Adams's first political action took place while she was a member
of her high school band. One day the members of the band, which was
integrated, decided to go to a nearby roller rink. Because two black boys
were part of the group, they were not allowed in. In response, Jane and
the other students wrote up a petition to protest the rink's action.

Exposure to what was occurring in Vietnam sparked the involvement
of other leftist youth. Fred Faust remembers attending a session in his
high school in south St. Louis where an army representative came to speak
and showed a film, *Why Vietnam?* Although Fred wasn't a strong opponent of the war, he had his doubts and saw the film as "shameless . . .
incredible propaganda." The next day Fred went to see the principal to
see whether another view could be presented. "Before I did that I called
Washington University; I just asked for SDS because I didn't know who
to call. . . . I got a spokesman for SDS who said yeah, they'd be happy
to come out and present another view." Fred didn't join any organizations during high school, but once he began college at Washington University he did become involved with SDS.

For others the spark to action involved exposure to a personal men-
tor or leader. YAFer Rob Tyler says he was inspired by Fred Schwarz,
the organizer of the Christian Anti-Communist Crusade,[2] during high
school when he watched Schwarz's programs on Hungarian freedom
fighters, Cuba, and other such topics on TV.

> So I got on a bus and went down [to the station] and I just loved
> it. I said, "This is what I've been waiting for. This is what the world's
> about. It's about the Communists." I had to do something about
> it. I was very concerned. . . . Then as I became more aware, [I re-
> alized] guys like Richard Nixon don't really fight Communists very

effectively; he's wishy-washy. There's other people much better. So I started gravitating in pretty heavy right-wing circles.

In short, by high school many future members of SDS and YAF were already defining themselves—and were being defined by others—as political beings. Some youth had even begun to incorporate an activist identity into their concept of self.


## HISTORY AS CATALYST

About a third of both left- and right-wing youth actually did become involved in political organizations during their high school years. The remainder were drawn in during their college years or after. The dramatic political and social events of the 1960s pulled people into making history, beckoning them to act on their beliefs. For SDS activists, the civil rights movement and the Vietnam War were the primary factors instigating action, while for YAF activists the 1964 Goldwater campaign and anticommunism were the main impetuses to action. These key historical forces provided the final essential ingredient to catalyze these youth into the political world.


### The Civil Rights Movement

In discussing which issue prompted their involvement, about equal numbers of SDS activists named either the civil rights movement or the Vietnam War as primary or cited both as equally important. Because civil rights protest built momentum earlier than antiwar protest, and because some civil rights organizations shifted away from working with white groups in the mid to late 1960s, later SDS activists were more likely to become active in response to the war.

Involvement with the civil rights movement initially ranged from participation in a few sit-ins and demonstrations, to help in desegregating restaurants, to membership in organizations such as the Southern Christian Leadership Conference, the Student Nonviolent Coordinating Committee (SNCC), or the Northern Student Movement. Some youth felt compelled to join in civil rights protest during high school. Rory Ellinger's first political steps took place in high school when he joined an NAACP picket of Woolworth's. Rory remembers,

Blacks could only order food to go out. If you were a black you came in and they served you in a bag and you had to leave. They all looked like preachers' sons or daughters, all dressed up. . . . I just was . . . moved. I was working as a checker at the Kroger's store and during lunch hour I went out and I saw these people [demonstrating]. I just stood there and watched and watched.

This experience spurred him to action. First, he participated in a few demonstrations. Then during college at the University of Missouri Rory became active in the peace and civil rights movement through the Catholic student movement. He became national vice president of Newman Club, a Catholic student organization, and began traveling around the country, giving speeches on Christian leadership and the civil rights movement. Through this group he also met Mary Varela, one of the early activists in SDS.

After graduation, Rory became active with the Young Christian Student Movement as a field organizer. He worked organizing civil rights and peace groups in Boston and Cleveland, raised money for SNCC, and worked as a demonstration chairman for the Congress of Racial Equality (CORE) in Chicago. His involvement in these organizations, and his association with Mary Varela, naturally led him to SDS.

Once these youth became involved with civil rights, they found their experiences transformative, propelling them to further action. Connie Brown first became active during high school in Wellesley, Massachusetts, when she, too, first joined a CORE picket of Woolworth's in a sympathy sit-in with the South. Once Connie started college at Swarthmore she immediately became involved with the Political Action Committee, a group that addressed a range of left-wing issues. However, Connie felt none of these causes were as exciting or as important to her as civil rights. Then, during the summer after her junior year, she and her sister drove to Cambridge, Maryland, to take part in one of SNCC's civil rights projects. Describing this as her "first real plunge out of my world," Connie's experience in Cambridge, living in the black community along with ten other students, changed her.

> It was exciting to be exposed to another culture and just exposed fast and have to absorb and . . . think and understand and try to figure things out. It was exciting what was happening in the community . . . which was . . . that everybody was all charged up and unified and happy and excited and thinking that something was really moving. . . . It quickly showed me a whole different part of life and how people are and how they can be. So that was really great and really important for me.

For some activists the decision to participate in the civil rights movement meant leaving behind a whole way of life and entering a new one. This was the case for Dorothy Burlage, who was raised in the South. Dorothy first became involved at the University of Texas where she began working with the YWCA and the National Student Association (NSA). When her sorority told her she had to choose between attending NSA meetings and remaining in the sorority because Greeks disapproved of NSA being interracial, she chose to leave and move into a desegregated dorm. Dorothy reflects on this decision. "When I chose it was like the door shut and I was no longer part of that southern culture that I'd been brought up in. . . . It was *very* scary. It was like once that ball started rolling . . . there was no going back."

Not only was there "no going back" but typically involvement with the civil rights movement led to involvement on other issues and with different organizations. Vivian Rothstein's story illustrates a common path of multiple activities. Vivian first became active with CORE at the University of California in Berkeley, organizing against discriminatory practices of the hotel and auto industries. Right after she turned eighteen Vivian was arrested, along with eight hundred other people, for lying down in the showroom of one of these auto dealers. That whole summer was spent in court. Vivian comments, "I sort of got swept into this whole political thing." The following fall Vivian became active in the Free Speech Movement and then decided she wanted to become a full-time organizer. In 1965 she went to Mississippi to work for SNCC and CORE, helping with voter registration and setting up Freedom Schools. The second day she was in Jackson, Vivian was arrested along with others who were challenging a ban against parading without a permit. Vivian spent about three weeks in jail.

> Then we went to this training program and . . . were dispersed in these counties. . . . I was sent to a little county right next to the county where [Michael] Schwerner, [James] Chaney, and [Andrew] Goodman had been killed. It was a very dangerous place. I was just plopped there on Red Dog Road in a little shack that was called the Freedom House. I worked with an eighty-two-year-old woman across the road and we just started organizing.

Several months later Vivian returned to Oakland, where she began working with ERAP (Economic Research and Action Project), an SDS project.[3]

In short, by the time many people joined SDS they already had been active for months or sometimes years, working with other organizations.

As Dorothy Burlage put it, "How I came to support desegregation is really the most critical question, not how I came into SDS. SDS was an aftermath of a really much more critical juncture." For those who cut their teeth on the civil rights movement, no other experience compares. Describing the movement as emotionally gripping, many viewed the spirit, the songs, the "beloved community" that endured violence and repression to achieve justice as a holy crusade, an unsurpassed heroic venture.

**YAF and the Civil Rights Movement**   As we might expect, the majority of YAFers did *not* become active in the civil rights movement. About half of YAF activists reported they either were opposed to the civil rights movement at the time or felt distant from the movement, that it did not pertain to their lives. The other half *did* feel sympathy for the civil rights movement. Although the majority of these YAFers did not become involved, surprisingly, four YAF activists were involved in some way with civil rights.

One of those who was drawn in, Mitch Petry, grew up in a middle-class neighborhood in Queens. He recalls watching the newsreels on television during junior high school, riveted by the way black people were treated in the South. He also remembers being impressed by the dignity and modesty of those claiming "the most basic of civil virtues." He wondered at the time, How can . . . a reasonable person not be revolted by what you see? Mitch calls the civil rights movement his "awakening politically." He says, "To kids who were socially conscious at all, the civil rights movement would seem to be the most important event happening historically." Mitch's first political action occurred during high school when he took part in local civil rights demonstrations. He also helped organize debates on civil rights in his school with a group that was affiliated with SDS.

Although three other YAFers also mentioned limited involvement with the civil rights movement, none described this issue as their primary impetus to action. Anne Edwards, who joined sympathy sit-ins at Woolworth's, says that her youthful idealism and belief in individual rights made her believe in the cause.

What is striking among YAFers who felt sympathetic toward the movement but did not participate in any way, is that several relate a "water fountain story" recalled from their childhood. In each case the person describes being appalled on discovering the separate facilities marked "white" and "colored," usually during travels through the South. Many of these YAFers believed that the civil rights cause was just but objected to some of the movement's tactics. They supported measures that used economic clout, such as boycotts and bus strikes, but opposed any reliance on the state to enforce equal rights, through the 1964 Civil Rights Act, for example.[4] Many YAFers feared these tactics would lead to the erosion of individual property rights or states' rights as well. As Lee Edwards put it, reflecting on his participation in King's 1963 March on Washington,

> I was deeply moved by the spirit of brotherhood and . . . love that permeated the great throng. But I could not accept their solution. Most blacks looked to the federal government to solve their problems. Conservatives saw the federal government as the problem. In truth, we spoke two very different languages, and there were few interpreters on either side.[5]

This opposition to collectivist solutions was closely tied to a prevalent belief that the movement was being led and manipulated by Communists. In contrast to reliance on government, many YAF activists advocated civil rights through the promotion of black capitalism.[6]

Libertarians in YAF were particularly torn by the dilemma posed by their belief in justice and their adherence to individual rights. Seeking a just and consistent policy, libertarians typically approved of desegregation of *public* facilities (which were supported by tax dollars) but opposed any forced desegregation of *private* facilities as an infringement on individual property rights.

Although YAF as an organization did not support civil rights, most opposition to the civil rights movement came from southern chapters.[7] One of the few leaders who did take a stand, Tom Huston, actively spoke out against groups such as the Ku Klux Klan and the National States' Rights Party and used his platform as president of YAF in 1966 and 1967 to call for "American Negroes to be made full-fledged citizens." His efforts were met with opposition from some quarters and even threats of bodily harm. Despite the varied objections raised against the civil rights movement at the time, numerous YAFers today express regrets at the failure of the right to take the lead in fighting for equal rights.

## The Peace Movement

The second historical catalyst provoking activism for youth on the left was the peace movement. For early SDS activists (those who became involved in SDS from 1960 to 1964) initial involvement typically focused on disarmament, while for later activists (those drawn in from 1965 to 1968) it was protest against the Vietnam War. Initial involvement ranged from participation in one or two antiwar marches or demonstrations supporting disarmament, to draft counseling, draft resistance, or becoming fully active in organizations devoted to peace.

SDSer Michael Kazin knew by the time he was in high school that he was opposed to the Vietnam War. In fact, he recalls some of his earliest political thoughts during childhood focusing on war, rejecting the whole idea of nuclear war and blaming the United States for "being the most guilty in the arms race." To express his beliefs Michael went to the April 1965 antiwar protest in Washington that was organized by SDS.

> I never had an experience like that before. The cherry blossoms were out; it was quite a beautiful time. People were saying great things. I soaked up all the speeches. I was still a liberal Democrat and so I liked the fact that people like [Senator] Wayne Morse had spoken as well as more radical people. . . . After that I sort of kept SDS in my mind as a positive thing.

Reflecting on the importance of the war to his activism as a whole, Michael says,

> I first got involved because of the war . . . even though there was all this sub-soil there anyway. But civil rights didn't really get me active in the way the war did. I'd already started thinking about [how] the world is in peril and the U.S. is potentially on the wrong side and thinking very much that killing in war was wrong.

As with civil rights, involvement in antiwar protest often had serious consequences in terms of changing priorities. Steve Kessler first became politically involved during his freshman year at UCLA when he went to a demonstration against Dow Chemical recruitment on campus. He then began to regularly attend antiwar demonstrations and protests against ROTC. At the end of the year, he recalls, "there was this call to resist illegitimate authority." Steve started thinking seriously about turning in his draft card. By the end of the summer, he made the decision and returned his draft card, refusing to be inducted. He calls this "the critical experience of my entire life. . . . Turning in my draft card was the . . . convergence of personal necessity with something that was politically critical." For more than two years Steve was caught up in his trial in which he was prosecuted for evading the draft.

Like Dorothy Burlage, some who became involved in the antiwar movement also felt doors close behind them as they decided to channel all their time and energy into protest against the war. Carl Oglesby followed an unusual route to becoming an activist. After finishing his bachelor's degree Carl began working in Ann Arbor as supervisor of the technical publications department at Bendix Aerospace Systems Division, a military industrial company. His job, which he held for eight years, required security clearance. By the time Carl discovered SDS he was thirty years old, married with three children, and owned a house with a white picket fence. In 1964 while he was at Bendix he began working for Wes Vivian, a local candidate running for Congress, writing position papers and campaign statements. By chance, Carl drew the straw to write up Vivian's position on the Vietnam War. The war was just beginning to get press and no one in the campaign knew much about it. As Carl studied the politics and history of Vietnam, he turned decidedly against the war. He wrote a position paper opposing U.S. involvement that was rejected by Vivian as being too radical. Carl recalls, "It was the first time anybody ever called me radical. I could have dropped my teeth. I saw nothing radical whatsoever about it. It just seemed stupid to go fight a war that you weren't going to fight hard enough to win, period."

Although Carl's paper was not used for the campaign, it was published in *Generation* magazine, where it drew the attention of SDS. A number of the early SDSers began visiting Carl and soon he and his wife, Beth, became integrated into the SDS network. By June 1965 Carl was elected president of SDS. He quit his job, sold the house, and moved with his family to Chicago to begin full-time work with SDS, earning $90 per week compared to the $10,000 annual salary he earned at Bendix. Carl reflects on this decision: "Really without Vietnam I would never have been pushed to the edge of making a choice and doing a thing like that. That really was something, to expose my family to so much uncertainty."

Some SDS activists say the civil rights movement stirred them to action and others point to the peace movement as primary; still others say it is hard to disentangle the two. These people say both causes felt equally important to their becoming activists. Many times people were simultaneously drawn into working on both sets of issues. Barbara Haber, for instance, first became involved in "ban the bomb" demonstrations at Brandeis. Soon after she became active in civil rights. For years Barbara was involved with both civil rights and protest against the Vietnam War. When asked which issue was more important in igniting her activism, she responds:

It's hard to measure. That's like saying was adolescence more important to you than the first three years of your life? . . . The civil rights movement was the first big thing I ever participated in and it was thrilling. That's where I got the sense of the beloved community, the possibility that came about through joint risk-taking for something worthwhile. . . . [But] the Vietnam War . . . shattered my comfort more than anything else in my life—my comfortable assumptions and my view of the world—and that taught me more about the dynamics of how the United States worked than anything else.

Whichever path a person took, through civil rights or through antiwar protest, each of these individuals arrived at the door of SDS. Joining SDS confirmed their involvement with politics, solidified their identity as an activist.

**YAF and the Peace Movement**    Unlike with civil rights, none of the YAF activists were sympathetic to antiwar protest *at the time they first became active.* Some libertarian YAFers were against the draft from the start and (as we'll see in chapter 4) when the Vietnam War escalated, libertarians grew increasingly opposed to it. The issue proved explosive to the organization. YAF's official position throughout the 1960s, however, was support for the United States fighting communism in Vietnam. In fact, a few activists say they were initially drawn to YAF because of its support for the war.

**The 1964 Goldwater Campaign**

No event compares to Barry Goldwater's 1964 presidential campaign in its significance for organizing youth on the right. Goldwater's campaign acted as a beacon for young conservatives much in the way the civil rights movement did for young leftists. All but four of the YAF activists in this study were involved in some way in the Goldwater campaign. For both traditionalists and libertarians, the Goldwater campaign was a primary route to activism and to YAF. Young people were involved in a range of activities from those who simply leafleted or stuffed envelopes, to those who were active on the local level organizing campaigns, campus groups, or Youth for Goldwater chapters in high school, to people who were full-time employees of Goldwater organizations.

One activist, Lee Edwards, even served as press secretary for Goldwater's presidential campaign.

Many youth had no previous organizational experience and were drawn into activism through the 1964 campaign itself. These people refer to Barry Goldwater as their "awakening" or, as one person put it, "the beginning of political consciousness." Some people became active during high school. Allen Brandstater was a senior in high school when he became involved with Youth for Goldwater.

> My first car was a '53 Ford; at one time I had eighteen bumper stickers on it. On the radio aerial I had punched out a can of Goldwater, which was ginger ale in a green can with gold lettering. I had a Goldwater pennant on top of my aerial. I'd go out 'til two and three in the morning with some friends and we'd [take down] Johnson/Humphrey stickers and put up Goldwater/Miller posters. I was a fanatic by the time I got to twelfth grade.

Other young people were drawn into the campaign during their college years. Sharon Presley's activism began with the Goldwater campaign while she was in college at UC-Berkeley. By then she had read Ayn Rand and considered herself a libertarian.

> So in 1964 I was walking on campus and there was a Cal Students for Goldwater table. At that time libertarians were favorable toward Goldwater because he was the closest . . . to what we believed. So I joined that group and became active; it was composed of both libertarians and conservatives. . . . But, of course, Goldwater was a very different kind of conservative from what we have today . . . because the conservatives of that time were not obsessed with religious morality issues. . . . The conservative movement was much more concerned with . . . economic issues and foreign policy. . . . So Goldwater to us seemed like a fresh breeze.

In fact, Barry Goldwater remains the only nonlibertarian presidential candidate Sharon has ever voted for in an election.

Many other youth speak of Goldwater symbolizing a new way, an opening on the political horizon. He acted as a beacon of hope for many young people on the right. Although Rob Tyler had been hanging out in right-wing circles since he discovered Fred Schwarz, his first full-fledged organizational ties were with the Goldwater campaign during his high school years. Rob started working "morning, noon, and night" organizing Youth for Goldwater chapters in high schools throughout the San Fernando valley in California. He reflects on what Goldwater symbolized.

> He represented a rebel. He represented a challenge to the eastern establishment. He represented West versus East. He represented a new approach toward international communism. He represented freedom from the growth of the federal bureaucracy. And he represented my personal freedom. I saw in him somebody that could bring about a new age in this country and Johnson was just the old politics.

Others, too, say they felt excited by Goldwater's challenge to the establishment and his commitment to individualism. The enthusiasm, passion, and idealism of youth intertwined with the campaign as Goldwater represented a break with the past, new possibilities. His talk of freedom and limitations of the state, his wariness of concentrations of power spoke to these youth, compelling them toward the political arena.

Given the idealism and reverence Goldwater inspired among these youth, it is not surprising that many people were crushed at Goldwater's landslide defeat. Maggie Kohls distinctly remembers the end of the election. She had been involved in the campaign since high school and became chair of Youth for Goldwater during college. For her "Goldwater was the answer to everything." Maggie recalls a specific incident in the aftermath of Goldwater's defeat.

> I remember running into one of the guys who worked on [the campaign] with me four months later. We hadn't seen each other since. Like everything died the day [Goldwater] lost. He was talking about something that happened and it was in terms of everything as preelection and postelection. You know, his life was divided that way.

For Maggie the loss was so devastating that she joined the John Birch Society, thinking "the world was coming to an end but I wanted to go down fighting."

Yet despite Goldwater's defeat, young people were able to get back on their feet and continue organizing. Alan MacKay remembers how he and his wife were "bitterly, bitterly disappointed" at the end of the election. Yet, he also comments,

> With the benefit of hindsight in history we realize that the presidential campaign, like nothing else, involves people, gets them started in the movement. . . . There were very few people, despite their disappointment, who said, "That's it for politics." The almost

universal reaction was "By God, we're not going to let that happen again. We're going to go out and take control of the Republican Party." . . . And it happened exactly that way. So the contribution of the '64 campaign can't be overestimated.

The conservative movement *did* gain by the 1964 election in a multitude of ways. For one thing, through Goldwater thousands of youth entered politics. The campaign transformed the uninitiated into activists
and united traditionalists and libertarians in common cause. As David
Keene puts it,

> For most of the conservatives of my generation the Goldwater cam-
> paign was the thing that got them involved. It did for us what the
> McCarthy or McGovern campaigns later did for the Democratic
> Party. . . . It's only a campaign like Goldwater's that is emotion-
> ally exciting and ideological and non-establishment that allows new
> people to come in. . . . Even if they lose, those people have gained
> the experience to go on, and many of them stay around for good.[8]

The campaign also instilled a sense of confidence in these young people,
ensuring that they would carry on, would continue to act on their beliefs. Participating in the campaign merely whet their appetite for activism,
convincing them to stay involved in the political world. In fact, many
people report that they continued working together with the same people
they met during the campaign, merely shifting to different issues. Sharon
Presley's group, for instance, Cal Students for Goldwater, became Cal
Conservatives for Political Action and continued working together on
the Berkeley campus.

Experience with the campaign also taught people organizing and
leadership skills that were useful for their subsequent activism. Dana
Rohrabacher became active in the campaign during high school. In addition to playing the banjo in a musical group called the Goldwaters,
Dana independently organized a Youth for Goldwater group of 120 students in his high school. He comments,

> In November 1964 there were Youth for Goldwater groups all over
> America and a lot of them were just like my own—totally inde-
> pendent but an *incredible* organization. The New Left didn't have
> anything like this at all. In retrospect when I look back at Youth
> for Goldwater, it's just *unbelievably* efficient and well-run and a
> potential force in the political scene.

Dana used the skills he had acquired in the campaign to begin organizing for YAF, soon rising to a leadership position in California.

Emmy Lewis, who left college at the University of Michigan after her freshman year in order to work full-time for Goldwater, reflects on the significance of the campaign,

> You hear so much about the left in the sixties. You rarely hear much about the youngsters in the conservative movement then. There were thousands, thousands across the country on campuses all over. We never got the publicity and we weren't interested in that. . . . We were out canvasing the precincts, trying to identify . . . young conservatives to run in the Republican precinct campaigns. We knew that's how you do it. You start from the grass roots up and Goldwater certainly mobilized and motivated scores more people because of his campaign. It was a very thrilling, exciting time.

Others, too, speak of the campaign as a crusade, a "star experience" that ushered them into political organizing.

Finally, the Goldwater campaign opened up organizational and friendship networks that were fundamental to the conservative movement over the next three decades. David Keene comments,

> The Goldwater election was the most important thing in the '60s. The people that you see in this town [Washington] today . . . the conservatives from the Heritage Foundation all the way over, are all people who were activated by the Goldwater election. It was the Goldwater election that allowed the conservatives to take over the Republican Party, allowed all their groups to get going and brought them all together in a community. So that was the central, most important event in the whole period.

Lee Edwards, in fact, argues that Goldwater helped turn a disjointed movement into a national political force that dominated the Republican Party for over a quarter of a century and prepared the way for Nixon's victories in 1968 and 1972 and Reagan's victories in 1980 and 1984.[9] In short, the significance of Goldwater's campaign for the building of a conservative youth movement, and for the building of a conservative force over time, cannot be overestimated.

One of the main benefactors of Goldwater's campaign was YAF. Because YAF was the leading conservative youth organization at the time, many of those who were drawn into the campaign also simultaneously discovered YAF. Numerous young people across the country who began by working for Goldwater ended up joining YAF. Some people recall meeting YAF members during the campaign who urged them to join in the aftermath of Goldwater's loss. Others saw YAF as a means to carry on the cause. For instance, after 1964 Rob Tyler and his peers began converting the Youth for Goldwater groups they had organized into chapters of YAF. He says, "We needed a vehicle to continue the momentum and that provided a really good vehicle."

For others the energy they transferred to YAF helped heal the wounds of the election. Kathy Rothschild remembers, "Oh sure, I was sad; I was disheartened. But the fact that we were involved in YAF—see we weren't *just* Youth for Goldwater. So it wasn't like close up shop and end. It was like okay, we go forward."

In fact, YAF itself was so intertwined with the Goldwater campaign that Lee Edwards comments, "Barry Goldwater made YAF but YAF also made Barry Goldwater—made him a national political figure and then the Republican nominee for President in 1964."[10] Clearly, it took the passion and excitement of the Goldwater campaign to inspire many young people to join the cause. Once involved, they continued their efforts wholeheartedly on behalf of YAF.

**SDS and the Goldwater Campaign**    Although the majority of SDS members opposed Goldwater, three SDS activists supported him in the 1964 election prior to their involvement with SDS. All three were political crossovers from their parents. None of these three actively campaigned for Goldwater although one did cast a vote for him. Two of the three also eventually became libertarian.

Within SDS a debate centered on what the Goldwater campaign meant and what stance SDS should take toward the 1964 election. This debate is evident through position papers circulated within the organization. Jim Williams, for example, argued that support for Goldwater came from a "proletarianized" middle class suffering economic insecurity. Predicting a move by the right to control the Republican Party, Williams called for active opposition to Goldwater through support for Johnson.[11] Richard Flacks also urged support for Johnson to defeat Goldwater. He argued that Goldwater represented white backlash against the civil rights movement and called on SDS to try to reach the white working class.[12] Al and Barbara Haber accused Flacks of misreading the significance of the campaign and opposed any support for Johnson, given what they perceived to be Johnson's move to the right. They urged SDS members not to vote at all.[13] Unable to reach a consensus, SDS took no official position on the 1964 election.

## Anti-Communist Issues

The second main historical catalyst to activism for YAFers was anti-communism. Both traditionalists and libertarians mention either specific historical events that triggered the need to become active or a general anti-Communist frame as the main reason for their political involvement.

The most common historical event named was the Hungarian uprising of 1956. Mike Thompson recalls the shock he felt in childhood on learning about this event.

> I remember going down and getting the paper in the morning during the Hungarian revolution. I was ten, twelve and still thinking something could happen. And then seeing the way we just did nothing. It was very difficult for me to understand how this country could do nothing after we basically encouraged [Hungarians] to do what they did.

Even though this incident was key to Mike's recognizing the importance of becoming involved, because of his age at the time he did not immediately join an organization. Rather, such events were decisive in fomenting the need for activism that many YAFers realized a few years later. Many discussed anticommunism as the catalyst to their involvement. Others named the construction of the Berlin Wall, events in China and Cuba, or the Bay of Pigs as historical junctures that sparked their belief in the need for activism. Yet in most cases the events themselves did not directly lead to involvement; rather, it took the Goldwater campaign or linkage to an organization embodying their beliefs, such as YAF, to actually transform them into activists.

For others no particular historical event instigated them to action. Rather, an awakening to anticommunism in general was the essential ingredient at the base of their activism. For example, Helen Blackwell had her "awakening" while in college at Louisiana State University. She was an art history major who, although fairly well informed, was not that interested in politics. Then the dean of women at her college, a conservative activist, called a meeting and Helen attended as representative of her sorority.

> What she did was show the film *Communism on the Map*. It was a whole day seminar. They took us out to a camp outside town and

there were speakers and a lot of material on the international situation at the time. That movie . . . was very dramatic because it
starts showing the countries as they turn red on the map as communism takes over. . . . I had known all that but I had never really
seen it displayed in such a dramatic way. Truly the whole experience just changed my life. I just was suddenly conscious that our
country was in real trouble and that most people weren't aware of
it, particularly the people in the universities.

Shortly afterward Helen learned about YAF and, with some friends,
started a chapter on campus.

Several YAFers say the reason they were not involved in the civil rights
movement was because saving the world from communism was their top
priority. As Rob Tyler put it, "It seemed like the Communist menace was
infinitely of a greater magnitude than backward conditions in the South."

**Anticommunism and SDS**    Although one SDSer, John Maher, did become
active in support of the people of Hungary while he was in college at
Harvard, as a whole the issue of communism found SDS youth in stark
contrast to those in YAF. The discrepancy is apparent in discussions of
Senator Joe McCarthy and the effects of the McCarthy era on people's
lives. The majority of parents of YAFers were strong supporters of
McCarthy and many YAFers also viewed McCarthy as a hero. At the
other extreme, most SDS parents (except those from crossover homes)
strongly opposed McCarthy, with one-quarter of SDSers in this study
having parents or other close relatives who were directly affected by the
blacklisting and harassment of the McCarthy era.

Barry Skolnick was one of those most dramatically affected. Speaking about his father, who was active in the Communist Party, Barry says,
"He was persecuted, hounded for his ideas all his life. He was put in
prison for his ideas. Jailed under the Smith Act. He was underground for
years. I didn't see him when I was a kid. . . . We had to sneak away to
see him. When I was five years old I used to have to have an alias." Traveling under a false name, Barry and his family would visit his father in
various places. Barry also recalls the FBI following him and his brother
when they were kids. Eventually Barry's father was caught and sentenced
to serve time. The Supreme Court ultimately overthrew this conviction
and Barry's father returned home.

More than any other historical event the McCarthy era separates the
worlds of the left and right. In a sense these youth were socialized into

contrary views of reality during these critical years. SDSer Bob Ross recalls the McCarthy era "the way a kid would—bad guys and good guys. We're [the left] the good guys. They're [McCarthy followers] the bad guys." Meanwhile Maggie Kohls, whose father thought McCarthy was a good guy, reached the conclusion: "This was a life-and-death struggle. We had to fight the Communists or we'd all be Communists." In short, communism was one of the essential dividing lines separating the worlds of the left and right, a morality struggle of good and evil, perceived in diametrically opposed terms. Rooted in different worlds and with contrasting assumptions about the world, each side found antithetical meanings in McCarthyism.

## JOINING SDS/YAF

Given the personal and historical catalysts motivating these young women and men, by the time most found out about YAF or SDS, they had already been involved in politics for months or even years. Whereas all the leftist activists became active in SDS during college or in the years after, nearly a quarter of right-wing activists became involved with YAF during high school, with the remainder joining during college or after.[14] One primary way that people found out about YAF or SDS was through *previous organizational affiliations.* Typically, once someone was involved "in the network," as one person put it, they'd find out about other meetings and organizations. Many times people held overlapping memberships in similar groups. One of the main routes to YAF, as discussed previously, was through the Goldwater campaign. Many youth also found out about YAF through involvement with Young Republicans. A few others were introduced to YAF through the Intercollegiate Studies Institute.[15]

Some people were drawn to YAF in opposition to other organizations. In particular, several people mentioned how they were turned off by the ever-recurrent conflicts in Young Republicans, the factionalism and fighting, the attention to procedures rather than substance, as well as the close ties to the Republican Party. At the same time they were drawn to YAF as an activist organization concerned with concrete issues. Others were drawn to YAF's broader philosophy, the fact that the organization "had a mission and a big picture," as one person put it. Barbara Hollingsworth explains her attraction to YAF:

> There was a lot of factionalism [in Young Republicans]; they had purges all the time. There was the political mechanics more than

the issues and that didn't interest me at all. [YAF] was issue-oriented. Whatever the issue was, we were very interested in exploring it. . . . So in that sense . . . on a personality level [we were] closer to SDS . . . because they were the cutting edge of issues. So we understood each other very well. Even though we were on totally opposite sides, we were just [interested in the] real intense political activity.

For those on the left the primary organizational routes to SDS were through civil rights groups or peace and antiwar groups. As on the right, overlapping membership in organizations was common, with many people attending meetings of multiple groups. Phil Hutchings, for instance, was active in a SNCC affiliate group, called the Nonviolent Action Group, at Howard University. He also went to demonstrations against the war. "It was all in that kind of cross-fertilization that I began to hear about SDS," he comments. In some cases individuals involved in one organization or cause were actively recruited by people in SDS. More often, though, people became involved in SDS because of the interconnection of the issues. In fact, some people had a hard time remembering the sequence of involvement with particular issues or groups: in their memories the elements all ran together.

The appeal of SDS for many youth was the organization's embrace of more than one issue. SDS filled "the need for something broader," as one person put it. Some people also said they desired more than pure activism and were drawn to the intellectual aspect of SDS. For Michael Kazin the people and the ideology of SDS alike attracted him. Michael began his years at Harvard by joining the Young Democrats, a group he had also been a member of in high school. But as he became more active on campus, he found himself drifting toward SDS, drawn to the analysis of the Vietnam War as immoral and compelled by SDS's ideology of participatory democracy. Michael also found many of the people in SDS charismatic. "The SDS people at Harvard seemed to be both serious and witty, very energetic, and yet intellectual. They were really models of the kind of man I wanted to be. . . . And the women were generally very smart, too, and sexy, which was not unimportant. They had a very unself-conscious way of carrying themselves." At the beginning of his second semester Michael resigned from Young Democrats and gave his full attention to SDS.

Michael's account points to a second route to SDS/YAF: individual ties. Closely connected to organizational networks, the other main route to SDS or YAF was through *friendship networks* or peers, personal contacts who introduced individuals to the organization. As other researchers have shown,[16] preexisting friendship networks are critical to mobilization. This is true for social movements of the right as well as the left. Typically, an individual met others who were part of SDS or YAF and slowly they became integrated with other members.

Some people specifically got involved through romantic relationships. SDSer Barry Skolnick was actively working in the draft resistance movement in Los Angeles trying to "hustle money" when he made contact with a woman, Karen, in New York who was working for the Vietnam Summer Project. For several months Barry tried to convince her that his group deserved funding. Barry was not only successful in getting funded but later, when he came to Chicago, he met Karen at the SDS office where she was working. They ended up getting married and, as Barry puts it, "She seduced me into SDS."

Similarly, Kitty Smith was recruited into YAF by her future husband. Kitty founded a Young Republicans chapter at her college. She met Lauren, her future husband, at a Youth for Goldwater mixer on campus. She learned about YAF through Lauren and admits that part of the reason she went to meetings was for social reasons. "I went to a women's college so it was lovely to go to a YAF thing because many times you'd be the only woman. It was a nice counterbalance."

In addition to organizational and personal networks, people who joined YAF named two routes to the organization not mentioned by anyone in SDS. A few YAFers were introduced to the organization through their parents. Kathy Rothschild, for example, went to the library with her mother one day while she was in high school. A flyer was put on the windshield of their car advertising a talk by John Stormer, author of the anti-Communist book *None Dare Call It Treason*. He was going to speak at a meeting sponsored by YAF:

> My mom had heard about Young Americans for Freedom. I went to an all-girls Catholic high school so my mom said, "Oh, I bet there'll be some real nice young men there. Why don't you go to the meeting?" Well, I wasn't sure. Then she said, "Well, we'll let you drive the car." Well, of course when you're sixteen and you have your driver's license, you'll drive anywhere. So I went to the meeting. I listened to John Stormer. I thought what he said was very

interesting. I was more interested in all the good looking high school men who I saw.

Kathy immediately joined YAF and became active in a local chapter.

The other route to YAF mentioned by some activists was through reading. For instance, Mary Fisk had not been involved in any political activities before college. When she read a letter to the editor of the college paper about the war in Vietnam, she liked what the young man had to say and looked him up. He was a representative of YAF and shortly after, Mary joined. Others found out about YAF through reading *National Review* or *Human Events,* wrote away and joined through the mail, and subsequently became involved with a chapter. No one in SDS, on the other hand, mentioned joining through sending in membership dues. As Judy Baker put it, "One didn't join SDS. One went to a meeting when they felt like it."

## POLITICS AS COMMUNITY

Joining SDS or YAF meant discovering a community, finding others with shared views and values. For many activists this community represented an answer to the sense of estrangement they felt during childhood or adolescence. Only a few YAF activists mention this sense of estrangement, but one-third of SDS activists discuss feeling different during childhood. Most often they relate the feeling to coming from a family that was single-parent, black, Jewish, or in some other way different from the surrounding community. The sense of separateness that SDSer John Brown Childs felt, for instance, came from his being one of the few black people in his neighborhood and school. He comments,

> Being black in a small town in Massachusetts basically surrounded by white people who say, "Yeah, you are a colored person" was fundamentally politicizing. . . . I never felt like I was a part of the world around me completely. . . . My critical facilities . . . got off to an early start in the sense that I couldn't say to myself—unless I really wanted to lie to myself—that I was just like everyone else around me.

John, as well as others in SDS, explicitly links this sense of difference to the feeling of standing apart from the world, fostering a critical stance toward society.

For other SDS youth feeling different had to do with their parents' politics. In particular, those whose parents suffered harassment during the McCarthy era were well aware of their differences from peers. Steve Goldstein remembers the ostracism he faced in his neighborhood at age five because his parents campaigned for Henry Wallace during a period of massive red-baiting. He vividly recalls, for instance, a gang of kids stopping him on the street and taunting, "You have red ankles. Your parents are Nazis." None of the neighborhood kids would play with him between ages five and eight. At the time he thought it was his fault. Other activists who say they felt different because of their parents' politics report feeling lonely, as if they never fit in.

Some SDSers say it was their own values or politics that made them feel separate from others. Carol Christman says she felt different throughout high school just because she thought sororities and other things her classmates were involved with were silly. She says, "I was a prom queen and head of the honor society but . . . there was nobody like me around. I felt very lonely." A few SDSers say they felt a craving for something more, a sense of a bigger world that would confirm their difference from others. Barbara Haber comments that many times she felt "different from people my age. . . . I always felt like I was a closet bohemian living out in the suburbs waiting until I grew up so I could leave."

One member of SDS and one from YAF, both describing themselves as "nonconformists" during their childhood, ended up becoming libertarians. SDSer Doug Knox says he grew up having a certain "the hell with the rest of you attitude" while YAFer Sharon Presley says being raised by a single mother and moving around a lot made her aware of her difference from others. "I was always in some subtle way unconventional, if not rebellious . . . with implicitly the idea that people didn't have any business telling me what to do as long as I wasn't bothering them."

The few other YAFers who say they felt different during childhood link it specifically to their own politics. Dave Schumacher says he felt like an outsider because of his unconventional libertarian views. "I didn't even feel comfortable at home. I felt as uncomfortable in many ways at school with classmates as with people who had conventional Republican or Democrat points of view and going home and talking to my folks."

Other YAFers comment as well on how their conservatism made them stand apart from others, especially when they were surrounded by people holding liberal views. In fact, although fewer YAF activists say they felt different during their childhood, once they became activists, many YAFers began to feel this sense of separateness. Particularly as the 1960s progressed, many YAFers recognized their own marginality as right-wing youth speaking out during times of increasingly leftist dissent.

For those activists who *were* aware of their difference at an early age, a few managed to feel positively about their marginality. SDSer John Brown Childs, for instance, says he felt "a sense of pleasure in not being in the mainstream." Others, though, suffered for their difference, feeling ostracized and alone during their growing-up years. SDSer Sue Jhirad, who felt she was an outcast throughout high school, explains, "I felt myself to be an oddball . . . maybe because I was Jewish, maybe because of my parents' politics. Because I just didn't look blonde and have a turned-up nose. . . . I would have given anything at that point . . . to be just like everybody else."

Yet this sense of separateness, whether welcomed or not, provided an outsider's viewpoint that became a crucial part of an activist's identity. As these youth developed a critical view of America and moved farther and farther away from the mainstream, this sense of being different served them well. As SDSer Bob Ross put it, "A certain marginality . . . is necessary to critical consciousness. There must be a place where you could put your foot which is outside the circle. . . . [It] gives young people a critical stance that they don't have to be like everybody else and that their ideas can be different ideas." Despite the isolation, they began to value the separate and distinct view of the world.

Once youth of the left and right became activists, they felt welcome relief in finding others like themselves. Politics integrated them into a community, offering a home to those who often felt like strangers. John Brown Childs, for example, discusses the solace he found in discovering other "marginal" people. Commenting on the group at the University of Massachusetts with whom he formed an SDS chapter, he says he found social support: "I could have just gone on being marginal the way I'd been in high school, but I was surrounded by other people saying, 'This is great. We're glad to be marginal. . . . This is a corrupt society; you don't want to be part of it.' . . . By joining SDS at least one had the sense of being fringe but part of a larger phenomenon."

Sue Jhirad also found comfort as a political activist, putting to rest her feeling of being an outcast. "Just the term 'the movement'—I could go to a rally in New York with 20,000 people at it and know half the people. . . . It was just a very warm feeling. There was this community atmosphere, people who were all around some kind of common cause."

Similar satisfaction in meeting kindred spirits is expressed by those in YAF. Connie Marshner, for instance, says she never fit in and "always stuck out like a sore thumb." Yet at the first YAF seminar she attended she heard Don Devine speak. "For the first time [I had] a sense that all the things I believed in might not be strange, interesting antiques, but that they might be viable ideas and there might be a lot of people who felt the same way." Joining YAF ended Connie's sense of isolation. She says, "Meeting the YAF people was the beginning of realizing this was not my own thing. . . . I really had a sense that there was a movement here, that this might have a chance of going somewhere."

Even those who did not view themselves as marginal still felt relief on meeting others of like mind. A few activists speak of the ways activism not only ended their isolation but boosted their self-esteem, released them from an unhappy home life, or gave them a sense of direction.

But for all these young people, whatever the complex components motivating their action, politics became intertwined with self, a deeply embedded part of their own identity. Rather than represent an acting out of irrational impulses or a sign of psychological disorder, as some analysts assert,[17] involvement in the political world brought a *realization of self* for these young women and men of the left and right. Distinct from their peers, if not in their backgrounds then certainly in their engagement with politics, they fulfilled long-held beliefs and desires through their activism.

## CONCLUSION

What is clear is that long before these young people reached the doors of SDS and YAF, politics was already an important part of their identity. The process of "cognitive liberation" essential to the formation of a social movement[18] occurs long before an individual is exposed to a formal organization or even introduced to a network of other activists. A complex array of external factors—social background, parental ideology and values, the political climate of the community, the influence of teachers, leaders, or books—intertwines with individual personality and experiences during childhood to create an affinity toward the political world. The other essential motivating factor, critical historical and political events, propels individuals to put their beliefs into action.

The stories of these activists also reaffirms the *social* nature of individual belief. The formation of consciousness, the initial steps in the political world, and eventual identity as an activist, all take place through interaction with others. Only through interaction with others does an individual "become political." As Johnston, Larana, and Gusfield put it, "Identity emerges through the mirror of social interaction. . . . Individual identity is quintessentially social."[19] In particular, friends and relatives are critical not only in forming links that pull an individual into organizations or networks of activists but also in forming political identity itself. The development of a subjective sense of self requires a community. In Erikson's terms, identity is located not just at the core of an individual but also at the core of his or her communal culture.[20] As we'll see in chapter 4, identity is neither fixed nor static. Once these youth began defining themselves through politics and became embedded in communities with others who shared their passion for politics, they continued to be transformed. Being political is a learning process, involving a series of stages of commitment, reconceptualization, and radicalization.

TOP: Vivian Rothstein (left) at a meeting with women from the Trade Union Federation during a trip to Vietnam in 1967. Courtesy of Vivian Rothstein.

BOTTOM: Vivian Rothstein (second from right) at the dedication of Transitional Housing, a project for homeless adults Vivian developed in 1996. Courtesy of Vivian Rothstein.

Bernardine Dohrn in 1969, going to Criminal Court in Chicago on charges of aggravated assault. Courtesy AP/Wide World Photos.

Bernardine Dohrn in 1995. Photo by Jim Zhiv; courtesy of Bernardine Dohrn.

LEFT: John Brown Childs
in 1964. Courtesy of
John Brown Childs.

ABOVE: John Brown Childs as a member of a community youth peace
organization, marching in support of the United Farm Workers Union
in Watsonville, California, 1997. Photograph by Ella Seneres.

TOP: Jeanne Friedman (left) at the Indochinese Women's Conference in Canada in 1971. Courtesy of Jeanne Friedman.

BOTTOM: Jeanne Friedman in 1997. Courtesy of Jeanne Friedman.

Terry Koch in 1965.
Courtesy of Terry Koch.

Terry Koch in 1997.
Courtesy of Terry Koch.

LEFT: Dorothy Burlage with Todd Gitlin during the 1960s. Courtesy of Dorothy Burlage and Todd Gitlin.

BELOW: Dorothy Burlage (left) with Alice Hageman in the 1990s. Courtesy of Dorothy Burlage.

LEFT: Michael Kazin in 1971.
Courtesy of Michael Kazin.

BELOW: Michael Kazin
in 1998. Courtesy of
Michael Kazin.

Naomi Schapiro in 1971. Courtesy of Naomi Schapiro.

Naomi Schapiro and her family in 1997. Courtesy of Naomi Schapiro.

ABOVE: Jim Shoch speaking at a political meeting during the 1960s. Courtesy of Jim Shoch.

LEFT: Jim Shoch in 1998. Photograph by Joseph Mehling/Dartmouth College photographer.

# CHAPTER FOUR

# TRADITIONALISTS, ANARCHISTS, AND RADICALS

Once activists joined YAF or SDS, their political education did not end. Through interaction with others, through conversation and shared experiences, commitment deepened. The events of the 1960s as well as their experiences as activists pulled members further into the political world. Many activists increasingly surrounded themselves with others of shared belief, peers who acted to confirm their view of the world. Traditionalists maintained their ideology, while activists in SDS and the libertarian right went through further transformations of belief and action, processes of radicalization that resulted in a shift in ideology and a changed identity. Participation in the political world transformed other facets of their lives as well. Particularly for those on the left, political activism often brought consequences in terms of greater risks as well as strained relations with parents.

## COMMITMENT TO THE MOVEMENT

Commitment to a social movement involves not only conviction about what is wrong with the world but also the decision to act on these beliefs, to strive for social change. Commitment also means a conception of oneself as someone who takes action in defense of deeply held values, someone who cares. In Kenneth Burke's words, "action is not merely a means of doing but a way of being."[1] As commitment to SDS or YAF grew, activists participated in a range of activities on both a local and a national level.

## Involvement in SDS

For the leftists in this study, the most common types of involvement in SDS were civil rights activities; participation in ERAP (Economic and Research Action Project)[2] or other community organizing projects; antiwar action including local and national demonstrations, draft resistance and counseling, teach-ins against the war, and organizing against ROTC on campus; and various other campus activities such as organizing around issues of free speech and university reform, forming study groups and putting on conferences, offering alternative classes, researching and protesting university ties to the military-industrial complex, and organizing campus workers. A few activists also participated in electoral campaigns, wrote for or edited local or national SDS newsletters, or worked on other SDS projects such as organizing workers in factories. Those who held national office were involved with recruitment, raising money, speaking tours, and promoting SDS.

Typically, individuals were involved in multiple activities and also shifted their involvement over time from one realm of action to another. Many times these shifts occurred through ties to others as activists pulled each other into new arenas. Phil Hutchings, for example, was in Washington, D.C., between 1962 and 1963 working with SNCC when he began attending some SDS meetings. In the fall of 1964 while he was doing some campaign work for Robert Kennedy, he ran into Tom Hayden at a party. Tom suggested he come to Newark to see the ERAP project there. A month after the election Phil moved to Newark to begin working with ERAP. He remained there until the early spring of 1965 when SDS president Paul Potter came to Newark to ask Phil if he would return to Washington to help organize the peace demonstration SDS was planning for April. Phil, who knew a lot about the D.C. community, was glad to help. After the march he returned to Newark where he stayed until 1968.

Meanwhile, in 1966 Phil also helped set up a SNCC project in Newark that worked closely with the ERAP project. Much of the work Phil did with ERAP and SNCC centered on housing—organizing rent strikes, getting people to fight their landlords for basic services, as well as organizing around welfare rights. Stokely Carmichael, whom Phil knew from college, was now the chair of SNCC, and urged Phil to commit himself more to SNCC. By this point the growing racial politics within the movement emphasized blacks organizing blacks. As one of the few blacks in SDS, Phil decided to shift his involvement to SNCC. He continued to maintain alliances with SDS, working together in coalitions and attending occasional SDS national meetings and conferences. In 1968 Phil moved to New York to take on a leadership role in SNCC. By this point he was no longer involved with SDS, although he continued to meet with SDS leaders on occasion.

As commitment deepened, some activists were drawn into the national level of SDS. Cathy Wilkerson, for instance, first became active working on a civil rights project in Chester, Pennsylvania, while attending college at Swarthmore. One day Cathy saw a sign on a campus bulletin board announcing the arrest of students involved in a school boycott and summoning people to continue the boycott the following day. She jumped in "feet first" the next day and was arrested. Cathy went to Chester every day after that, nearly flunking out of college. She became immersed in organizing and opposition to segregation.

At the end of her sophomore year Cathy was in a quandary about what to do next because she was leaving for the summer. She went to the leaders of the SDS chapter to discuss it. "They just sort of laughed . . . like it was a ridiculous problem and they weren't really interested. . . . That's when I just got totally disgusted with these people and dropped out of SDS." At this point Cathy also tried to drop out of college, desperately wanting to participate in Mississippi Freedom Summer. But parental permission was required and Cathy's mother refused to let her go. Cathy returned to school but was involved only minimally in politics.

After she graduated in 1966, Cathy decided to give "straight politics a try" and began working for a congressman. While working for him, Cathy decided she wanted to go to the national SDS convention being held in Clear Lake, Iowa. Upon hearing of her plans, the congressman prohibited her attendance. Cathy regretted missing the meeting "where the old-guard male intellectuals from the East Coast were thrown out and more informal midwestern radicals came in." In November, soon after the election, Cathy went to Chicago and stopped by the national office of SDS.

I walked in . . . and there was Greg Calvert [SDS national secretary] and all of these midwestern folk. . . . The editor of *New Left Notes* had disappeared a week ago and no one had seen hide nor hair of him since. He was on a cloud of marijuana somewhere out in Kansas and he was never going to come back again. I had never met Greg in my life. He didn't know anything about me. After we had talked for an hour or two, he said, "You're a warm body . . . will you be the editor of *New Left Notes?*" So I said Yes.

Cathy stayed in Chicago for six months as editor of the SDS paper. She tried to change it "from being the old ideological rag with these . . . three-page debates on Communist theory . . . into a news sheet of campus demonstrations."

Cathy recalls one of her first tasks: retyping the entire mailing list of SDS onto address cards so it could be bundled by zip code.

> There were four of us who did this. It was an incredible job. We stayed up for three days, night and day, nonstop, drinking wine, eating, talking. We used to go down to this little cafeteria that would serve chili for forty cents. We had little money. . . . [We] became very close very fast. . . . Life was just a daily struggle. We worked twelve hours a day, seven days a week. I lived in this little shack, literally, with one space heater, with no furniture and spaces between the floorboards with the cold air coming up, with a mattress on the floor. It was totally primitive but it was wonderful. It was really one of the greatest six-month periods of my life because everyone was for real.

That spring Cathy and others working in her office decided to put democracy into action. Believing that the leadership of SDS should continuously be infused with new recruits, they all decided to return to grassroots work on a local level in different cities. Cathy decided to move to Washington, D.C., because there were no active SDS chapters there at the time. It seemed an important place to organize, and Cathy knew the city. She found a huge house with eleven bedrooms for $250 a month and recruited other activists to fill the house. Everyone had part-time jobs. Cathy worked in a drugstore and began organizing SDS chapters. By the end of the year they had started chapters at every university in the city; they also became involved with draft resistance. Cathy continued attending national meetings of SDS and was elected to serve on the national interim committee. By then she was fully committed to SDS; it had become a way of life.

### Involvement in YAF

Like their SDS counterparts, YAF activists also became involved in simultaneous activities and shifted their focus over the years. Right-wing youth most commonly were involved in the following YAF activities: anti-Communist action, such as organization of consumer boycotts against corporations selling products to Eastern Europe or in support of "captive nations"; activities to support the war in Vietnam including campus demonstrations, shipment of medical supplies and reading material to Vietnam, and education around the war; activities to counter the left on campus, for example, counter-demonstrations, support for ROTC, and recruitment of conservative faculty; involvement in electoral politics including the Goldwater campaign as well as other national and local candidates; and educational activities such as speakers' bureaus and work on local or national YAF publications. Those in the national leadership were busy with recruitment of members, growth of chapters, fund-raising, public speaking, and writing for national publications. For both SDS and YAF different campuses emphasized different types of activities. In YAF, for instance, the University of Kansas chapter focused mainly on education while the chapter at Stanford worked to counter SDS and other leftist groups on campus.

Kathy Rothschild's trajectory typifies the varying activities of those in YAF. Kathy joined YAF during high school in St. Louis after immersing herself in the Goldwater campaign. Kathy became press director of her YAF chapter.

> One of the useful things that YAF did was that they really understood—as Phyllis Schlafly does—that it's much better to train people to do something than to just come in and do it for them. . . . Whenever YAF would have a state convention we focused on workshops to train you—how to write a press release, how to deliver it. . . . The national headquarters published very useful tools like a little book on how to get the press to cover your event. . . . I basically took that little booklet, wrote the press releases, hand delivered them to the *Globe Democrat* and the *Post Dispatch,* and we started getting a lot of publicity for what we were doing and more members. So it was very successful.

In 1968 Kathy enrolled at Meramac College, a community college within walking distance of her home. She wanted to stay at home so that she'd have access to her own phone, room, typewriter, and desk to continue her "political operations." Kathy soon became a campus leader. Her YAF chapter helped organize the National Student Committee for Victory in Vietnam. She remained active in supporting the war throughout the early 1970s. Kathy and the other Meramac YAFers were also

available to aid the nearby Washington University YAF chapter in holding counter-demonstrations to the left. Kathy says her "great claim to
fame was keep[ing] the American flag from getting burned" during one
of the campus demonstrations at Meramac.

During this time Kathy and others also helped a local congressman in
his campaign to retain the right-to-work law and worked with Youth for
Reagan in 1968, raising money so they could go to the Republican convention in Miami Beach. After college Kathy moved to Washington and
got her first job working for Dave Jones, former executive director of
YAF, who headed the Charles Edison Youth Fund.

Another activist, Harvey Hukari, became involved with YAF in 1964
while attending San Francisco State. He took over the chapter there and
primarily was involved with counter-protests to antiwar demonstrations.
Believing the whole dialogue on the war was one-sided, Harvey felt the
need to present opposing arguments and began organizing counter-teach-
ins to educate students about Vietnam. At this point there were no violent confrontations between the left and right.

In 1966 Harvey transferred to Stanford. Finding the Young Republican group "too moderate and not as interested . . . in confronting the
left," Harvey started a YAF chapter. In addition to holding counter-
demonstrations, the Stanford chapter pushed to get more conservative
professors hired, organized to retain ROTC credit, published a weekly
newspaper, and worked on political campaigns. During the late 1960s
some of the confrontations with the left erupted into violence. Harvey
continued to be active in YAF through 1970.

As with SDS, the deepening commitment of some YAF members led
them to involvement with the national level of YAF. For example, Allen
Brandstater first organized a YAF chapter in Glendale, California, while
he was in high school in 1965. He became very active and, along with
other YAFers, started working with Youth for Reagan during the pri-
maries of 1966. Allen recalls some of the anti-Communist activities YAF
organized during those years:

> YAF focused on things such as we were fighting the Communists
> in Southeast Asia but the Firestone Tire and Rubber Company was
> building a huge tire factory in Communist Rumania. The Chase
> Manhattan Bank was arranging one hundred million dollar loans
> to the Soviet Union at 2 or 3 percent so they could buy American
> subsidized wheat. The IBM corporation was selling sophisticated
> hardware and software directly to the Soviet Union; and the Ford

Motor Company was proposing to build—and did build ulti-mately—the largest truck factory in the world in Siberia. A lot of young conservatives like I [did] thought, Why are we fighting com-munism in Vietnam and losing all these young American lives in order that the major American corporations can make billions of dollars on the blood of young Americans?

SDSers also distrusted big corporations—but for diametrically opposed reasons. Whereas those in SDS increasingly were suspicious of corporate capitalism, the underlying motive for Allen's and other YAFers' opposi-tion to corporations was anticommunism, stopping any trade with "cap-tive nations." Allen helped others in his chapter picket IBM headquar-ters in Los Angeles to protest its trade with the Soviet Union. They also picketed the Soviet circus and the Bolshoi Ballet when they came to town. In addition, viewing YAF's mission as educational, as being "a training ground for leaders," they brought in local conservative leaders to speak.

Allen ended up working himself up through the ranks of YAF. While he attended the University of Southern California, he became executive director of California YAF, held a position on the national board, and became western regional director.

When I was executive director here in California, our state orga-nization raised about $60,000 in 1967. That was unheard of for any YAF organization. We had a nice suite of offices that were in a brokerage firm. We had four full-time young people working for us. . . . I liked it. It was like being a young businessman with my own office and a nice carpet on the floor, glassed-in enclosures. . . . It led to a lot of friendships and associations.

The description of his office contrasts sharply with Cathy Wilkerson's description of her time working in the national office of SDS. As execu-tive director Allen raised money, put on press conferences, and wrote news releases. He says, "I was more an administrator in the movement than a campus activist."

Dana Rohrabacher also became active on the national level, but as a campus activist. Previously involved in Youth for Goldwater, Dana was introduced to YAF while he was attending Harbor Junior College. He remained active while also attending Long Beach State, during which time he organized several YAF chapters. Once the Reagan campaign came along in 1966, Dana jumped on the bandwagon, using YAF as the base for Youth for Reagan. "We expanded the chapters of Youth for Reagan into every high school and college . . . and then used those chapters to become YAF chapters after that. So by the end of the Reagan campaign in '66 we had a very well functioning group of people . . . actually in the same area that I represent in Congress right now."

In 1967 Dana went to Vietnam as an election observer and spent the next six weeks there. When he returned he took over the state chairman position of YAF. During this time Dana says he became a "hyper-activist"— organizing, raising money, putting on seminars.

> At this point there was a real split in YAF between the campus ac-
> tivists and the people that were basically political activists. The po-
> litical activists were people who wanted to work in campaigns. The
> campus activists were people who were very interested in fighting
> the ideological battle of Marxism. Marxism was making enormous
> headway on our campuses and universities. There needed to be an
> ideological fight. . . . I was the ultimate campus activist. I was down
> on the quad every day debating with a Marxist.

Dana remained in YAF until 1969. After the 1969 YAF convention he shifted his activities to libertarian causes. Like his counterparts in SDS, he was fully immersed in politics.

## THE NARROWING OF SOCIAL TIES

For many activists on both the left and the right, growing commitment to the movement meant a narrowing of their circle of friends. As politics became the main focus of their life, people increasingly found themselves surrounded by others of "like minds." Being with those who shared similar views and values provided a sense of support, solidifying commitment. Peers were essential in reaffirming activists' subjective view of the world. They confirmed that you weren't alone in acting on your convictions, that you were doing the right thing. As SDSer Dorothy Burlage put it, "All along the way there were people who would get me to the next step. . . . They validated what we were doing." Peers also fostered collective en-thusiasm that sustained morale during the long months of organizing.

In addition, peers played an important role in pushing forward an ac-tivist's beliefs. Those who had been involved longer served as role mod-els and educated others about issues and theory. YAFer Don Ernsberger says the people he met during the Goldwater campaign were already read-ing Ayn Rand and "were primarily more libertarian than I was and they pulled me that way. . . . We used to argue things and [they] eventually pulled me into a more consistent position." One friend was particularly influential in logically convincing Don that "libertarian" was the right label to call himself. These other activists provided a vocabulary that allowed a reconstruction of identity, creating further commitment to the movement.[3]

Other YAFers were particularly inspired by conservative leaders whom they got to know. Several YAFers mention personal relationships they had with figures such as Stan Evans or Frank Meyer, who encouraged them and furthered their thinking. David Keene, for instance, developed a close relationship with Frank Meyer, a former Communist who was a leader of the Old Right.[4] Calling him "the conscience of the early conservative movement," David recalls visiting him about once a month at his home on a mountain in Woodstock. He also remembers phone calls he received from Frank in the middle of the night. "Frank was a great influence. If you were involved he would call you at 2:00 in the morning, after [his] breakfast, and harangue you and want to know what you were doing. And check to make sure you weren't deviating too much from the principle. . . . He was very important to most people of that generation."

SDSers were also pushed forward by their peers. Rory Ellinger was particularly inspired by Mary Varela, an early SDSer who attended Port Huron. He recalls an incident during his days as a leader of the Catholic student movement.

> I'd give a talk on Christian leadership and I'd give some bull about praying hard, being a good example. Then Mary Varela was coming up to me . . . telling me I was full of crap. She started telling me people are dying in Vietnam, people are dying in Mississippi and you're talking about leadership. Leadership is standing up being counted, is fighting for racial justice.

Mary not only inspired Rory to join SDS but changed the direction of his thinking.

Others, too, give accounts of being "moved to the left" by their peers. SDSer Bernardine Dohrn remembers the impact of the friends she made at the University of Chicago: "I fell in with a lot of people who were from left families, a lot of New Yorkers and a lot of people who were politically active. It took me quite awhile to even know what they were talking about. They had a whole frame of reference. . . . Immediately it was a very political world. . . . So immediately my frame of reference broadened enormously."

Some activists discuss how particular friends challenged their ideas or exposed them to new thoughts or readings, opening them up politically and intellectually. They spoke of people who taught them a "way of seeing." In this sense activists were educated into a political perspective. The ideas they brought with them were further shaped through their interaction with others. Among peers activists learned a framework for understanding injustice, for articulating who or what is responsible for social problems, as well as strategies and goals of social change. Talking through experiences and analyzing social issues established a frame, a way of seeing the world. Berger and Luckmann talk about secondary socialization when "significant others" challenge the taken-for-granted reality of the world by posing altered views of reality. These significant others play a central role in the reality-maintenance of this altered worldview. In particular, conversations provide an ongoing vehicle to maintain and reformulate subjective reality. We talk through various experiences, thereby allocating them a definite place in the world.[5] In this way ongoing conversations with other activists not only sustained commitment but also helped individuals maintain and modify their political beliefs.

While on the one hand peers became the reference group and created the frame for seeing the world, on the other hand a world inhabited solely by others of the same political persuasion was insular. It offered protection and support as it shielded individuals from outside ideas. But constant association with like-minded activists also created a frame with a single lens. Thus, many activists were cut off from those with varying perspectives. This was particularly true for those in SDS. SDSer Andrea Cousins recalls how her world narrowed during this time:

It really was a sense that we were this new world. I lived on 149th Street . . . and worked on 147th Street. . . . [I] lived with Sharon [Jeffrey, one of the founders of SDS] and with another friend. And felt that I didn't even have to have a telephone, that everything that I needed was right there. Everybody that I really cared about, if they weren't there, then I didn't need them. I really felt like we were the whole world.

Andrea says anyone who wasn't an activist or who didn't share her views "just sort of dropped by the wayside. . . . Everybody that wasn't involved, as far as I was concerned, was out of this world."

Another SDS activist, Jim Shoch, remembers the intensity of his world once he became completely committed to politics. "All the time all you did was political work. . . . It's a frenzied life . . . reminded me of Erving Goffman's *Asylum*. It was like this intense experience. Your whole life was this organization—social, political . . . we lived in houses of four and five each. . . . Once you got into SDS, that was your world."

In short, there were both benefits and drawbacks to this narrowing of social ties. Bernardine Dohrn sums up the positive and negative aspects of this exclusive world:

> In terms of who I hung out with and who influenced me . . . the strengths of [the movement] were that . . . we felt that things were connected and things were coherent and made sense. Everybody's efforts related to everybody else's efforts. . . . We could help figure things out together, complicated things that happened and we didn't expect. But the disadvantages were definitely becoming insular and living inside a bubble and not seeing the world from other people's points of view, from other people's life experiences. And that definitely became telling, no question about it.

Whereas few SDSers mentioned any enduring relationships with those of different political persuasions, a substantial minority of both libertarians and traditionalists reported they maintained at least one friendship with someone who held opposing views. These YAFers had friends who either were in SDS, were Marxists, or were active in some other leftist group. Some say they commiserated with these friends about common problems in organizing a movement while others say their relationship was purely social, politics was set aside.

## PATHWAYS OF TRADITIONALISTS

All youth became increasingly committed to political activism, but during the course of the 1960s traditionalists retained their fundamental beliefs while both libertarians and leftists went through processes of radicalization, shifting their ideology as a result of their experiences. Although several traditionalists in YAF mention "flirting with libertarianism" during the course of the 1960s or temporarily "falling away from religion," none report a fundamental shift in their core beliefs or values. Traditionalists maintained their same ideology during these years.

In fact, the ostracism traditionalists increasingly faced as the 1960s progressed merely acted to reaffirm their beliefs, further binding them to the conservative cause. Just admitting one was a conservative caused a reaction during those years. Alan MacKay comments, "The word 'conservative' was a curse word, almost like standing up in public and saying 'I am an alcoholic.' . . . People would be shocked and taken aback. He's actually admitting it."

Many traditionalists mentioned the discrimination they faced on campus as outspoken conservatives facing the left. Scott Stanley put it this way:

> Our ideas were [the] subject of ridicule and attack and viciousness on the college campus. Everyone hears endlessly about the McCarthy era, but there's no talk about the terrible harassment that went on against college students and professors who were anti-Communists and anti-collectivists. . . . It was terrific. . . . One of the things that movements need to coalesce and survive is, of course, harassment, and we felt ourselves persecuted for our ideas.

The ostracism conservative youth faced forged tight bonds and solidified their sense of mission. Barbara Hollingsworth recalls the atmosphere she faced at the University of Illinois–Chicago Circle campus: "There was no one particular event as much as the whole mood of the left at that time was so—shrill is the word. You couldn't talk with a lot of them on any level. . . . This really sealed my beliefs even further. . . . It was hard to debate because they'd say 'Ah, you're just a fascist' or whatever. . . . It made me more aggressive." Barbara says even when she was called "fascist" or "Nazi" she interpreted this as a positive sign that her activities were having an impact.

Lee Edwards eloquently conveys the way in which ostracism strengthened people's commitment.

> You have to understand that we were forged throughout the entire sixties. My God, to be a young conservative in the sixties was to be . . . an untouchable, a pariah, a Jew in Syria, a black in South Africa. . . . So we fought back. . . . Your abilities—intellectual abilities, political abilities—are all heightened in that kind of an atmosphere. We were in the front lines of political and philosophical debate and activism in this country. And we were very good at it or else we would have been demolished. . . . So there's a certain amount of self-confidence which came up in that. . . . There was a feeling in those early years of growing awareness of our power and our abilities and of the difference that we could make. . . . Solzhenitsyn speaks of how even in the gulag that one little tendril of grass comes up through the concrete. In a way we felt that way as well.

We were determined not to be silenced . . . not to be defeated. There was a sense of a crusade, a mission.

Many traditionalists report feeling increasingly on the margins, outsiders during these years, viewed as fanatics and extremists. Unanimous to these accounts is the belief that opposition merely fueled commitment to the cause. Even those traditionalists who originally saw possibilities for common cause with SDS in the early years of Port Huron, through mutual belief in participatory democracy and local initiatives, saw few shared beliefs by the mid- to late 1960s. As more and more campuses erupted in violence, traditionalists viewed their relation to SDS as antagonistic. While some traditionalists respected their opponents, seeing them as decent and reasonable, others described them as opportunistic and destructive, the enemies of all they held dear.

## PROCESSES OF RADICALIZATION

Unlike traditionalists, leftists and libertarians were radicalized through their experiences as activists. By a variety of means—through intellectual growth, a deepening knowledge of politics, experiences of frustration at the lack of social change, confrontations with government and evidence of police brutality—individuals were transformed. Others were worn down by the unending events of the 1960s—assassinations, the war, ghetto riots, government repression. Different people took varying paths to radicalization.

I speak of *radicalization* here not just as a changed perception of reality, a shifting of beliefs, but also in terms of a changed sense of self, an altered identity. For many of the activists on both the left and the right this shift brought, in Keniston's words, "a realization—sometimes slow and sometimes sudden—that one has changed; the common experience of 'finding oneself' acting, reacting, thinking, and feeling in ways that at an earlier stage of life would have been inconceivable."[6] As with Keniston's sample of radicals on the left, libertarians on the right also went through varying processes, some more gradual, others instantaneous, by which particular experiences and events led to a transformation of belief and identity. Such stock-taking was not only an individual process but also took place within the context of a group.[7] Radicalization is a relational process; together people construct meaning in understanding dramatic events and experiences. Such incidents precipitating a revision of identity occurred concurrently to activists on the left as well as the right.

## Radicalization in SDS

Some SDSers name one particular event or experience as the critical rad-icalizing experience of their lives. A few say that their first political act—typically, simply joining a demonstration—was the watershed event. Bernardine Dohrn recalls the significance of the first time she joined a picket line in a demonstration against HUAC:

> I stood across the street and I watched for half an hour. I just couldn't imagine—it seemed so embarrassing to me to join this little group of people and walk around chanting in a circle. . . . I felt an outsider. I wasn't part of the group. But I have a very clear sense that walking across that street and falling into that picket line and hearing my own voice chanting was a walking away from the past.

This sense of crossing a boundary was also conveyed by Carol Christ-man. Carol says in an instant she moved from being a "good liberal" to having her world explode and moving to the left. She recalls,

> The way I got organized was through police brutality. I was at the University of Wisconsin at the famous Dow demonstration in 1968 and really wasn't involved. . . . I was walking to class and people were demonstrating outside the building where Dow was and came back over the hill. It was like something outside my ex-perience was going on. It sounded like a war zone. Of course, I've [since] learned to recognize the sound of tear gas canisters. But it sounded like bombs going off . . . and people were running out with blood just covering them . . . superficial head wounds, very dramatic. . . . It was the first violence on a white campus in the country so . . . I had no way of understanding what was hap-pening. The crowd started running and people were freaking out. Someone said, "Cops are beating people in there" and psycho-logically . . . something happened. It was like my head was in fast motion.

For both Bernardine and Carol these events marked a shift, an im-mediate change from an earlier "prepolitical self" to the initiation of be-coming a "committed activist," yet radicalization did not end there. Carol discusses the gradual transformation by which she eventually identified as a radical, becoming in time a Marxist-Leninist.

> I remember first going to antiwar demonstrations and people were chanting, "Ho, Ho, Ho Chi Minh." [I said to myself] "Eeeww . . . don't say that. It's going to turn everybody off." And somewhere somehow . . . I became comfortable with that and the next thing you knew I was chanting "Ho" and then debating how many angels could dance on the head of—I became very ideological. So there were lots and lots and lots of incidents. It really was so evolutionary.

Most SDSers speak of their radicalization in similar terms of a gradual shift of perspective brought on by numerous experiences. The crossovers in particular illustrate this process, the small group of SDSers who ended up at the opposite end of the political spectrum from their parents. Crossovers represent more extreme versions of radicalization as their ideas changed most dramatically over time. One of the most dramatic cases of a shift in ideology is evident in Cindy Decker's story. Cindy first got involved in politics through a family friend who was active in the John Birch Society. This woman helped sponsor Cindy to attend the Freedom School in Colorado Springs. Cindy says the two weeks she spent there "changed my life." She was exposed to ideas she had never heard about before. She says, "It hadn't occurred to me that not having a government was a viable alternative . . . [or] that not having a God was a viable alternative. . . . I got my mind blown all at once and no drugs!" As a result of these experiences Cindy changed from being a John Bircher to becoming a libertarian.

Cindy also met her future first husband at the Freedom School. Together they became involved with the Minutemen, a paramilitary right-wing group. At the time Cindy felt civilization was about to collapse and was drawn to the survivalism of the group. She became heavily involved, working at the Minutemen national headquarters, running training sessions in the Ozarks, and "helping line up relationships to run machine guns." She did all these things and at the same time felt "God, these people are truly bonkers!"

About a year later in 1964 Cindy began attending the University of Kansas. Once on campus Cindy found herself drawn toward people who were working against the war.

> On an issue-by-issue basis I absolutely agreed with them. I was arrested in a sit-in. . . . I was real interested in the civil rights move-

ment, very supportive of it. I absolutely was opposed to the war in Vietnam. I was absolutely opposed to the draft. I absolutely was opposed to any kind of racism. So the people I gravitated to on an issue-by-issue basis were all the SDS types.

Cindy, along with others, helped build the fledgling SDS chapter on campus. But Cindy's motivation at the time was in part "to keep an eye on all the lefties on campus." At the same time, Cindy was attracted not only to the politics but also to the lifestyle of SDS.

I was very much a child of my generation in terms of lifestyle. I found the burgeoning of consciousness and the letting down of a lot of inhibitions, the adventure of forging a new lifestyle . . . exciting and interesting and far more attractive . . . than staying in some . . . restrictive mainline right-wing political hierarchy. . . . A bunch of us just really walked a line between very different kinds of worlds. I was probably the most extreme case. . . . I'd been hanging out with all these right-wing paramilitary types who were fascist pigs. . . . I'm not using the word "fascist" in a loose way. They were neo-Nazis. . . . I absolutely was horrified with their view of interpersonal relations. They hated Jews and niggers and I didn't. I had none of those feelings at all.

Saying she felt politically schizophrenic during this period, Cindy comments, "I didn't fit in politically any place."

Cindy became active in SDS working on antiwar and antidraft issues. She felt allegiance on a personal level to the people in the organization, particularly the small anarchist faction where she felt most at home. By 1966 Cindy had moved to Berkeley and was involved in SDS's national interim committee and national council. She also became involved in an SDS project aimed at organizing tuna cannery workers. Cindy was open about discussing her past as well as her libertarian views and says the people she knew just accepted her peculiarities. Cindy remained active in SDS through the early 1970s.

For Aldyn McKean, another crossover, the catalyst in his conversion to the left was the Vietnam War. Aldyn arrived at Harvard in fall 1966, a young Republican from Idaho. He joined the Young Republican Club but found himself gradually drifting leftward. His first progressive act was signing a petition to support Cassius Clay's refusal to go into the army based on being a conscientious objector. Although initially Aldyn was supportive of the war, as he began to read more and started going

to teach-ins, his views on U.S. involvement in Vietnam shifted. He remembers Professor Stanley Hoffman's teach-in on the history of the war
as being particularly important.

> He talked about how the U.S. had signed the Geneva Accords and
> that there were supposed to be elections in 1956. And that the U.S.
> had deliberately prevented those elections from happening and de-
> liberately prevented the unification of the country because clearly
> they knew that Ho Chi Minh would win if they held them. That
> they had then set up this corrupt regime and supported it and,
> when they decided that Diem was not working out, they got rid of
> him. . . . When someone as knowledgeable and articulate as Stan-
> ley Hoffman . . . lays out the documentary evidence which proves
> that that happened, then [someone] like me, who was raised to be-
> lieve in America and our government . . . suddenly all this gets
> called into question. And that's what began to happen.

It was not simply the war per se but Aldyn's exposure to people whose
perspective resonated with his own concerns that provoked his switch
in beliefs. They gave voice to views that made sense to him. Through
others he learned a framework to understand the war. Shortly after this
teach-in, Aldyn participated in his first demonstration, a sit-in against
the Dow recruiter on campus. He continued going to local demonstrations, to antiwar marches in Washington, and eventually he ended up
joining SDS. Aldyn moved from being tangentially involved with SDS to
becoming a full-time radical. He became part of the Progressive Labor
(PL) faction of SDS and was asked by leaders of PL to go to Vietnam to
organize the troops against the war. In 1971 Aldyn enlisted in the army
(see chapter 7).

In fact, the Vietnam War was an important catalyst of radicalization
not only for crossovers but for many activists in SDS. A number of people
name the Vietnam War as the impetus that pushed them to a more militant stance. Like Aldyn, Jim Shoch started out supporting the war during his high school years. He took the position that "the more the world
was under Communist control, the less was free in the world." Considering himself a liberal anti-Communist, Jim went through a transition
when he got to Stanford. Some of his dorm-mates were already against
the war and by the end of his sophomore year Jim also took this position.
Jim began organizing people on campus to wear black armbands every
Friday to protest the war. At this point, however, he thought demonstrations blocking induction centers were too militant. He recalls thinking,

"It's one thing to desegregate a lunch counter when that was the source of the oppression, but this seemed much too symbolic and militant. I wrote some article for the *Stanford Daily*, 'Anatomy of the Failure.' I felt when looking back three years later, what a joke, considering what I got into." Jim's comment typifies many activists' experiences; in relatively short periods of time, individuals went through rapid changes of beliefs and tactics, embracing ideas that formerly would have been unthinkable.

The following fall Jim joined SDS and for the next several years became intensely involved as an activist. Much of Jim's further transformation came through reading. He remembers going home one spring vacation and reading an article in the paper about the Geneva accords and the elections to unify North and South Vietnam and how the United States agreed to abide by the election but in fact did not. Jim considered this a "complete breach of every notion I [had] about the U.S. as a just and democratic country . . . this contrast between . . . notions of equality and justice and decency and democracy and here the reality was clashing against the values I'd been raised with." Like Aldyn, the gap between the ideals of America and the reality of U.S. action in Vietnam provoked a shift in belief.

Jim began to read "like a maniac" to find out more. The single most important converting factor, he says, was reading *Containment and Change*, written by SDSer Carl Oglesby and Richard Shaull. It completely changed Jim's view of "how things worked." By discussing capitalism and imperialism, the book made Jim aware of broader systematic patterns beyond the Vietnam War. At this point Jim "decided I was no longer a liberal or even a left liberal, but I was now a radical. Not clearly a socialist, not clearly a Marxist yet, but clearly moving in this direction. I would certainly have called myself an anti-imperialist by the end of the summer." For Jim the shifts from calling himself a liberal, then a radical, and then an anti-imperialist were symbolic expressions of much more comprehensive changes. His exposure to peers who articulated views against the war, combined with his own reading, led to his shift in identity.

Integral to many activists' accounts of radicalization is the disillusionment these youth felt over the role of the American government. A recurrent theme in their stories is a growing frustration at the lack of government response throughout the 1960s—from pushing for civil rights to ending U.S. involvement in Vietnam. Again, it was the gap between the ideals of American democracy versus the reality of confronting federal inaction and government repression that provoked a requestioning of belief. Sue Jhirad captures this sense of erosion of belief in government. For her, disillusionment began during her work with the civil rights movement when she witnessed the "relative indifference of the federal government to the pleas for help at that time." Sue says this began the long process of disillusionment with the American power structure she calls her radicalization, "the feeling that there was something wrong 'at the root of things.'"

Sue's disillusionment continued with her involvement in the antiwar movement. By the late 1960s, after years of political organizing, Sue felt frustrated by the lack of visible change and increasingly angry at the "day-to-day things that were happening . . . the war kept going on and the lies kept accumulating and things just kept getting worse and worse." She says this anger made her and other activists move from their original belief in nonviolence and faith in rational persuasion to five years later wanting to stop the war no matter what. After endless atrocities, the tactics became more and more militant.

> The demonstrations took on a different character. They were much more disruptive. People went to demonstrations dressed for combat. The early demonstrations we dressed up to look impressive to the power structure and to the newspapers and wanted to look normal and reasonable. By '67, '68, '69, people were wearing shoes that were comfortable for running from being clubbed, and carrying handkerchiefs in plastic bags with water so you could avoid tear gas, and going in affinity groups—not alone—to demonstrations. The whole thing had taken on a sort of military cast.

It was not just government intransigence but also government repression and police brutality that radicalized people. Numerous people were changed by witnessing police brutality, what Klandermans refers to as "consciousness-raising during episodes of collective action."[8] Sue says,

> Just the experience of being beaten up by police, seeing how vicious they could be . . . and seeing the persecution of the FBI coming after us, seeing that there was a whole police network. You might think you were doing this fairly innocuous antiwar work, but I was visited by the FBI. People were harassed. You began to see there was something going on, as far as the state goes. . . . People's awareness of things just evolved.

Sue describes a process common to many leftists: as government harassment and repression against the left escalated, many activists were provoked to a more extreme position. This experience is echoed by many

SDSers who give accounts of the squelching of underground papers on campus or tales of police brutality, incidents that alienated youth and drew lines between "us" and "them."

In fact, such incidents of repression by police or university officials radicalized thousands of youth, even those who had more moderate views or were previously inactive.[9] Doug Knox comments on the impact of witnessing a particular incident of police brutality against protesters who were lying down in front of buses at induction centers.

> No question in my mind that for my own case it had a big effect on my attitude toward police. . . . Seeing police behave in an incredibly brutal fashion, just maliciously beating people up. And these were pacifists, people that were just limp. They could have picked them up carefully and put them in these wagons. . . . That had a big effect on me psychologically. You can't always pinpoint, okay at this point the existing political structure becomes delegitimized in your eyes, but I'm sure that had a major impact.

Such incidents of overt repression raised consciousness about the entire system, further delegitimizing authority.

Finally, radicalization was also tied to the seemingly unending series of historical and political events crammed into the decade. In particular, during the last years of the 1960s it seemed the country was coming apart. McAdam comments,

> It's very difficult for someone who didn't live through that period to understand that months—not simply years, but months—make a difference. What it felt like in January of '68 on the college campus bears precious little relationship to what it felt like in December of '68. You've moved politically and culturally light years from these positions. There is simply that much groping for a new ground. It just continues to spin out of control in that fashion.[10]

Both events and the reactions to events occurred so quickly that there was little time to digest what was happening, let alone to reach a reasoned response. At the same time, after years of commitment many activists felt worn down, discouraged by what they perceived to be a lack of any real change. Cathy Wilkerson recalls,

> There was Vietnam. There were [Black] Panthers being murdered. There was murder and mayhem. So we felt compelled to get the answer immediately so we could act on it. There didn't feel like there was any space to be complicated or to accept that life was

complicated. We had to simplify it and move on. . . . Every night
we would gather and watch Vietnam on the TV, and watch black
people be attacked and murdered. . . . It just never stopped. . . . I
felt like we really needed to be disruptive to stop what was going
on, that it was wrong to sit by and let it happen.

Todd Gitlin speaks of the contraction of time experienced by the New
Left as a result of the momentum of the war, government repression, and
the "hermetic quality of movement experience. Inside the movement, one
had the sense of being hurled through a time-tunnel, of hurtling from
event to event without the time to learn from experience."[11] This com-
pression of time and the immediacy of the need to respond, to attain civil
rights, to stop the war, to end repression, further contributed to the radicalization process as individuals wholeheartedly dedicated themselves
to the movement.

Integral to this radicalization process was a shift in identity, a relabeling of the self. Many activists on the left went through a process by
which they embraced the label "radical" to locate their politics. The transformation from liberal to leftist to Marxist to Maoist or anti-imperialist signified a change in ideology. By naming themselves, activists made
their identity real; they defined themselves within the spectrum of leftist
ideology, marking the boundaries of belief. Michael Kazin, who recalled
his own series of changes, tracks the process: "It was roughly from 1961
I would have considered myself a liberal Democrat; to '64 when I [was
a] left-liberal Democrat; to '66 when I would have called myself a radical; when I joined SDS to '68 when I would have called myself a revolutionary; and '67 to '69 when I would have called myself a revolutionary
Communist."

Through such labeling, activists communicate to themselves and to
others their shift in consciousness. Labels are displays of commitment
that convey identity to self and to others, knitting together the community. Activists' need to locate their beliefs grew even more urgent by the
end of the decade as the left erupted into sectarian politics. For those on
the right, adopting the term "libertarian" signified a similar process of
radicalization.

## Radicalization of Libertarians

Libertarians in YAF also went through processes of radicalization. Like
some in SDS, a few libertarians also point to one particular incident as

"*the* radicalizing event" in their political development. Rather than a long-term gradual process, for these individuals the rupture in belief is instantaneous. Maggie Kohls was transformed instantly with the realization "that hit me at once like somebody slapped me in the head." She explains,

> I remember standing in the middle of the living room when this hit me. . . . It was the result of getting divorced; and I was sexually active. . . . It hit me that morning that the reason I was anti-Communist was because they [Communists] take away your freedom. Yet in the Birch Society we were against anything to do with sexual freedom. . . . I'd grown up so conservative and being part of this Movement to Restore Decency where nobody was supposed to do anything. It suddenly dawned on me that I was having fun for the first time in my life. I wasn't hurting anyone. I was doing things that I certainly thought I would never do. It just dawned on me I had no business all this time telling other people what to do. . . . That was the day I became a libertarian.

This realization led to a "total relaxing of everything" as Maggie became "a much looser person." Eventually Maggie met other libertarians and became politically active once again.

More commonly activists went through a series of gradual changes during which they discovered their libertarian beliefs. Sharon Presley describes the development of her beliefs and her growing alienation from traditional conservatives. Sharon first became active in a YAF chapter at UC-Berkeley during the Goldwater campaign, working alongside traditionalists. Sharon was particularly drawn to Goldwater's support for civil liberties. Sharon, along with others in her chapter, was also involved in the Free Speech Movement (FSM).[12] The Berkeley administration banned all political tables on campus. Because the ban meant the Goldwater table was also prohibited, Sharon became active in early protests to support free speech.

> We felt the University was very high-handed. But then when [the FSM] moved into civil disobedience, we became more reluctant to be involved. . . . So most of us withdrew from support of the Free Speech Movement not because we disagreed with the ultimate aims, but because we were . . . reluctant to get involved in civil disobedience. . . . Looking back, I'm embarrassed that I even thought civil disobedience was inappropriate. . . . Because by as little as a year

later, the libertarians among us had realized that civil disobedience is a strategy which sometimes has value and is entirely appropriate. But we were just groping for our way at that time, so we shied away.

Still active in Republican politics at this point, Sharon spoke to conservative groups about the FSM. Although there were no serious repercussions to her participation, she says this involvement "helped propel us away from more traditional approaches."

After Goldwater's defeat Sharon also became active with Students Opposed to Conscription, believing the draft violated the most fundamental principles of individual liberty. The YAF chapter, now called Cal Conservatives and made up mainly of libertarians, increasingly felt the strains of working with traditionalists. Sharon comments,

> We could agree with them on the economic issues and for a brief time on foreign policy—to my embarrassment—which we later changed our minds about. Because there was a time when we were for the war in Vietnam—how embarrassing to remember that now! It didn't last too long! We caught on a couple of years later, but at that time we were still into the anti-Communist thing.

As with the left, it was not uncommon for libertarians' beliefs to change over a relatively short time.

By 1966 Sharon's YAF chapter ran into serious trouble with the national organization. Sharon recalls,

> Some funny things started happening. Like the head honchos in YAF had begun to catch wind of us . . . and realized that they had some pesky libertarians on their hands. Two of the members of our group had been former chairmen of California State YAF and they were also known to be druggies. What we got from the grapevine was that they [the national YAF office] were absolutely petrified that we as a chapter would come out with statements advocating the use of drugs. . . . So they pulled our charter. They kicked us out. We were the first libertarian deviationists from YAF.

The purging of this chapter was a foreshadowing of things to come (see chapter 7). Sharon felt she could no longer work with traditionalists, that their goals were too different and the similarities too superficial. Sharon also took a stance against the Vietnam War during this period, although she did not participate in antiwar activities. Once she began graduate school at San Francisco State, all her activities were directed toward the Alliance of Libertarian Activists. By 1967 Sharon identified as an anarchist.

Dave Schumacher also went through a gradual process of radicalization. Unlike Sharon, though, from the start he felt discomfort as he searched for a political position that felt consistent with his beliefs.

> It was almost like . . . going shopping in a sense because I would read things that the ACLU [American Civil Liberties Union] was involved in, cases they would be defending, and say, "Yeah, I agree with that." [But] there were a lot of things that the ACLU was doing that I just *didn't* agree with. Then there would be some statements or positions that you'd see, like SDS when they got started. You'd say, "Well okay, this is something that I can agree with, but I don't agree with 90 percent of the rest of this."

Dave opposed SDS's belief in the redistribution of wealth but agreed with its opposition to the war. By 1964, while working with YAF, Dave realized that his stance against the draft and against the Vietnam War differed from the views of many of his fellow activists. He was bothered by the inconsistencies he saw in conservative Republicanism. At that time, he recalls, "I was just working my way through those conflicts, contradictions, all those issues, on my own. But I didn't have a name for it."

Once he began college at Princeton, Dave became active in antiwar demonstrations. Although he knew people in SDS, he disagreed with their support of the North Vietnamese. He says,

> I was opposed to the war but not for the same reasons that a lot of other people were. In SDS and in YAF . . . it seemed to me that it was a package deal you had to take. If you thought the war was bad, that meant you were in favor of Ho Chi Minh and radical Marxism. I would always be trying to pick and choose . . . and make it work with something that I believe. And that just was hard to do.

After reading Ayn Rand and attending objectivist lectures, Dave began identifying as an objectivist, which was "one more level of feeling more comfortable and more consistent." As the war escalated and YAF "became more and more rabid" in supporting the war, Dave says he began weaning himself from YAF. Meanwhile Dave became more active in protesting the war, attending big antiwar demonstrations in Washington and Fort Dix, and campus sit-ins at Princeton. As a member of the undergraduate council Dave also proposed a resolution to get ROTC off campus, which was eventually adopted by the university. Throughout these activities Dave continued to feel frustrated with both left and right; as he put it, "right church, wrong pew," not feeling comfortable with either constituency.

For many libertarians as for SDSers, the Vietnam War and government repression contributed to the radicalization process. Many activists who became libertarian were opposed to the draft from the start, believing conscription by the state violated the most fundamental principle of individual liberty. Viewed as involuntary servitude, the draft became particularly contentious during the Vietnam War because it was an undeclared war and because libertarians increasingly saw the war as immoral. Although some traditionalists were also against the draft in principle, their belief in the need to fight communism led to unqualified support for the war. Thus, as Dana Rohrabacher puts it, "when libertarians saw people basically evading the draft or going to Canada . . . they did not see that as an attack on the country. . . . Traditionalists, on the other hand, although they were officially against the draft, really took that very personally," viewing it as unpatriotic and irresponsible.

Many libertarians became active in the antidraft movement, attending protests, participating in demonstrations at induction centers, and helping to close draft boards. In 1967 Don Ernsberger, for instance, successfully worked to get YAF to adopt the notion of a volunteer army. Don recalls the draft being a dividing line between traditionalists and libertarians: "The conservatives always insisted if you're drafted you served. [They thought:] It would be nice to have an all-volunteer army. We'd like to push for it. But when push comes to shove, you serve your country. Whereas our [libertarian] view was when push comes to shove, you go to Canada, you go underground, you resist." Among the libertarians he knew, Don says, an underground was in place. Although less organized than that on the left, it offered refuge for men resisting the draft.

Libertarians' stance against the draft placed them in an uneasy alliance with the left, yet it was really the Vietnam War that radicalized many libertarians, bringing elements of the left and right together. Libertarians went through a shift from the mid to late 1960s, during which time they turned decidedly against the war. Paralleling the case of some SDSers, Gus DiZerega's perspective changed through reading and intellectual reasoning. Gus read both right- and left-wing histories of the Vietnam War and, through rational judgment and analysis of the evidence on each side, found he could no longer justify the war.

My reasons for being against the war were that we were killing a great many people who didn't have a choice because they lived under a right-wing dictatorship. If there was going to be a right-wing or a left-wing dictatorship, it didn't seem to me worth killing people over. So it was unjust to the Vietnamese. . . . It was also very, very destructive for our own country because of the precedence of undeclared wars and the internal divisiveness that was going on.

Dave Walter's shift in perspective was gradual. Dave initially believed what he calls "conservative propaganda" supporting the war, considering the war essential to help the people of Vietnam fight communism. Slowly Dave began changing his mind. Ironically, it is what he learned about Vietnam in his ROTC courses that finally convinced him to change his views. At first he was angry that President Lyndon Johnson was holding back the United States from winning, not providing enough men, afraid of bombing Hanoi. But soon he questioned the very basis of the war.

At first we became angry with the way the U.S. was conducting the war and we attributed that to the evil Democrats or the evil liberals. [But] after awhile you saw so many atrocity pictures and you read so much about the South Vietnamese Army being a bunch of brutes and the people not backing them, and said, "What are we doing here?" The Vietnamese aren't willing to fight the Communists. Polls were taken . . . that showed that all they wanted was the war to stop. . . . If they weren't willing to fight for themselves, why should we get involved? . . . So my anticommunism didn't change; it was just that . . . the ends don't justify the means. You can't deny freedom to Americans in the name of fighting for freedom overseas.

By 1968 Dave advocated that the United States pull out of Vietnam.

Although libertarians took a strong stance against the war, unlike their leftist counterparts they believed that both the North *and* South Vietnamese were corrupt. Several libertarians commented that even though they worked with the antiwar left, they remained disturbed by the leftist embrace of Marx, Mao, or Lenin. Thus, despite their shift to an antiwar stance, libertarians remained suspicious of communism, still questioning the motives and interests of the North Vietnamese.

Even with these differences from the left, many libertarians became involved in the antiwar movement during the late 1960s, participating in demonstrations, moratoriums, and teach-ins against the war. While some libertarians participated by attending a few peace rallies, others became full-fledged activists in the movement. Some YAF chapters that were primarily libertarian turned their full attention to opposition to the war. Dave Walter comments, "At some point before the purge there were actually YAF chapters that were out joining antiwar marches. So there was a real . . . personality crisis in YAF. Some chapters were this and some chapters were that."

Don Ernsberger was the chair of the Penn State YAF chapter. By 1968 this chapter was the largest in the country, boasting 285 members. Both traditionalists and libertarians were members, but libertarians were in the majority. The chapter actively worked against the war. Don recalls, "I went to all the [antiwar] demonstrations. At Penn State the Libertarian Club was active with the Student Mobe [Mobilization to End the War in Vietnam]. SDS was in it and we were in it and we worked together on certain things." In particular, SDS and Don's YAF chapter worked together in protesting the war, ROTC, and military recruiters on campus.

Once active against the war, many libertarians went through further radicalization. Like their leftist counterparts they, too, became disillusioned with government. Just the act of opposing the war led some activists to question their government. Louise Lacey comments, "I was against everything. I was against the government period. It's bad enough that they steal your money with taxes, but then to spend it on requiring people's bodies and just taking your life away from you was the ultimate in something I just didn't believe in." Others, too, say their shift to an antiwar position was accompanied by a more critical stance toward government.

Disillusionment with government also was provoked by government repression. As with members of SDS, libertarians were horrified by police brutality and harassment of protesters. Once he became involved in the antiwar movement, Dave Schumacher was further radicalized by the government's reaction to protesters.

[At] the march on Washington I can remember going underneath the Justice Department and [Attorney General] Mitchell standing out there on the balcony and watching . . . and there were helicopters and the police. . . . I reacted very, very negatively to the way the government was responding to protesters. There was a lot of suppression—you know, the flag burning and draft card burning—

the government responded to those in a fascist way. . . . I just never could understand why other people in YAF didn't see that association. . . . I was totally mistrustful of Nixon, Mitchell. . . . I hated Henry Kissinger. . . . When you see the way the administration responded to opposition to the war and the things that were going on—domestic surveillance and the efforts to control personal behavior. The drug laws were being passed and stuff like that. It was objectionable.

Accompanying this turn against government, by the end of the decade over half of libertarians interviewed shifted their identification, using the term "anarchist" to describe themselves politically. Dana Rohrabacher comments on the transformation by which he became an anarchist. "I came to the point where I just was an advocate of no government at all. I was never a nihilist, but I came to the point where I was an individualist anarchist, where I didn't believe in any government. I was the ultimate idealist in that sense."

Rob Tyler's embrace of anarchism came about while working with the left as an antiwar organizer. Even though he opposed the Leninists working for the cause, he began to feel more and more affinity with anarchism: "I was seeing myself more on the Emma Goldman, Kropotkin— I was reading *all* that stuff—Proudhon, and all the anarchist stuff. It just made a lot of sense to me. So I found myself not just a libertarian, but finally I was an anarchist."

These shifts in identity parallel transformations of those in SDS. The choice of a label to adopt became increasingly important as the decade wore on. Sheldon Richman's experience is typical. When Sheldon arrived at college in the fall of 1967, he heard the word "libertarian" for the first time. He began meeting libertarians and was introduced to the writings of Ayn Rand. At this point Sheldon called himself a Randian. As Sheldon's views developed, he became more critical of foreign policy and shifted to a position against the war. At this point he used the term "libertarian" to describe himself. By 1969, heavily influenced by Murray Rothbard,[13] Sheldon saw a philosophical contradiction in being for individual rights while also supporting a monopoly state. At this point he decided "anarchism was the legitimate position."

Like SDS members whose radicalization was accompanied by shifts in identity—from leftist to radical to Marxist or revolutionary—so, too, many libertarians went through transformations in self-labeling, distinguishing themselves as "libertarians" and consequently moving on to call themselves "anarchist" or "anarcho-capitalist." Intrinsic to the process of radicalization, then, is the transformation of self. The labels capture a shift in worldview: what problems are critical, who or what is responsible for these problems, what makes up the vision of an ideal society. Self-labeling also conveys identity and commitment to those outside. Calling themselves radicals or anarchists locates individuals within a larger community.

These shifts in belief also signified an opening between the worlds of the left and right, a convergence between elements within YAF and SDS that indicated overlapping interests and values. Unlike traditionalists in YAF who saw no common ground with SDS, many libertarians found common cause with SDS. Some libertarians even worked in coalition with those on the left and, as we'll see in chapter 7, a few even ended up joining SDS.

## THE CONSEQUENCES OF RADICALIZATION

Radicalization also marked activists through the concrete consequences such beliefs and actions had on their lives. McAdam distinguishes among the risks of activism, referring to the "costs" involved in terms of the time, money, and energy required of an individual, as well as the anticipated dangers (legal, social, physical, financial) of engaging in particular types of activities. For example, signing a petition is low cost but may incur high risks in terms of consequences, as it did during the McCarthy era; whereas organizing the homeless has high costs in terms of time and energy, but low risks in terms of consequences. In studying Freedom Summer volunteers, McAdam concludes that individuals who initially engage in low-risk activism are drawn into more costly forms of participation through integration into a network of committed activists who take greater risks. McAdam argues the other key ingredient to high-risk activism is being "biographically available," that is, being free of personal constraints such as full-time employment, marriage, or children. Only those who do not have competing responsibilities that pose obstacles to participation are willing to be risk-takers.[14]

Yet what we also need to understand high-risk activism, based on the experiences of those in YAF and SDS, is a third factor: the degree of repression directed against a given social movement. Virtually all the activists in both SDS and YAF were biographically available; they were young, without careers, and the majority were single and without family responsibilities. All of those interviewed were also well integrated into circles of other committed believers. Yet even among highly committed members of YAF and SDS, all individuals were not equally likely to engage in high-risk activism. The higher risks taken by some activists are directly related to the differential response by government. In particular, government repression was directed toward the left and not the right.[15]

Traditionalists in YAF were the least likely to face any kind of organized resistance by government. They held demonstrations and marches, but none reported any negative consequences to such action in terms of being arrested or jailed, beaten by police, or harassed by the FBI. Thus, the costs incurred were relatively small, requiring few risks.[16]

High-risk activism *is* evident among libertarians. At least half of the libertarians were involved in demonstrations in which they were teargassed and witnessed police brutality. Because so many libertarians during the late 1960s became active in antiwar protests, not only were they exposed to individuals willing to take higher risks, but they themselves directly encountered repression against their activities. Thus, unlike traditionalists, higher costs were associated with libertarian activities.

SDS activists, however, encountered the greatest resistance and therefore paid the highest costs for political involvement. Not only did SDSers face tear gas and police brutality, they also were more likely to be arrested, jailed, and put under surveillance or harassed by the FBI. In addition, several SDSers were thrown out of school as a result of their participation and two activists in this study went underground by the end of the 1960s.

Some SDS activists unintentionally ended up taking higher risks. Andrea Cousins recounts an experience of confronting the police while attending a demonstration in Boston with a friend:

> Some tactical police were hauling [my friend] off and twisting his arms and beating him on his kneecaps with their sticks. I was just falling after them and imploring them to please stop . . . that they didn't have to twist his arms and beat him. I went and tapped the shoulder of one of the guys and he arrested me in turn and threatened me a lot. . . . I was watching them hit Bob's knees and this guy, Dennis, was saying to me that he should be doing the same to me. They made us sit on the ground and fingerprinted us and put us in jail. I only stayed there for a few hours but it was really very, very, very, very frightening. I felt like I was lost to the world.

Andrea was literally dragged into taking higher risks. Her arrest was not a conscious decision she made beforehand; rather, she acted spontaneously against the brutality she witnessed.

Cindy Decker, on the other hand, consciously decided to risk arrest during a sit-in at the University of Kansas. Although this was not a difficult decision for her to make, the experience changed her.

> It wasn't just the event of getting arrested, but the entire process around it [that was radicalizing], the interpersonal dynamics that are associated with it. . . . I didn't have any trouble at all making a decision to sit down and get arrested. . . . But I watched other people just sit, wring their hands, and cry because they couldn't figure out what to do. I didn't realize it was such a big deal. . . . Then following that event there were a series of meetings with the university establishment. I was amazed to find myself speaking out against them because it wasn't really something I'd considered.

Witnessing the arrests and people's reactions to them pushed Cindy to take a more vocal role in opposing the campus administration, furthering her commitment to the movement.

Another SDS activist, Vivian Rothstein, explains why it was so difficult for some people to face being arrested, the real consequences of such decisions. "When I got arrested in San Francisco, I knew at that time you couldn't be a teacher in California if you were arrested. There were a lot of jobs you couldn't get and it was a big decision to make. I made it consciously because I was only eighteen and I thought it was the kind of life I wanted to lead, to be an activist." Vivian made a calculated decision to risk arrest, recognizing the implications of her action in terms of her future job prospects.

Other SDSers mention being followed, having their offices raided, drugs planted, and provocateurs infiltrating local chapters as a consequence of their actions. In some cases parents of activists were also affected. Several SDSers mention the FBI harassing their parents. In Carol Christman's case, when government officials began asking questions of neighbors in her parents' community, Carol's father decided to take early retirement from his government job, frightened that he would continue to be hassled.

As activists witnessed brutality or were the targets of repression and harassment, they were pushed to take greater risks. The effects of repression led to further radicalization. For libertarians and leftists, then, a cycle of radicalization occurred. Certainly being biographically available allowed activists to engage in acts and embrace beliefs that might have otherwise been too threatening. Derek Barron remarks,

> We were all college students and in a position to take risks that we wouldn't dare consider taking now because we're all fat and mar-

ried or close to be[ing] married . . . [with] children and all that. But at that time we were willing to consider almost anything. So the idea of trying to bring about a revolution in the country to reverse the direction that the country seemed to be taking was very attractive to a lot of us.

Yet it was not just ideology or biography, but concrete acts of repression that escalated the likelihood of high-risk activism. Given the combination of this brutality and repression, as well as the frustration activists felt at the slow pace of social change, many activists were pushed to more extreme tactics—not just engaging in civil disobedience but accepting disruption, violence, or even armed struggle as the only means to achieve change. In some cases, government provocateurs also prodded people to militancy. Such tactics in turn led to greater repression and further radicalization.

### Relations with Parents

A final effect of radicalization was strained relations between activists and their parents. While the majority of YAF parents remained supportive of their offspring's activism throughout the 1960s, expressing pride in their involvement or providing money, shelter, or other forms of aid for the movement, only a quarter of SDS parents remained wholeheartedly supportive. This outcome corresponds with previous research that finds a greater degree of generational conflict among left- versus right-wing youth.[17] The lack of support among SDS parents was in part a result of activists' radicalization and the greater costs and higher risks SDS members faced. However, despite the fact that libertarians were also radicalized, few faced strained relationships with parents. Parents of libertarians were just as likely to be supportive of their offspring as parents of traditionalists. Thus, once again the costs of activism were greatest for those in SDS.

Activists with parents who opposed their involvement ranged from those who experienced estranged relations, in which parents and children "felt alienated from each other," to those parents who expressed overt disapproval and even hostility. One of the few libertarians who felt strain was YAFer Dave Schumacher. He remembers arguing with his parents about the Vietnam War, racism, and other matters. Because of this he felt uncomfortable at home. In particular, Dave reacted against his father's authoritarianism.

The thing I objected to in the family setting [were] things my father would say—"You do it because we say you're going to do it" and that kind of thing. I didn't accept it in the family and I don't accept it in life. . . . The way I tried to establish my own identity was to just continue to force them to respond to things rationally. It was a problem. I took a beating. He took a beating.

The opposition of SDS parents was often extremely heated, erupting into intense conflict. Steve Goldstein, a red-diaper baby, speaks humorously about the conflict he faced. Because of their split with the Communist Party during the 1950s, Steve's parents felt hatred toward the party and objected to his leftist activities. "They had a lot of contempt for [the party]. So their great fear was that I would become a professional revolutionary. So naturally I did. I hadn't even thought of it until they suggested it." His parents were particularly upset when he joined Progressive Labor.

My father and I had battles, four or five hours of screaming at each other. [But] they didn't stop talking to me. I have to say in retrospect they were pretty incredible. . . . They never threatened to cut me off. I would have cut me off in a second, but they never did. . . . That was pretty principled because they really disapproved of what I was doing *intensely.*

Some relations became so strained that all communication ended. Jim Shoch faced one of the most dramatic breaks with his parents as a result of a film made about Stanford SDS in 1969. Jim was interviewed as a leading campus radical. During the filming Jim basically called his father a racist. His parents were horrified. Jim explains how it happened.

I get sick to my stomach thinking about it. . . . This was . . . just three or four minutes of a forty-five-minute interview that basically ranged all over the map . . . my analysis of the world and imperialism and this and that. [The filmmaker] asked for some family background and so without thinking—it never even really occurred to me he'd use this . . . I said, "[My father] wears three-piece suits to every occasion. He infrequently speaks in words of less than ten syllables. And his liberal facade will on occasion break down and he'll call blacks 'niggers.'" . . . Which he had done in some hotel room on a trip to London one time in a furious argument when pushed. . . . But I was pissed off at him and his lifestyle and his wealth and this kind of liberalism. . . . I just couldn't *stand* liberals at the time. . . .

We were all into renouncing white skin privilege and so it seemed like I [was] explaining part of my radicalization. . . . I wasn't hostile when I was saying it. . . . It came across as an observation of my background and some of the things that had shaped me.

After the film was shown, Jim and his parents didn't speak for over a year. There was one point, about six months after the showing, when Jim wrote them a letter of "mild apology." When his parents came out to San Francisco to attend a convention, Jim met them at their hotel room. But the attempt at reconciliation failed.

I told them that I possessed arms and [was] trained in their use and suggested that they become the same because the revolution was coming [laughs]. As far as I could tell they were going to be on the wrong side. That didn't go over too successfully! My father was icy cold and I left. It was clear that they didn't want anything to do with me. They didn't say, "You're disowned.". . . It wasn't like "We renounce you as our son." It just ended very icily.

A year later Jim wrote a long letter of serious apology and shortly after that, they resumed talking and repaired their relationship. But clearly the costs of Jim's beliefs were tremendous in terms of the pain of these antagonistic family relationships.

As the 1960s progressed and segments of SDS moved toward embracing Marxism, some SDS parents, particularly those who lived in the shadow of McCarthyism, feared their offspring's drift toward communism. It was for this reason that Phil Hutchings's parents opposed his politics.

[My mother] was always worried that I was going to knock some girl up and come home and have five kids to support and my life would get ruined . . . or I might become a drug addict or a Communist. It was all in the same breath. These were the four or five no-no's. . . . But it was more like society had put certain things on leftism. . . . People like Paul Robeson had disappeared because he had been progressive and McCarthyism had been very strong. My father was in a government job and just remembering what McCarthyism had done around people with government jobs. It was not even so much that the ideas themselves were considered. It was just like what would happen. . . . It was more of a protective thing.

When Phil went to Cuba with the Venceremos Brigade, he became even more distanced from his father. His father couldn't understand why Phil would cut sugarcane for Castro, an enemy of the United States, when there were plenty of improvements to be made at home. Phil comments, "You could talk it all into the ground and never get anywhere on this."

But looking back, Phil empathizes with his father's dilemma, saying his generation represented the first time black people could actually get decent jobs and be upwardly mobile, a possibility not available to his parents. "It's like I was throwing it away from their standpoint. I was just throwing those opportunities away." This fear of the repercussions of activism was much more evident among parents of SDS activists than parents of YAFers. In addition to ideological differences that provoked generational conflict, parents of SDSers worried about interruptions of careers, unfinished education, and lost opportunities as they watched their young become more and more absorbed in the world of activism.

As one might expect, the majority of SDSers who crossed over from the politics of their parents also faced tensions with their parents. One crossover, Cindy Decker, recalls the conflict she faced with her father. One particular incident stands out in her mind:

> I was on my way to the SDS national headquarters in Chicago and he was driving me to the bus station. He did one of these Why don't you go back to Russia? numbers. I looked at him and I said, "I want you to understand that I don't consider Russia to be an ideal place at all. I don't consider Stalinism to be an ideal form of government. What I want to do is make the United States, which I love a lot, a better place for people to live."

This fusing of activities on the left with Russia and communism was assumed by other crossover parents as well. Calling her parents "dyed-in-the-wool Republicans," Lynn Dykstra says her parents hated all of her activities. In reaction, Lynn stopped discussing her politics and hid her involvement, trying not to get her name or picture in the paper. "[My] father . . . was sure that we were all getting duped by the Communists, that the Russian Communists had sent all these spies over to set up SDS and it was all being run by and paid for by foreign agents and we were just stupid. That was so ludicrous that I knew he was wrong." Lynn's experience is unusual, however, in that her parents eventually shifted their own beliefs, becoming more liberal; in 1972 they even voted for McGovern.

Not all crossovers faced opposition from their parents, however. Although Bernardine Dohrn's parents didn't change their beliefs, they were unusual in their unwavering support for Bernardine throughout the 1960s, even when Bernardine went underground. Despite the fact that her parents never understood her actions, and even though her involvement caused them hardship, Bernardine's parents stood by her side.

> They were quite wonderful and quite loyal. . . . When we went underground, they had no way [of understanding]. Now as a parent I can see that nobody would have any way [of knowing]. . . . The idea that anybody in the world would have agreed with us or that we had support—it was just beyond their experience. . . . [But] they had this absolute position and the parts of the family that denounced me, they refused to talk to any more. . . . They talked to the FBI several times a week for ten years and were very polite to them. But I was a good girl and [they thought] whatever I was doing had some sense that they [just] didn't understand.

While a minority of SDS members had their parents' encouragement and support, the majority who faced parental opposition and hostility paid an even higher price for their participation. The pain, difficulty, and loss of family relations resulting from activism is, then, another hidden cost of political commitment. Any discussion of the consequences of political activism must take into account the personal anguish and psychological expenses created by such generational conflict.

## CONCLUSION

Integral to sustaining a social movement is building solidarity by developing and maintaining loyalty and commitment.[18] Activists in both SDS and YAF went through parallel processes. For members of each organization the movement first enticed and then increasingly absorbed their focus and energy. Growing commitment to the movement brought them into circles with other dedicated activists and expanded their involvement, enmeshing them even further in the political world, pushing them forward in their beliefs and action.

Individuals cement these bonds to a social movement through interaction with others. As Klandermans puts it, "Collective beliefs are created by individuals not in isolation but in the course of communication and cooperation."[19] Talk is central to building solidarity. Through ongoing conversations and shared experiences, other activists reaffirm and extend political ideology. Fine discusses the importance of talk as a way of processing experience and building a shared identification. One type of talk critical to social movements is "war stories," narratives of experiences that members have gone through in the context of their participation.[20] Individuals who have undergone deeply moving experiences seek group support for understanding these events. Through shared emotional reactions they build and sustain solidarity. "Emotions provide rich, first-hand, and powerful content for the construction of identity. Whether a person wishes to or not, a surge of emotion becomes immediate evidence that she or he relates in that powerful way to self, another person or event, or a collectivity."[21] This emotional "at-homeness" in a movement is essential to solidarity's survival.

Yet building solidarity also entails excluding others. The narrowing of social ties, what Taylor and Whittier call "boundary maintenance," marks group relations by highlighting differences between activists and those outside. Boundaries heighten the we/they distinction by which social movements sustain their collective identity. But not all movements equally engage in exclusionary behavior. As we've seen, SDS members were more likely to narrow their social worlds. As they became radicalized and became more and more critical of the dominant society, SDSers drew their circles tighter around them. "Maintaining an oppositional identity depends upon creating a world apart from the dominant society."[22] This narrowing of ties was exacerbated by the amount of repression used against leftist protesters.

Meanwhile, although YAF members also built solidarity to maintain collective identity, they were more likely to sustain relations with people holding different or opposing views. Their oppositional identity to the dominant society was never as severe, nor did YAFers suffer the harassment and repression by authorities that SDSers faced.

We've also seen the divergence between the pathways of traditionalists and libertarians or leftists. While traditionalists retained their beliefs, libertarians and leftists went through similar processes of radicalization. Through exposure to others, through refinement of their beliefs, and as a result of their concrete experiences in protest movements, these activists shifted ideology, transforming their identity to become "radicals" or "anarchists." Radicalization, too, is a relational process. Only in interaction with a community of others did radicalization take place; in turn, the sense of radical identity sustained the community. Radicalization also meant these individuals, particularly members of SDS, faced higher risks and paid greater costs for their activities.

Two other experiences radicalized some members of SDS and YAF: participation in the counterculture (chapter 5) and feminism (chapter 6). Both of these experiences played a key role in bringing together elements of the left and right as well as in fragmenting each movement.

# CHAPTER FIVE

# THE COUNTERCULTURE: LEFT MEETS RIGHT

Many people remember the 1960s not only for the protest movements of that era but also for the counterculture. Images of bearded and mustached long-haired men, women with flowing hair and skirts, tie-dyed shirts and faded overalls, music festivals and head shops, organic food stores and homemade granola, Indian bedspreads, lava lamps, and the smells of marijuana and patchouli oil textured the late 1960s and early 1970s. A common assumption might be that youth on the left embraced the counterculture while those on the right rejected it. But in fact activists in both SDS and YAF differed in their reactions to the counterculture. A portion of activists in both groups rejected the counterculture, dismissing it as self-indulgent and destructive, while another portion in each organization embraced this youth movement. For libertarians in YAF the counterculture offered a means to reformulate beliefs, provoking radicalization that forged further bonds with their counterparts on the left. Thus, the counterculture served as a meeting ground for the varying interests and overlapping impulses of this divided generation.

The use of the term "counterculture" here specifically refers to the dress, music, drugs, sexuality, and "alternative lifestyles" associated with the cultural changes of the 1960s.[1] These lifestyles also signified a renunciation of conventional values—the rejection of conventional manners and morals for an emphasis on spontaneity and self-expression; the opening of the self to feeling and immediate experience over repression of gratification; the replacement of traditional attitudes toward career, success, and money with a devaluing of materialism and a search for jobs that emphasized self-realization and social contribution; and an emphasis on naturalness expressed by the rejection of the use of cosmetics, perfumes, and deodorants, by the embrace of nudity, and the eating of organic foods.[2]

Thus, the style and behavior of those who took up the counterculture signified an oppositional stance to the dominant society. As Whalen and Flacks comment,

> [T]he most evident meaning of long hair and blue jeans was that one was deliberately trying to look like anything but a conventional adult. . . . To be seen as a hippie in the mid-sixties was . . . not simply to be part of a new fashion trend; it was instead interpreted by many as a commitment to an alternative life course, a sign that one had made a break with the values and ways of life defined by one's parents, school, and community.[3]

Music was an integral part of the counterculture, a further expression of opposition to established rules and institutions. Flacks argues that the movements of the 1960s are difficult to grasp unless we recognize the way music crystallized the identities of alienated youth and provided the underpinnings for collective gatherings.[4] Folk music characterized the early 1960s, giving voice to protest and bonding people together in solidarity, and rock music symbolized the mid to late 1960s: Bob Dylan went electric and the Beatles, Rolling Stones, Grateful Dead, Doors, Janis Joplin, Jimi Hendrix, and a host of other groups gave voice to a more widespread youth culture.[5] As Marcus puts it,

> The music was something that you could talk about with your friends and that you couldn't talk about with people who were older than you. It gave people a sense of generational solidarity and a sense that they were different and a sense different from the rest of the country, different from any other generation in American history, that they were in some ways special and blessed and it gave them a sense of being embattled, of . . . being considered outsiders, reprobates, bad people.[6]

Rather than a single, unified entity, in actuality the counterculture incorporated a range of beliefs and practices. For instance, the counterculture embraced diverse—and even contradictory—values. It encompassed both an urge toward individual expression and self-gratification, and an urge toward collectivism and community. It is, indeed, this diversity of beliefs and practices that allowed people of varying backgrounds and ideologies to commonly identify with an oppositional culture.[7]

Although cultural radicalism has accompanied leftist protest movements of the past,[8] the counterculture was able to reach a much larger audience because of postwar America's middle-class affluence. A rise in the discretionary income of teenagers created an economic base for youth culture, as the leisure and fashion industries expanded to serve this "teenage market." The ability of the mass media (e.g., radio, television, records, movies) to promote and disseminate youth culture further accelerated this generation's collective identity.[9]

## SDS AND THE COUNTERCULTURE

Within SDS, division over the counterculture corresponds to the date when individuals became active. There is a notable difference between the hostility expressed by the early activists (who became active in SDS from 1960 to 1964), versus the more accepting embrace of the counterculture by later activists (who became active from 1965 to 1968).

Many early activists viewed the counterculture as self-indulgent and narcissistic. For instance, one early activist, Sue Jhirad, comments,

> I was less into the cultural aspects than the political aspects. . . . Some of that may have been a question of age; by the time the counterculture really hit strong, I was already in my mid-twenties. . . . I had grown up in the fifties. . . . I look[ed] at some of [the counterculture] as kind of silly, self-indulgent. . . . I was . . . antagonistic to some aspects of it. . . . I just didn't really identify with it in a strong way.

Certainly the fact that many members of the early group were older and were affected by the more conservative cultural styles of the 1950s explains part of the difference in stance toward the counterculture. But early activists' objection to the counterculture did not simply reflect differences in age or style. Carl Oglesby speaks about his hostility toward the counterculture: "I was always annoyed at people who thought that the counterculture was in and of itself the revolution and that all we needed to do was all get high and listen to rock music. . . . Drugs had become kind of a metaphor of revolution and I felt that really was wrong, that saying change your head, that wasn't a revolution."[10]

Some early activists point to particular aspects of the counterculture that they opposed. Vivian Rothstein comments on the drugs and fashion of the youth culture:

When I was in Berkeley drugs were an important part of the student movement. . . . I actually saw some of my friends become heroin addicts. So I got very frightened of drugs. They either became heroin addicts or they . . . fried their brains on LSD. So I really moved away from the drug culture and so I didn't like that part of [the counterculture]. And . . . we were . . . serious about what we did and wanted to look like ordinary people. . . . I never believed in dressing in rags because I'd worked with people who had to dress in rags. I knew poor people . . . didn't like to be dressed like that. I felt it was ridiculing poor people to dress like that.

In particular, many early activists were afraid that elements of the counterculture harmed the movement, making it harder to organize politically. For instance, Dorothy Burlage says, "I was never into drugs. . . . I didn't want the drugs being associated with the politics. . . . I didn't want to muddy the waters in the South. . . . I mean if people smoked pot, that was one thing. But to make that an issue and to *contaminate* a vision of changing race relations in this country with that, seemed to be not helpful."

Like Dorothy, Bob Ross also objected to the counterculture from a strategic vantage point, seeing it as an obstacle to political organizing. In order to successfully advocate socialism, Bob believed, you had to look as nice and normal as possible, rather than look exotic and risk alienating others. Because of this and for ideological reasons Bob adamantly opposed the counterculture, fearing its detrimental effects.

I saw [the counterculture] happening in front of me. I knew that it was becoming primary. I didn't like it. . . . I thought it was destructive to the construction of a popular movement. It was isolating; and elements of it, of course, were just purely reactionary. . . . [I] thought that an awful lot of the rhetoric coming out of the so-called young Turks—they were called Prairie Power—was not at all socialist or favorable to the working class. Because a lot of it was countercultural and I just didn't see that as the cutting edge of socialist revolution. . . . I didn't [agree] with what I saw as anarchistic ideas—and I mean that technically, not connotatively.

Bob's comments point to the growing divisions that occurred in SDS from 1965 onward. As a result of SDS's role in organizing the first large national antiwar march in Washington on April 17, 1965, SDS "went public."[11] In the aftermath of the march, the media gave unprecedented attention to SDS, labeling it the leading organization of the New Left. As a result, membership skyrocketed. In December 1964 SDS membership was 2,500 with 41 chapters; by October 1965 membership escalated to 10,000 with 89 chapters.[12] This upsurge in membership had two important consequences. First, it fundamentally changed SDS from a small group based on face-to-face interaction into a large-scale organization. From the mid-1960s on SDS became so large that the experience of being in the organization shifted from one in which members were integrated into a large circle of friends to an organization in which individuals knew only local or at best statewide members and often felt estranged from the national leadership. In fact, as the 1960s progressed, more and more tensions developed between the local and national levels of the organization.

The second change accompanying SDS's growth was the entry of new waves of activists who often differed from the "old guard." Unlike the older generation who mainly became active through civil rights work, from 1965 onward most new recruits were brought in through opposition to the Vietnam War. Todd Gitlin says these new members shifted SDS's center of gravity from the East Coast to the hinterlands—to the South and the Great Plains.[13] Called "Prairie Power" these new recruits also differed ideologically from the early activists. According to Gitlin,

> [They] accepted the prairie identification as a symbolic badge of Americanness and populism. . . . Whether or not they came from an actual prairie, these Prairie Power people wore their hair longer and seemed looser in style, less formal and mannerly than the Old Guard generation. They were more likely than the Old Guard to call themselves anarchists; when they formulated a political position at the 1966 convention, it went by the name of student syndicalism. Within SDS they stood for campus organizing and against the centralized national office; many were students themselves, in fact, when most of the Old Guard had left the campus. In style they were proto-hippies.[14]

The pattern generally holds true that early SDSers opposed the counterculture whereas the later generation embraced it, yet in actuality there were people who bridged the gap between these two positions. Jane Adams, for example, began working with SDS during 1964 and was older than most of the later activists. But in her role as regional organizer in the Midwest, and as temporary national secretary during the summer of 1966, Jane also embodied Prairie Power.[15] Jane held ambivalent views of the counterculture. On the one hand, Jane said she was simply "too straight . . . too political, and maybe too intellectual" to fully accept the counterculture. Having grown up on a farm, she had a "pretty jaundiced view" of the back-to-the-land movement. There were also particular aspects of the counterculture that Jane found objectionable. For instance, she opposed the attitude of "what's mine is yours and I don't have anything so gimme." Criticizing the youth movement as "insensitive and almost predatory," she says it was particularly exploitative of women.

> There's sexual freedom and then there's sexual exploitation. . . . It was still a male culture. I remember one group that [was] real counterculture. They weren't political at all. . . . The women did all the cooking and all the cleaning, and would wait on [the men]. . . . It was worse than anything I'd ever experienced.[16]

Because of these macho strains and because Jane was older than many others, she felt distanced from the counterculture.

On the other hand, Jane also felt that the cultural dimensions were important. She believed in building counterinstitutions that directly confronted "the powers that be," seeing such utopian experiments as models of different ways of being. She criticized the old guard in SDS for not recognizing the ways the counterculture appealed to people. In particular, she relates an incident in 1966 when an Oklahoma SDS chapter got busted for marijuana. This provoked a big debate within the national office of SDS. Several people, outraged at the drug use, attempted to expel the chapter.[17] As it turned out, what the cops uncovered was not drugs and the charges were dropped. But meanwhile the incident exposed a division within SDS. Jane recalls,

> All of my friends had been smoking dope for a long time. Many of them had been taking acid or other psychedelics—peyote and whatnot; I mean this cactus ranch was part of the vernacular. And that was just a complete disjuncture for these East Coast older—not so much in age older, although there was some age difference—but generationally older. . . . That was one of the major differences.

In fact a couple of years later Jane and her partner opened up a head shop in Oklahoma in the hope of "bring[ing] together the cultural and the political revolution."

John Brown Childs is another early activist who embraced part of the counterculture. Yet he points out the different meaning the counterculture had for him as a black activist:

> I saw [the counterculture] as one current. I had this other current, which was the black community and what was going on there. That was countercultural, but in a very different kind of way. So I was part of that, too. I didn't see the white counterculture as the only way to go. It looked like it was useful because it . . . was eroding the traditional white hegemony. These were people who were just . . . thumbing their noses at what existed and they were rejecting Western culture and trying to live like Indians on communes. . . . To the degree that black culture became something that people respected . . . I was sympathetic to [the counterculture].

John also points out that for him the sexual liberation associated with the counterculture represented a lifting of the restrictions dictated by segregation, the freedom to cross the line and sexually relate to whomever he wanted to. Thus, the counterculture had a different meaning for him than it did for white activists.

There were even a few exceptions among the early activists, those who wholeheartedly supported the counterculture. Barbara Haber, for instance, says that by the late 1960s she was becoming a hippie.

> I wore my hair in braids, I smoked dope, I wore long dresses and sandals. Lived in collectives, made my own bread, ate granola, ate yogurt, was a vegetarian for awhile. . . . And dabbled in psychedelics and . . . tie-dyed things and macramé. . . . I was more into the human potential movement than some people, real interested in psychology and stuff like that. . . . Everyone I knew . . . men grew their hair long, they wore beards, they wore ponytails. Everybody had embroidered work shirts and we tie-dyed everything we could. . . . We definitely were political and we wanted all hippies to be political.

Barbara says the counterculture was an integral part of her experience during the 1960s. "From the beginning how we lived our lives everyday was part of what it was all about. . . . It was a given long before I ever could articulate it."

Barbara's perspective is an uncommon one among the older generation of SDSers. The counterculture was not the only factor that divided early and late SDSers but, as we'll see in chapter 7, the older generation's stance toward youth culture did play a part in the explosive SDS convention in 1969 that led to the demise of the organization.

In contrast to most early activists rejecting the counterculture as a diversion from politics, later activists embraced the counterculture in beliefs and lifestyle, seeing it not only as a valid part of 1960s activism, but as an essential part of the political movement. The building of alternative lifestyles and parallel or counterinstitutions was experimental and, in Breines's terms, "prefigurative," embodying the values and ways of the ideal society.[18] SDS member Judy Smith captures the feeling of the import of the counterculture: "The counterculture was a very important part of what linked us. Dress, dope, music, were our break with the standards of what was expected of us. No one could do it alone, and the counterculture provided a glimpse of what a movement might provide in terms of new identities, new comradeship, new ways of seeing."[19]

Indeed, the counterculture became central to the identity of these political activists. Judy Baker, one of the later generation of activists, said,

I really felt . . . that we were going to create a culture that really worked. . . . In 1966, 1967, '68, the counterculture and the political movement were the same; if you asked people what they belonged to, they belonged to everything. . . . It was a very, very open time. . . . I really don't think [the history of the sixties] has been written yet. Until people can get a sense of what it was like to sit in a t-group [therapy group] and talk about what you really think but you have not been saying because you didn't want anybody to know; or you could sit in a women's liberation group and say, "My husband has never done a dish in his life and he's never going to." . . . I don't think people want to remember it because it really does challenge a person to be real.

Terry Koch, another later activist, attributes his embrace of the counterculture to the unity of politics and youth culture in the St. Louis community. "What to me was wonderful about St. Louis was that if you were a poet, if you were a black jazz musician, if you believed in abortion rights . . . it was the same as being in the antiwar movement. You were all in it together because you're in St. Louis and you're surrounded by a bunch of rednecks. . . . It was all one and the same." By necessity, political and countercultural communities came together in the face of opposition. Terry says the two communities were also linked financially as SDS used to regularly receive money from drug dealers. "We got cash donations for bail, for leaflets when we needed one. I knew who was dealing and I would say, 'You're making money off our community. Share it.'"

Saying at the time that he identified as "a countercultural activist," Terry saw youth culture as an important part of the politics of the times. "I saw it not only as not being a diversion. I saw it as being very much making room for a new order, a new society. I felt when Che Guevara talked about the new man, it could include smoking pot [laughs]. The two to me were right together. . . . We saw youth culture as being a facet of making change."

Jeanne Friedman, a later activist who was at Stanford, identified with the counterculture as well, although she also recognized the difficulties of bringing together the two communities. She believed the counterculture and left-wing politics were "natural allies," and yet sometimes it didn't work out because the counterculture "carried within it a lot of people who were profoundly anti-Communist and anti-ideology," advocating simply that "Everybody do your own thing." But Jeanne saw herself as a meld of the left *and* the counterculture.

> I thought [the counterculture] was very liberating and very fulfilling. . . . Basically I liked those people. I found them creative and bright and their hearts were in the right place. It's just the world was not amenable, I thought, to being changed solely by good vibes. . . . The hippies were going to have to get a little more organized. . . . But the politicos were also going to have to mellow out a little bit, right? . . . The counterculture was very, very important.

A few other later activists also expressed mixed feelings about the counterculture. They were drawn in but remained critical of the politics (or lack of politics) of the youth culture. Michael Kazin was one of those divided in his judgments. As he wryly comments, he brought the counterculture and politics together at a party one night when he took his draft card, rolled it into a joint, and smoked it. And yet he was also skeptical of the counterculture.

> I liked rock music and I did LSD, mescaline, peyote, and lots of marijuana, [but] I didn't feel allegiance with what seemed to be the ideology of it. I was always political . . . and I thought it was flabby thinking and people were fooling themselves about how people were

going to change. You know, the old "You have to change yourself first to change society" kind of thing. . . . I was always on the side of the politicos.

Yet later Michael comments that the women's movement was the "political translation" of the counterculture; feminism made clear that individual transformation was absolutely vital. Recognizing the importance of this, Michael says he gained insight from the counterculture.

Although the majority of SDSers conformed to this pattern of early activists rejecting the counterculture while older activists identified with it, the one consistent exception were SDS members who joined the Progressive Labor (PL) Party.[20] Formed in July 1962, PL was a Marxist sect whose original coordinating committee consisted entirely of members of the Communist Party who had been purged for being Maoists.[21] By the mid-1960s PL declared itself an anti-imperialist organization aimed at organizing the working class. Sale reports that by the end of 1965 organizational difficulties led the leadership of PL to "assert a new rigidity, tighten its ranks." The changes included a strong stance against the counterculture. "The New Left style that was coming to be associated with the hippies was held to be unpopular with the working masses and denounced as 'bourgeois'; marijuana smoking and drinking were discouraged, couples living together were asked to get married, beards and long hair were frowned on, casual blue-jean attire was renounced."[22]

Thus, PL members who joined SDS in the early 1960s as well as those who joined later united in their opposition to the counterculture. Steve Goldstein, an early activist who joined PL, objected to the counterculture on political grounds. He saw drugs as an impediment to building a movement; one couldn't organize while being stoned. Further, drugs were an avenue by which the government could infiltrate the movement. PL's official position viewed drugs as a tool of the ruling class used to pacify people in order to prevent collective struggles. Some also argued that entrapment of drug users was one of the chief tools used to bust organizers and discredit the movement.[23] Therefore, PL members argued, it was important for SDS to take a strong stand against drugs. In 1969 PL member Jeff Gordon introduced a resolution urging SDS to condemn the use of drugs as "one of the major weapons that the ruling class uses to . . . prevent struggles from taking place."[24]

Other PL members saw drugs and the counterculture as individualistic and a flight from reality. Norm Daniels remarks,

I liked the music and I certainly liked the sexual liberation of the sixties. . . . But I also didn't believe for a minute the view that we can't change the world unless you have a revolution in your own head. . . . I thought [it] was just a lot of baloney. My recollection of the sixties and the early seventies was not a period of sitting back and taking drugs and listening to revolutionary music and so on, but grueling hard work, enormous tension, fear, poor health as a result of constant exhaustion. . . . So I saw the cultural revolution . . . as a great diversion. I thought [communes and alternative lifestyles] was just escapism.

Echoing some of the early activists' concerns, other PL members believed long hair and a countercultural appearance alienated the working class.

Besides activists in PL, individuals who ended up joining other Marxist-Leninist groups also tended to be antagonistic toward the counterculture. Again, membership in these sects cuts across year of activism in creating opposition to the counterculture. For example, later activist Jim Shoch, who got involved with the Revolutionary Union at Stanford, comments,

I felt like a foot in and a foot out of [the counterculture]. I certainly smoked a lot of dope; that part I had no trouble with. . . . [But] I was never a hippie. You couldn't be a hippie in the Revolutionary Union. . . . We thought it was totally apolitical. . . . We were . . . turning on, tuning in and dropping *in*. . . . I didn't want to grow my hair long, live in filthy apartments in the Haight, and just hang out smoking dope. I really was intensive political. I didn't see most counterculturists as engaged as I felt it appropriate to be. . . . [The counterculture] in its totality [was] a bit too self-indulgent and too withdrawn from . . . engaging the dominant culture.

One of the very few who "deviated" from this correct line on the counterculture was PLer Aldyn McKean. Although at the time Aldyn had not yet come out as a gay man, he particularly objected to the homophobia within PL.

There is no question that there was . . . severe homophobia. PL was probably the worst. . . . It was really more attitudes. . . . The typical thing would be simply not feeling that it was an important issue. . . . That what's important is building the revolution and . . . you can't organize workers if you indulge in any kind of—they didn't go for long hair and smoking pot. So clearly being openly gay would be anathema. I can remember one person in particular saying, "Well what do you want? Do you think PL should write a sex manual?" as though the question was about sex as opposed to about oppression and rights. . . . The issue was never about sex. The issue was that if you're a gay person and you want to live your life openly, that you then face discrimination, oppression, physical violence, etc., etc., just as other oppressed groups do.

Aldyn's discomfort with PL's position, as well as his identity as a gay man, eventually led him to leave PL.

Given these intense divisions within SDS over the counterculture, it is not surprising that individuals' stance toward youth culture became one of the issues that split apart SDS during the late 1960s.

## YAF AND THE COUNTERCULTURE

Although we might expect all YAF members to be against the counterculture, in fact, as with SDS there was a deep division among activists. But for YAF this split was not based on the year of entry into activism; rather, it corresponded to the ideological divisions between traditionalists and libertarians. A common joke around YAF in the 1960s was that traditionalists wore colorless ties, sat straight, and prayed while libertarians wore necklaces and slurped their soup. Like early activists in SDS, traditionalists abhorred the counterculture. Both traditionalists who joined YAF before 1965 as well as those who became active in the later 1960s opposed the counterculture. Lynn Bouchey put it this way:

It was a generally unpleasant, unpleasant time. . . . I thought the music was nasty; I thought people were nasty. They dressed horribly. . . . It was a time I'm glad is gone. I see no romance to it. . . . I loved the early sixties, you know the Beach Boys, that sort of time. . . . But I was *totally* turned off [by the counterculture]. . . . The potheads and this sort of thing I found a waste.

Like early SDSers, many traditionalists viewed the counterculture as self-indulgent and destructive. For instance, Anne Edwards discusses the counterculture as being "imposed" on people. "We all had to suffer through it. . . . It was a very damaging time because of drugs. There were drugs before . . . but never were they combined with the self-righteousness of the antiwar movement and the music. . . . That was a very rotten combination of events that came together all at one time."

Yet, unlike the early SDSers, traditionalists also opposed youth culture from a religious standpoint, believing it was immoral. Emmy Lewis comments,

> You could say, "Well, it doesn't hurt anybody else." But what does it do to you? Does it rob you of your spiritual side? . . . Maybe there's no sense of their relationship beyond the material, immediate, temporal world. . . . The thing that's maddening is when you are slovenly and unclean you're hurting yourself. And the songs of the left. . . . If you listen to the words . . . that talk so crudely about sex, it reduces Man to being an animal. . . . They don't recognize or see or want to elevate Man to his higher natural state.

Lee Edwards, another traditionalist, says he couldn't relate to the music, clothes, language, or drugs: "I was critical of the counterculture. I thought it was dangerous, hedonistic, self-centered, disruptive." Lee was part of the *counter*counterculture; he worked with Ed Butler in forming the square movement in the late 1960s. Declaring "Square power is on the rise," they started a magazine called *Square,* put on square conferences, and had a television show with square writers and square entertainers like John Wayne. At a Freedom Rally organized by YAF in 1969 that was devoted to victory over communism, 15,000 self-proclaimed "squares" sang, "We don't smoke marijuana in Muskogee. We don't take our trips on LSD. We don't burn our draft cards down on Main Street. 'Cause we like living right and being free."[25] In Lee's words, the square movement "was very consciously against the counterculture."

In fact, the culture many traditionalists were engrossed in during their college years sounds much like the mainstream culture of the 1950s. Jo Ann Gasper recalls the student tradition at the University of Dallas of the annual groundhog party held during the cold days of February: "The notion was that we would greet the groundhog with beer and get the groundhog so drunk it wouldn't see its shadow and wouldn't go back in its hole and then spring would come." Fran Griffin recalls wearing skirts to class throughout her college years. She lamented the day the campus got rid of the dress code because "everyone began dressing so sloppy."

Even those traditionalists who marginally participated in the counterculture continued to hold antagonistic views. Mary Fisk, for example, says she rejected all of the counterculture: "It goes back to the Catholic foundation of folk beliefs that these people were not living up to being the best a human being could be. They were typically gratifying whatever whim or desire or need they had. So I didn't have any respect for them. I would consider their activities immoral and oppose it." Yet Mary also had friends who were part of the counterculture.

I visited some communes. I had friends who were hippies. When I went to the communes, I very much was impressed by this very peaceful, totally accepting atmosphere of whatever you are or whatever background you have, they'd just love you and welcome you and "glad you're here." So morally and emotionally I would be against this . . . but when I was there I enjoyed it.

On weekends Mary went to Greenwich Village and even smoked marijuana on occasion. Only one other traditionalist mentioned trying marijuana. Despite their exposure to marijuana, neither reported any change in their fundamental opposition to youth culture.

Another traditionalist, Mitch Petry, went to Woodstock. Yet even there he maintained his traditional attitudes and felt different from others attending. Describing himself as "pretty square," Mitch recalls his experience:

I dated a girl at the time who wanted to go up there and so I went with her. . . . We went to hear Jimi Hendrix and . . . the Eagles and a bunch of other groups. But the point is I wasn't drug-taking and I didn't dress differently. I had long hair at the time, but . . . I was pretty much on the straight and narrow. My values were basically middle-class working stiff, didn't come from money so I had to worry about responsibilities of a job. I remember being at Woodstock and thinking, I need to be back by a certain day for job reasons and school reasons. That might not have been on the minds of a number of other people. So when you say did I identify with them, no.

In particular, Mitch remembers the disturbing atmosphere of Woodstock once the thunderstorms began. "What struck me was . . . after the initial expression of universal love . . . when the rains came people were running for cover. . . . People were selfish, people weren't caring for each other. . . . It was terrible." In striking contrast to praise of the collective spirit and caring witnessed at Woodstock, Mitch comments that perhaps the storms were a deliberate act by God to convey the lesson that moral actions are more important than preachings of brotherly love.

One of the few traditionalists who had anything good to say about the counterculture was Alan MacKay. Although he did not attend Woodstock, he recognized both the positive and negative aspects of youth culture.

There was truth and validity in a lot of the things that were said on behalf of the counterculture. One of the things that they were saying was there's an awful lot of hypocrisy in American institutions. I agree with that. . . . There was a spirit of generosity . . . of sharing and of brotherhood . . . that was a positive thing. . . . If there was an awful lot of drug abuse, there was an awful lot of promiscuity, those are the bad sides.

Alan recalls enjoying wandering through the tent city set up in the Boston Common one summer during the 1960s.

The air was redolent of marijuana. . . . It was a very friendly atmosphere. These people were gentle people. I felt very comfortable with them. . . . Whenever you're talking about what thousands or millions of people are doing, it's a danger to overgeneralize. . . . No social phenomenon is ever a single thing. . . . The counterculture movement gave rise to some very good things. It's helped the concern for the environment. It's helped a concern for nutrition. . . . And it's always healthy to test the premises that the last generation lived on and see whether or not they continue to make sense.

Alan's sympathy with the counterculture is atypical. The difference between the overwhelmingly negative response to the counterculture by traditionalists and the stance of libertarians in YAF is striking. Like later SDS activists, libertarians embraced the counterculture in their attitude and lifestyle.[26] For instance, when Dana Rohrabacher was asked if he felt an allegiance with the counterculture during the 1960s, he replied,

[We did] identify with the counterculture. The traditionalists were people who . . . wore their suits and ties and slacks and nice shorts; and the rest of us, we were basically in our raggedy blue jeans and listening to rock music and wearing worker shirts and growing our hair longer and listening to the Doors and groups like that. . . . The libertarians in YAF really identified with the freedom that was being expressed by the Woodstock generation. . . . Libertarians got very deeply involved in the new culture . . . where the traditionalists I don't think ever went through that at all [laughs]. They were just back there in 1965 right where they started.

Dana recalls the particular affinity he felt for the music of Bob Dylan.

Bob Dylan's music meant a lot to me at the time. . . . I identified [with] a lot of Dylan songs. . . . I remember . . . his experiences . . .

and social commentary. . . . A lot of the traditionalists looked at Dylan as somebody who was an enemy. . . . He was a Commie or something. I thought of him as a poet and as someone who was talking about truths through experience. During that time period when I was really attracted to the counterculture, I was trying to find ways of seeing the world through other people's eyes in order to find if I could capture more insights into the world. . . . Dylan certainly . . . tried to give you those insights.

For Dana the counterculture philosophy represented "a revolt against constraints and against institutions." He says, "I saw more of a free spirit philosophy being expressed—and that attracted me a lot."

Dana also notes that West Coast libertarians were more involved in the counterculture than those on the East Coast. Eastern libertarians were more involved with Ayn Rand and the philosophy of self-interest while Dana and other libertarians on the West Coast were "much more involved with the Grateful Dead and with rock and roll and, in my case, body-surfing, and our emphasis was all individual freedom."

Among this sample of libertarians, those on the West Coast were in fact more likely to wholeheartedly embrace the counterculture. Marilyn Bradley speaks of the transition she went through on arriving in California:

I thought I had died and gone to heaven. I came out here without a pair of blue jeans; I was wearing penny loafers and little Villager skirts. So I was going through this incredible personal transformation and wrestling with . . . issues personally. . . . I looked like a hippie but I took baths. I smoked dope and did acid. . . . There were no rules when I came to California, just sort of let go. Which is exactly what I needed to do to mature.

Gus DiZerega already identified with the counterculture when he decided to leave Kansas and move to California. He arrived in Berkeley with shoulder-length hair, wearing a fringed leather jacket, and riding a motorcycle. Gus says he supported the counterculture "over the heavy-duty politicos." He believed those in the counterculture were "closest to living life the way I thought it should be lived." While Gus's Protestant sense of responsibilities compelled him to fight the state—to be "a politico"—he thought the counterculture had an enormous impact. Like the later generation of SDSers, Gus viewed the counterculture as a fundamental part of his politics.

Those libertarians who grew up in California also expressed an affinity for the counterculture. Although Harvey Hukari says he never took drugs, as a youth living in San Francisco, he went to rock concerts at the Fillmore, spent time in Haight-Ashbury, and read many countercultural underground newspapers. Harvey claims he was drawn to the ethic of the 1960s, "the opposition to government control and the idea . . . that individuals ought to be free to do whatever they want to do as long as it doesn't harm someone else."

Similarly, Sharon Presley comments, "I absolutely identified [with the counterculture]. I was living in San Francisco at the height of hippiedom. I can remember going down to Haight Ashbury, thinking that this was neat. . . . I saw it as people just being what they wanted to be. That was to me the essence of the counterculture."

For many libertarians the counterculture symbolized individual freedom, liberty of the mind and spirit. It also represented a stance against institutions, being critical of the system. Louise Lacey grew up in Marin County, California. When asked what the counterculture meant to her, Louise replied,

> Sympathetic people . . . people who shared my values. . . . The media said that the counterculture was made up of hippies who didn't believe in the work ethic. Now that wasn't my experience. The people I knew were working damn hard trying to make a living not being part of the system. . . . What they didn't go for was the traditional concepts of what it meant to be responsible. I had to reevaluate my ideas about what responsibility was and . . . what success was, what were worthy goals, personal goals.

Louise says the music of the times played a vital role. The lyrics of groups such as the Grateful Dead and the Jefferson Airplane conveyed important "interpersonal messages that had a political foundation." As an example Louise says the song "Wooden Ships" by Crosby, Stills, Nash, and Young "reinforced our feeling that we were cast adrift in an alien world and that it was up to us to make new values and create something new in the way of a future. . . . We had hope." Like later activists in SDS, libertarians found in the counterculture a new way of being, prefigurative of the new society.

Whereas these West Coast libertarians were vocal advocates of youth culture, the few libertarians who had more mixed reactions to the counterculture all came from the Midwest or the East Coast. Yet even these activists all identified to some extent with youth culture. Marick Payton, who grew up in Kansas, says on the one hand he was culturally "rather too conservative to be that comfortable" with the counterculture. Yet, on the other hand, he still felt some allegiance:

> The only drug I ever tried besides alcohol was pot. I never went on to LSD and all the other interesting stuff that everybody else around me was into. I was kind of cautious and conservative. Certainly enjoyed my number of years as sort of a free love advocate. So that part of it was quite convivial actually. [I didn't] like the corporate culture and liked bellbottoms and tie-dyes and things like that. . . . Had long hair. . . . So for a quiet, conservative, midwest sort of guy I enjoyed the sixties a lot and miss it a lot.

Sheldon Richman, who was raised in Philadelphia, is one of the only libertarians who felt apart from the counterculture. Although he says he identified "only slightly" with youth culture, even he had his sympathies.

> My roots in the movement were very strongly Randian. So I was concerned about what I saw as nihilism or irrationality or mysticism in the counterculture. . . . It seemed to be opposed to reason and science, technology, industrialization. Those were all things I was . . . in favor of so that kept me from being a full-fledged member of the counterculture. On the other hand, my attitude is that people ought to be free to experiment in different ways of living. I don't think we know everything there is to know about the best way to live. . . . One of the ways you find out is by some brave people trying different things. So in some sense I was sympathetic to [the counterculture] and identified somewhat with it.

Although the only drug he ever tried was marijuana, Sheldon knew people who lived together and thought it was "perfectly all right," saying he "wasn't held in check by traditional morality." Unlike traditionalists who were horrified by the experimentation of the 1960s, Sheldon had faith in trying alternatives.

In short, in contrast to traditionalists, even libertarians who say they felt less connected to the counterculture still had contact and felt some allegiance to it. Any differences among libertarians about the counterculture did not pose major problems. Sheldon Richman reflects,

> There was no tension between the libertarians who didn't think of themselves really as counterculture in the full sense and the ones that did. We all got along fine. That's what made us different from the traditionalists. They would have looked at someone wearing

long hair and a beard and sneered and figured "You're a socialist" or call them a Commie or something like that. So the attitudes were very different.

In fact, what is apparent is that the allegiance libertarians felt with the counterculture during the late 1960s led to a growing rift within YAF. Sheldon Richman recalls the conflict over cultural issues between libertarians and "trads," as traditionalists were called. "Culturally [the trads] were conservative. They knew who they didn't like. They didn't like liberals. They didn't like liberal Republicans. They didn't like hippies, new left, and [they] felt libertarians were part of that. So they didn't like them in a cultural sort of emotional sense."

The feeling was mutual. Libertarians increasingly felt their differences with traditionalists. Sharon Presley says that in terms of personal lifestyle she felt more comfortable with the left than with conservatives.

> I recall a time when the idea of living with someone and not being married, you didn't talk about it much. But we [libertarians] were doing it and . . . I didn't see any problem with that; but the conservatives still were having a problem. . . . Then, of course, the drug issue. . . . I experimented with a couple of things just out of curiosity, but it never was anything that I was doing much of. But I figured if people wanted to do that, it was their business and nobody else's. So in those kinds of issues I started feeling increasingly uncomfortable with conservatives. . . . So on all these aspects of conventionality, where the conservatives were so stuffy, and I said, "What's the big deal? Long-haired hippies? Who cares what length somebody's hair is? Like big deal—what does that have to do with a person's worth?"

This division between libertarians and traditionalists over the counterculture was also played out in a fascinating debate that took place in *New Guard,* the YAF monthly magazine, in commentary on the movie *Easy Rider.* A 1969 review by Stanford YAF chair Harvey Hukari applauded *Easy Rider* as dealing with "the quest for freedom from societal restraints, the task of finding one's self and difficulty of being an individual in an indifferent or hostile atmosphere." The movie shows us "an America where individuals with long hair are treated as outcasts, where redneck southerners deal harshly with those who choose to be different and where most of the 'straight' people are mindless, drab and bigoted."[27] In another positive review, *Easy Rider* is labeled a "remarkable commentary on America" that presents an "America that excuses its collective bigotry by hiding or legitimizing it in the name of democracy."[28] These words are striking because they could as easily have come from someone on the left.

In response to Hukari's review, David Brudnoy called the movie "implicitly subversive of important values. . . . It's cool porn, subtly subverting, cleverly luring the . . . uncorrupted to worship at the shrine of Our Lady of Grass." Brudnoy objects to the message of the movie, which he sees as "what's wrong with America is 'straight' America," as "hippieism . . . always drug accompanied, is great stuff," and "straights are . . . simple wits at best, at worst savages."[29] Supporting this view, one person wrote a letter to the editor deploring *Easy Rider* as "a cheap representation of drugs, sex and filth with no responsibility to God, family or country."[30] Clearly, what is playing out here is not only the divergence of opinion over the counterculture, but also a battle over the meaning of America, a struggle over who and what is responsible for the problems ripping apart the nation.

### The Role of Drugs

Within this growing divide between libertarians and traditionalists, one major area of difference concerned the use of drugs. Only two traditionalists admitted ever trying marijuana, whereas only two libertarians claimed to have used no drugs at all. All remaining libertarians smoked marijuana, with nearly half of those interviewed also using hallucinogens.

The use of drugs created ground for common cause between the libertarian right and the countercultural New Left. As Willis points out, during the 1960s drugs acted to unite individuals in opposition to straight society.[31] Part of the process entailed a transformation of the self by which a person became desocialized from conventional culture. Wieder and Zimmerman argue that the process involved a disengagement from major social institutions.[32] Illustrative of this, a Rand study in 1966 found that those who took LSD remained the same except for responses to a scale that rated "ways to live." Stating that one dose of LSD stimulates enormous changes, the report concluded:

> Whereas the person taking the test might have said, "It's important for me to get a corporate job. It's important for me to have a good car," after one dose of LSD they were saying, "I think maybe a contemplative lifestyle might be what I want to have. I think I'd

like to travel before settling down. I think maybe I want to look for some spiritual value in my life."[33]

YAFer Louise Lacey witnessed this transformation. Louise says that besides Ayn Rand, the other "clarifying and motivating" experience for her was music and drugs. "Smoking dope and taking acid and listening to music [made me see] the larger whole. I identified with the whole instead of just myself. LSD tends to do that to you. It's the kind of experience you don't go back from. . . . It's why I dropped out in the first place." After gaining new insight from psychedelics, Louise decided that "I no longer wanted to be among those who were autopsying the putrid corpse of the body social. I wanted to create positive alternatives instead."

For the left as well, using drugs became part of the process of questioning society. Bernardine Dohrn comments,

> I think that drugs—the nonaddictive drugs—marijuana primarily, but then the hallucinogenic drugs—were primarily a part of breaking out of the molds that we were being raised to occupy. . . . I was never very involved with drugs . . . but to the extent that I experimented with those things . . . and there was a year or two when I was involved to some extent with drugs—they helped give us a sense of another reality . . . or spiritual and esthetic dimensions to things. So I think that it was great.

Both the actual experience of taking drugs as well as run-ins with the state as a result of drug use brought together the worlds of the right and left. The radicalization evident in Rob Tyler's story is typical. Having been active in YAF for five years, Rob was in the top leadership of the California branch. Drawn to the music of youth culture, he heard Jim Morrison sing "Light My Fire" one day in spring 1967 and knew then that he was going to smoke dope. Reflecting on this he says,

> The whole drug thing really impressed me. . . . It gave me literally a new way of thinking. It changed the rules suddenly. All of a sudden I was an enemy of the state. I was doing something illegal and the government could come down and bite my ass. I didn't like having to be put into that position, doing something I thought was absolutely none of their business . . . and was exercising my personal freedom. So when I was smoking over at the Republican National Convention, that shocked a few people because they knew me as a pretty conservative activist. I began to feel less akin to conservatives.

Rob claims to have become the Johnny Appleseed of YAF, turning on others ripe for change. He set up what he termed "little fronts" such as the "Bob Dylan Appreciation Society" where he would invite people to his house to listen to Dylan and "smoke tons of dope." His use of drugs accentuated the differences he felt from traditionalists: "We were drug-using fiends. I'd go to my own board meeting stoned and wearing this Air Force jacket . . . because I was in the reserves at the time, stoned the entire weekend. I just could not relate any more to the trads."

By the late 1960s, Rob said, he "became very upset with the right-wing Christian types," particularly with their attitudes toward individual freedom. Meanwhile, his counterculture experience brought him to realization of common ground with the left.

> Timothy Leary and reading Baba Ram Dass . . . was just amazing. It wasn't right or left. It was *be here now.* . . . It was a different lifestyle. . . . The greening of America—that was us. . . . I began to see that there are people on the left you *can* work with. . . . The counterculture was a great common ground. We had all these common values—love and peace and freedom from government interference and personal growth. . . . I was an enemy of the state. . . . Drugs and the war were the catalyst . . . and the lifestyle that Nixon and his gang didn't approve of.

Rob says as he encountered new people, he changed: "A number of things had to be analyzed and reviewed and I couldn't hold onto the old prejudices." He gained a better understanding of the black struggle and of sexual discrimination. He comments, "It was difficult, but what I remember clearly was constantly being amazed at how much change I was going through at the time. Every three months . . . I was at a *totally* different mental place. It blew my mind. I didn't know when the damned thing was going to end."

Change came very rapidly, on the right as on the left. Rob's transformation involved not only a shared experience in the counterculture but also the recognition of common issues with the left. The use of drugs, and his stance against the war, led him into direct confrontation with the state. Saying he "reached a point that the American government was my enemy," Rob became an anarchist.

A parallel perspective occurred to SDS member Fred Faust, who said, "There were common grounds with the Right. They were against Big Brother, against narcs on campus. There were common grounds when it came to getting Big Brother off your back." In fact, the crackdown by campus and government authorities against drug users radicalized the left as well as the right. SDSer Lynn Dykstra relays a story of a drug bust at the University of Illinois in which a number of campus dealers she knew were arrested. Some people arrested had only very small amounts of marijuana, yet the police stormed into dorm rooms and dragged them off to jail. Lynn says this event radicalized her; it "drew lines between 'us' and 'them.'"

Such experiences led not only to alienation but to a questioning of governmental authority. A study by Mankoff and Flacks of students at the University of Wisconsin found that as drug use spread, an increasing number of college youth experienced harassment by officials. Such repression led to the delegitimation of institutional authority, radicalizing youth along the way.[34]

Thus, government repression forged a link between the left and right. By labeling casual pot smokers and small-time dealers as criminals, the state unintentionally "weakened the authority of authorities."[35] Such action turned libertarians, as well as the countercultural New Left, into enemies of the state with a common concern for protection from government interference. Rod Manis, who served as chair of California YAF, wrote,

> Members of my generation who have turned on with psychedelic chemicals are especially aware of the insanity and tyranny of government. They know from their own experiences that there is little harm in the use of these drugs. Many realize that if man is going to be able to enjoy, even just cope with the fantastically complex society and world of the future, he will have to have the help of mind-expanding drugs.

In response, Manis called for the expansion of personal freedom through "abolition of the draft, censorship, and all laws that regulate or restrict pot, acid, narcotics, alcohol, cigarettes, gambling, contraception, abortion, prostitution, cohabitation or any act that does not violate the property rights of others. . . . Our bodies belong to us and we alone should decide what we do with them."[36]

While the call for social freedoms brought libertarians into common cause with the countercultural left, it exacerbated tensions with traditionalists. Dana Rohrabacher reflects on the main factors that divided YAF:

> The two things that eventually split the youth of the right wing were the draft and legalization of marijuana. Those two issues were cen-

tral issues. . . . Milton Friedman, who was the conservative guru . . . [was] in favor of marijuana being legal and . . . not in favor of the draft. . . . It's consistent with his free enterprise philosophy. Well, the libertarians started evolving into that and pretty soon you got into a situation where on the fundamental issues of the day . . . the libertarians were more in tune with what the left was advocating than [with what] . . . the conservatives were advocating.

In short, division over cultural issues intensified the political differences between libertarians and traditionalists, creating a fundamental schism in YAF.

## CONCLUSION

Divisions within both SDS and YAF over the counterculture not only created tensions within each organization but also brought together the worlds of the left and right. In particular, the use of drugs, and the reaction from and to authority as a result of this drug use, further contributed to the radicalization of libertarians in YAF. Thus, the counterculture became a meeting ground not only in terms of shared lifestyles and values but also in terms of a common frame of understanding as the countercultural New Left and the libertarian New Right faced common enemies.

This case indicates that social movement mobilization is not always a predictable process. The intersection with people outside the boundaries of the New Left brought in new constituencies. Unexpectedly, then, the *cultural* aspects of the leftist movement appealed to new audiences of support among the counterculture. Libertarian belief and action increasingly overlapped with sectors of SDS. As we'll see in chapter 7, these sectors converged around a common hostility toward the state, a strong impulse toward personal freedom, and a call for decentralization and local control of neighborhoods, schools, and the police.

At the same time the libertarians' allegiance with the counterculture, combined with their stance against the Vietnam War and their reaction to government repression, translated into an ever-widening gulf between libertarians and traditionalists. Eventually these differences would erupt and lead to the purge of libertarians at the 1969 national YAF convention. But before turning to that, we must first consider another set of divisions that occurred among members of SDS and YAF, one that focused on issues of gender.

# CHAPTER SIX

# THE WOMAN QUESTION

In addition to the counterculture, the issues of gender and feminism variously divided SDS and YAF activists during the late 1960s. Demographically, women in SDS and YAF had remarkably similar backgrounds—the main difference being that the majority of SDS women's mothers had paid employment and few mothers of YAF activists did. Also, their parents raised them with similar expectations about their future lives.

Whatever the common elements in their upbringing, there are critical differences in their experiences as female activists. Surprisingly, there were divisions among women in both groups as to whether they believed women were treated as second-class citizens. While many SDS women perceived their secondary status and reacted against sexism within the movement, a vocal minority claim no discrimination from their male peers. Within YAF most women say they were welcomed and respected in the movement; yet a minority voice of YAF women, both libertarian and traditionalist, recognized their secondary role and viewed the men in the movement as sexist. What explains these differences among women? What factors contributed to the divisions in their experiences?

## THE UPBRINGING OF FEMALE ACTIVISTS
### Social Background

Before considering women's objective position in each organization, let us review the background differences between women on the left and the right. Both groups came from backgrounds of privilege (see chapter 2). The majority of fathers of all female activists earned a college or graduate degree. Further, the overwhelming majority of fathers of both groups of women were employed in upper white-collar jobs; only a very few were employed in blue-collar jobs.[1]

One key difference between SDS and YAF women, however, concerns their mothers. While the mothers of both groups of women have similar educational backgrounds, with over one-third of all mothers having a college degree,[2] there is a striking contrast in the proportion of mothers employed. SDS women have the highest proportion of mothers who had jobs outside the home during activists' preteenage years, slightly over one-half, while only one-fourth of the mothers of YAF women worked outside the home. The majority of mothers with jobs worked in the female sector of the labor force.[3] In short, the majority of women in YAF grew up with mothers who were at home, while the majority of those in SDS had mothers who worked outside the home during their childhood. Given this difference, we might expect SDS women to have received stronger messages about their own future careers or general support for feminism. Surprisingly, they did not.

### Parents' Expectations

Women activists in both SDS and YAF, raised during the late 1940s and 1950s, grew up during a time of traditionalism regarding men's and women's roles. In the aftermath of World War II, during which unprecedented numbers of women entered the labor force, there was a concerted effort to get women to return home, to the suburbs, to bear and raise children.[4] This general climate of traditionalism affected the aspirations of women on both left and right.

Although female activists, like the population as a whole, grew up amidst traditional expectations, the majority of these women were raised in affluence and in homes where their parents stood out in terms of their involvement and commitment to politics. Thus, not only the material means existed for them to go to college, but access to issues of public debate throughout their childhood opened up new horizons and possibilities. Given this juxtaposition of traditional norms with advantaged and politicized backgrounds, it is not surprising that we find a mixture of messages conveyed by parents. Some women in each group were raised with traditional expectations about gender, some women had parents with nontraditional expectations of their daughters, and some women received contradictory messages about their futures. What *is* unexpected is that approximately the same proportion of women on the left and the right were brought up with traditional, nontraditional, and contradictory upbringings.

Like most girls raised during the 1950s, a portion of both SDS and YAF women had parents with traditional expectations of their daughters. Typically, YAFer Jáime Ryskind states, "When I was growing up . . . you either were a teacher or a nurse, if you didn't get married, or a wife. Really those were the options." Hoping to get married, Jáime grew up thinking she'd be a secretary.

Similarly, SDSer Bernardine Dohrn was the first generation who attended college in her family and her parents also expected her to be a teacher or a nurse. Bernardine recalls, "They expected me to get A's and do well. But they expected me to get married and have kids and have something to fall back on and [to] be economically secure and live in the suburbs." Once Bernardine was in college, her parents opposed her goal of attending law school, insisting she get her teaching certificate to secure her future.

Other women in SDS and YAF were given contradictory messages about their futures. In some cases parents had discrepant expectations of their daughters. YAFer Louise Lacey, for example, says her father told her she could do anything she wanted to do. In contrast, her mother expected her to be a nurse, librarian, or teacher. Louise comments, "My mother used to say, 'It's just as easy to fall in love with a rich man as a poor man.'"

Others say they received mixed messages from each parent. On the one hand, SDSer Andrea Cousins was never encouraged to make money or become independent. "Implicitly the idea was to get married and that my husband would support me . . . and that I would do something interesting . . . that would help other people." On the other hand, Andrea's father, the author and editor Norman Cousins, hoped Andrea would help him with the editing of *The Saturday Review*. Andrea sums up the dilemma:

It was very confusing to me for many years because I was being encouraged in all sorts of implicit ways to be like my father; but I was a woman and was supposed to marry someone like my father. . . . [It involved] not knowing how to be a woman and be like my father, not knowing how to marry someone like my father and be like my father, not knowing how to marry someone like my father and be like my mother if I was supposed to be like my father, not knowing how to be like my mother if being like my mother was supposed to be the opposite of being like my father. You know, that puzzle, a conundrum of sorts I now think a lot of women find themselves puzzled by, but I thought was my own private weird problem.

For SDSer Dorothy Burlage the mixed messages she received had to do with being raised female in Texas. Saying Texas women had a tradition of being more assertive than southern women, Dorothy absorbed a mixture of "southern belle–type stuff" and also learned to ride horses and shoot and camp and handle herself in an independent way. In addition, because Dorothy's father died when she was young, her mother had always worked. Dorothy comments, "I had all the rhetoric of not being a strong woman and all the role models of being one."

In other cases women felt their parents' support ran contrary to the general culture of expectations for girls. For instance, YAFer Carol Dawson says her father was very encouraging and proud of her accomplishment. "My father was very supportive of me as a person. He thought I could do anything that I wanted to do, which was kind of unusual in that day and age for a father to have those kinds of goals for his daughter." But Carol says she felt constrained by the options available to her.

All of us during that period, in the fifties and early sixties, there was always an attitude that no matter how successful you might have been in college or in an early career, that you would eventually settle down and raise a family and melt back into the background and not cause a fuss. One part of me accepted that and another part of me didn't.

In contrast to these women, at least a third of women in each group were raised with nontraditional expectations. Parents of these activists encouraged their daughters to choose a career and to be independent. For example, SDSer Cindy Decker recalls,

My parents were always very supportive of my having a career. If somebody asked me what I wanted to be when I grew up, starting when I was twelve it was always a doctor. Before that I wanted to be an archeologist. But I always had a professional career goal that included going to school a lot. . . . It never occurred to me that I couldn't do those things if I wanted to.

Similarly, SDSer Carol Christman says her parents would have liked her to be an ACLU lawyer or a college professor. She comments, "I grew up absolutely believing I was going to be somebody. It wasn't like I was expected to be somebody's wife." On the right, traditionalist YAFer Helen Blackwell also says her mother encouraged her to be independent.

It's funny—my mother in some ways was more like the feminists than I am . . . not that she had any of their hostility to men or any of the perversions or negative aspects of it. But she believed that women should . . . have a career and be able to provide for themselves if they ever needed to . . . just so they could be independent. So she encouraged me to do that—which I didn't really do! [laughs].

Libertarian YAFer Sharon Presley says her mother, who raised her alone, never had any traditional expectations: "One of the wonderful things about my mother is she never tried to pressure me into being X, Y, or Z. So I grew up never ever believ[ing] all of the sexual stereotyping crap. . . . Basically always, from the time I can remember, I knew that I wanted to go as far with my education as I could, which basically meant a Ph.D." In the seventh grade Sharon wanted to be an archeologist studying ancient Egypt, then she briefly flirted with interior decoration, followed by the fields of nuclear physics and chemistry. Saying she was a tomboy as a youth, Sharon comments, "My mother never tried to push me in any direction. She never did say, 'Nice girls should wear dresses. Don't get your dress dirty.' . . . And because she worked and was independent and supported me, I have that independent role model."

In fact, what is striking is not only that equal numbers of YAF women were encouraged to take nontraditional paths, but that a minority of *both* SDS and YAF women report that their mothers were feminists. On the left, Jane Adams's mother and grandmother were feminists "from early on." Jane says, "My mother's earliest memory is sitting on a curbstone watching her mother in a suffrage parade." Jane's mother raised her to believe "I was intellectually as good as anybody" and expected Jane to have a professional career. During the late 1960s and early 1970s Jane's mother became very involved in women's consciousness-raising groups.

SDSer Naomi Schapiro's mother became a feminist because of the restricted options she faced in her life. Although she was a brilliant student who graduated from high school at fifteen, her mother had no support from her family to go to college. Naomi also recalls her mother, disillusioned by her activities with the Communist Party, telling her, "Here I was this working-class woman with no college education and there wasn't any way I could do anything but be a tiny cog in the wheel and go sell *Daily Worker* on the corner." Because of these experiences, Naomi's mother was very resentful and was determined that Naomi would go to a good college, become a doctor or a lawyer, and be at the top of her field.

Contrary to expectation, all the YAF women who report their mothers were feminists during their childhood are traditionalists. For instance, throughout Mary Fisk's childhood, her mother was employed as an electronics engineer, an extremely male-dominated profession. Mary says she was very proud of her mother.

> She was just a radically liberated woman . . . the only female on the East Coast who was an engineer. Each man had one product line that he had developed; she had three. I was very aware of sexism. . . . I was more aware than other girls that there are huge barriers [for women]. When I knew she was doing three times the workload for half the pay, it definitely made an impression on me.

Even more remarkable is that two women who became key leaders of the pro-family movement during the 1970s, Jo Ann Gasper and Connie Marshner, both report their mothers were feminists. In fact, Jo Ann found herself on the opposite side of the generation gap from her mother during the 1960s. Her mother was liberal on social issues, believed in equal pay for equal work and the right to abortion, supported "flower power and . . . the youth movement," and even tried smoking marijuana. Jo Ann reflects,

> My mother was not a militant feminist, but she was very much a feminist. My grandfather had three daughters. He told them that they could be one of three things: they could be a housewife . . . a nurse, or . . . a teacher. One is a housewife, and one is a nurse and one is a teacher. Now my mother happened to be the nurse. And she was very much distressed that opportunities were closed off to her just simply because she was a woman. . . . She wanted me to become a physician. My stepfather wanted me to become a lawyer. So I guess I disappointed both of them and became neither. To this day she is a *very independent* woman.

Connie Marshner, the other leader of the pro-family movement, says her mother "was a feminist before the term even existed." Her mother grew up in a matriarchal family. Connie recalls hearing about her mother's maiden aunts, Aunt Rose and Aunt Alice. Aunt Alice worked for a publishing company for twenty-five years. "She never married any man because, as they were fond of saying, she loved her own way more than she loved any man. And [Mother] kind of admired that."

Connie's mother had specific plans for her daughters. From the time Connie was three, her mother wanted her to be the head dietitian at a leading hospital in Boston. Meanwhile, she told Connie's sister that she would grow up to be the president of IBM. Connie also grew up with strong messages about the need to be independent.

> I can remember from my earliest days Mother going on about how the Married Women's Property Act in England . . . was the most important thing that was ever done because before that your husband controlled the woman's money, and she couldn't even have her own checkbook. . . . And if her father left her a fortune, her husband could spend it, and she didn't have any say about it. Most kids in eighth grade are not really interested in the effects of the Married Women's Property Act. But to me that was something to think about. . . . She had very advanced ideas. . . . I remember her saying, "God, when you get married, your life is over. Then when you have children, that's the end of your life."

Connie also vividly recalls the day when she came home from school in the sixth grade and her mother was excited about Betty Friedan's new book, *The Feminine Mystique:* "I remember her saying, 'You won't understand the world until you read . . . *The Feminine Mystique.* . . . You won't understand how awful it is to be a woman until you read this book.' And for one reason or another I never—I mean with that kind of recommendation, you don't want to read the book!"

When Connie and her sisters turned fifteen, her mother gave each one of them a diamond ring. The idea was that her daughters would go to college and should not be in any hurry to get a ring from some boy. Connie notes the irony of her mother's views, given Connie's eventual leadership of the pro-family movement.

What these stories point out is that there is no simple relationship between parental expectations and beliefs about gender and children's adoptions of those beliefs and ideals. As Gerson so eloquently demonstrates, sometimes children adopt the ways of their parents in becoming adult men and women, sometimes they rebel against their parents' ways, and sometimes circumstance and unexpected life events lead them in new directions.[5] Despite these different messages conveyed to women on both the left and the right, all activists were unusual, however, in that they defied tradition by becoming vocal and active political women. Once they joined YAF or SDS, what experiences did they face as women?

## THE OBJECTIVE POSITION OF WOMEN IN YAF AND SDS

Looking at the objective position of women in each organization, we find evidence of male dominance in both SDS and YAF. For one thing, men monopolized leadership positions in both groups. Within YAF individuals elected to the board of directors as well as the state chairs were disproportionately male throughout the 1960s. For example, in 1966 out of thirty-eight state chairs listed in a YAF memo, thirty-seven were male. A similar list in October 1969 again shows only one woman state chair.[6] Similarly, within SDS there were only two female national officers during the entire 1960s.[7] SDS men also monopolized executive committee and national council memberships. Evans finds female membership on the executive committee increased from 14.3 percent in 1961 to 23 percent in 1962 and 26 percent in 1963, only to plunge to 6 percent in 1964.[8] Thus, major decisions on a national level were predominantly in the hands of men in both organizations. In addition, the vast majority of written materials and position papers issued by both groups were authored by men.[9]

Further, the culture and style of each organization display signs of male chauvinism. For instance, the written materials of both groups reflect the sexualization of women. SDS's paper, *New Left Notes,* ran occasional drawings and cartoons deriding women. In one case a cartoon that appeared in the January 8, 1969, issue provoked a response. Accompanying an article on the Cuban revolution, the cartoon showed a "sexy broad being dragged off by her hair, presumably to get fucked . . . dressed like a Playboy bunny." In a letter to the editor, Frinde Maher complained about the sexual exploitation in this portrayal as well as the denigration of women's liberation. Commenting on the message conveyed by this depiction of a female revolutionary, she writes, "She is saying that it is 'in' to be liberated, that you can still project a sexy image and that in fact liberation is 'attractive' to men; that revolution is glamorous and exciting and that if you come on over you can have a piece, too."[10] Another cartoon cited by Evans also reflects the disparagement of women's liberation. The cartoon appeared in a 1967 issue of *New Left Notes* and shows a girl, wearing earrings, polka-dot minidress, and matching visible panties, holding a sign that reads We Want Our Rights and We Want Them Now.[11]

The sexualization of women in YAF publications was even more overt. The YAF monthly magazine, *New Guard,* regularly featured a "Miss YAF." For instance, the text next to the April 1968 Miss YAF pinup reads:

Charisse might be an exquisite wine, or perhaps an exotic French perfume. Fortunately for Texas YAF, Charisse is . . . an articulate student conservative and active YAF booster. The 5'7"; brown-eyed high school junior has an exhausting number of recreational "escapes."[12]

Another article, entitled "California YAF's Better Half," includes posed pictures of women from YAF with a text that reads,

Proving that beautiful girls can be political as well as poetic has been another of YAF's achievements, accomplished with the willing aid of the nine attractive young conservatives pictured here. In addition to "dressing up" various Cal-YAF functions with their presence, each girl also helps to reflect accurately the real image of young conservatism in California.[13]

Other YAF publications unabashedly use adjectives such as "gorgeous" and "cute" in discussing women in the organization.[14]

Although by these objective measures there is clear evidence of sexism in both organizations, the picture is more complicated in terms of women's subjective perceptions of their roles in each group.

## SUBJECTIVE PERCEPTIONS OF WOMEN'S ROLES

Regardless of present-day views of feminism, there is a division among both left- and right-wing women as to whether or not they perceived discrimination in SDS and YAF during the 1960s. This is unexpected in two ways. First, many accounts of the rise of the women's movement of the 1960s and 1970s point to New Left women as the instigators of the second wave of feminism, arguing that women in SDS and other leftist groups were motivated to form a movement in their own interests because of discrimination by leftist men.[15] Yet the evidence here suggests that while many women did have this experience, other women in SDS *deny* discrimination by leftist men. Second, the common perception of women on the right assumes they do not recognize women's secondary status or sexism among men. Equally surprising, then, is the minority voice of women who *did* perceive discrimination within YAF during the 1960s.

## Perceptions of SDS Women

The majority of women in the present study *did* talk of discrimination within SDS. Of these women, nearly all were later activists, having joined SDS from 1965 to 1968. Women discussed a variety of issues illustrative of women's position in SDS.[16] Several women mentioned the lack of women in leadership roles, citing examples of men chairing meetings, dominating speakers' lists, and generally acting as experts and theoreticians of the movement. Naomi Schapiro recalls her experience during the Harvard strike in 1969. Although women were arrested out of proportion to their numbers, when it came to voting for a steering committee, the top ten people elected were all men. Naomi and another woman were added to the committee because the men were so embarrassed that there weren't any women.

Barbara Haber, one of the few early activists who discussed sexism in SDS, says she was shocked by her treatment: "I had been a bright kid at Brandeis. I had been a political leader. So I came on the scene and I expected to be valued, treated with respect, welcomed into leadership circles. Instead, I started being treated like a secretary or something." Barbara says even Al Haber, the founder of SDS whom she eventually married, sometimes treated her like a secretary.

> He used to write me these little memos on yellow pieces of paper and attach them to things . . . giving me these little instructions. . . . I was brought up to think I was special, to think that I was smart, and to think that I was going to accomplish something. In graduate school . . . I was a good student, had a fellowship, and was treated by my professors as someone with promise. But in SDS I couldn't get no respect. I was constantly being diminished and I often felt all confused and crazy.

Even those women who made it into the top positions felt they were treated differently from men. Bernardine Dohrn speaks of the difficulty she had being one of the few women leaders. "It was crazy the way that kind of tokenism is crazy. On the one hand, I felt that I was often caricatured, stereotyped, diminished. On the other hand . . . I felt like [I] was an important role model."

When Jane Adams became national secretary during the summer of 1966, she discovered she was the only woman in the national office. She also discovered there were consequences to being a female leader. As she put it, "It was very clear that my being an independent woman was

having some fairly serious consequences on my sex life, my love life."
Jane says her position and her refusal to acknowledge male power alienated men.

Besides being excluded from leadership roles, women complained
about being relegated to do the mundane tasks of the movement, the daily
chores: photocopying, phone calls, and making coffee. Beth Oglesby says,

> Women were doing too much of the office work. Women were do-
> ing the footwork of the organizing . . . even in the ERAP projects—
> taking the mothers to the welfare office. They were doing the phone
> stuff. They were doing the mailings. . . . And it's the men who talk,
> and it's the men who theorize, and it's the men who make the de-
> cisions. Except for a few articulate women, most of the women were
> not listened to.

This, too, was a common complaint: not only were meetings dominated by men but when women spoke, they were not taken seriously. In
short, women felt silenced and made invisible. Barbara Haber discovered that some men in SDS seemingly were allergic to what she had to
say: they just couldn't hear her words. Eventually she worked out a deal
with her husband, Al, so that whenever she said something, he would
repeat it so that finally it would get recognition.

Evans argues it was not so much a lack of knowledge or intellectual
sophistication that kept women from speaking; rather, it was more a
matter of style—the competitive, domineering manner that was foreign
to many women.[17] Some women mention this intimidating style and even
say it was an impediment to joining SDS. Naomi Schapiro went through
a painful process of learning to speak out. She remembers being intim-
idated at her first SDS meeting at Harvard in the fall of 1967. "I want
to say it was so male. . . . All these people arguing and fighting and using rhetoric that I didn't really understand . . . so that I felt like I couldn't
say anything. . . . [It was] not particularly welcoming. . . . So it took me
awhile to get involved because it wasn't that easy to do." Once involved,
Naomi forced herself not to remain silent. She pushed herself to talk
but each time she felt like "a nervous wreck." Naomi also made herself
read a lot of leftist literature she was just beginning to understand so
she could use the right words "because if you used the right words,
people would listen to you."

Judy Baker says when she tried to challenge this setup at Harvard SDS,
she ran into hostility.

I would get up at meetings and I would demand to be the chair-person and I would say, "We need a man and a woman up here. . . . I want you women to speak out." . . . People would get very angry at me. Oh absolutely, and say, "Look, you're diverting this, this meeting is not to talk about men and women. This meeting is to plan a demonstration around racial pay differential or rent control. . . . We don't have time for this bullshit. We'll deal with that later." . . . I was always surprised when I was criticized.

Another criticism women raised was that the fate of women in SDS was determined by their relationships to men. In particular, a woman had a better chance of "succeeding" in the movement if she was the girl-friend or wife of a male leader. Cathy Wilkerson was well aware of this problem of male sponsorship. By 1964 Cathy had quit SDS twice because she was so turned off by the style of the organization.

I went to a couple of meetings [my freshman year] and it was clear that girls didn't talk and that the only way a girl could be anybody was to flirt with one of the boys. . . . So I didn't go any more. . . . I dropped out of SDS again after [my sophomore] year. . . . The stuff around women was just atrocious and didn't ever change. . . . There were all these very articulate male leaders and the only women who seemed to be accepted were the women who were in relationships with them—with some exceptions. . . . There was no women's movement at that point so . . . there was no legitimacy for relationships between women. If you wanted to make it in the political world, you had to concentrate on the relationships with men.

As Evans put it, a woman's status could rise or fall according to changes in her sex life.[18] Many women felt that, above all, they were seen as sexual beings, not taken seriously in their own right. As Cindy Decker recalls, "Guys were always coming on to me. They couldn't see beyond the fact that I was an attractive female to dealing with me as a person and dealing with my ideas. I was extremely resentful." This sexualization of women was also evidenced in Fred Faust's recollection of one male leader's comment about the Friday night SDS meetings at Washington University. Stealing a line from Ralph Ellison, the leader said, "The class struggle turned into the ass struggle when men tried to figure out how they were going to get laid."

The cumulative effect of these experiences was that many women began to see a contradiction between the movement rhetoric of equality and the reality of women's place in the movement. Women faced the fact that SDS was not truly the participatory democracy they had imagined. Cindy Decker recalls the feeling she had during the late 1960s.

> I was more frustrated by the position of women within the movement than anything. Which was a constant source of discussion because here were all these sanctimonious young men going around pontificating about how the world was a bad place and we really ought to change the way people related to black folks and . . . brown folks. But they treated women in totally abysmal ways. That was real frustrating for most women in the movement. It was a constant source of conflict.

All of these issues—the lack of female leaders and the intimidating style of SDS, the exclusion of women from speaking, women doing the mundane tasks, and the treatment of women as sex objects—became the topics of much discussion among the early groups of women who organized consciousness-raising groups in SDS. As Marge Piercy put it in her essay "The Grand Coolie Damn," which rallied women in the New Left to feminism, "The Movement is supposed to be for human liberation: how come the condition of women inside it is no better than outside?"[19]

Yet not all women in SDS agreed with this perception of the New Left. A vocal minority of women in this study *deny discrimination*. All of these women were early activists, those who joined SDS from 1960 to 1964. These women argue the whole characterization of SDS as sexist is overblown.[20] The voices of this group of women have rarely been heard, partly because they felt silenced by the feminist movement. These women speak of being censored for this interpretation of reality.

Although some of these women acknowledge that not all SDS members were treated the same, they see it in terms of insiders and outsiders, *not* in terms of men and women. They point, for example, to women leaders who commanded authority as being part of the inner circle. As Andrea Cousins put it,

> It was more like the in-group vs. the out-group. . . . People who were sure of themselves and who were smart enough to have a lot of authority. Betty Garman seemed to be one of the boys. . . . Casey [Hayden] seemed to me to be one of the boys. . . . And I looked at people like Mickey Flacks as being just as "in" as Dick was. It seemed to me like it was more a class thing than a gender thing.

Some of these women insiders were married to or partners of male leaders; others gained respect on their own. Further, these early women who deny discrimination perceived *all* female insiders as having confidence and smarts, regardless of their relationships with men. Helen Garvy attributes differences in leadership not to gender but to variations in style.

> I saw it as not male-female, but as quiet versus loud and stylistic differences. . . . People who are loud tend to get more credit than people who work quietly behind the scenes. At times that gets annoying. That's something that the movement as a whole . . . needs to deal with. . . . I just happened to know a lot of men who never got credit for stuff who feel the same way. They were my friends.

Arguing that who gets recognized is a matter of loudness rather than gender, Helen believes men who worked quietly were equally likely to be ignored.

Denying that gender was a basis of division, these women say they did not feel discriminated against by their male peers. For example, Dorothy Burlage perceived both men and women as making important contributions. "I remember feeling, I wish I was as good an organizer as Sharon [Jeffrey] or I wish I was as articulate as Casey [Hayden]. I was as impressed by these women's skills as I was by the men's. So it wasn't like I thought the men are doing all the great things and they have all the options."

Helen Garvy also denies she was treated differently and points to women's *choice* in taking on particular tasks.

> A lot of women's anger . . . comes from doing things that they didn't want to do and resenting it. I don't think I've ever done anything I didn't want to do. Therefore, I don't have resentment about stuff. . . . It's a complex issue because it goes back to a lot of the way women are socialized. . . . It's true that a lot of times if cooking needed to be done or coffee needed to be made, women did it. . . . Part of that's because somebody said, "Okay, who's going to make dinner?" and some woman would get up and volunteer. . . . It never occurred to me to get up; I was involved in conversation. . . . I also know that a lot of the biggest male chauvinist pigs, so labeled in SDS . . . did their share of the cooking.

Rather than mistreatment, Helen says she was encouraged by her male colleagues.

Now maybe [men] thought that I was totally inferior to them. But I never perceived that. Not only that, but . . . there was a lot of support and encouragement. It's something that really needs to be said, from men who were considered traditional male chauvinists and who got dumped on a lot by the movement.

Helen recalls her own experience working in the national office as assistant national secretary. When Clark Kissinger, then national secretary of SDS, was busy with other tasks, Helen had to plan a national council meeting, something she had never done before. When she expressed her doubts to Paul Potter (then president of SDS) and Todd Gitlin (past president) over lunch one day, they encouraged her, reminding Helen of her knowledge of the issues. She comments, "Any time I would say, 'Well, I'm not sure that I can do this,' they would say, 'Yes, you can.' Todd was a real important person . . . partly because I knew him the longest. . . . [He] knew me and knew what I could and couldn't do." Helen concludes, "People treat you a lot the way you expect to be treated."

In a similar way, Vivian Rothstein says the movement gave her a chance to develop and be respected at a time when there were few such avenues for women. At the time no school counselors sat down and talked to a woman about what college she wanted to go to or what she wanted to do with her life, whether she wanted to become a professional. Vivian felt she was valued more on the left than anywhere else. "No one really took me very seriously. That was one reason that I liked the movement, because I was taken seriously."

Once women began to organize within SDS, some of these early women felt distanced or even critical of feminist meetings. Dorothy Burlage admits she didn't feel any allegiance with the women's movement at the time.

I went to some of the meetings, but I kept thinking—I'm embarrassed to say it—This is frivolous, that there were people who were genuinely poor and . . . people who were genuinely discriminated against because of color. And I didn't see women as such an oppressed class at that time. I became more sympathetic over time. . . . But initially I thought it was sort of diversionary from issues of race and class.

Other women say they, too, didn't feel it was personally important or relevant for them to join with other women.

Even those early women who did end up joining feminist groups say their motivation was *not* based on criticism of New Left men. Andrea Cousins reflects,

> [My involvement in the women's movement wasn't] a reaction toward the left, but it's as if all of us [women were] like minnows. . . . That was the way we were swimming. . . . I was obviously so much in struggle with myself about power and being a woman and competition for boys and sisterhood. The idea of women getting together was such a soothing idea to me; and getting the guys out of the picture was so soothing. But more than anything, the idea that the personal was political was crucial to me. . . . That the things that I really was in pain about could be part of the political community in a way that SDS and civil rights had not ever been able to do.

Vivian Rothstein says her involvement in the feminist movement during the 1960s grew from her understanding of women's unequal place in society, rather than hostility toward leftist men.

> I became a feminist through really valuing underrepresented people getting power. . . . So I didn't come to it from being pissed off at the left . . . although I think women were undervalued in SDS. But that was going on in the whole society. We were less undervalued [in SDS] than in the rest of society. . . . The common thing is that women on the left were so mistreated and it made them feminists. That's really not my experience and I don't really agree with that theory, frankly. . . . I don't think that that's what built the women's movement. Just like no one ever burned a bra. There are lies that are told . . . not lies, but misinterpretations.

In short, while some women felt a growing discontent with their role in the organization, others say they felt respected and affirmed in SDS, much more so than in the larger society.

### Perceptions of YAF Women

Women in YAF, unlike their counterparts in SDS, have not produced volumes of discussion on their position in the movement. The majority of YAF women denied their secondary status in the organization, saying they did not encounter any discrimination. A common refrain was that YAF was in a state of growth and that everyone was welcome. For instance, libertarian Maggie Kohls says, "Any group that's struggling and trying to grow tends to be less prejudiced against . . . minorities or women. . . . You want members more than you care what they look like. . . . I didn't feel there was any particular prejudice against me, but . . . I'm blind to that sort of stuff."

Similarly, traditionalist Dawne Winter comments, "I didn't feel that I was being put down because I was a woman. . . . When you're a minority movement like that, you appreciate everyone who comes in. So it doesn't matter whether they're male or female, white, black, yellow, red, whatever."

Several women interviewed were the chair of their YAF chapter. They uniformly said they felt free of discrimination. These women felt autonomous and respected. Barbara Hollingsworth says,

> I always felt very free. . . . I never felt discriminated against as far as YAF was concerned. Probably that was because they were so happy to have somebody that a warm body was better than nothing. . . . All of our meetings . . . it never even occurred to me that it was strange that a woman was in my position. . . . It's only in retrospect that I realize that. . . . It was probably sheer numbers more than anything else. It was just so few of us. . . . YAF just never developed a hierarchy that probably the left did. . . . Since we were so small, [women] always had a prominent role.

Emmy Lewis, who was the only female statewide chair of YAF, says she never witnessed any signs of bias. She concludes it is a woman's attitude that determines how she is treated.

> Sometimes women who are so caught up in this preoccupation of looking for areas where they may be discriminated against . . . sometimes they, I wouldn't say encourage it, but if you're looking for trouble, sometimes you get it. It's a philosophy and an attitude that you carry with you in your life that determines how things work or . . . how you respond to situations. All my life . . . people have been wonderful to me. . . . If you think like a victim, you are one.

One of the few women who held national office in YAF, Carol Dawson, also says she was treated equally. "I don't remember thinking that I expected to be treated any differently and I wasn't. I just felt that I was equal when we all sat around the table discussing things or we were putting a magazine together. My opinions counted as much as anybody's and it never really was an issue." Thinking about her position on the first national board of YAF, Carol says,

I just felt like I was one of the boys. . . . Never occurred to me that there should be any difficulty whatsoever with a person of my gender being in a position in an organization. It wasn't until much later, until I'd had children and then went back to work, that I discovered that it could be a problem. . . . You know, I read the same feminist literature everybody does. We've all had these experiences. But then, no, it just didn't seem a problem. . . . [I] didn't think they treated me any differently. I would have noticed if they had.

Not only did the majority of YAF women feel welcomed and valued; several women also commented that they liked being one of only a small number of women active on the right. In particular, they liked being surrounded by men. For example, Fran Griffin reflects,

Here I [was] at an all-girls campus and I'd go to these meetings that would be predominantly men, and that was sort of nice. And then it would be easy for me to get girls to come because I'd say, "Well, they're mostly men that go." . . . So they'd all want to come. . . . It was nice being around a lot of men that were smart and interested in the same political ideas that I was. I thought that it was great. So it didn't really bother me that there weren't a lot of women there. . . . [The men] seemed happy to have a few women there, too, instead of just looking at men all the time. So, no, I didn't feel any discrimination I can think of.

Yet, surprisingly, there was a minority voice within YAF of women who *did* perceive discrimination. These women talk of the problems caused by male conservatives. Some women complained about being viewed as sexual objects. Mary Fisk, who held a position as editor of *New Guard* and was on the national board of YAF, recalls, "I was smart and pretty and a lot of guys would just hit on me."

Another woman who complained about this, Marilyn Bradley, says she was a "victim of the age." In the late 1960s she appeared as Miss YAF in *New Guard* "wearing little skimpy clothes." Marilyn comments, "I [was] a sex object. . . . I felt like I was window dressing at the time. But I didn't really know how to handle it either. I was kind of wide-eyed and naive and a watcher. That was the role of women and nobody questioned it. So there I was, watching." Yet, ironically, the editor of *New Guard* who chose her for Miss YAF, Arne Steinberg, was also very encouraging of her abilities. He tried to get her to write and take on more intellectual tasks. Marilyn says, "He was the only one in the movement who thought I was smart. They all thought I was pretty, but none of them thought I was smart."

Anne Edwards also was aware of sexism within YAF. She recalls a time when she wrote a letter to *New Guard* in support of an article on conservative feminism, only to be told by the male editor that her letter would not be printed because the issue was not important. Anne comments, "I think very often that some of the problems in life were caused by male conservatives."

It is illuminating to compare these women's comments to remarks by some of the activists in the sample who participated in both the left and the right. Louise Lacey, who was involved with YAF and later with New Left organizations, says the left was more sexist than the right.

> One of the things I didn't like about the left during the sixties was how hostile they were to their women. That's one of the things that kept me away from a lot of what they did. . . . Because on the right maybe they have this tradition of partnership or something. . . . Certainly in my own peer group there wasn't any of that crap or at least I didn't experience it.

In contrast to her libertarian peer group, Louise charges leftist men with "not listening to [women], interrupting, and not letting [women] hold responsible positions."

Cindy Decker disagrees. She maintains that sexism existed equally across the political spectrum: "The guys on the left had their rhetoric, [which] was a little more delicate. But their behavior was absolutely totally as exploitative as men on the right. It's just that the men on the right were out there with it." Perhaps the discrepancy between leftist men's egalitarian beliefs and their actions made their sexist behavior more apparent than men on the right, who never advocated an egalitarian line.

In short, while the majority of women in YAF deny being treated differently, this small group of women, including both libertarians and traditionalists, experienced discrimination on the right and identified sexism among their male peers.

## WHY WOMEN DIFFER

Given these differences in perception over women's roles, how do we understand such divisions? Why do some women in each organization recognize discrimination, while others say there was equality? One explanation for why more SDS women recognize discrimination than do YAF women concerns the fact that a higher proportion of mothers of SDS activists were employed outside the home. Research shows that children whose mothers have paid employment are more likely to have nontraditional views of gender than children whose mothers stay at home.[21] Given that twice as many SDS women's mothers had jobs, it is not surprising that their activist offspring are much more likely to recognize sexism than their YAF counterparts. Since the same proportion of women in YAF and SDS were raised with traditional or nontraditional expectations, we cannot look to differences in parental expectations to explain which women recognize sexism. Rather, the reality of seeing their mothers balance work and home life made a difference for young girls on the left, providing them a basis by which to evaluate their future position as women.

There are two other key factors that help explain the differences among women: organizational factors and the availability of a language to express discontent.

## Organizational Factors

In SDS all the women who deny discrimination are early activists. Early activists' experience of being in SDS was fundamentally different from later activists' experience.[22] Early activists were involved in a small, tight-knit organization in which face-to-face interaction was common. The earliest members were even handpicked by founding members to fit into the group. As pioneers speaking out amidst a time of apathy, early SDSers relied on one another and welcomed others of like minds. Bound together in a beloved community, a type of gemeinschaft, people knew each other and worked together as a circle of friends. As Dorothy Burlage characterizes those years,

> Everybody was so giddy with the opportunity to do something meaningful. . . . The Victorian worries were gone and people were free to be friends without the normal expectations that had been there in the fifties and they were free to try to change the world. . . . It felt so good, we didn't pay a lot of attention to some things that you might have otherwise questioned, like men's and women's roles. It seemed so insignificant compared to the general excitement and enthusiasm, that it wasn't a big issue.

These early members knew one another well and shared a sense of mission. The nature of such group ties prohibited women from speaking out against their brothers. The bonds of trust and overwhelming sense of community during the early 1960s meant women were resistant to destroying this feeling of family. Depending on others like themselves to sustain their activism, they acted to protect the fledgling movement they had created.

In the aftermath of the successful antiwar march in April 1965, as SDS membership dramatically increased, the fundamental experience of being in the organization changed.[23] As SDS grew it also became more diverse, with conflicting ideological tendencies. People were no longer hand-picked to fit into the group. The expansion of SDS also meant that people no longer knew everyone in the organization. The vast majority of activists did not become involved on a national level; at best they knew most members of their chapter. Helen Garvy speaks about how SDS's growth changed the nature of group meetings.

> A lot of the change . . . had to do with the [fact that the] groups got larger. Then it becomes much more shouting matches. People who are good orators and were not intimidated about getting up on speaking platforms tend to become much more important than when the national council meeting is in a room this size and everybody knows each other and . . . respects the work that the other people are doing. It's real different. . . . I always felt that people respected me because they knew what work I did. They could see it.

In addition, the growing factionalization and impulse toward ideological purity that characterized the later years of SDS led to a lack of cohesion, a fragmentation of the organization (see chapter 7). Thus, the bonds of gemeinschaft were broken, the sense of community no longer superseded the differences among members.

Jeanne Friedman speaks about the experience of ideological purity in Stanford SDS during the late 1960s: "One way the sexism was manifest was that you had these men . . . telling you what correct ideology was. . . . The men were the ideologues . . . telling very politicized women . . . who were able to read and think themselves. . . . It would translate as sexism under the guise of ideological struggle. The men were the experts and the women didn't know anything."

Many women found the dynamics of these later years alienating. Naomi Schapiro recalls the infighting she encountered during the Harvard strike in 1969.

> There was a lot of very ugly factional stuff that happened right on the eve of the strike. . . . I really experienced it as a very male

way of relating. . . . It was hard to deal with. I just remember some very ugly internal meetings right before the strike happened that really disgusted me. . . . Just disgusted me being part of the whole thing.

Evans also argues that the later SDS was less hospitable for women. She says from the mid to late 1960s the notion of community suffered as competition increased. As a result, the unconscious male dominance within SDS became more overt.[24] Evans comments, "SDS had grown too large and too diverse to re-create the earlier sense of unity and community. Its unwieldy size and ideological conflicts intensified the attributes that had always made national meetings difficult for women: jargon, verbal competitiveness, wrangling, and posturing."[25] At one of the early meetings organized to discuss women's issues in SDS, Evans notes, older women had a hard time identifying with the anger of younger women, who never felt as accepted or respected as the older generation.[26]

Not only was the sense of community destroyed, but also because these later activists were not the founders of SDS, they were less invested in maintaining unity. No longer were activists single voices speaking out in the darkness. By now multiple organizations existed on the left; one could choose between an array of possibilities for involvement.

Organizational factors also help to explain why most women in YAF did not perceive discrimination. Like the early activists in SDS, members of YAF struggled together in a relatively small movement *throughout the decade of the 1960s*. In fact, the majority of YAF women who deny discrimination resemble those involved in early SDS: pioneers bound together in common cause, happy to find others of like mind. Unlike SDS, however, as the 1960s progressed, YAF activists *increasingly* became a minority voice speaking out during a liberal era. This sense of alienation in YAF members grew throughout the 1960s, particularly as the New Left gained in strength and number. Their feeling of being ostracized for their unpopular views only intensified their sense of mission (see chapter 4). In this context it makes sense that many women report being welcomed and appreciated in the movement. Further, because YAF never grew to the size that SDS did, the organization never had to deal with issues accompanying such expansion. Although ideological factionalism *did* develop within YAF, these tensions focused on conflicts between libertarians and traditionalists, *not* on differences connected to gender (see chapter 7). In part this lack of attention toward gender reflects the absence of a language to articulate discontent.

## A Language of Discontent

A second factor that explains the variation in whether or not women recognize discrimination is access to a vocabulary to express discontent. One of the critical requirements for any social movement to form is the availability of a language to voice grievances. Early SDS women did not have access to such a vocabulary. There was a certain taken-for-granted quality to their experiences. As Connie Brown explains,

> I felt conscious of not being able to talk [in SDS meetings], but I would say that my consciousness of feminism was not very much. . . . What I remember is just the feeling . . . would be more on a family level. Like within the family you might think, Oh God, he's the boss and he makes us all do what he wants . . . just *take it for granted that that's the way it is.* Here we had these very high-powered men in our project. We might not like it, but *we would assume* that that was who was going to run things. (emphasis added)

Another early activist, Barbara Haber, speaks directly to the lack of a language to express such feelings. "My experience [in SDS] first of all was of incredible sexism, *for which I did not have a word.* . . . I knew that I hated it and I was miserable and I knew I was being excluded. What I didn't know was that being a woman—it took me a long time . . . before we started talking about that" (emphasis added).

By the mid to late 1960s a framework *did* develop by which to identify and name sexism within the movement. Although two older activists were the first to raise the issue of women's position in the movement, the issue lay dormant for a couple more years. In 1965 two early SNCC activists, Casey Hayden and Mary King, wrote the seminal paper "Sex and Caste: A Kind of Memo," addressed to "a number of other women in the peace and freedom movements." They drew the analogy between women and blacks being part of a caste system that excluded both groups from hierarchical structures of power. King and Hayden also contrasted the movement's egalitarian ideas with women's actual subordinate role.[27] Although a reading of this memo prompted a group of women to walk out of a national SDS conference a month later, women didn't begin to seriously organize within SDS until 1967.[28]

By the late 1960s the language of black power and colonialism pervaded SDS. Ideological debates were filled with arguments about the struggles of third-world people. In contrast to the early women, then, later activists were surrounded by the language of oppression. This available vocabulary gave legitimacy to women's concerns. Like the first wave of feminists who learned from their participation in the abolitionist movement, these activists learned to apply the framework of race to their own lives as women. Later activists inherited these ideas and used them to understand their own position in the movement. The civil rights movement provided a "master protest frame" within which women came to understand their unjust positions. Snow and Benford, drawing from Erving Goffman, argue that frames allow individuals "to locate, perceive, identify, and label" events within their life space or the world at large.[29] They can reframe what they had taken for granted as a problem to fix, an injustice to right. Women were able to draw on the ideological understanding of the black struggle for their own struggle as women and to mobilize.[30]

In short, later activists not only had a different experience within the organization but also applied a vocabulary to the analysis and open discussion of their experiences of sexism. As later activist Carol Christman put it, the younger women were "able to give names to [their] sense of frustration. . . . By the time I came along a revolution was occurring."

For many women becoming feminists was similar to the process of radicalization they had gone through during their early years of activism. Some women talk of the process of learning a way of seeing. They were, in a sense, educated into this perspective. Carol Christman comments, "Getting connected with feminism was a whole set of learning experiences."

Although many early SDS women also became feminists, their stories have an element of resistance that later women's stories lack. For some early activists, their identity as radicals superseded their identity as women. As pioneers, some speak of how they saw themselves as exceptional and just "one of the guys." For instance, Sue Jhirad says, "I resisted for a long time thinking of myself as a woman because of this . . . exception. I was a leader and I could do it, and I was just one of the guys basically. . . . Many things happened to me . . . in my life which were strongly women's issues, but I wiped that out and never thought about it consciously."

For these women the radicalization to feminism often was abrupt. Sue recalls her first inklings of consciousness at a time when she was trying to balance her commitment to antiwar work with having a job, working on a Ph.D., taking care of her baby, and doing all the housework. Ignoring her feelings of frustration, Sue decided to organize women into an antidraft group in Boston. She initiated a meeting that included a group of her women friends. Sue was furious when these women, instead of organizing, took up the topic of why women are oppressed. Sue remembers,

> I thought it was secondary to the issue that men were dying in Vietnam. . . . All my anger and frustration about my situation was stuff that I never articulated politically *because I had no framework for it.* Which is an intriguing phenomenon, how a strong, independent . . . woman would allow herself to become just a household role without even seeing that there was anything wrong with it. [That] tells you something about *what life was like before women's liberation ideology even existed.* (emphasis added)

Soon after this event, Sue began going to some women's meetings and recalls a sudden awakening she had at one such meeting.

> I just had this complete and total revelation that suddenly everything was turning inside out. I began to see all these things that happened to me in my life of having been raped, having been beaten up by my boyfriend, having a very authoritarian father, doing all this housework. I began to see for the first time. . . . These were political questions. And I got very engaged in the women's movement at that point.

By naming her experiences and seeing the political dimension to her own personal troubles, Sue was able to become part of a collective response that resonated with the widely shared experiences of other women.

Barbara Haber went through a similar change from initial resistance to a sudden radicalization to feminism. Her change in perspective was accompanied by much pain and confusion. Barbara recalls her experience during an SDS convention at Champaign-Urbana.

> The women went off to have their own separate meeting . . . and I didn't go with them because I was very frightened of going off. I was married and wanted to stay married. More than that even . . . I wanted the approval of the male leadership. I was the daddy's girl. . . . My whole life was geared around getting male approval and I wasn't getting it. And I wasn't going to give up because I'm very obstinate.

Instead of joining the women, Barbara chose to join a group of men. As she listened to their discussion about sex and whether women were passive, and tried to put in her own two cents' worth, Barbara discovered she was a feminist. She remembers her resistance, of being afraid of losing "what I was still striving for." Barbara's ambition was to crack the barrier and be accepted by men as the exceptional woman. She was torn between two contradictory views.

> There was still that old idea that I could be "the special woman," the one as smart as men, who men would respect as an equal. The idea that if women couldn't get that respect, it meant we really were inferior. The self-hate, the disidentification with femaleness was still strong in me. On the other hand, I had the growing sense in my gut, "[The women are] right, they're my sisters and my only path to survival is to be with them." But that felt like a terrifying shift.

Barbara's description illustrates the threat posed by identifying as a woman and feminist, not only in terms of the fear of alienating men, but also in terms of a shift in her sense of self.

In short, while many women in SDS became feminists, the emotional pathways were different for younger and older generations. Whereas the early women felt a strong sense of community within SDS and were reluctant to break the bonds of unity with men in the movement, later women's experiences within SDS were more alienating and divisive. At the same time that these younger women were pushed toward feminism from their negative organizational experiences, they were pulled toward feminism by the surrounding ideology of equality and oppression that resonated with their own experiences as women.

One final way that later women were pulled toward feminism is through the counterculture. The language of the counterculture intersected with feminist beliefs. Both emphasized the importance of lifestyle, of the personal as political. By rejecting middle-class standards and lifestyles and embracing sexual freedom, the counterculture called into question basic institutions such as marriage and the family, causes that were critical to feminism.[31] As we saw in chapter 5, later activists embraced the counterculture while early activists tended to dismiss it. This, too, made later women more prone to recognize discrimination.

Turning to YAF, in addition to the positive organizational experiences that most women report that led them to deny discrimination, we find no language of discontent on the right. Because the right tends to focus on liberty rather than equality, no appropriate framework was easily available in the way that it was for the left. Because the civil rights movement was not central to the vast majority of activists on the right, there was no analogy to blacks or pervasive "master protest frame" by which women could understand their own position. This lack of a comparison group also helps explain why the majority of YAF women did not recognize discrimination.

Why, then, did a minority of YAF women perceive sexism? The picture is not as clear-cut as it is with SDS women. The few women who did recognize discrimination are not linked by age, ideology, or distinct organizational experiences. All of them, however, had some experience that brought them into contact with the ideology of equality. Traditionalist Anne Edwards, for instance, was one of the few YAFers who *did* participate in the civil rights movement. During her sit-ins at Woolworth's she certainly was exposed to the language of equality. In fact, in discussing sexism Anne makes the comparison, saying, "I think that female[s] who wanted to drive a truck or play quarterback should have [been able to do it] because of the law of the land. . . . Just as with civil rights—I don't think there should have been obstructions put in the way of women." Her experiences with civil rights gave Anne a framework for understanding her own situation as a woman.

Mary Fisk is another traditionalist who identified sexism within the movement. Mary is the activist whose mother was an electronics engineer, whom Mary described as "radically liberated." Certainly Mary's experience of seeing her mother "work three times as hard as men, for half the pay" provided a vocabulary by which to name her own experiences. She became increasingly disturbed, for example, by the leadership of Phyllis Schlafly within the conservative movement. Mary says, "Phyllis Schlafly bothered me, for reasons of my orientation. I didn't like that whole image, that that's what people thought conservative women were like. I thought she talks a traditional role but she jets all over the country with a nanny taking care of her kids. It's hypocrisy."

The other women who identified sexism in the movement were libertarians. During the 1960s libertarians took a stand in support of women's right to abortion, sexual freedom, and gay rights. These positions no doubt brought libertarians into contact with a language of equality. Further, as we saw in chapter 5, libertarians also embraced the counterculture. Through the counterculture as well these women likely discovered a common vocabulary with the incipient feminist movement. In fact, one woman, Marilyn Bradley, says her own involvement in the "human potential movement" brought her directly to the doors of feminism. "Therapy is the key . . . looking inward instead of looking at the world. And feminism was a part of the opening up process. As I was making my connections for myself, I would go out and do talks. I would encourage other women to do the same. You know, 'We're struggling together.'" In fact, to one degree or another, all libertarian women ended up becoming feminists by the 1970s (see chapter 8).


## CONCLUSION

In sum, women who were later activists in SDS encountered a large and increasingly divisive organization. This experience, combined with the prevalence of an ideology by which to express their discontent, made many later activists critical of their own position as women within the movement. Early women activists, in contrast, were much less likely to perceive discrimination in SDS and did not become feminists because of mistreatment by leftist men. Their strong ties to male peers caused those who did become feminists to see a clash between their identity as women and their identity as radicals. Their path to feminism posed more of a threat to their notion of self. Within YAF, while most women perceived equality and felt supported by men, the minority of women who recognized discrimination had individual experiences that exposed them to ideas about equality, giving them a framework for understanding their own situation as women.

As we'll see in chapter 7, these issues of gender and feminism had a critical role in the divisions within SDS. During the late 1960s groups of women began debating women's roles within SDS, meeting to discuss women's issues, and organizing a movement on their own behalf. The tensions caused by feminism, which divided both men from women and women from one another, contributed to the explosive national convention of 1969, an event that signaled the organization's demise.

YAF, too, went through internal struggles during the late 1960s. But gender had no role in the ideological conflict that tore the organization apart. Rather, the growing gulf between libertarians and traditionalists led to YAF's own explosive national convention in 1969.

Yet whether or not women identified sexism within YAF or SDS, what is clear is that during the 1960s women in both groups gained valuable tools and resources through their activism and eventually applied them to organizing other women (see chapter 8). Women on the left focused on fighting for feminist goals. Women on the right chose either to organize for feminism or to oppose feminism and fight to retain women's traditional place in society.

# CHAPTER SEVEN

# PARADISE LOST

During the last years of the 1960s activists in both SDS and YAF became polarized and embattled. While some SDS activists became completely immersed in a world of total politics, others were alienated by the changes and left SDS. Meanwhile, the gulf between libertarians and traditionalists in YAF grew wider. Their conflicts signified a growing intersection of interest between the left and the right as the ideology and identity of libertarians moved closer to those in SDS. These internal differences erupted into explosive national conventions of each organization in 1969.

## TENSIONS WITHIN SDS
### The Growth of Militancy

The late 1960s witnessed further radicalization within SDS. A number of factors contributed to this spirit of militancy and escalation of tactics. First, the stream of political events that occurred in the late 1960s created a sense of apocalypse, feeding the notion that immediate change was essential. The assassinations of Robert Kennedy, Martin Luther King Jr., and Malcolm X; the killing of Fred Hampton; ghetto riots; the trial of the Chicago Eight; the confrontation between protesters and police at the Democratic National Convention; the student takeover of Columbia University—combined with the escalation of fighting in Vietnam and the events in France in May 1968—all added to a sense that the world was coming undone.

Bernardine Dohrn discusses her reaction to the killing of Black Panther leader Fred Hampton by Chicago police as well as the general feeling of 1969.

> The assassination of Fred Hampton . . . was another one of those moments which definitely pushed us into a much more militant and dramatic series of steps because it was so blatant . . . so outrageous, and they were so naked in their lies about it. . . . The whole world seemed to be coming apart, and SDS went from being a fairly modest-sized national organization to enormous in that year because of the war and because of Columbia and because of Paris and everything that was happening in the world. So it was an overwhelming situation.

Accompanying this sense of urgency were weariness and anger at the government's failure to respond. As conditions seemed to worsen and no change was evident, activists grew tired and frustrated, and many came to believe that more extreme actions were needed to stop the killing and to create social change. It seemed as if either apocalypse or revolution was imminent. By 1969, Steve Kessler says, it was clear that "the resistance strategy didn't work." He believed that either there would be massive repression and the government would "lock us all up," or the movement would grow so large that the government would "be swamped."

Many people concluded it was essential to throw themselves fully on the side of "making the revolution." Politics became a way of life as activists breathed, ate, slept, and dreamed their beliefs. Surrounded by others with shared views, activists were prodded on to further radicalization. Michael Kazin speaks of the reasons for his own move to militancy during the late 1960s.

> The rational side is [that militancy is] what it seemed to take to stop the war; seemed like nothing else was working and like also the moral thing to do. . . . People were getting the shit kicked out of them, the Vietnamese and . . . third-world people. The more personal, emotional side of it . . . is that people I looked up to were going that way and I was following them to a certain degree. I was a leader in a small scale . . . in the Harvard chapter, but I was also a follower. . . . The cool people in the world seemed to be revolutionaries. . . . So it's hard at this point to separate how I felt individually from the wave I seemed to be part of. . . . SDS conventions were important in that I could go into these places, '67 and '68 es-

pecially, hear people I looked up to call themselves revolutionaries and Communists. . . . It wasn't so crazy to talk about yourself being a revolutionary.

Michael points to the continuing importance of peers and role models in moving activists to a more militant position. Such people acted as guides into a revised view of reality, mediating this altered worldview to other activists.[1]

The move to more extreme positions was also provoked by the increased repression protesters faced during the late 1960s. The FBI counterintelligence program aimed at the New Left, COINTELPRO, was in full swing by 1968. More and more SDS members experienced incidents of FBI surveillance, harassment, and encounters with infiltrators. Not only did their encounters further fuel the flames of distrust of government, but they also generated paranoia in the movement.

This paranoia, in turn, led to the increased insularity of activists. The need to establish trust meant that activists became more and more concerned with surrounding themselves with others like themselves. This combination of the need for trust, insularity, and the belief that it was necessary to be full-time revolutionaries created a social movement dynamic that fostered dogmatism. Individuals felt continuous pressure to act in the correct political manner. Thus, the urgency of events pushed people to militancy as others in the movement pulled them into it. As Andrea Cousins explains,

> There was . . . a kind of ethos . . . that you're supposed to be politically active all the time, that if you were serious about [politics] you . . . put that first. . . . And if you weren't doing that, you were really being self-indulgent and you were not doing the right thing. . . . We oppressed each other with a tremendous sense of moral principle. We were in such a kind of straitjacket, having to prove to each other that we were doing the right kind of political work, and thinking the right way. . . . There was such a hierarchy . . . with people who were right and people who were wrong, tremendous self-righteousness.

Phil Hutchings recalls how "correct-line-ism" dictated all aspects of life so that even cultural styles were subject to censure. He says at a certain point if you weren't walking around in army boots or green military jackets, "you weren't part of the in-group." Phil had friends who felt guilty about wanting to dress up because then people would think "they were turning petit-bourgeois." This dogmatism demonstrates once again the centrality of social processes not only in the positive construction of social movements but in the negative aspects of peer pressure as well: social support transformed into group censure, ostracism, and new forms of oppression.

Once the dynamic of dogmatism was in place, it led to polarization. Dorothy Burlage discusses this process that, she says, grew much worse by the end of the 1960s.

> There was that *whole* thing that people would get into about who was the most correct. . . . You had to be more radical and more radical and more willing to take risks to *prove* yourself. . . . It was really divisive. People weren't allowed to live their lives in a normal way either. . . . I remember being at people's houses when they had children and thinking . . . they were ostracized because they were taking care of children instead of being political. It was quite rigid.

Some activists who were married felt on the defensive for being in a "monogamous heterosexual marriage"; others with children felt completely unsupported in the demands of parenting. There was little room for the private demands of family life. Barry Skolnick says he and his wife, Karen, "took a lot of shit" for having a baby in 1968. "They thought that [the baby] was going to enslave Karen, that I had done this to her. That even getting married, having the state sanctify your relationship, was counterrevolutionary."

Finally, the escalation of militancy was intricately bound to the ideological divisions within SDS during the late 1960s. Like many social movement organizations, SDS succumbed to factionalization, with each sect demanding ideological purity from its adherents. The polarization resulting from these divisions furthered the insularity of activists as people sought out others aligned with their position. This, too, upped the ante of militancy.

## Ideological Factionalization within SDS

While many activists in SDS reached the conclusion that a revolution was necessary to change American society during the late 1960s, the content and tactics of that revolution, and who would lead it, became sources of intense conflict. By the time of the national SDS convention in 1969 the main divisions were between Progressive Labor, Weatherman, and those who remained unaffiliated with either faction.

**Progressive Labor**  Maoists formed the Marxist sect of Progressive Labor (PL) in 1962 after they were expelled from the Communist Party. By
the mid-1960s PL declared itself to be an anti-imperialist organization
aimed at organizing the working class. PL began making inroads into
SDS by 1966, mainly by mobilizing students against the war. Although
by this point the Communist exclusion clause had been removed from
the SDS constitution,[2] PL seemed to pose little threat. Founded on the
principle of democratic centralism, PL's tight cadre style, its adoption of
conservative dress, and the embrace of Mao seemed alien to many members at the time.

Yet during the late 1960s, as SDS activists became radicalized and with
PL's concerted effort at recruitment, membership in PL began to increase.
In 1967 PL made a serious attempt to recruit SDS members through its
"worker-student alliance" (WSA) program. WSA called on students to
join with the working class by supporting striking workers, advancing
campus workers' demands, and involving workers in antiwar actions.[3]

Following a traditional Marxist line, PL aimed at organizing the industrial proletariat. Afraid of alienating American workers, PL advocated
"base-building" rather than resistance. Thus, PL opposed confrontations
on campus that might alienate workers and rejected student power issues
as elitist. Seeing the main struggle as being between the working class and
the bourgeoisie, PLers viewed racism as a tool of the ruling class, with
blacks being the most exploited of all workers and women being a special oppressed part of the working class. Both blacks and women needed
to align with the working class in its fight against capitalism. Any effort
at separate organizing was "revisionism," PLers believed, and only wors-
ened divisions among workers. The Black Panthers as well as separate
black student organizations were "bourgeois" and "reactionary." Similarly, PL viewed "women's issues" as secondary to organizing workers.[4]

Further, as discussed in chapter 5, PL took a hard line against the counterculture and the use of drugs. Fearful of alienating workers, PL denounced youth culture as bourgeois and individualistic. It discouraged
all drug use, renounced beards, long hair, and blue jeans, and asked co-
habiting activists to get married. Sale describes PL men as "noticeable
for their purposely straight dress, starched workshirts and coats-and-ties,
fifties-short hair, and smooth-shaven faces."[5]

PL provoked strong reactions within SDS. Todd Gitlin points out that
one clear effect of PL was in helping "Marxize SDS . . . as Marxism and
then Marxism-Leninism became SDS's unofficial language." Gitlin quotes
Greg Calvert commenting on the conversions he witnessed: "In about a

six-month period suddenly everybody in SDS said, 'I am a Marxist,' or 'I am a Marxist-Leninist.' . . . People you never would have suspected of having read Marx at all suddenly became 'Marxists.' Overnight."[6] PL played an important role, then, in shifting activist identities to Marxism.

In fact, when Bernardine Dohrn was elected as interorganizational secretary at the SDS convention in 1968 she declared, "I consider myself a revolutionary Communist." Mike Klonsky, elected national secretary, described himself the same way. Rather than aligning with PL, however, Dohrn became part of Weatherman and Klonsky aligned with RYM, an acronym for Revolutionary Youth Movement.

**Weatherman**   Weatherman grew out of a section of SDS that became known as RYM, named after Mike Klonsky's 1968 essay "Toward a Revolutionary Youth Movement."[7] This influential paper advocated that SDS expand beyond its base of students by looking toward youth, particularly working-class youth, as a revolutionary class. Klonsky specifically called for organizing youth in community and junior colleges, high schools, and trade schools; inside the army; and among the unemployed. The paper provoked sharp debate at a SDS national council meeting in December 1968, with PL denouncing RYM's emphasis on students and youth, rather than the working class, as vanguards of the revolution.[8] Beyond indicating the conflicts developing within SDS, the meeting marked an essential shift as it was the first time the majority of members advocated building a class-conscious revolutionary movement.

The actual use of "Weatherman" as a position didn't emerge until the 1969 SDS convention in Chicago. The name was taken from Bob Dylan's song "Subterranean Homesick Blues," "You don't need a weatherman to know which way the wind blows." The name appealed to youth, with its overtones of antiauthoritarianism and independence, and it also implicitly spurned PL, inferring that you don't need a top-down centralist organization to tell you how to make a revolution.[9] Even the choice of quoting a counterculture figure like Dylan repudiated the politics of PL.

The first Weatherman document, distributed at the 1969 convention, challenges PL's worldview. The statement identifies the primary struggle in the world being between U.S. imperialism and national liberation struggles against imperialism. While Weatherman views workers and oppressed peoples of Asia, Africa, and Latin America as the vanguard of the revolution, the revolutionary vanguard within the United States is black liberation. Unlike PL, Weatherman saw racism not just as a tool of the ruling class but as fundamental to all of society. Blacks are not just exploited as workers but are also an oppressed nation suffering colonial exploitation within the United States.

The main task for white activists is to support black liberation as well as national liberation struggles—the National Liberation Front in Vietnam, the Cuban revolution, and other third-world movements. Youth, particularly working-class youth, have a special role in supporting these struggles since they have less of a stake in the system and are hurt most directly by imperialist oppression through unemployment, "jail-like schools," and having to fight in imperialist wars. At this particular historical juncture, Weatherman argued, neither professionals nor the white working class are revolutionary because they take advantage of their own racial position of "white skin privilege." Rather, it is up to American youth to escalate protest at home and to show solidarity with anti-imperialist forces.

While recognizing the importance of the "woman question," Weatherman labeled as reactionary all women's groups that were not "self-consciously revolutionary and anti-imperialist." Calling separate women's groups "bourgeois" and "counterrevolutionary," Weatherman argued that the base for a revolutionary women's movement must be the most oppressed sectors: black, brown, and white working-class women. Women workers must play an essential role as fighters and leaders of the anti-imperialist movement. In short, while PL saw women's liberation as secondary to class conflict, Weatherman viewed women's liberation as secondary to the struggle against imperialism.

Finally, Weatherman called on young white militants to form a revolutionary party, a centralized, cadre organization. Rather than PL's call for "base-building," Weatherman called for resistance—and even armed struggle—as the only path to revolution and establishing world communism. Weatherman was also distinct from PL in style, embracing the counterculture both in ideology and lifestyle. It endorsed the use of marijuana and LSD, criticized the family as bourgeois, and called for sexual liberation and "the smashing of monogamy."

Five activists in this study became members of PL. Steve Goldstein, who joined PL when he was eighteen and eventually became a national leader, says the conflict between PL and Weatherman was explicitly "over whether you felt the problem in our society came from the working class or from the ruling class." In Steve's view, while PL aligned with workers, Weatherman believed black people and minorities were good but white working-class males were bad. While writing off the majority of white workers, Weatherman supported the Black Panthers, who had a good side but also "a lot of bad side . . . gangsterism and a lot of super-macho bullshit." Steve comments that people in Weatherman "were much more rigid, mechanical, sectarian than we [PL] were. The only thing is they were stoned all the time so you couldn't tell."

Aldyn McKean also became active in PL. He says after years of working in SDS, he eventually had to choose sides, torn between the appeal of PL's politics and the lifestyle associated with RYM and the New Left. He didn't feel comfortable in either caucus. He tended to socialize more with New Left people but agreed more with the analysis of the Worker-Student Alliance [PL] people.

I used to make fun of PL. . . . I used to [think] these were the people with the short hair and they didn't really rate. . . . We used to make fun of them because they were all standing around waving Mao's little red book, even though in fact that was not something that PL did. But that was the image, brainwashed Maoists. So then I went out and became a brainwashed Maoist myself.

Five other activists in this sample ended up joining Weatherman. Cathy Wilkerson says she was attracted to Weatherman because the group put the fight against racism at center stage.

They also claimed to have close relationships with the leaders of various militant black organizations, including the Panthers. I was very naive about the level of integrity in those relationships. Many of us . . . had done antiracism organizing, but when the Panthers began getting killed by the police and their work came under constant attack, we turned to those whites who appeared to be the most committed to supporting the Panthers. I was in Chicago when Fred Hampton was killed. I got woken up at 5:30 in the morning and told that the Chicago police had broken into the apartment and shot Fred in his bed. And that was it. I felt like I had no right to be alive. If I was not also under attack, I was doing something wrong. The murder of Fred organized three-quarters of the membership of Weatherman into Weatherman. . . . People just shed [every]thing. . . . The other part of it was that there was nothing else.

Cathy says the choices available were between becoming "an organizer around working-class issues and fighting with the unions," joining Weatherman, or becoming a feminist separatist. Because Vietnam and international issues were so essential to her, she felt closest to the politics of Weatherman.

Michael Kazin also briefly joined Weatherman at Harvard, where he had been cochair of SDS. Whereas he had first felt opposed to Weatherman, he even more vehemently opposed PL. For one thing, he and his friends were focused on the war and on black power. "Where the black movement led, I and other people in SDS generally felt we should follow. That's why it was so shocking that PL opposed Panthers, because even though now I think they were probably more right than wrong, to oppose the Panthers at the time was like . . . blasphemy."

Having spent the summer of 1969 in Berkeley, Michael stopped at the national office of SDS in Chicago and talked to Mark Rudd. He found Rudd's arguments supporting Weatherman convincing. When Michael asked, "Isn't Weatherman adventurist," Rudd replied by asking, "When have we really done enough to help the revolution?" Michael agreed that nothing had been won yet and "we really should keep doing more." Plus the politics of Weatherman was "an extension—a crazy one—but nevertheless an extension of a lot of the politics of my side in SDS." Like Weatherman, Michael was oriented toward the third world and saw his role as supporting other people's revolutions while also trying to disrupt this country and stop the war. In addition, many of Michael's friends were joining Weatherman "so it seemed like the thing to do." This combination of the affinity for the ideas promoted by Weatherman or PL, along with the influence of friends, explains activists' choices.

**The Unaffiliated**    The majority of SDS activists remained unaffiliated. Among these, some opposed both PL and Weatherman. Although Sue Jhirad had many friends in PL, she was critical of both groups. Sue didn't join PL because they were "manipulative" and "too doctrinaire." She was going with a guy from PL but at a certain point it became clear that he was sleeping with her in order to recruit her. Yet the development of Weatherman also scared her. As someone who always tried to unite people, Sue disliked the splits within SDS. She was particularly alienated by PL's "way of dealing with people" and with its decision to join SDS en masse, "which many people saw essentially as a takeover." Sue considered PL's infiltration of SDS a big mistake, predicting it would "wreck" the organization.

Carl Oglesby also disagreed with both sides. On the one hand, he ardently opposed PL:

They were anti everything left-wing. They would figure out left-wing reasons to be against anything that was revolutionary or even socially positive. They would fight the black leadership of the civil rights movement because it was insufficiently radical. . . . They would say Castro's government was a lie in the face of socialism. They would attack on behalf of socialism, on behalf of the revolution. . . . And at each new meeting PL was getting more vociferous and more daring. They would have more people in their Worker-Student Alliance who would sit in ever larger blocks waving their little cards, their credentials always perfectly in order.

On the other hand, Carl also opposed Weatherman. It was, in fact, people in Weatherman who eventually drove Carl out of SDS, claiming he had "bad politics," that he wasn't sufficiently revolutionary. When Carl thinks back on the politics of Weatherman now, he is torn.

In a sense the Weathermen looked more foolish than they really may have been. To get back into their shoes is to look at a world of considerable apocalyptic frenzy. . . . On the one hand . . . I get mad at them for . . . the self-satisfaction of their stupid little mud pies of theory. . . . On the other hand, they sensed something very true about America of 1969 and '70. They sensed that the threat of police state repression was magnitudes greater than conventional discourse understood. They sensed that the antiwar movement would be the recipient of the powers, that we were the targets. . . . And they realized that in that set of circumstances a movement leadership essentially had to choose between the existing underground or not existing at all. . . . I don't think it was easy for them to change their lives the way they did, to spit out their middle-class background. . . . What they did was courageous, if not always really smart.

Other SDS activists were sympathizers with one faction or the other but, because they had reservations, stayed unaffiliated. Above all for many activists the divisiveness and conflict of SDS during the late 1960s was confusing and alienating. Dave Strauss was disturbed by the transformations he witnessed in his good friends as some of them joined Weatherman, likening the effects to scenes in old Korean War films where somebody is brainwashed. One day Dave would be talking to people about something and the next day they would be entirely different; he couldn't understand what was happening. He felt isolated and confused and ended up leaving SDS.

Witnessing bitter quarrels, John Brown Childs felt alienated.

It was very disturbing . . . watching the fighting that was going on. Some of which, obviously, as we know in retrospect, was managed by the FBI as the COINTELPRO program. But I can't blame it all on the FBI because [they were] . . . only able to do that [because of] a certain receptivity on the part of people to think badly about others. . . . The FBI definitely exacerbated it. They had informants all over the place . . . provocateurs. But they made use of existing dogmatism against dogmatism, vanguard group against vanguard group. That's where I really developed my wariness of positions that claim absolute answers to problems.

Jane Adams, another activist who felt caught in the middle of the conflicts, was grief-stricken by what occurred during the late 1960s as "everybody seemed to be going off in the wrong directions." Amidst all the factionalism, Jane kept feeling she should know what to do. She says, "Every once in a while I still feel like had I known what to do, maybe things would have come out differently because I had a lot of influence. . . . Every once in a while I go back and try to rewrite history." Clearly for some activists the anguish of those years remains vivid.

In addition to the ideological differences between PL and Weatherman, two other issues were central to the divisions within SDS: women's liberation and the use of violence to create social change.

### Women's Issues

Tensions over women's issues also split SDS during the late 1960s. Echols and Evans document the organizational changes as SDS struggled to come to terms with feminism.[10] The main issues dividing activists centered on how women's liberation fit into the revolution as well as SDS's stance toward an independent women's movement. On one side were those who insisted on the primary importance of women's oppression. Rather than seeing women as superexploited workers (as PL did) or as secondary to the fight against imperialism (as Weatherman argued), these activists viewed the liberation of women as central to the struggle. They called for the elimination of male supremacy within SDS as well as for the importance of women organizing among themselves. They supported women forming an independent movement that would work in coalition with SDS.

Again, activists felt forced to take sides in this pressing ideological debate. Jane Adams was one of the women who recognized the importance of women organizing. In 1967 at the SDS National Convention in Ann Arbor Jane met with other women at the first "Women's Liberation Workshop" and helped draft a statement analyzing sexual inequality. They declared, "As we analyze the position of women in capitalist society and especially in the United States we find that women are in a colonial relationship to men and we recognize ourselves as part of the Third World."[11] Maintaining that women's subordinate status within SDS inhibited the revolutionary struggle, they called for an educational campaign to address women's liberation in SDS and for SDS men to confront their "male chauvinism." The statement provoked a heated response, particularly by men, who were furious by the third-world analogy.

But it was not just men who opposed women organizing. Jane also recalls the fights among women.

> The whole issue of whether there should be separate caucuses for women became a real acrimonious issue. I felt that women . . . needed our own space. . . . We should work within SDS, but we should also have our own organization. . . . The women who were more identified with classically Marxist kinds of positions . . . were opposed to that because that was leading to disunity. I argued . . . that you could have unity with diversity.

Besides those calling for an independent women's movement that would work in coalition with SDS, were women who called for a separatist movement of women organized completely apart from men. Beth Oglesby became involved with the separatist women's movement. After separating from Carl, she joined consciousness-raising groups and women's liberation groups in San Francisco. She recalls the nature of the splits among women there.

> We had the separatist feminists, who were mostly white middle class, just feminist issue people. Then we had socialist nonseparatist women who wanted to work in political groups with men. And then we had the lesbians who were the only . . . racially mixed and class-mixed group. . . . I was not interested in the Marxists who felt that if we could just [get] rid of imperialism, then guys would do all right by their women. I thought . . . that it was going to take a little bit more than that.

Beth moved to Boston to work with Bread and Roses, a socialist feminist group organized by and for women that worked in coalition with the male left. A few months later Beth came out as a lesbian and began identifying as a radical separatist feminist.

On the other side of the issue from those promoting an independent women's movement were those who saw women's liberation as secondary. As discussed before, both PL and Weatherman saw women's issues as subordinate to the primary contradiction of class conflict, racism, or anti-imperialism. For these people women's liberation was branded as individualistic and psychological, aimed at personal liberation rather than political change. Separate women's organizations were viewed as bourgeois and divisive to the revolution, resulting in false consciousness in which sex was placed above class, race, or imperialism. Only communism would truly liberate women. Cathy Wilkerson recalls the enormous degree of conflict created by these issues in her women's group, which was formed in Washington in 1968 and included both SDS and ex-SDS women.[12]

> There was always a tension in the group about what was feminism? Was it separatism, was it a fight for equality within the left, or in society at large? . . . We struggled with it for many months. . . . As it happened, many of the women who became more and more identified with the women's movement were . . . in relationships with men. Most of the SDS women were not, or if we were, we were not married and . . . lived in communal houses whereas the others lived in nuclear families in apartments. We didn't shave our legs; they did. All of that stuff was a big deal at the time. Every personal choice seemed laden with significance. Because we had no language to explore the deeper issues, our differences came out around other things. There started to be some baiting that went back and forth. "SDS women worked with men so we weren't sincere about our commitment to feminism." And we would bait them about racism. . . . There was no way to have a subtle position. . . . It was like the armed struggle debate. You had to be for it and that was it, or you had to be against it totally. . . . Nobody could deal with life is complicated and it requires complicated analysis and solutions. To say that separatism is right sometimes and wrong sometimes, you would be smashed. You could never survive.

As Cathy so clearly articulates, the politics during these extreme times pushed activists to the limits. The pressures for purity meant there were no shades of gray. Divisions over "the woman question" created much hostility between women and men as well as among the women in SDS.

## The Issue of Violence

The other central issue that exacerbated divisions in SDS concerned the role of violence as a means of social change. The intensity of events, combined with frustration with the lack of change, led some activists to embrace violence as a tactic. Debate over the use of violence was common during the late 1960s. Jim Shoch talks about his own acceptance of the need for armed struggle.

> It wasn't such a difficult transition actually, believe it or not. . . . The Black Panthers were around and the RU [Revolutionary Union][13] was very much influenced by the Panthers. . . . They seemed exciting, charismatic, effective. . . . There was just a lot in the environment. . . . The radicalism seemed to have an armed character to it, at least in the way it was propounded. . . . It didn't seem like some big decision: "I'm no longer a pacifist." I can't remember if I ever was a pacifist. . . . There wasn't any theoretically coherent spokesperson for a parliamentary road to socialism around.

As a member of RU, Jim participated in required weapons training every two weeks.

While violence was "in the air" for some SDS activists, compelling them to take up arms, other activists condemned such action, holding fast to their belief in nonviolence. Early activists were more likely to take this stance than later activists. Dorothy Burlage, for example, contrasts the violence she faced in the South fighting for civil rights with the adoption of violence as a tactic by northern SDSers.

> In the South people really were getting killed and so you didn't play with guns and you didn't play with violence and you didn't provoke it intentionally. . . . In the North it was anything from a cavalier disregard to excitement. . . . I always thought northerners took too many risks unnecessarily for reasons that I couldn't understand. It didn't seem to me necessary to create such violence to promote the issues. So I didn't identify with it and I didn't sympathize with it.

Jane Adams was also acutely aware of the implications of embracing violence. She read about the violent tactics of some East Coast SDSers while living in Oklahoma, where at most forty other people were actively against the war and where long hair "meant you got your life threatened after a football game, particularly if you lost, because all the jocks would be coming looking for a hippie, for somebody to beat up. It was not friendly territory." Recognizing that the embrace of violence was pure posturing, Jane thought it was crazy, knowing it "could get us wiped out." Both Jane and Dorothy point out the varying impact of violence in different regions of the country.

The shift to violence had a much more personal meaning to Cindy Decker. Because Cindy had experience with guns, some people turned to her for training. Cindy recalls, "SDS had taken a conspiratorial turn. . . . The fact that I could shoot guns, and I was a hell of a good shot, was extremely attractive." Although she did teach some people how to shoot, Cindy became more and more disturbed by this turn of events that reminded her of her initial involvement with the right-wing paramilitary movement.

> I considered my move from Minutemen into SDS to be a personal liberation of sorts. And watching SDS turn back into the Minutemen . . . that's how I saw it. . . . I had moved from paranoia, secretiveness, isolation . . . into openness. It was like moving from the shadows into the sunlight. . . . I didn't want to close back up.

Yet many of those opposing violence felt outnumbered, on the margins. These activists said there was no place for them in the movement; they felt left behind by those who were prepared to kill and die.

Some activists saw this embrace of violence as a distinctly male phenomenon, a way for men to prove themselves. Dave Strauss comments that talk of "offing pigs" and other such posturing was a type of rite of passage. Violence represented a coming of age, as it had for generations of men who took risks and fought during wartime.

This macho stance was particularly associated with the politics and style of Weatherman. Echols remarks that Weatherman was obsessed with smashing "honkieness" and "wimpiness." Part of the effort to liberate women involved women's adopting a male stance, becoming "street-fighting women," tough and ready for combat.[14] Michael Kazin reflects on this point in talking about the few months he spent with Weatherman.

> There was something to the feminist critique of I wanted to be a tougher man and I didn't want to be bookish Michael, I wanted to be Mike, fist-and-learn-karate and this kind of thing. . . . Men [were] certainly trying to prove themselves as revolutionaries. . . . A lot of men, me included, were into this cult of violence. . . . Of

course, the violence that all but a very small proportion of what white radicals took part in was mostly throwing rocks at windows. They were hardly revolutionary guerrilla tactics. Kind of a joke in retrospect.

Michael says men were more drawn to violence than women and also recalls women in Weatherman trying to be strong as they put on their army boots, hoping to "masculinize themselves."

But Weatherman Cathy Wilkerson saw a difference between some men's penchant for violence and the militancy of women in Weatherman. Women were militant by an "instinct that responds to injustice. It needs to be taken care of now and you do what you have to do. You put your body on the line and don't even think about it." Cathy points to a whole tradition of women being militant defending their families and children. Many SDS actions similarly were meant to convey a sense of urgency: overturning the tables of ROTC recruiters or disrupting speakers. Women had no trouble with this kind of militancy that didn't hurt other people. Cathy was attracted to such actions because she felt it was vital to be disruptive to stop what was going on, that sitting back would make her complicit. But ideas about armed struggle and actually physically hurting another person, she says, were positions women were reluctant to take.

Regardless of whether women and men approached violence differently, Weatherman's stance toward violence was one more area of conflict with PL. Many in PL were disdainful of Weatherman for its embrace of armed struggle. Judy Baker was particularly opposed to the use of bombing and terrorism that Weatherman advocated once it went underground. Like many in PL, she believed such actions alienated workers. While she felt a move toward greater militancy during the late 1960s, Judy never condoned bombing and tried to talk people she knew out of using such tactics.

Debates over violence, women's issues, and other ideological differences led to an escalation of conflict within SDS. By the spring of 1969 internal strife resulted in splits and even the dissolution of SDS chapters, including ones at Brandeis, Berkeley, Columbia, Texas, and Michigan State. Sale comments, "The era of bad feelings was clearly at its peak."[15]

Accusations abounded and even fistfights broke out between warring factions. Sue Jhirad vividly recalls the deterioration of debate and civility within Harvard SDS by the end of the 1960s. "[The factions] were really hateful toward each other. . . . It was . . . very much [a] male-led, male-dominated way of doing things, with a lot of nastiness. . . . My last memory was at this SDS meeting in Boston seeing [a male SDSer] . . . and he was just screaming and yelling at this PL person. . . . It was very ugly political splits." There was tremendous bitterness at Harvard as a result of the split between PL and non-PL members, including allegations that some SDS leaders were FBI agents. In fact, both PL and Weatherman accused those on the other side of being government agents. Judy Baker comments on her view of Weatherman. "I thought that the FBI organized them; I still think the FBI organized them. And if the FBI didn't organize them, then they should have. . . . I hated what they did. I hated what they stood for. I hated them on a personal level. And I thought that they exploited women in a way that . . . just turned my stomach."

On the other side, Carl Oglesby comments on PL,

> There was an enormous transformation going on in SDS, mainly because of the Progressive Labor Party, which I always will think of as cops. I think that PL was police-controlled. . . . I think the Progressive Labor Party was a counterintelligence ploy that originated with the New York Red Squad and that somehow it evolved into something that was run on a national basis. . . . They were, after all, the hammer of the hammer and anvil that destroyed SDS.

Accusations of being racist, anti-Communist, or counterrevolutionary were also common charges employed by all sides during the late 1960s.

## THE TOTALITY OF POLITICS

The drama of the historical events of the late 1960s heightened the sense of the political domain. As militancy grew and conflict escalated, politics did not merely intensify but became a totality for many activists. As Whalen and Flacks put it, the extremity of the times made it necessary to abandon all personal interests and dedicate oneself wholeheartedly to "making the revolution."[16] Particularly for those activists who became involved in PL, Weatherman, or other sects, politics dictated all aspects of life. They came to identify themselves solely in terms of politics and pushed aside all other concerns.

Illustrative of the transformations that took place among some activists is Lynn Dykstra's story. Lynn compares her experience in Weatherman to that of Patty Hearst, the newspaper heiress who was kidnapped in 1974 by the Symbionese Liberation Army, an extreme leftist sect, and ended up adopting their beliefs. Lynn felt immense sympathy for Patty Hearst and understood what had happened to her and how she came to accept all the things she was told. The transformation of Lynn's own beliefs was gradual and, she says, must be seen within the context of the times.

> It can start out as brainwashing, but it evolves. . . . It's the acceptance of a belief system that within its own system makes perfect sense. . . . But you don't get brainwashed to be something completely different than you are. There are little bits of what is said that fit with . . . your values and your background and . . . those things then get pushed into this system you're getting taught. . . . Some of the things I thought and said as a Weatherman make no sense now but they made perfect sense at the time. . . . That we were going to tear down the United States government and create a completely different world. And we were going to do it violently and that was perfectly right to do. . . . It has a lot of religious fervor . . . to it. And made perfect sense within the context of this little group of people, but not taking into account reality and the rest of the world.

Berger and Luckman speak about secondary socialization when individuals commit themselves in a comprehensive way to a new reality, for instance, giving themselves to the revolution with the whole of their lives. The final consequence of secondary socialization is the readiness to sacrifice the self to this new reality.[17] By the time of the 1969 SDS convention Lynn had contemplated losing her life to the revolution: "It was more of a martyrdom feeling that we were right and they were wrong and if they shot us, it would just help our cause. But we weren't trying to get killed. . . . None of us were *that* crazy."

Lynn, and other activists in her situation, in effect became segregated from the inhabitants of other worlds, disaffiliating themselves from previous connections. As Berger and Luckmann put it, individuals are "no longer 'yoked together with unbelievers,' and thus [they are] protected from their potential reality-disrupting influence. . . . People and ideas that are discrepant with the new definitions of reality are systematically avoided."[18] Lynn began working and living with a cadre of four other activists. Eventually she found the group stifling. "It was really getting to be very vicious and very radical and very controlling. So that the things we were fighting against . . . were suddenly appearing in the midst of us. Instead of feeling like you had freedom of choice, you were starting to lose freedom of choice, and that was one of the values we had."

In particular, the group came to dominate decisions "around lifestyle, behavior, ways of talking, attitudes." Lynn recalls the group dynamics.

> When you have a small group of people and you're living together
> and you think you're all going in one direction and you fight about
> things like "Do we spend our money on new guns or . . . on food?"
> or "Do we give to the poor or don't we give to the poor?" or "Do
> we need new clothes or not?" or "Do we steal them?" or "Can you
> be friends with people from your past or not?" They didn't want
> me to be friends with people from my past and that was too much
> of them to ask. . . . It's like a very bad marriage that's going down-
> hill rapidly.

Feeling more and more isolated, as if her "world was actually shrink-
ing," Lynn eventually broke away from the group.[19]

Leaving such groups that demand complete commitment and total im-
mersion is often difficult. Cathy Wilkerson, also a member of Weatherman, faced this situation. First, in order to be accepted into the group,
Cathy had to endure intensive criticism of her feminism.

> I had to undergo a forty-eight-hour criticism of my women's poli-
> tics, forty-eight hours straight . . . days and nights. By the end of
> which I renounced everything I believed in basically. . . . I think that
> I would have recovered, but then Fred [Hampton] was killed by
> the police and a number of other things . . . happened in rapid suc-
> cession. So that by the end of three months I was so disoriented
> that I really did sort of sell away my own independent thinking
> for about five years. Then the Townhouse [explosion] happened
> and . . . that was the last nail in the coffin. . . . But there was this
> feeling . . . just let me put my body on the line. I'm so worthless.
> I'm so . . . filled with guilt. . . . You watch these massacres on TV
> every night . . . and it was so horrible that . . . you said, "My ex-
> perience is not so important as this experience."

As Cathy's poignant quote illustrates, some activists who became increasingly horrified by the events of the times, by the killings and war
and injustice, and by the intransigence to change, became completely en-
gulfed in radical action. Being a revolutionary became their sole identity
as everything else faded in significance. The collective identity of the
group replaced individual identity.

Saying there was a certain point at which she "became a zombie,"
Cathy reflects on the group process.

> There's a dynamic that happens when you join these groups . . .
> because you developed this fantasy that the group is the leader of

the revolution and it's the only group that has the right analysis of what's going on in the world. . . . So if you're not in the group . . . you're a bystander to history. . . . It's very intense and, once you buy into it, then you become more invested in staying into it. . . . Then . . . after the Townhouse happened, I had a vested interest in buying into it because then I knew I would have to stay underground and who else was I going to hang out with? But it was a very sick organization . . . because it was so isolated.

Cathy became completely absorbed in the group and lost her political bearings so that she "couldn't think independently enough to have doubts. . . . I really didn't have a critical thought for five years. . . . It became a totally negative fight rather than fighting to create something better. . . . Then the organization fell apart. Thank God, praise the Lord!" Only when the group dissolved did Cathy find her bearings. It is not that she then abandoned her identity as a radical; rather, she found a way to keep that identity in coexistence with the rest of her life, with her entire self (see chapters 8 and 9).

Members of Weatherman were not the only ones who suffered from the totality of politics during the late 1960s. Aldyn McKean recalls the difficulty of his situation. By the fall of 1969 Aldyn had joined PL and become "a full-time SDS automaton." He recounts,

There was a certain point where I was living with a woman who was also in the WSA [Worker-Student Alliance] caucus of SDS and we would get up in the morning at 6:00. . . . We would go to a subway stop and pass out literature . . . to workers coming to work, and then we would go organize students, and we would go to our collective meetings, and it was the whole day. . . . And there were a bunch of us from SDS who were working at the Roy Rogers hamburger joint and we ended up having a strike there [laughs]. It really was a full-time job. . . . At a certain point I was really not happy. . . . It was drudgery after a while. . . . It had gotten to the point where I was operating completely out of guilt.

John Maher, another member of PL who worked in factories for several years trying to organize workers, comments that "more and more, [PL] became a cult."

Even activists who remained unaffiliated with any sect felt the pressure to let politics consume them. Steve Kessler comments on the overwhelming sense of politics during the late 1960s, saying his activism "literally and figuratively" became his whole life. He explains, "I didn't really allow for an independent identity outside of politics." Clearly, then, for a number of activists in SDS politics not only became a central part of their identity, but by the end of the decade had taken over their lives, completely overshadowing all other sense of self. The political self assumed a "master identity," dominating all other identities, and permeating everyday life.

## THE DRIFT AWAY FROM SDS

While some SDS activists became consumed by politics, other activists began to drift away from the organization by 1969. The tenor of the times, the shift to conflict and violence, alienated many people, particularly the early activists. Helen Garvy recalls her reaction to the shift in tone during the late 1960s as new people came into SDS.

> There started to be a lot more arguments. . . . I had no interest in long involved policy debates that weren't connected to action. . . . Then a lot of the craziness started and . . . my response . . . was, "I don't want to spend time arguing with the people who tried to infiltrate SDS." . . . My reaction was to just take my marbles and do what I wanted to do. . . . So I was officially a member, I would get *New Left Notes*, I would every so often write stuff or talk to people, but I was more into doing what was important to me.

Another early activist, Dorothy Burlage, also felt "less in tune with the national leaders" and was disturbed by the ideological turn of the late 1960s. Saying she started out "as a simple kid," Dorothy found that SDS became much too complicated "when they were arguing whether the Chinese version was right or the Russian version was. It was over my head . . . and it seemed irrelevant." She was also uncomfortable with the style of SDS in the late 1960s, which she called "unnecessarily rude." Dorothy withdrew from SDS although she remained politically active.

Derek Barron felt the whole movement lost its bearings in the late sixties as "the left lost touch with itself and the way in which it was perceived in the larger society." Derek found the changes within SDS "absolute craziness": "I had not the slightest inkling of how this could lead to widespread social change. It just seemed incredibly self-destructive to me. . . . It was clear that things . . . were developing in the movement in a way that I just didn't really have any interest in being a part of." The idea of being a full-time revolutionary didn't appeal to Derek. Instead,

he committed himself to finishing college and made the difficult decision
to go to law school.

Carl Oglesby didn't simply drift away but was driven out of SDS by
some members of Weatherman because of his stance on Cuba.

> Everything went crazy. I finally had a feeling of home in the move-
> ment and suddenly I didn't have any sense of home in the move-
> ment. I was being attacked by people that I used to think were pretty
> neat, because I was not taking revolutionary positions. I went to
> Cuba, tenth anniversary, 1969, wrote it up for *Life* magazine. I
> thought it was a pretty good piece. Took such shit inside of SDS,
> (a) for writing for an imperialist rag like *Life* magazine, (b) for then
> proceeding to write a critical article about Cuba. . . . I was pretty
> tired and bummed out at this point. It had been nonstop New Left
> politics for four years and I'd gone through a lot. . . . SDS wasn't
> fun any more.

In short, by the time of the 1969 SDS convention many early activists
already had distanced themselves from SDS and no longer felt emotionally "at home" in the movement. Very few early activists attended SDS's
final convention.

## THE 1969 SDS CONVENTION

The details of the final days of SDS are well documented.[20] In brief, the organization broke apart under the weight of factionalization during the
national SDS convention held in Chicago in June 1969.[21] Among the
fifteen hundred delegates, a third were PL members or sympathizers, another third belonged to Weatherman or its RYM allies, and the remainder were newcomers, anarchists, or unaffiliated leftists.

One of the most explosive moments came during the first day of the
convention, when the Weatherman/RYM coalition welcomed the Black
Panthers, anathema to PL. In order to discredit PL's antinationalist position, Weatherman/RYM had invited members of the Puerto Rican
Young Lords Organization, the Chicano Brown Berets, and the Black Panthers to speak. After denouncing PL, Rufus Walls, a Black Panther leader
from Illinois, unexpectedly launched into a discussion of women's liberation, declaring the Panthers supported free love and "pussy power."
The crowd, stunned, erupted in response, chanting "Fight male chauvinism." Walls yelled back, "Superman was a punk because he never even
tried to fuck Lois Lane." The hooting and chanting in reaction to this

remark was so intense that Walls was forced off stage. This speech was particularly embarrassing to RYM members as they had been trying to gain support by attacking PL's stance on women's liberation. The next Panther leader, Jewel Cook, merely inflamed passions by returning to the topic, again endorsing "pussy power" and reiterating Stokely Carmichael's infamous statement that "The only correct position for women in the movement is prone." At this comment, the hall broke into pandemonium. Hundreds of shocked delegates booed amidst deafening chants.[22] A fistfight broke out by the end of the evening.[23]

The next day the Panthers returned, declaring PL either had to change its position on nationalism or else be considered "counterrevolutionary traitors." PL members responded by chanting, "Smash Red-baiting. . . . Read Mao." Although the tension-filled convention continued, the final act occurred the following evening when Weatherman/RYM decided to expel PL and its allies for being "objectively racist, anti-communist, and reactionary."[24] Declaring themselves to be the real SDS, Bernardine Dohrn led seven hundred delegates out of the convention hall, chanting, "Power to the People" and "Ho, Ho, Ho Chi Minh."[25]

The day after, Sale reports, there were two SDSs as well as a number of people in between. Many Old Left–type sects remained with PL-SDS and continued to debate traditional sectarian Marxism. Yippie collectives, the Panthers, and assorted others stayed with Weatherman/RYM. A group of anarchists, disgusted with both sides, left the convention, and marched to the headquarters of the IWW (Industrial Workers of the World). Many unaffiliated leftists felt confused, with no place to go.[26]

The irony of SDS politics, as expressed in this final convention, is noted by Richard Flacks, one of the original Port Huron members. By the time of the convention SDS had

> turned into the very opposite of what its founders had intended. SDS had begun with the intention of avoiding dogma, doctrine, top-down discipline, factional warfare, and sectarian style and language. Its purpose was to create the basis for a left that could appeal broadly to the American people. By its final convention in 1969, SDS had not only fallen prey to all the supposed failures of the Old Left, it had become an incredible caricature of its worst excesses. Monolithic, slogan-chanting factions met in open combat over obscure points of dogma, beyond any hope of intelligibility.[27]

Subsequent to the split, both PL and Weatherman/RYM declared themselves to be "the real SDS." Each faction met separately, passed resolutions, and elected its own set of officers. Weatherman/RYM retained control of the national office in Chicago, including the printing presses, mailing lists, files, and treasury. Yet once they separated from PL, divisions between Weatherman and RYM emerged. During the convention RYM supporters articulated their disagreements with Weatherman in a position paper entitled "Revolutionary Youth Movement II."[28] In brief, although RYM-II agreed with Weatherman in viewing imperialism as primary, unlike Weatherman the RYM faction argued that white workers had the potential for revolutionary change. Accusing Weatherman of abandoning its responsibility for organizing white workers, RYM-II believed blacks, women, and students would take a key role in raising the consciousness of the white working class. RYM-II also supported women's liberation and opposed male supremacy.

In the aftermath of the split, RYM-II and Weatherman ran separate slates of candidates. Weatherman won all three national positions. The two major issues Weatherman focused on in the months after the convention were enlistment of working-class youth to join in the revolution and actions against the war. In October 1969 Weatherman promoted a national action called the "Four Days of Rage." Hoping for crowds of thousands, in actuality two to three hundred Weatherman members met in the streets of Chicago and tried to "bring the war home" by battling the police. Meanwhile, RYM-II held its own peaceful demonstration in Chicago. Activists identified with RYM-II felt more and more alienated from the politics of Weatherman. By the end of the summer many RYM-II sympathizers decided to go their own way and continued to organize, taking jobs in factories and community colleges, working with people on welfare, and putting out a newspaper entitled *Revolution Youth Movement.*

Meanwhile, PL moved its version of the national office to Boston and continued to focus on the Worker-Student Alliance. Many members took jobs in factories in order to understand the working class and to recruit workers. PL continued to focus on organizing at factories and "smashing racism" during the early 1970s. The organization was strong in Boston, New York, and scattered other locations but was unsuccessful in expanding its base.

In 1974 PL finally broke apart, or "self-destructed," as Steve Goldstein put it. Steve tells the story of how Milt Rosen, one of the founders of PL, gathered the top leadership of the organization together and said, "I'll tell you the kind of people I want." He pointed to a white wall and said, "I want to point to that wall and say, 'That's a blue wall' and [have the members] . . . say, 'Blue.'" Realizing that PL had begun "the process of Stalinizing us," Steve quit. Soon after, the organization dissolved.

Among the thousands of SDS activists who remained unaffiliated, some chapters disassociated themselves from both sides, declared themselves independent, and continued to work on local issues. But in the aftermath of the convention many other SDS chapters collapsed without the presence of a national center. Doug Knox describes how the Stanford SDS chapter fell apart after the June convention. "The people here felt, 'Well, what the hell do we care. . . . The national office [is] a bunch of jerks; they want to go blow up everything. And there's another group of crazy Maoists that want to be even more far-out. We can just persist at our local level.'" Although the final SDS convention seemed like a "bolt from the blue" to most Stanford members, in fact the national debates quickly penetrated into the local level. Within six months Stanford SDS was polarized and people started to meet separately.

In the months after the convention the Harvard SDS chapter witnessed growing hostility between PL and Weatherman. Michael Kazin decided to quit Weatherman because of the sense of impending violence.

> In my heart of hearts I was very scared. . . . My leaving Weatherman was occasioned more by my fears of killing and being killed, by the sort of . . . Nietzschean violence of PL. . . . We were calling ourselves SDS and . . . we kept them out physically. . . . There was some talk of them crashing the meeting with clubs. . . . We were talking in our Weatherman collective [that] it might come to a shoot out. . . . Things were pretty crazy. . . . 1969, early '70, were not the sanest moments in the history of the American left. . . . I was scared to death, scared of death. I thought, I believe in violence, I believe in revolution, but I don't want to die against PL. I don't want to die killing people from this left sect.[29]

During an all-night meeting Michael convinced his collective to expel him. Before he left, he gave the collective all of his money, about two thousand dollars.

In early 1970 Weatherman went underground and split into small secret cells, each working to bring the war home. With armed struggle as its aim, the Weather Underground began using acts of sabotage and terrorism in order to hasten the revolution. On March 6, 1970, while Weatherman members Terry Robbins and Diana Oughton assembled a bomb in the basement of a townhouse owned by Cathy Wilkerson's father, the bomb exploded, killing Robbins, Oughton, and Ted Gold. Cathy Wilkerson and Kathy Boudin managed to escape unharmed and immediately went underground. For many people "the townhouse" incident marked the final breath of SDS.

## TENSIONS WITHIN YAF
### Ideological Factionalization

YAF, too, suffered from factionalization during the late 1960s. As libertarians distanced themselves from their traditionalist peers, many discovered a growing convergence with sectors of the New Left.

The War   As discussed in chapter 4, the war in Vietnam was one major factor that created a schism between traditionalists and libertarians. Not only the issue of the draft but, increasingly as the 1960s proceeded, the perception that the Vietnam War was misguided, wrong, and even immoral separated libertarians from traditionalists. By 1969 many libertarians and traditionalists found themselves on opposing sides. While libertarians were protesting the draft and demonstrating against the war, traditionalists were rallying in support of U.S. involvement. Traditionalist Lee Edwards was the coordinator of a rally held in Washington on Veterans Day in 1969 to support the men fighting in Vietnam. He recalls,

> Our meeting occurred just a few days before several hundred thousand peaceniks demonstrated in the nation's capital against the war. . . . Our program was prudently balanced, including Republicans and Democrats, conservatives and liberals, a Boy Scout for the Pledge of Allegiance, a beautiful young black girl to lead the Star-Spangled Banner, and a folk singer named Tony Dolan, who later became one of President Reagan's top speechwriters.[30]

Meanwhile libertarians grew more and more hostile to the state's draft of individuals as well as to American involvement in what they saw as an illegal war. In 1969 YAFer Ron Kimberling made a statement declaring he was "opposed to the U.S. imperialist venture in Vietnam, which is being conducted in a manner that seriously undermines freedom for the Vietnamese and for citizens in our own country, who are being subjected to fascism in the name of freedom."[31] This language is strikingly parallel to that of the New Left.[32] Many libertarians participated in moratoriums, teach-ins, and antiwar protests. On some campuses libertarian groups took the lead in organizing sit-ins and demonstrations against

ROTC.[33] Some libertarian YAF chapters even worked with SDS in organizing against the war.

**Government Repression and Police Brutality**   A second dividing line between libertarians and traditionalists concerned government repression and police brutality. While traditionalists remained hostile to the antiwar movement and student protest on campuses and supported measures to maintain order, libertarians were radicalized by the repression and brutality used against protesters (see chapter 4). In 1967 YAFer Bill Steel, for instance, witnessed the police beating demonstrators during a Vietnam War protest at Century City. He was shocked into feeling he had been "supporting the wrong side," and shortly afterward he began campaigning against the draft.[34] This opposition to government further separated libertarians from traditionalists and brought libertarians into common cause with the left.

**The Counterculture**   A third factor that contributed to the widening gulf between libertarians and traditionalists was the counterculture. As discussed in chapter 5, traditionalists abhorred the counterculture while libertarians embraced it both ideologically and in their own lifestyle. In particular, the use of drugs brought libertarians and the left together. It was not only the actual use of drugs but also government repression faced by "freaks" that led to a questioning of authority and cemented bonds between libertarians and the countercultural New Left.

For some activists drugs became a proving ground of their libertarian credentials. Don Ernsberger comments that although he thought the draft was the "most important litmus test," many libertarians, particularly those on the West Coast, viewed the legalization of marijuana as most important.

> There were a lot of libertarians who . . . [had] a basic mental assumption that if you don't smoke marijuana, you're not a libertarian. . . . There was a student from Northwestern University . . . and he was a solid libertarian ideologically, but he wore a jacket and a tie. . . . He was absolutely disinterested in drug use. And there were libertarians . . . who would say, "Don't trust him. He's not one of us. He doesn't even smoke dope" [laughs].

Dave Walter remembers attending libertarian conferences during the late 1960s where people self-consciously flaunted their smoking of marijuana while speakers addressed the group.

In short, there was a growing distrust between libertarians and traditionalists as their interests diverged. While traditionalists viewed libertarians as flag-burning, dope-smoking leftist sympathizers, libertarians viewed traditionalists as law-and-order, drug-suppressing authoritarians who were obsessed with communism at the expense of civil liberties.

## CONVERGENCE OF THE LEFT AND THE RIGHT

At the same time that the gulf between traditionalists and libertarians grew wider, there was a growing convergence between libertarians and sectors of the left. In particular, they had a common hostility toward the state. Libertarians radicalized by opposition to the war, government repression and police brutality, and by state legislation of drugs, began to see government itself as the enemy. This view further exacerbated tensions between traditionalists and libertarians. Whereas traditionalists continued to believe that communism was the main force of evil, libertarians began to feel that the U.S. government and domestic fascism were equal or even more dangerous threats to individual liberty.

As more and more libertarians began to view the state as the enemy, they discovered common ground with the New Left. Both decried the fate of the individual living under the shadow of the corporate state. Both worried that government had become uncontrollable, was veering toward totalitarianism, and was intervening both internationally and domestically in areas it did not belong. Both feared Big Brother, believing the government had no business interfering in people's personal lives. Both believed government, rather than offering solutions, had become part of the essential problem.[35]

Typically, this view of the U.S. government created a schism as more and more libertarians felt alienated from the conservative movement. The late 1960s witnessed accusations by libertarians charging YAF with being run by reactionaries and bigots. The right was accused of being a "wasteland of authoritarianism," bordering on fascism. As Karl Hess, former speechwriter for Barry Goldwater turned libertarian, put it: "To really love this land, you must first learn to loathe this nation and the system for which it stands."[36] In an article in *Playboy* in March 1969, Hess also declared that libertarians should work to end the whole concept of the nation-state and concluded: "The style of SDS so far seems most promising. . . . It is itself loosely knit and internally anti-authoritarian as well as externally revolutionary."[37]

The shared antagonism libertarians and the New Left felt toward cen-

tralized authority was connected to a common belief that people should
control their own lives. Both opposed the growth of bureaucracy and
sought to return power to the individual. Libertarians shared the New
Left ideal of building "a new community which will reaffirm the dignity of the individual in the face of the corporate state."[38] Both sought
to replace the centralized, hierarchical, top-down power structures of
the state with decentralized, self-governing communities. In their critique of bureaucracy both also denounced the "education factory system" by which large universities rendered the individual student a number, a nameless, faceless IBM card. In place of mass society, they called
for a society of decentralized institutions in which individuals participated in the decisions affecting their lives. Both libertarians and the New
Left advocated neighborhood government, local control, and community policing. Both were skeptical of the paternalistic welfare state and
supported self-help and self-determination in poor and black communities. Both sectors also ardently defended civil liberties. They opposed
government restriction of abortion, drug use, pornography, and mutually consensual sexual acts. As libertarian David Friedman put it, "We
believe in a totally free society in which every man can think, say and
smoke what he likes, do business with anyone on any mutually agree-
able terms, and sleep with anyone willing to sleep with him."[39] This attitude, too, revealed the gap between libertarians and traditionalists, as
traditionalists vehemently opposed abortion, gay rights, drug use, and
free love.

    In fact, the stark differences between libertarians and traditionalists
erupted over the issue of flag-burning, which occasioned long and angry
debates within YAF during the late 1960s. Allen Brandstater vividly recalls arguments on the topic.

> We [traditionalists] felt that the muscle and fiber of YAF was be-
> ing challenged by a group that had more in common with the left
> than they did with the traditional right. . . . I remember one con-
> versation . . . we talked about the outrage that some of us felt when
> we'd see leftists in different campuses on TV at night burning the
> American flag. Bill [Steel] took the position . . . "Well, who cares,
> if it's their property. It's only a piece of cloth." I said, "What do
> you mean, it's a piece of cloth? It is emblematic. It's the American
> symbol of this country." . . . It was really that conversation when
> I realized how far afield we had grown in the conservative move-
> ment between the traditionalists and the libertarians. Their view

was, "Well, if you spent nine dollars and you purchased an American flag and you want to burn it, it's your property and you ought to be able to do that. Or if I purchased thirty dollars' worth of heroin with my money and I want to inject it into my veins, I ought to be able to do that." This was really the formative . . . issue which created a festering sore that ultimately led to the major split in the summer of 1969.

As the worlds of libertarians and traditionalists moved farther apart, the worlds of libertarians and the left grew closer together.

## INDIVIDUAL TRANSFORMATIONS

The convergence of left and right is most apparent in the lives of individual activists. Libertarians took varying paths toward the left. Three people's experiences are illustrative. Gus DiZerega's dramatic change began in 1965 during the third meeting of the YAF chapter he organized at the University of Kansas. He describes what happened.

> I'll never forget the meeting. . . . This woman walked in and sat in the back. . . . She had long hair and a short skirt and boots up to here, sort of mid-sixties Peter, Paul, and Mary type garb. Didn't look like a conservative, but she sure looked good! I could tell that she also didn't think too much of what we were saying. And I, to my own admission anyway, had never lost a political discussion ever. So after the meeting was over, knowing full well what I'd hear, I said, "Well, what did you think of the meeting?" "I think you're a bunch of fascists." "How so?" "Fascists believe in big government. You believe in the draft, don't you?" "Well, yeah." "Doesn't the draft mean big government controlling people?" "Well, but we need it to fight the Communists." All of a sudden I'm on the defensive, which I wasn't used to. . . . I figured the best defense when you have an untenable position is a good offense and I said, "Well, you socialists believe in big government." She said, "I'm not a socialist; I'm an anarchist."

At that point conceptual frameworks began "to get real bent" for Gus. He was being "pummeled intellectually" by this woman, who was the secretary of the local SDS chapter. Gus recalls, "This was just too weird; I'd always heard [SDS] believed in big government . . . and here's somebody who said she's an anarchist and then said she believed in free markets. . . . It's like taking intellectual acid, it's what's going on here?" The woman invited Gus to an SDS meeting. So he went and was warmly welcomed. At the time, Gus says, SDS was a warm and decent organization, not in any sense revolutionary. They were pro–civil rights and antiwar. Gus was quite taken with the personal decency of the people he met and contrasted it with the "political machinations and interest in political power" he found in YAF.

Although Gus was drawn to SDS on a personal level, he soon began feeling an intellectual connection as well. When some SDS activists gave Gus literature to read, he was surprised to discover that the case the left made against U.S. involvement in Vietnam was more convincing than what he read on the right. Gus was also introduced to the journal *Left and Right*. First published in 1965, the editors of *Left and Right* were Old Right leaders Murray Rothbard, Leonard Liggio, and George Resch. They started the journal to try to bridge the communication gap between left and right. The journal helped Gus understand the connections in his own beliefs.

Gus secretly began attending SDS meetings. Once the word got out, "the more Republican politician types" in his YAF chapter voted Gus out of being chair. In late 1966 Gus joined SDS.[40]

> I decided I was tired of . . . right-wing politics, tired of that type of ego tripping. I'd viscerally liked the left a good deal more, would stay with them and would argue a pro–free market position, but mostly focus on the antiwar stuff. . . . At that time I'd become pretty much a good orthodox libertarian anarcho-capitalist.

Gus's activities in SDS included antiwar organizing, student rights, and "generalized attacks on the state."

Ironically, about a year later as Gus was passing out antiwar literature on campus, a woman approached him about helping her form a YAF chapter; by now the first one had fallen apart. Because Gus felt SDS had "no sense in economics," and hoping to see a free market case made on campus, Gus helped organize the chapter and even served as secretary-treasurer. The following fall when the former chair of YAF left, owing to succession of office Gus ended up becoming the YAF chair once again. By a quirk of fate at the same time his SDS chapter was experimenting with decentralized leadership and his turn came up, so Gus simultaneously became chair of SDS. He says he didn't find it disturbing to be in this exceptional position. "Mostly it was hard to explain to people. I didn't have much personal difficulty with it. I never felt that I was contradicting myself because I was in each for very clearly defined reasons. . . . My support of the right had solely to do with economics. . . . My support of the left had to do with everything else."

The SDS chapter found Gus's dual role amusing, particularly as many of them identified as anarchists. The YAF people were less sympathetic. Once the national office of YAF found out about Gus's dual position, they wrote to the university to disaffiliate from the campus chapter. Gus says, "I figured I was the first member of YAF to be purged for left deviationism. . . . So at least it gave me probably the sole historical claim to having been simultaneously chairman of both SDS and YAF."

By this point Gus grew weary of traditionalists in YAF. He concluded: "I'm tired of conservatives. I'm tired of their self-righteousness. I'm tired of their intolerance. I'm tired of their authoritarianism. To hell with them." Gus became a libertarian SDSer, supporting the free market, "but in every respect being a pretty orthodox New Lefter and anarchist." In 1968 Gus wrote an article for SDS's publication *New Left Notes,* entitled "Opening to the Right." He called for a dialogue of ideas and coalition between the New Left and the antistatist, anti-imperialist, pro–civil liberties strand of the Old Right, seeing their ideals as "remarkably similar."[41]

Gus continued to be active in SDS until 1969 but then became alienated by the sectarian politics of the national organization. His early sympathy with people on the left who were not "shrill ideologues" had gone, and by the end of the 1960s the faction fights and embrace of violence drove him away. "I tried to talk myself into being a revolutionary on a couple of occasions, but it didn't really stick very well." Once SDS disintegrated, Gus decided he'd had his fill of organized politics and dropped out.

Marick Payton is another YAF member who ended up sympathizing with SDS. Unlike Gus, however, Marick's experience with the left led him away from libertarianism. Marick too was a member of YAF in Kansas, at an earlier time than Gus. While he was in YAF, a man Marick knew who was affiliated with the John Birch Society hired him to go and report back on the SDS conference in Champaign-Urbana. Marick already had friends in SDS and rode with them to the meeting. He recalls traveling to the conference as a "wonderful bohemian" experience, riding with six people in a VW bug, "driving night and day, sleeping on the floor in these big collective gatherings."

Marick made no secret of being a member of YAF. Much to his surprise, the SDS people he met didn't care. Because he was open-minded and interested in learning about the issues, people welcomed him. Marick says at this point SDS had a "love generation trusting spirit . . . before they started being beat up by the cops everywhere and persecuted by the FBI. . . . [They] felt themselves having nothing to hide." The meeting prompted Marick to rethink his beliefs.

> I began to recognize a real common shared moral interest with the New Left. It was my introduction to the New Left in a really personally powerful way . . . living with them . . . and hearing their debates and feeling their commitment to these issues. . . . It took me from being . . . a fairly smug, self-satisfied libertarian rightwinger . . . [to understand] that folks on the left were motivated by highly admirable values, something that the anti-Communist types could never give them. There was that opening in my own thinking to at least appreciate their motivations.

These personal connections changed his perspective, as they had for Gus. Upon his return, Marick realized he was "absolutely sympathetic" to SDS and wrote a report on the conference that "to the Birch folks sounded like I had been absolutely corrupted." Marick felt a kindred spirit with SDS on an array of issues.

> The concern with the rights to full and equal access for minorities, pacifism, antimilitarism, civil liberties issues. . . . The whole gamut of freedom to speak, freedom to publish, freedom to travel anywhere, anytime, to hear anybody talk on any subject . . . those kinds of issues. The military industrial complex was an issue . . . [the] synergy between the big corporate world and America's militarism. . . . [SDS's] concern for the plight of poor people. . . . I wasn't at all interested in their solutions, but the legitimacy of the concerns and . . . the reality that substantial percents of people didn't have . . . a decent shot at the good life, was a shared concern.

Although Marick never joined SDS, he continued to have friends in the organization. He also participated in the antiwar movement. Once he moved to Berkeley, Marick also became involved in activities around People's Park in 1969. He says, "Just viscerally it felt good, opposing the establishment."

Meanwhile Marick had more and more doubts about the property rights aspect of libertarianism. He questioned the assumption made by libertarians simply accepting the existing unequal distribution of property as a starting point. He felt that by accepting disparities of access and privilege, libertarians made "an enormous moral cop-out by refusing to address the issue of how one provides true equality of opportunity." Here, too, Marick felt a common bond with those on the left. Becoming more and more concerned about issues of social justice, he finally broke with the libertarian movement.

Louise Lacey, a third libertarian who discovered common cause with the left, started drifting leftward by the mid-1960s. Louise started a YAF chapter with some friends in San Francisco during YAF's early years, 1960–1961. At that time she was greatly influenced by Ayn Rand and became involved in objectivist circles. In 1963 she quit her job as a secretary and moved to Chicago to take a job as a writer, including writing for an objectivist magazine. During this period she, too, discovered the journal *Left and Right*. Louise found the arguments compelling.

Unlike Gus and Marick, Louise was then abruptly catalyzed leftward by an intense, visceral reaction against the state. In 1966, shortly after Louise returned to California, she began working for the leftist magazine *Ramparts* as research director for the Kennedy assassination project. This was an exciting time for Louise. Although she already identified as an anarchist, Louise became one on a "gut level" through her experiences reading the twenty-six volumes of the Warren Committee Commission testimony on the assassination.

> It was like getting diarrhea in Mexico. It came like that. I ran for the bathroom and I threw up, and then I turned around and sat down and shit. That happened to almost everyone who was there. It was a body experience of purging. I wanted to cry because all of the beauty of our original government [was] lost. . . . It gets uglier and uglier and uglier. . . . It's inevitable. When you get a government this big and organized this way, it's going to be corrupt. . . . I understood . . . that the state will never wither away. . . . Its nature is to keep growing and gathering power. . . . What you have to do to a state is beat it to death, figuratively.

During this time Louise also became involved in the antidraft movement. She came to the conclusion that her views about politics were not that different from leftists' views, the main difference being in how to implement their ideas and whose money would be used to do so. Since neither of these was an issue at *Ramparts*, she supported the magazine 100 percent.

Whereas many libertarian YAFers recognized common cause with the left by the end of the 1960s, less common were SDSers who sought out those in YAF. Doug Knox is one of the few SDS activists who had friendly relations with YAF; he is also one of the few SDSers who identified as libertarian. During the years Doug was involved with Stanford SDS, he recognized his differences from others in SDS. Always an avid reader, he recalls, for example, reading about Ho Chi Minh and his "incredible police state [and] despotism." He tried to talk to other SDSers about his views but found it counterproductive. Because he shared leftist concerns about the military industrial complex, state capitalism, imperialist ventures, and the corporate system, he felt comfortable working with SDS. But Doug never gave up his economic views. He was particularly affected by Ludwig von Mises's book *Socialism,* which systematically critiqued socialism as an economic system. Asked if he discussed these ideas with others in SDS, he replied,

> Not really. I'd casually say something like, "It's not going to work very well. Look at poor communism" or something like that. But . . . most of these people [were] pretty unsophisticated themselves. I mean this is like a romantic myth of North Vietnam. . . . They don't really know what it entailed. It doesn't mean they're not adamant in claiming they do, but they don't really.

Throughout Doug's political evolution he remained skeptical of state power. His work against the draft merely intensified this belief. In his junior year at college, Doug became very interested in Yugoslavia, attracted by the idea of market syndicalism and producers' cooperatives. But after study and analysis, he grew skeptical of this, too.

While active in SDS, Doug also knew people in the Stanford YAF chapter. On occasion they'd invite him to speak, for instance, in debates on U.S. foreign policy. He recalls, "If I was a special guest [at YAF meetings] they would say, 'Understand that Doug Knox is SDS trash but has an interesting point of view here.'" Doug did not find it difficult to cross the political divide. "I thought they were definitely wrong-headed on the Vietnam War but not every tactic or thing done by SDS did I agree with either. So there was room for seeing some merit on both sides."

In fact, much earlier Doug was introduced to the commonalities between the left and the right. While in high school he came across an article by the historian Ronald Hamowy in *The New Republic,* entitled "Left and Right Meet." Hamowy discussed the common threads between radical libertarianism and the New Left: the critique of the welfare state, the hatred of bureaucracy and top-down organization, the ideal of participatory democracy. By chance when Doug came to Stanford he discovered Hamowy was teaching there. Doug called him up to ask how he could become involved in the libertarian movement. Hamowy laughed, explaining there was no libertarian movement on campus. He did tell Doug about a libertarian conference in southern California that Doug attended. Hamowy also encouraged Doug to organize students independently of SDS. By 1969 Doug formed a new group at Stanford, the Radical Libertarian Alliance (see below).

Doug was invited to go to the national conventions of both SDS and YAF in 1969 as a reporter for the *Stanford Daily* and for *The Resistance,* a paper of the draft resistance movement. He decided to go to the YAF convention because he heard that libertarians were going to make a serious attempt at changing the organization. Doug remained active in SDS until the organization fell apart in the aftermath of the 1969 convention.

Another SDSer, Carl Oglesby, was also an important link between libertarians and the left. Many libertarians cited Oglesby's book, *Containment and Change: Two Dissenting Views of American Foreign Policy,* as an inspiration to their thinking.[42] The book aimed at providing a democratic and libertarian foundation for the antiwar movement.[43] Oglesby urged the libertarian right to see common ground with the New Left in their stance against imperialism and militarism. Warning of the "superstate . . . the state rampant, the iron state," he argues that the libertarian tradition of individualism and voluntary association is central to the "Negro freedom movement" and the "student movement against Great Society-Free World imperialism."[44] In his postmortem essay on SDS, "Notes on a Decade Ready for the Dustbin,"[45] Oglesby again found common ground with libertarians, identifying the draft, high taxes, inflation, and "Big Brotherism at all levels of government" as essential social problems.

Carl was well known and admired by many libertarians. Louise Lacey recalls seeing Carl on television in 1966 talking about the left and the right. She was so impressed with him that she called him up and they began corresponding, eventually becoming friends. Carl was also invited to speak at libertarian conferences and meetings during the late 1960s and early 1970s. Calling himself "a bit of an isolationist," Carl also knew and worked with Leonard Liggio and Murray Rothbard in efforts to bring the left and the right together.

In short, sectors of the left and the right converged around a common hostility toward the state, a strong impulse toward personal freedom, and a call for decentralization and local control of neighborhoods, schools, and the police. As Phillip Abbott Luce commented at the time, "The unlimited personal 'libertarianism' of the farthest-out YAF cliques would create a society virtually identical to that envisioned by the New Left's dreamier anarchists."[46]

While libertarians discovered common ground with the left, traditionalists hardened their opposition to SDS. Branding SDS the "Student Demolition Squad," traditionalists escalated actions against the left on campuses during the late 1960s. One strategy initiated by California YAF in 1967, entitled "the Blue Button Campaign," distributed over 100,000 blue buttons to students in colleges to support efforts against those "trying to destroy the university." Ron Docksai explained at the time that the blue button was "a symbol of opposition to the violence and terrorism of our nation's new Nazies [sic]—the radical, left-wing militants who believe in no-one's rights but their own."[47] Declaring, "We have not been heard because we have been studying. Now we must be heard!" YAF urged the public to continue supporting universities, arguing that the majority of students were grateful for the education provided to them.[48] One person who proudly donned the blue button was Governor Ronald Reagan.[49]

Traditionalists also took direct action against universities to stop the left. At Adelphi University, Wayne State, Ohio State, and Wisconsin, YAF brought injunctions or threatened to sue the university for suspending classes during moratoriums, arguing that the suspension was a breach of contract causing YAF members to lose the option of attending classes.[50] Other YAFers demanded the expulsion of students taking part in campus disturbances and the dismissal of faculty who encouraged student unrest.[51] Counter-demonstrations erupted into actual violence between the left and the right at the universities of Wisconsin, Columbia, Yale, Maryland, and elsewhere.[52] Further discussion about actions against the left was planned for the 1969 national YAF convention. The theme of the meeting was "Sock It to the Left."

## THE PURGES BEFORE THE CONVENTION

Even in the months before the August 1969 YAF convention the tensions between libertarians and traditionalists erupted into overt conflict. Two states in particular went through major purges: Pennsylvania and California. Both were strongholds of libertarians. In March 1969 the California board removed co-state chairmen Bill Steel and Dana Rohrabacher from California YAF. Pat Dowd was named temporary state chair. The official reason given for the dismissals was "philosophical conflicts and other incompatibilities with members of the board."[53] In private, journalist Terry Catchpole said YAF leaders told him Steel was removed for "anarchy, libertarianism, and subversion."[54] Two weeks before the convention the California state board of directors discharged Allen Brandstater, charging him with disobeying the state chair, gross fiscal irresponsibility, insubordination, and misuse of funds. In response, national chair Alan MacKay dismissed Dowd along with the entire state board.[55]

Meanwhile libertarians in Pennsylvania organized a slate of candidates to challenge the national slate at the upcoming convention. Don Ernsberger, one of the organizers behind this effort, began sending out a newsletter so people could exchange ideas about what was going to happen at the convention. By summer his list included about two hundred libertarians across the country. Don also sent out a letter to YAF supporters explaining the position of libertarians. Assuring his readers that libertarians would only use democratic procedures to change YAF, Don wrote,

> This letter is to inform you that the Libertarian Caucus is not about to seek to ruin YAF. In fact the very purpose of our effort is to build YAF into an even stronger Pro-Freedom organization. Our purpose is not to split YAF into two ideological warring camps but rather to make the National organization into a fair coalition of Traditional Conservatives and Libertarians, all who are working for the same general goal—A Free Nation.[56]

The hope that traditionalists and libertarians could work together peacefully was short-lived. In July the national board removed Dave Walter as state chair of Pennsylvania YAF. The state chair was elected by delegates at the state convention; libertarians predominated in Pennsylvania. Between conventions, however, the state chair could be removed unilaterally. Dave Walter comments, "When it became obvious that I was backing the libertarian slate at the '69 convention, they just removed me and put Jay Parker in charge."

In Jay Parker's opinion, many of these libertarians, people whom he had initially brought into YAF, had gone too far. "When these individuals became antitraditional and only pro–Ayn Rand, and then just beyond the pale, it just got out of hand. . . . No one is more of a fierce individualist than I was back then, but I believed in an ordered society, and I believe in God. So that was a rub as well."

Many libertarians believed the purges were part of a national effort by traditionalists to take over YAF. According to Sheldon Richman, in every state where there was a libertarian, they were forcing him out and putting in someone that the national organization approved of. "It was motivated by ideology. They didn't want the libertarians in leadership positions. . . . It threatened their own plans and they associated it with . . . being close to leftism because it was permissive."

Don Ernsberger describes the tactics he witnessed as traditionalists maneuvered to attain their agenda.

> We knew what happened in New York was going to happen again; that there were all these clubs brought in that were . . . paper clubs, clubs that were basically thrown together because there was a convention coming up. . . . In Philadelphia we [libertarians] had . . . the YAF office for the city . . . but there was also a group of people called Edmund Burke YAF . . . in the northeast corner of the city, all Catholics, all real traditional conservatives. . . . They mailed into the national office a computer list of the entire zip code 191 and they said, "Here's our members." . . . The national office was conservative and they gave them the city. . . . We actually got affidavits from people saying, "I'm not a member of this group; I've never heard of them" and we took it to St. Louis. . . . At one point . . . we had this big fight over delegations and we produced evidence and had tape recordings of people saying that they . . . never heard of this group. But when the final vote came . . . the vote was done by the national committee . . . and so they threw our delegation out.

Clearly, ideological differences were the main motivation for the purges, but traditionalists were also concerned about practical matters. The participation of libertarian YAFers in antiwar demonstrations, their allegiance to the counterculture, and their perceived callousness over the burning of the flag did not bode well for the organization. Traditionalists were worried about YAF's image and how aberrant acts would affect fund-raising. Don Ernsberger says at the time libertarians thought it was all ideology, but looking back there was another element.

> There were people who ran YAF who realized that the financial base of that organization was primarily older people who were conservatives. When they wrote a check out for $100 to Young Americans for Freedom, their image was, "My money's going to go to Washington and it's going to support some clean-cut, God-fearing, patriotic young kids who are on these campuses with the evils of

leftism everywhere, and they're there with their flag and they're fighting for what I believe in." So the structural issue that we minimized . . . was could YAF survive if it came out as a libertarian organization? Or would it suddenly lose its funding? There are people who I see now, a lot of the old YAF people . . . who still argue that the reason we had to be purged was . . . for the health of the organization [so that] we did not appear like a bunch of dope-smoking, long-haired aberrations of conservatism.

Traditionalist Mitch Petry agrees that YAF was protective of its image.

To the extent [libertarians] talked about unifying with SDS on Vietnam . . . there was no chance for us to work with them. . . . We had a very big organization. . . . None of us on the board were on salary, but we traveled to different campuses, we had a big organization, we had a regular staff. So money needed to be raised for these things. The money came from donors, contributors, and it would be just impossible to explain to them why we were joining with a group that was involved with SDS. . . . To explain it that way was really tough politically.

Given the ideological conflict, the purges, and the concern over YAF's image, traditionalist Mike Thompson says the leadership of YAF knew ahead of time there was going to be a confrontation at the convention: "We had already taken the action to get rid of them [the libertarians]. . . . We had already taken some of those actions of dechartering chapters. . . . What St. Louis was, was their challenge to us." The challenge proved to be fatal for libertarians in YAF.

## THE 1969 YAF CONVENTION

Among the twelve hundred members attending the 1969 YAF convention, held in St. Louis from August 28 to 31, an estimated 20 to 40 percent were libertarians.[57] There were two organized groups of libertarians. The Anarcho-Libertarian Alliance, led by Karl Hess's son, Karl Hess IV, included about fifty to one hundred members. They arrived with black flags unfurled. The Libertarian Caucus, led by Don Ernsberger and Dana Rohrabacher, claimed about three hundred members.[58]

Dave Schumacher attended the convention as part of the Virginia delegation as an unaffiliated libertarian. He felt YAF had detached itself "from what it really should be" and that the organization was inconsistent.

Over time YAF had become more anxious, more feverish, more re-actionary. . . . When I was first associated with it, there was a lot of emphasis on economic freedom and libertarian values. . . . YAF people always [were] waving the flag and talking about Jefferson. . . . In fact, there's a lot of allusions in YAF's literature and their . . . organizational culture to 1776, the Liberty Bell and so on. . . . They obviously just really were getting away from that. . . . There was something wrong.

Dave was relieved to find other libertarian YAFers who shared his views.

Other people had come to the same conclusion. You know that movie . . . *Close Encounters of the Third Kind?* You know how everybody goes to that same point in Wyoming? That's the best way that I can describe it, that people all on their own, all of a sudden saying, "Hey" . . . the same kind of feelings and converging on the same point. So when I went to St. Louis with a group from Virginia and Washington, we all felt it was kind of celebratory . . . because we felt finally somebody is trying to . . . bring YAF to [its] senses.

Don Ernsberger says from the start there was a noticeable difference between libertarians and traditionalists attending the convention.

The typical young conservative at St. Louis wore a suit and tie, had pretty short hair, probably recognized grass if they smelled it, but probably [was] not in any way involved with drug use, thought of themselves as, "If drafted, I'll go and kill Communists." . . . And most of them were probably totally unfamiliar with Bob Dylan songs and things like that. We [libertarians] used to play guitars and banjos. So if you looked at the meeting of our group and the meeting of their group, they were night and day.

On August 28, several hours before the opening session of the convention, a copy of a letter by Murray Rothbard circulated through the crowds. The letter was addressed to libertarians urging them "to leave a house of false friends for they are your enemies." Rothbard lambasted the right for being "run by ex-Communists and monarchists cloak[ed in] authoritarian and neo-fascist policies." Referring to the police brutality at the 1968 Democratic Convention, Rothbard declared,

When Mayor [Richard] Daley's cops clubbed and gassed their way through Chicago last year against unarmed demonstrators, the only libertarian reaction was to revile Daley and the cops and to support the rights of the demonstrators. . . . Our stand should be on the . . . side with the people, with the citizenry, and against the State and its hired goon squads.

He ended the letter, "Why don't you leave now and let the 'F' in YAF stand then for what it has secretly stood for all along—'fascism'?"[59]

Meanwhile, traditionalists were disturbed by the presence of anarchist libertarians. Mitch Petry remembers being very antagonistic to them because they adopted the word libertarian. "We didn't see them as libertarian. We saw them as anarchists. . . . At the time David Friedman, son of Milton Friedman, was involved with that group. I remember talking with him at length and great disagreements we had over their using terminology which in retrospect seems so trivial, but at the time was so important to us." Rumors that Karl Hess—not a scheduled speaker—would address the convention also stirred up traditionalists.

Although scattered groups of libertarians refused to stand at the recitation of a prayer or during the pledge to the flag, no animosity surfaced until right before William F. Buckley was introduced to speak. Then the most dramatic evidence of factionalism occurred when Pat Dowd, former California state chair, was prevented from seating himself on stage next to Buckley. A delegation of California libertarians protested, demanding that Dowd be seated. To traditionalist cries of "We want Buckley!" libertarians chanted, "We want Hess!" Traditionalists then chanted, "Sock it to the Left!" to which libertarians responded, "Sock it to the State."[60]

When Buckley finally did speak, he commended the delegates for their healthy disagreement. He also called for a reaffirmation of traditional conservatism, saying that freedom is for those who agree to live within the framework of our traditions. Those who deny such traditions, Buckley proclaimed, lose the right to freedom.[61] In stark contrast, Hess, who spoke later that night under the St. Louis arch, denounced the right for abandoning the rights of the individual. According to Hess, the chief threat to liberty in the United States was not the radical left but the near-omnipotent U.S. government. He concluded that libertarians on the right must join forces with the New Left.[62]

Tensions escalated the next day when libertarian delegates ran into difficulty receiving their credentials to admit them to the voting sessions. Dave Walter recalls the measures taken to restrict libertarians:

[I remember] battles on the floor . . . challenging [the] paper chapter delegates. . . . Some chapters had libertarians and some of their people couldn't come and so the trads brought in any old person to serve. I think it was David Friedman who stood up at the convention and said, "This guy's not in our chapter. He doesn't live there." . . . [But during] the voice vote they accept[ed] him as a delegate. . . . If they had just said, "Look, we got the votes" and had been nice . . . maybe the split wouldn't have happened. But there was so much hostility generated by these tactics. . . . It was obvious that if Jesus Christ had walked in and said he was a libertarian delegate, they would have shouted him down [laughs]. . . . There were people at that convention who probably had been in YAF three days. . . . [But] since they controlled the credentials . . . they'd get anybody they wanted in as a delegate. And they did.

SDSer Doug Knox, who was covering the convention for two papers and felt closest to the anarcho-libertarians, comments on the costs of such tactics. "It was very vicious. These people [traditionalists] later became the hatchet men of the Republican Party and they were very good at it. But a lot of people get bruised in the process. . . . Meanwhile the established traditionalists . . . were winning everything essentially."

One libertarian candidate who ran for the national board was nominated as "an enemy of the state." His platform included declarations that "the police today . . . are becoming armed forces training not to defend the people and their property, but to defend the politicians, their prerogatives, and state-capitalism" and ended with the leftist slogan All Power to the People.[63] He was soundly defeated as were all other libertarian candidates. The entire traditionalist slate was elected to the national board.

The libertarian platform resolutions were also voted down. Resolutions calling for immediate withdrawal from Vietnam, legalization of marijuana, and denunciation of domestic fascism were defeated while traditionalists successfully passed resolutions calling for an end to East-West trade, support for South Africa and Rhodesia, victory in Vietnam, opposition to campus radicals, and domestic law and order.[64]

Libertarians also were frustrated in their effort to change the wording of the Sharon Statement. They proposed adding "domestic statism" to "international communism" as the twin menaces to individual liberty.[65] Sheldon Richman remarks,

We wanted to *add* to [the Sharon Statement] "domestic statism" and we couldn't get them to consider that. . . . We thought it was a deep philosophical debate. They saw it as simply a power struggle . . .

it was a concession they didn't need to make. They had the votes. They controlled all the key posts. . . . They were also responsible to some of the elders, like Buckley, and it would have been a bad sign. . . . And if you look where they are today, they've all fulfilled their dreams. They wanted to be Republican operatives. . . . So they weren't going to jeopardize their careers. . . . It was always . . . a career thing for them. Look what David Keene is now . . . he's the head of the ACU [American Conservative Union], he's now the consultant around Dole's campaign. . . . For them to acquiesce . . . to say there was something that was on a par with the menace of international communism . . . would have tarnished their reputations with the people that were more important to their careers, the older people.

Alan MacKay conveys the traditionalist perspective:

There was discussion about changing the Sharon Statement . . . and my attitude on that was, It's pretty good; it isn't perfect but it's pretty good. And if you start to fuss with it, you're going to redo the whole thing, throw out everything that we had all these years. It is a broad statement of conservative principles and anybody who is uncomfortable with it doesn't belong in YAF.

Despite the libertarian losses, newly elected national chair David Keene assured libertarians they still had a place in YAF and promised no more purges. At the same time Keene denounced the faction of "self-styled anarcho-libertarians" and said they should decide whether to remain in YAF or join SDS.[66] Despite Keene's assurances, many libertarians felt defeated. Sheldon Richman says, "The libertarians pretty much got smashed. . . . All the candidates lost. . . . It was a turning point because we realized that the libertarians weren't going to be ever at home with the conservatives. They didn't really want [us] there." In particular, Sheldon recalls the deep animosity aimed at libertarians at the convention:

There was this big exhibition hall where people had booths. . . . Anytime . . . it was obvious that the libertarians were gathering . . . the trads . . . would start to taunt the libertarians, hollering, "Laissez-fairies" [laughs]. And claiming that civil disobedience was bad. Of course, every night they were doing under-age drinking in Missouri, so they didn't seem to be all that careful about obeying the law, which was something we pointed out to them. They said we were drug users. It was the typical stuff that the worst sort of conservative engages in when he's near a libertarian.

Dave Walter also remembers the taunts of traditionalists:

There was open homophobia . . . talk about queers. Everybody who was against the war was a queer. . . . It's strange because Bob Bauman was chairman of YAF when I joined and I recall him as one of these holier than thou types, very moralistic, married to a very straight Catholic girl, sex was evil and all this sort of stuff. . . . They were chanting, "Laissez-fairies!" So if you were against the war, you were obviously homos. [Bob Bauman later became a member of Congress and, during his time in office, announced his homosexuality.]

The issue that finally broke the convention into two hostile camps was draft resistance. Two draft resolutions were proposed. The first, called the Goldwater plan, promoted a volunteer army and the gradual abolition of the draft. The other resolution advocated active resistance to the draft by illegal or legal evasion.[67] The delegates endorsed the Goldwater plan but traditionalists added a clause to condemn draft resistance and the burning of draft cards. At that point libertarian Dave Schumacher stepped forward, grabbed a microphone in the center of the floor, and announced that it was the right of every individual to defend himself from violence, including state violence. He pulled out his draft card and, "holding it aloft like the torch of liberty—YAF's official symbol," Dave burned his draft card in the middle of the convention floor.[68] The meeting erupted into an angry mob, as traditionalists shouted, "Kill the Commies!" Dave recalls,

I was surprised. I really wasn't prepared for the viciousness of the traditional Republicans. . . . It really brought . . . into focus for me that they really didn't have any tolerance for personal liberty, freedom of speech. In many ways it was just like the young Communists—very orthodox and if you deviate from the orthodoxy, you are not only socially ostracized, but they [attack you]. . . . Actually I got out okay, because there was a ring of people around me in the auditorium who really were assaulted. When they saw what was going to happen, they . . . [tried] to prevent it from happening.

Traditionalists quickly passed a resolution expelling Dave from YAF. Traditionalist Alan MacKay recalls the scene: "I was presiding. I called for immediate revocation of his membership. . . . The convention over-whelmingly voted in favor of doing that. Although Milton Friedman's son [David] . . . was furious at me . . . screaming . . . 'You can't do this! You can't do this!' I just really thought that it was time to grow up."

Three hundred and fifty libertarians suddenly reacted in violent opposition to their former conservative allies. As Jerome Tuccille put it, "After a few confused moments of punching and shoving and general commotion, the division was complete. There could be no turning back."[69] Another anarchist libertarian, J. M. Cobb, who drove to St. Louis following a Phil Ochs/Rennie Davis rally in support of the Chicago Eight, commented, "The draft card burning and the violent reaction to it was the most significant event of the convention because it proved to every libertarian that he could not make common cause with the traditionalist conservatives except on libertarian grounds and libertarian issues. YAF cared more about obeying the laws than about ending the draft."[70]

While some libertarians argued they should remain in YAF as a moderating influence, others called for a united front with the anti-Marxist left in fighting against state capitalism and for social justice.[71] One group of libertarians stormed out of the meeting, denouncing domestic fascism and calling for resistance to the Vietnam War, legalization of marijuana, and unity with SDS.

Later that night while libertarians met, crowds of traditionalists stomped through the floors of the hotel shouting, "Kill the libertarians!" Tuccille recalls, "Suddenly it dawned on the minority opposition exactly who their main enemy really was. The New Left? New Leftists had never demanded the blood of the anti-statist right."[72] Former libertarian moderates now painted placards with slogans such as "Smash the State!" and "I Am an Enemy of the State!" Later in the night members of the Libertarian Caucus and the Anarcho-Libertarian Alliance met with two anarchist chapters of SDS to set up a communications network. The loosely knit organization was called the Society for Individual Liberty (SIL).[73] Dave Walter comments on the need for a new organization.

It was strange getting to St. Louis and finding out that we were large enough that we could be independent. Right up until the end of the convention, we were trying to extract promises. We would stay and work [in YAF] if this, this, and this happened. David Keene had made a number of promises. He would visit Pennsylvania and California and try to be a mediator in the disputes, [but] he never did. Plus when David Schumacher burned his draft card, a riot almost ensued. And the laissez-fairy stuff and the hostility from the trads. It was obvious that YAF couldn't survive with both of us there.

Libertarian Rob Tyler says the convention was his last attempt to work with conservatives.

I wore a suit for the last time in years in 1969, hustling for votes, going from delegation to delegation, trying to be a reasonably moderate libertarian when I bristled with that term. Then finally when we got our asses so badly kicked, put on my nice blue jeans and my blue-collar work shirt so they could really know where I was at. . . . We lost and that was it for YAF.

Pausing a moment, he reflects, "I guess I was going through a lot of growing up . . . and a lot of experimenting. Showed up for the convention, made a shot there, didn't get high for a few days, and tried to appear straight. And then I was lost, I was out of the womb." In the weeks and months after the convention, in fact many libertarians, both voluntarily and involuntarily, were cast out of the womb.

## THE AFTERMATH OF THE CONVENTION

### The Purges

Immediately following the convention the national board met and moved to expel any YAF member who burned his draft card or who had dual membership in SDS and YAF. Pat Dowd, one of the few libertarians remaining on the board, objected to the proposal, stating that some YAF members joined SDS in order to educate its members. Despite his objection, the resolution passed. It read: "The National Board of Directors declares that membership in the SDS is inconsistent with the Sharon Statement of YAF and that such membership will be grounds for expulsion from YAF."[74] At a subsequent meeting a similarly worded resolution also declared anarchism inconsistent with the Sharon Statement and grounds for expulsion.[75]

In the weeks and months after St. Louis traditionalists systematically purged libertarians from YAF. Several libertarians, including Karl Hess IV, were removed for activities "contrary to the interests of YAF."[76] Despite Keene's pledge that no purges would take place before he visited California, in October the national board revoked the membership of

California libertarian leaders, including Bill Steel, Dana Rohrabacher, Ron Kimberling, Rod Manis, and John Schureman.[77] Keene also suspended the active status of twenty-six chapters. Members of these chapters immediately held a press conference and announced their "liberation" from YAF.[78]

Soon afterward Pat Dowd was also removed from California YAF, charged with "not representing all of the state and not working with the staff." In a letter to YAFer Wayne Thorburn, Dowd wrote that he was shocked to be ousted after dedicating over five years to YAF and always acting "in good faith." He felt disillusioned and bitter about the organization.

> Maybe I am just too idealistic in believing that actors in the political game will deal reasonably and justly with each other when power is at stake. . . . The last National Board meeting dismayed me greatly. The Board members acted like chauvanistic [sic] madmen purging people right and left for no other reason than they disagreed with the individual's brand of conservatism.

Dowd condemned the board for its action, saying it "reeks of thought control" and asked, "Is YAF to demand a loyalty oath on every word and phrase of the Sharon Statement?"[79] These are indeed ironic words, given that loyalty oaths were a main impetus to the founding of the organization. Being purged from YAF became a badge of honor. Fellow libertarian Berl Hubbell wrote Dowd at the end of October, stating: "I was beginning to worry that the NO [national office] didn't think I was important enough to purge. I'm glad they salvaged my ego."[80]

Mitch Petry, who was involved in the national leadership at the time, says he felt regret at participating in the purges but was also disturbed by libertarian actions.

> Frankly, I was personally bothered by [the purges]. . . . Anyone who is involved in [an] organization where you . . . bring people in, the idea of suspending memberships bothers you. [But it also] bothered me that they used the name libertarian [to explain the purges], because they were suspended . . . for draft card burning and other things. There was a huge hotel bill we had to pay in . . . St. Louis by some destructive attempts to set rooms on fire. . . . It [was because of] criminal activity . . . rather than violations of the Sharon Statement . . . that we took action. But in retrospect it's really tragic when this sort of thing happens.

One of the unintended consequences of the purges was the birth of the libertarian movement.

## The Formation of the Libertarian Movement

In reaction to the convention and to the subsequent purges, dozens of libertarian chapters in California, Texas, Pennsylvania, and other states began pulling out of YAF. About half of the YAF chapters in California resigned or let their charters lapse.[81] The Stanford chapter, headed by Harvey Hukari, quit in a flourish when Harvey and fifteen other members burned their YAF cards in front of TV cameras with the ashes falling into a symbolic lily-white coffin.[82] Renamed the Free Campus Movement, the members proclaimed that they wanted to continue working within the conservative movement but "no longer wished to associate themselves with the racist, authoritarian personalities who dominated YAF."[83] Ironically, the Stanford chapter had been honored at the St. Louis convention as an outstanding club.[84]

Meanwhile SDSer Doug Knox organized the Radical Libertarian Alliance (RLA) at Stanford. One of the flyers rallying people to the group began with a quote from the Port Huron Statement: "We regard men as infinitely precious."[85] A campus publication, "The Last Radical Guide to Stanford," described the RLA as being part of "a nation-wide network of anarchists who are working to end the Indochina war and destroy the U.S. government. As radical decentralists, they seek to abolish the state and put all social organization on the basis of voluntary association."[86]

Other YAF chapters also formed new libertarian organizations. Fifteen chapters in the Los Angeles area charged YAF with being dominated by "reactionaries and bigots" and formed the Student Libertarian Alliance. Among other things it opposed increased taxes, punitive drug laws, harassment of hippies, and "the takeover of consumer-oriented enterprises by the 'military-industrial complex.'"[87] At American University the YAF chapter was taken over by libertarians who used YAF funds to publish a magazine that included pro-Weatherman articles by Karl Hess.[88] The Temple University YAF, headed by Sheldon Richman, decided to drop its affiliation with YAF and rename itself the Temple Libertarian Alliance.

In addition, many former chapters joined the Society for Individual Liberty, the organization created in St. Louis.[89] In September following the convention Don Ernsberger appeared on TV, announced his resignation from YAF, and reiterated his pledge to work with SDS at Penn State.[90] He and Dave Walter became the directors of SIL, with head-quarters in Philadelphia.[91] By 1970 SIL had 103 chapters on campuses around the country as well as two in Canada and one each in Sweden, India, and Australia.[92] SIL coordinated libertarian groups around the country and also gave the first forum to David Nolan, the catalyst be-hind the Libertarian Party, which was founded in 1971. Nolan had been active in Young Republicans at MIT and in California. Although he was not a member of YAF, many ex-YAF libertarians became involved in the early years of the Libertarian Party.

The libertarian movement was blossoming in different places and in dif-ferent ways. The Student Libertarian Action Movement (SLAM) was cre-ated in Arizona, with chapters in Georgia and Colorado.[93] An anarcho-capitalist group at Wesleyan adopted the principle of alliance with the New Left and renamed itself the Earl Francis Memorial Chapter of SDS, vowing to fight against Marxism within SDS.[94]

By 1970 there was also an array of journals for libertarians to read. *Left and Right: A Journal of Libertarian Thought* was probably the most influential among activists. In the 1965 inaugural issue Old Right lead-ers Murray Rothbard, Leonard Liggio, and George Resch wrote: "The present day categories of 'left' and 'right' have become misleading and obsolete and . . . the doctrine of liberty contains elements correspond-ing with both the contemporary left and right."[95] In addition to several libertarians in YAF who discussed the importance of the journal, SDSers Doug Knox and Carl Oglesby also mention its role in their thinking. Carl Oglesby comments, "*Left and Right* was the most influential . . . it told me what I wanted to hear . . . it's hard to exaggerate how important it was to me. . . . Murray [Rothbard] and Leonard [Liggio] gave me the philosophical foundation . . . my bearings."[96] In addition to *Left and Right*, other libertarian publications included *The Match* (published by SLAM), *Man and State*, Ronald Hamowy's *New Individual Review*, and *The Libertarian Forum*.

## Meetings of the Left and the Right

At the end of 1969 and throughout 1970 libertarians also initiated meet-ings of the left and the right. Rampart College sponsored a left-right con-ference in 1970. Karl Hess spoke, urging support for the Black Panthers and opposition to state repression. One of the other speakers was Carl

Oglesby. Oglesby spoke about how the New Left was dominated by a vanguardist rhetoric. Trying to bridge the gap between left and right, Oglesby declared, "In the past you've always wound up calling somebody you disagreed with a pinko or Marxist or fellow-traveler. Well, I'll tell you in advance. I'm all of those things. So that's out of the way. Now we can talk." Many activists from the right were enchanted with Oglesby's honesty.[97] Meanwhile Dana Rohrabacher and Rob Tyler also began organizing to bring together the left and the right. In the aftermath of the convention they issued a public statement repudiating the "conservative establishment." Rohrabacher, in an indictment of the right, declared, "We recognize the fact that the U.S. in its economic and social manipulation of individuals' lives and property, is reminiscent of fascist tyrannies of the past. . . . We side with classical revolutionary 'rightists' such as Albert Jay Nock who said, 'The antithesis of radical is superficial.'"[98]

During 1969 and 1970 Dana and Rob initiated a series of left-right conferences at the University of Southern California. Rob recalls the thinking behind these meetings:

> We encouraged people to leave YAF. We had these annual conferences at USC—Psychology of Freedom, the Left/Right Festival of Liberation, bringing in the left. Victimless crime was one theme. . . . Ed Royce, [who] is now a state senator, was going to those things.[99] And a guy named Steve Simms was flying down from Idaho to go to these; he's now a U.S. senator from Idaho. . . . We had Carl [Oglesby] at our Left/Right Festival of Liberation. We really went out of the way to actively recruit . . . people in the left that we could identify with. . . . It was a genuine dialogue that we initiated. We also had a debate between Tom Hayden and David Friedman.

The Left-Right Festival of Mind Liberation, held in March 1970, was one of the most successful events they planned. Five hundred delegates met to discuss possibilities for right-left cooperation. Besides Carl Oglesby, leftist Paul Goodman also spoke, along with representatives of the libertarian right. Dana remembers the ideals of the festival, the hope of forming a coalition between libertarians on the right and the pro-freedom elements on the left.

> There was an anarchist element in the left who we met over the years and had discussions with. They were essentially anti-private property but also anti-government. And we were pro–private property and anti-government. . . . In fact, at one point the libertarians

felt that we were going to be like the New Left; it was going to be a mass movement of libertarians and that we were going to be the vanguard . . . in this new freedom movement. But that never worked out; [it] was just unrealistic. That was just pipe dreams. . . . But the discussions were very interesting and at a very high level of intellectual sophistication. Most of the people I work with right now in Congress—very, very few of them understand Marxism to the degree I understand it. Because they never got . . . into the different levels of argument . . . to understand why people believe what they believe.

The common ground of the discussion was libertarianism. Libertarians of both the right and left believed in the value of individual liberty and thought the government had no business interfering in individual lives. Both worried that government was becoming uncontrollable and feared the state was becoming totalitarian. Both believed in returning power to people at a local level, calling for a radical decentralization of government.[100] As we'll see in chapter 8, although the ideal of uniting the right and the left into a mass movement never materialized, libertarians and New Leftists followed similar paths in their lives after the 1960s.

### The End of the Sixties

The blowing up of the townhouse in 1970 signified the demise of SDS, yet YAF survived the 1960s and still exists today. In 1970 YAF celebrated its tenth anniversary at a banquet in Hartford, Connecticut. Awards were given to William F. Buckley, Barry Goldwater, and Ronald Reagan. Among other festivities, the audience joined in singing "Mine Eyes Have Seen the Horrors of the Militant Extreme."[101]

In 1980 YAF held a twentieth-anniversary event at the Grand Ballroom of the Mayflower Hotel in Washington to review the events of the past two decades, to pay respect to conservative leaders, and to cheer the hoped-for victory of presidential candidate Ronald Reagan. Writing about the event for *National Review,* M. Stanton Evans, the author of the Sharon Statement, commented that while New Left groups had all but vanished, YAF was still full of energy. YAF's conservative beliefs, once considered hopelessly romantic, were now in the mainstream. He wrote, "On the evidence of this anniversary, the effort has been far more successful than any of us back there at Sharon could possibly have imagined."[102] YAF had indeed come of age.

## CONCLUSION

Both YAF and SDS encountered parallel processes of ideological strain and conflict during the late 1960s. Given the ardent attachment activists felt to each movement, along with the radicalization of both libertarians and leftists, it is not surprising that factionalization occurred. The transformation of ideology, combined with the rapid succession of historical events of the late 1960s, and in the case of the left, increased repression of protesters, meant that activists in each organization felt the need to stake claims, stand firm, and close ranks.

On the one hand these social movements offer an enlarged sense of self, infusing activists' world with meaning and providing a sense of worth and excitement as individuals join with others in a community to create social change. Shared beliefs and experiences forge bonds of solidarity within the movement. On the other hand, group bonds can become stifling. As William Gamson states, "At some point, social support can become social pressure."[103] With the growing rifts within SDS and YAF, differences became conflicts and the thrust toward ideological purity prevailed. In the extreme, some activists—particularly on the left—went through a complete transformation of identity as the collective identity of the group superseded all other selves, providing the sole meaning in life as politics permeated everyday life. Such "conversion experiences" signify a change in individuals' "sense of ultimate grounding"[104] so that experiences, both past and present, that were formerly interpreted in one way "are now given new meaning and rearranged, frequently in ways that previously were inconceivable, in accordance with the new master frame."[105] Rather than enlarging the self, in these cases politics engulfs the self.

As a result of the growing divisions within each organization, both SDS and YAF suffered from tumultuous national conventions in 1969. For SDS the conflict ended in the dissolution of the organization, the splintering of the left, and eventually the decline of this generational unit. For libertarians, the short-run effect of their split with traditionalists was being purged from YAF; yet in the long run, libertarians built a strong independent movement. Meanwhile, for traditionalists their triumph not only left YAF intact but also began their ascent as a generational force of the 1970s and 1980s.

ABOVE: Mike and Kit Thompson with Senator Barry Goldwater, 1976. Courtesy of Mike and Kit Thompson.

LEFT: Mike Thompson in the 1990s. Courtesy of Mike Thompson.

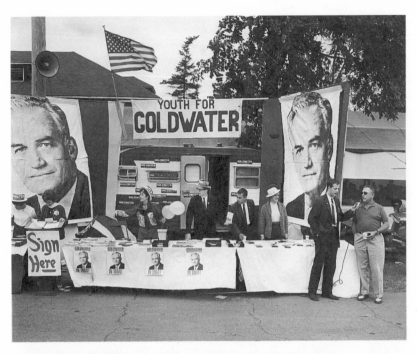

TOP: Emmy Lewis (at left, in the straw hat) campaigning for Goldwater in 1964. *Detroit News* File Photo.

BOTTOM: Emmy Lewis meeting with President Reagan in 1995. Courtesy of Emmy Lewis

ABOVE: Harvey Hukari speaking at a student government hearing in the 1960s. Courtesy of Harvey Hukari.

LEFT: Harvey Hukari in the 1990s. Courtesy of Harvey Hukari.

TOP: Sharon Presley in 1965. Courtesy of Sharon Presley.

BOTTOM: Sharon Presley in the 1990s. Courtesy of Sharon Presley.

LEFT: Louise Lacey
in 1966. Courtesy
of Louise Lacey.

BELOW: Louise
Lacey in the 1990s.
Courtesy of
Louise Lacey.

LEFT: Lee and Anne
Edwards in 1968. Courtesy
of Lee and Anne Edwards.

BELOW LEFT: Lee Edwards
with President Reagan
in 1981 to present a copy
of Lee's book, *Ronald
Reagan: A Political Biography.* Courtesy of Lee
Edwards.

Anne Edwards, member of board of directors of United Seniors Association, Inc., with Speaker of the House Newt Gingrich, 1996. Photograph © 1996 JoAnn Simmons-Swing; courtesy of United Seniors Association, Inc.

ABOVE: Allen Brandstater, executive director of California YAF, introducing then-governor Ronald Reagan at YAF's 1968 California state convention. Courtesy of Allen Brandstater.

LEFT: Allen Brandstater in the 1990s. Courtesy of Allen Brandstater.

ABOVE: Kathy Rothschild protesting against IBM in St. Louis, 1968. Courtesy of Kathy Rothschild.

LEFT: Kathy Rothschild with her husband, Rick, in 1998. Courtesy of Kathy and Rick Rothschild.

TOP LEFT: Dave Schumacher attending a conference on "Overcoming World Hunger" in 1969. Courtesy of Dave Schumacher.

TOP RIGHT: Dave Schumacher with Karl Hess during a retreat in Fort Collins, Colorado, 1987. Courtesy of Dave Schumacher.

BOTTOM: Dave Schumacher in the 1990s. Courtesy of Dave Schumacher.

# CHAPTER EIGHT

# PICKING UP THE PIECES: THE 1970S

Given the tumultuous and apparently ceaseless events of the 1960s, how did activists fare during the 1970s? How did they integrate these dramatic experiences into their lives and carry on their politics? And what kinds of work did they do? Traditionalists, libertarians, and leftists faced different situations in the aftermath of the 1960s. The left went through further conflicts and splits during the 1970s as leftists coped with loss of membership in a group that had been their home for years. With the demobilization of their movement's organization, libertarians too had to forge a way during the 1970s. But, unlike SDS, the libertarian movement was blossoming at this time, offering a new place for libertarian activists. Meanwhile, traditionalists inherited YAF and continued on, facing a smoother path during the 1970s in terms of their politics and work lives.

Despite these differences, politics remained central to the identity of the majority of activists on both the left and the right throughout the 1970s. Identification as an activist was a part of daily life, not only through a continuing commitment to politics, but also in choices about work and lifestyle.

## PATHWAYS OF SDS MEMBERS THROUGH THE 1970S
### Politics

The majority of SDS and YAF activists remained politically active during the 1970s. For those on the left, the disintegration of SDS meant that activists channeled their energy into other groups and issues. Some activists found another organization that embodied their beliefs and transferred their commitment and skills to this group. Sue Jhirad, for instance, began the decade involved in antiwar work and the women's movement. By the time the war ended, Sue had received her doctorate in literature from Harvard and was teaching at MIT, a position she held for two years. She began to reevaluate the direction of her life and decided she wanted her work to be directly tied to her politics. Sue had felt for a long time that one of the weaknesses of the left was that it hadn't reached the working class, that it had been more of an intellectual middle-class movement. Some of her close friends were living in a commune and were involved in a Marxist study group; they concluded that going to work in factories was important political work. Sue became active in this group, which eventually became part of the October League, a Marxist-Leninist sect. The group's long-term goal was to form a working-class Marxist-Leninist political party; the short-term goals were to organize unions and push for more democracy within existing unions. Sue quit her job at MIT and went to work at a sweatshop in an electronics company. She remained in the group for nine years, during which time she also worked as a drill press operator, on an assembly line at General Motors, and as a welder at General Dynamics.

Whereas Sue was committed to one organization throughout the 1970s, many other activists became involved in a series of organizations over the course of the decade. Their experience reflects the ideological conflict that tore apart numerous leftist organizations at the time. Jim Shoch's experience is typical; Jim's commitment to organizations shifted as each group faced internal splits. At the end of the 1960s Jim was immersed in antiwar activism at Stanford. By this point Jim decided,

> I no longer was some kind of libertarian socialist. I was a Marxist-Leninist. As we reflected on how would socialism spread to other Americans . . . we needed an historical agent. . . . Students weren't enough. Blacks weren't enough. . . . So we pretty uncritically just said, "Where to go? Well, the working class." So at the time some Maoist variants of Marxism-Leninism were on tap and what was available . . . was this Revolutionary Union [RU].

During the three years that Jim was active, RU went through a split over ideology. Jim recalls the conflict being over "the precise character of armed struggle in the American Revolution. . . . We wrote detailed papers . . . [such as] if, when the ghettos go . . . the role of white revolutionaries [was] to create diversionary action so that the occupied troops could not get to the ghettos, run supplies through police lines. It was bizarre levels of detail as to just what this protracted urban guerrilla warfare would look like."

After the split, Jim joined those who formed a group called Venceremos. Dedicated to armed struggle, Venceremos became heavily involved in the prison movement. The time Jim spent in Venceremos was intense, including weekly five-hour meetings. The group lived together in order to save money for the cause. In the early years, in an attempt to organize the working class, Jim worked as a shipping and receiving clerk and tried to make contact with the United Electrical Workers. Moving in and out of the labor market, other members lived on welfare. In order to subsidize the revolution, Jim also used a good portion of the $25,000 his grandfather had left him. Jim comments, "There was a lot of unemployment, worked half the time, half the time not. But the time you weren't working, just full-time you were in politics."

By the summer of 1973 things "were getting crazy in the organization." Jim had the sense to quit a month before the group fell apart. After the organization dissolved, "in the midst of an identity crisis," Jim moved to San Francisco. He groped around for another organization. He says, "There was [only] one six-month period where I was not up to my eyeballs in the leadership and maintenance of a socialist organization." First, Jim became involved in housing politics. Soon after he joined a group called the San Francisco Socialist Coalition. He worked with others to set up a group called Power to the People that launched a public power campaign. In 1976–77 the coalition merged with the San Francisco Liberation School into a regional organization called the Northern California Alliance (NCA), which was "basically socialist antiracist, antisexist, anti-imperialism." Jim was involved with the organization for a year and a half. The NCA had a variety of projects including publishing a leftist paper, organizing office workers, as well as a group of health workers, a public sector committee, and a housing committee. Eventually NCA also self-destructed, torn apart between "Maoists, a few Trotskyists, a few independent Leninists, and some populists." Jim objected when one of the leaders tried to push the group in a Maoist direction.

It was clear the idea was to centralize the operation. So I basically precipitated a fight by dropping out of this . . . committee and saying, "I can't go along with this." We had this bloody battle for nine months and study groups and discussion. . . . And this speech I gave, "We've got to root this out and call it what it is: Stalinism," and impassioned arguments back and forth. It finally split and half of those people went on to become Line of March.

During the late 1970s, after the split in NCA, Jim became involved with the New American Movement, organizing around housing. He was also very active in San Francisco city politics, including electoral campaigns. Meanwhile, in terms of work, unlike Sue Jhirad, Jim's employment was not the locus of his political work. Jim supported himself through a variety of jobs over the years. Once he moved to San Francisco, began working as a delivery truck driver. Then he worked as a forklift driver in a plastics factory for two years. Jim chose jobs that wouldn't deflect him from politics.

There were some bouts of unemployment, but it was basically a ten-year decision to do some kind of manual work. . . . I thought you were a socialist, this is what you did. You just fought professionalism. . . . What [the jobs] allowed me to do is . . . vegetate, not think much, and then I'd have nights and weekends free for millions of meetings. . . . I had lots of energy left over. I was going to meetings four and five nights a week and on the weekends. I kept it up for a long time.

Jim's political beliefs prohibited him from considering a professional job. He recalls one day in 1975 as being particularly poignant. At the time he was delivering IBM typewriters to high-rise buildings downtown.

If there's a more demeaning job on the face of the earth, I can't think what it could be. . . . Even the secretaries pat you on the head and say, "Put it over there, boy." I'd been sent to Stanford to run the country, not to be a typewriter delivery person. So you're driving around . . . and there's newspaper boxes, thousands of them, on every corner. Everywhere I turned the headlines were screaming . . . "Saigon Falls, Saigon Falls." So here I am this delivery truck driver. I mean utterly, completely changed my life in as dramatic a fashion, other than getting killed, that I can imagine. I just spent the whole day crying. I was just thrilled the war was over, reflecting on what it had been for me. . . . Kind of like my childhood . . . this was indelibly etched. It was [an] amazing, amazing day. . . . I was totally joyful. It seemed like a complete victory for everything we all had done. But I kept reflecting also on choices that I had made. . . . It's not like . . . "Gosh, now I can go back to resuming my old life." . . .

Everything that had happened and how I'd ended up there and how
my life . . . was going to remain completely different from what it
otherwise had been had that war not come along.

Jim eloquently captures the unexpected transformations he encountered
as a result of his commitment to the movement, the mixture of emotions
as he recognizes the irreversible changes in his life. After years of menial
labor, Jim decided he wanted more meaningful work. In 1979 he took a
job as a community organizer for the Gray Panthers, an activist organization fighting for the rights of older people. He stayed there through
1982.

## Women Organizing Women

For many women in SDS the feminist movement provided continuity and
helped sustain commitment to politics. As the left was torn apart, women
used the skills and knowledge they had gained to help build the women's
movement. The skills and resources women acquired as community organizers, their growing sense of self-worth and independence, and the
theoretical understanding they gained of inequality and oppression were
all applied to mobilize for women's equality. Beth Oglesby, for example,
transferred all of her energy and resources from the left to organizing
women. After she split up with Carl in 1969, Beth remained in San Francisco and became completely involved with the women's movement. "By
the time the Townhouse happened . . . there was no way I wanted to be
part of that. . . . At that point . . . I found the women's movement,
which was just so nurturing and so different. It wasn't about guilt and
you should be doing this. It was just about self-discovery." Beth was active in early consciousness-raising groups and the San Francisco Women's
Liberation Group. She came out as a lesbian and began to define herself
as a separatist feminist.

In 1970 Beth moved to Boston and became involved in Bread and
Roses, a socialist feminist organization that appealed to her because it
was a separate women's organization but also worked in coalition with
men on issues of antiracism and anti-imperialism. In 1971 Beth took part
in the ten-day takeover of a Harvard building by women demanding
the establishment of a women's center. Later that year Beth got together
with other SDS people and they started a daycare center. Work in the daycare center took over Beth's life and consumed her energy for the rest of
the decade.

Many other SDS women became involved in the women's movement. Not all women, however, found feminist activism rejuvenating. Both early and late SDS women were involved with feminism, but early women were much more likely to report negative experiences in the women's movement. A substantial number of women encountered dynamics similar to those common in leftist groups: dogmatism and demands for political correctness. Like many leftist organizations, many women's groups also went through ideological splits and factionalism during the 1970s.[1]

Vivian Rothstein had mixed experiences in the feminist movement. The early years of her involvement were exhilarating. By the late 1960s Vivian had turned her full attention to organizing women and was one of the founding members of the Chicago Women's Liberation Union (CWLU). Vivian worked exclusively in the women's movement for three years. The women in CWLU set up a Liberation School, where hundreds of community women met and took classes. CWLU also ran a newspaper, an abortion referral service called Jane, a women's clinic, and started the Women's Liberation Rock Band. Vivian remembers the excitement of using the knowledge she had gained on the left on behalf of women.

> A lot of left women who had been political activists . . . came . . . with this sense of excitement and commitment and a lot of skills. Which is what . . . we got out of working in SDS. . . . There was no place for us to take leadership. So we took it into the women's movement. There was really no other place where we could use what we knew and where we could be treated the way we wanted to be treated. . . . There was a lot of momentum in the women's community that didn't exist in the mixed community any more. It felt great. But then these sectarians came in and said, "You're all middle-class white women." It was . . . this self-hatred. That's what ultimately destroyed the Women's Union. But for several years we forestalled it and it was great.

As the initial feeling of collectivity, of building a movement together ran into ideological dogmatism, the energy and resources used to initiate projects now turned inward. Vivian recalls, "It was these left sects that didn't believe in an independent women's movement who spent a lot of time trying to destroy us. We fought off the Socialist Workers Party. . . . But then these other sects came in . . . and they would push their line. . . . They didn't believe in bourgeois women's organizations. We ended up spending so much time fighting them, it was really a shame."

The push toward ideological purity not only destroyed the organization but also left its scars on individual activists. Vivian felt personally attacked by others in the women's movement.

> I felt a lot of criticism from the women's movement. . . . At first I got some criticism for being a leader. . . . [Then] I felt some criticism around being in a monogamous marriage. . . . We tried to have an open marriage. I just got mired in all sorts of personal shit along with a lot of other people. We were trying to be the new socialist men and women. It just about killed me.

At the time Vivian was living in a political commune in which everyone shared money and possessions. Some people had paying jobs; others threw themselves into activism. Vivian's husband became romantically involved with her best friend, another member of the commune. Vivian says she barely survived the experience.

> The combination of my living situation, my personal life, and my politics just closed in on me. . . . I felt criticized at all levels. . . . I felt like I barely got out of the women's movement with my life. . . . A lot of people experienced a lot more pain than we've ever talked about. . . . Women were using their feminism as an excuse . . . to really do what men and women have always done to each other.

There were also strains developing in the women's movement that Vivian didn't believe in.

> Robin Morgan wrote some poems about who the enemy was. For her the enemy included Dave Dellinger and Tom Hayden. . . . Then Jill Johnston was saying that if you're pregnant, you should have amniocentesis, and if you're pregnant with a male child, you should kill it. I just didn't believe in that shit. I hated it. I felt the women's movement was no longer a place for me, that there were a lot of politics . . . built on hatred.

Given these experiences, and recognizing the desire to save her marriage, Vivian and her husband, Rich, decided to leave Chicago in 1974 when Rich got a job with the Clothing and Textile Workers Union in Denver. Despite her disillusion with the women's movement, Vivian continued political work throughout the 1970s. She worked for the American Friends' Service Committee on issues concerning Vietnam and on the Middle East Peace Education Project. Later, when Rich was transferred to North Carolina, Vivian began working as the public affairs coordinator for Planned Parenthood.

Several other early SDS women also spoke about their ambivalent experiences in the women's movement. These activists were particularly put off by the intolerance of the feminist movement in the early 1970s. Barbara Haber comments that the feminist movement "defined what was the right kind of woman. There were all these conflicting messages, like you had to be lesbian, you had to be militant, but you weren't allowed to be too this or too that." As with SDS, group dynamics alienated some members. Yet despite the schisms and pressures faced by peers on the left and in the women's movement, activists held true to their beliefs and continued to find ways to make social change. Many of them, however, also faced dilemmas concerning their work lives.

## Work

In addition to trying to make politics amid the splits, splinters, and disarray of the left, activists struggled with how to make a living. The basic problem was how to reconcile becoming an independent employed adult with living as a radical. By this point most activists had either dropped out of school or finished their undergraduate degrees and needed to make money to support themselves. Unlike traditionalists in YAF who faced smoother transitions between adolescence and adulthood, between college and career, many SDS activists followed more tentative routes, patching together a living in order to sustain their politics.[2] Thus, for most leftists the 1970s included much shifting around—both in terms of political groups and in terms of jobs. Rather than a linear process in which they worked in jobs aimed toward building for the future, many activists assembled a series of odd jobs in order to sustain their politics.

Helen Garvy, for example, was involved in a variety of work situations during the 1970s. At the end of the 1960s Helen moved to San Francisco and started a nonracist, nonsexist school for children. She says, "I wanted to raise kids who could see through bullshit, whether it came from the right-wing, from liberal Democrats, or from SDS demagogues, from leaders who would get up on the soapbox and say, 'Follow me, I've got this little red book.'" Helen saw the school as a continuation of her activism and worked full-time at the school without getting paid. But she didn't talk to other SDSers about it because they didn't think her work was politically important. Meanwhile she took odd jobs to get by, including working as a janitor to get a rent reduction on her apartment, working a swing shift at the post office during Christmas, and delivering leftist papers in the community. At one point Helen and a friend also opened "an unorthodox bike shop" in which the prices were listed as "whatever the customer can afford."

After four years of working at the school "twenty-four hours a day," Helen felt burned out. She "started seeing psychology as quite political," viewing therapy "as not making people fit into the world, but helping people to survive in a fucked up world." Helen began working at a mental health clinic, another counterinstitution, and remained there for another four years. In short, Helen varied between taking temporary jobs to sustain her activism in the school with shifting her energy into being a therapist, in which she viewed her paid work as an extension of her politics.

Like Helen, a lot of activists held a variety of jobs throughout the 1970s, moving from one job to another, at times interwoven with bouts of unemployment, in order to support themselves while they poured their energy into their activism. For years people were marginally employed or patched together a life in which their work would either not interfere with their politics or was an extension of their beliefs. Both YAFers and SDSers accumulated skills and resources through their activism, but those on the left used their experience to further their participation in social movement organizations and issues, not to build individual careers. Thus, most leftists—in contrast to traditionalists in YAF—continued to define themselves as outside the mainstream and to work outside mainstream institutions during the 1970s.

Rory Ellinger was one of the few SDS activists who continued to work *within* mainstream institutions during the 1970s. Yet even he felt conflicted between activism versus career and moved in and out of the mainstream throughout the decade. During the late 1960s Rory went from being the president of SDS at the University of Missouri to being press secretary for Senator Tom Eagleton. But when Eagleton asked Rory to stay on after he won the 1968 election, Rory chose to return to campus politics in Missouri. Unlike traditionalists, he chose local activism over mainstream politics. Rory reflects on this decision:

It probably was a bad decision. . . . I went from . . . Eagleton's office, from all these very influential political people, big lawyers and very wealthy people, who we used to call "silk stocking," "corporate liberals," and went back to campus in '69. I grew a beard and I led the march on the state capitol. . . . The members of the state senate wanted to have me arrested. . . . The buildings burned at Lincoln and they were going to indict me.

In 1970 Rory returned to school to work on his doctorate. Most of his time, however, went into activism.

Throughout the early 1970s Rory moved back and forth between student activism and mainstream liberal politics, between the campus and the community. Because of his position of prominence, Rory was appointed by the mayor to serve on several boards and commissions in Columbia, Missouri. In 1972 he became the head of the Cerebral Palsy Foundation and later became the head of the Missouri Association for Social Welfare. The only SDS activist in this sample who chose to run for office during the 1970s, Rory ran for the legislature in 1972, won the Democratic nomination, but lost the general election. After this he decided to go to law school. While in law school he continued to be politically involved, working on electoral campaigns, serving on the board of ACLU, and supporting efforts to pass the Equal Rights Amendment.

Rory is atypical in his involvement with the mainstream. Most SDSers felt an aversion to being absorbed in mainstream politics or institutions, fearing co-optation of their deeply held beliefs and values. Central to their identity was a stance critical of the mainstream. Further, pressures by peers prohibited some activists from pursuing graduate education or committing to jobs too close to the mainstream. The fear of being considered a traitor, a "liberal" in the terminology of the day, caused turmoil and anguish as some activists felt conflict between personal ambition and commitment to their political beliefs. Andrea Cousins recalls her predicament in facing these issues.

> I was very interested in dreams and the unconscious. I loved symbolic structure and I loved analyzing it. But I couldn't find a way to do it that would be kosher politically. . . . I always felt this conflict between what I thought was good politics and what I would personally like to do. . . . I just hated organizing, hated it with a passion. But that was the thing to do. I really just wanted to be in people's kitchens; I wanted to be talking about their histories. I always felt like an army marshal knocking on doors. . . . I hated wanting people to do things, to get them to this meeting or that meeting or whatever.

Andrea eventually returned to graduate school to study anthropology.

Yet even the decision to go to graduate school caused anxiety for some activists. Michael Kazin recalls a Weatherman friend who told him, "If you didn't drop out of school, that was making bets against the revolution. . . . Any kind of normal life was making bets against the revolution." Some activists anticipated criticism or even ostracism as they faced choices about their future. Once again, peers acted as a means of social control, circumscribing behavior.

Other activists felt clueless and directionless about how to even return to the mainstream, given their radicalization during the cataclysmic events of the 1960s. Even if they recognized a desire for some kind of mainstream work, they felt confused about how to return to the "normal path," after being so consumed by radical politics. Some activists had no idea how to translate their movement skills into regular jobs. Dave Strauss says that during the 1960s he never felt confident about his abilities. Further, the prohibition he felt against discussing his future left him feeling isolated and confused.

> I was having trouble seeing where I was going. Because one of the things we were very bad at was understanding our skill development. I learned a tremendous amount that has been invaluable to me, but I didn't know it at the time. I thought I was just failing and everybody in the group [was] failing. . . . People sometimes would tell us . . . "Boy, you guys are really great. . . . You could be head of this corporation." I didn't feel like I could be head of any corporation. I felt like if I wasn't doing [this], I'd [be on] unemployment. . . . I never felt terribly well skilled.

Again, in contrast to traditionalists, who had an easier time translating their activist skills into mainstream positions, SDSers faced much higher costs for their activism not only during the 1960s but throughout the 1970s as well. Traditionalists did not have to make difficult decisions about being arrested, knowing they were closing off options for the future. Dorothy Burlage notes this difference, commenting that while the right "just stayed on track . . . we all fell off." Dorothy recalls worrying about her own future, wondering how she would make a living when the movement was over.

Despite the pressure not to pursue careers and the confusion felt by some SDSers, a number of activists *did* begin careers during the 1970s. Those who chose this path brought their politics to their occupation, seeing their work as an extension of their beliefs. John Brown Childs describes the process by which he decided to return to graduate school to pursue a career as an anthropologist. Like Andrea Cousins, he realized his talents were not in community organizing. After five years doing various kinds of community work, John realized there was a lot he didn't understand. He began to think it would be more useful to get a degree and use that degree as a base. "My going back to school . . . meant approaching the community from a different angle . . . coming at it as an intermediary, bridging kind of person, offering some skills, like analytical skills."

Yet even these activists who committed themselves to a professional career struggled with their choice and continued to have doubts each step of the way, questioning whether they were doing the right thing. After a difficult process, Derek Barron entered law school at the end of the 1960s but was uncomfortable with his decision.

> Even after I started law school, I had deep questions about whether I made the right choice, a real ambivalence about being there, a resistance to associating myself in any way with what I had perceived to be the corporate establishment and corporate law and business law, commercial law—any of that stuff—I didn't want to have anything to do with. At that time the great attractiveness of law school—we used to talk about this all the time—was that you didn't have to commit yourself to anything when you were in law school. You could maximize your options. . . . When you get out, you've got this graduate degree and you can go off and run a carnival, for crying out loud. . . . So I went to law school without any . . . real intention of being a lawyer.

Midway through his second year of law school, Derek was bored. He had spent the summer working for Ralph Nader in Washington, but he didn't consider that really practicing law. Before he quit, he decided he should have some practical experience. A law school friend introduced Derek to one of the leading civil liberties lawyers in the country. "He was the person every radical in the city turned to for legal advice when they were up a tree and couldn't get down." They immediately hit it off, Derek was hired, and after he graduated, he began working for this lawyer full-time. As his work became congruent with his beliefs and with his identity as an activist, "I began to see how the law could be an instrument for social change, for protecting the oppressed and vulnerable from the power of the state. I began to learn how to do it . . . not simply stand around and complain [or] organize a group of people to throw rocks . . . but to really do it." Derek's struggles over his career have no counterpart in the experience of traditionalists in YAF I interviewed. None expressed similar misgivings about integrating their politics and their work.

During the 1970s a number of SDS activists finished their degrees and began professional jobs. Among the women these included jobs as a teacher, a nurse, a doctor, and, for several, a therapist. Among SDS men, three worked as college professors, three as lawyers, and one as a teacher. Further, by the end of the decade many more SDS activists had returned to graduate school and were preparing for professional careers. By 1979 over half of the SDS activists (55 percent) had either earned graduate degrees or were currently enrolled in graduate programs.[3]

### Licking the Wounds and Healing the Self

While SDS members forged their way through the splits and politics of the 1970s, as some members found a path toward a professional career, the 1970s was also a time of burnout, of confusion, of reassessment. For many people the 1970s represented a coming to terms with the 1960s, a process of recovery from the dramatic and nonstop events and experiences they encountered as activists when they stepped off the path to "normal adulthood." There was no clear path showing activists how to proceed. Their identity as radicals interrupted or redirected earlier expectations of finishing college, becoming established in a job, getting married, starting a family, and settling down. Instead, many activists felt unsettled, uncertain where to go or what to do or how to reconcile their identity as a radical with the rest of their lives.

Phil Hutchings found the late 1960s and early 1970s very disorienting. Phil was struggling to find his place beyond being a "movement junkie."

> When I first met . . . the sit-in people in 1960 when I was a freshman at Howard, this whole scenario . . . how I saw myself moving in a more middle-class pattern, and getting a career, and getting married, getting a degree—it was like here were kids who were sixteen and seventeen who through their own action . . . were changing laws, making history. It was like you didn't have to wait. . . . If you really wanted to do good, you could do it now. . . . Here was the movement. Get involved. I just threw myself into that and that was a total head trip. . . . it was like a whole new opening to how one could live their life. . . . So it was very hard, as those heydays began to decline in the late '60s, to figure out how you could continue to get that feeling of making history. . . . I compare it a lot to a drug addict. . . . I kept wanting to get another high—a new demonstration, a new issue. Maybe it'll be *this* movement or *that* movement . . . but never getting the same type of high.

Accompanying his search for a movement high, Phil also felt at a loss about what to do with his life. There was little discussion in the movement of how people were going to settle down for the long haul. Phil began asking himself critical questions:

> Were we going to live in the ghetto forever? . . . Was the object to . . . bring [everybody] down to a certain level? . . . We clearly didn't have the power to make the poor people richer, so . . . [were] the middle-class people supposed to come down and live on . . . $10,000 a year? . . . That became obviously ridiculous. . . . People would go out and they would want better things. . . . You want a television, you want a couple pairs of suits, or you'd want a better job or . . . want to get married and need a job that could pay for kids. . . . You might want to not live in the ghetto all your life. It's fine to do it when you're in your early twenties . . . but you'll want different things and life wasn't going to always be that way.

Recognizing that people's needs and desires change as they get older, Phil realized that his problem was not just his own but was a political problem the movement was not addressing. Phil felt people shouldn't be attacked for wanting a life beyond politics; it was wrong to assume because of these other desires, they were selling out. He recognized as well his own feelings of political burnout, confronting the fact that he could not continue doing grassroots organizing, walking up and down streets knocking on doors eight to ten hours a day.

Many SDS activists report feeling burned out during the 1970s. They dealt with it in a variety of ways. A few retreated to the country. By the end of the 1960s Carl Oglesby's marriage had broken apart and Weatherman had pushed him out of SDS. Bruised, he says, he "lost any sense of purpose." Carl moved to Vermont to live on a commune and spent a year or so recovering.

> I felt isolated, cut off, abandoned, unappreciated, abused . . . lonely. . . . I went through a personal burnout period in 1970, '71. I left the movement to its own devices. I became very self-consciously a *non*leader. . . . I went to live in the countryside. There were maybe a half dozen, sometimes a dozen other people living at this very spacious place, all of whom were more or less in the situation of burnout that I was in—wondering what to do, wondering if there was anything to do . . . politically scared of the Weathermen, scared of the FBI even more, beginning to be quite desperate. . . . And many

of us wondering whatever was going to happen to this country, but no longer feeling that anything that we did made much difference.[4]

Despite these feelings, Carl kept up his political activities through writing, giving talks and workshops in Boston, going to marches, and by sponsoring a weekly political discussion group at the commune, which typically was attended by anywhere from one hundred to two hundred people. But Carl's time at the commune drew to an end when "the Weatherman influence came around the back door." A filmmaker living at the commune brought guns to the farm and persuaded a number of people that the revolution was around the corner and that all serious radicals had to take up arms. At about this time a theater company in Boston decided to produce one of Carl's plays, so Carl picked up and moved to Cambridge.

By the early 1970s Barbara Haber also felt the weight of the events and experiences she had been through but found a different path of relief. As the 1960s came to an end, the world seemed to be collapsing around her. Rather than move to the country, Barbara turned to spirituality and therapy. She comments on her feeling at the demise of SDS,

The more long-term disintegration of this organization that, love it or hate it, was my home . . . and was my identification, was very traumatic because . . . I thought it would go on forever. . . . Life at that point for me was . . . a blur of dramatic events, most of them negative. It was not surprising to pick up the paper . . . and find out that people I knew had blown themselves up in the Townhouse. It was not surprising to find out that somebody had blown up the Math Science Building at Madison and someone got killed. It was not surprising to hear that the United States was in Cambodia. It was not surprising to find out that students got killed at Kent State and Jackson State. . . . Things happened constantly. . . . It was a bombardment. It was like wait, wait . . . it's all going wrong. . . . So for all of those reasons, therapy had a lot of appeal and so did spiritual things—meditation, Eastern philosophy, needing to get another handle on it somehow.

Barbara withdrew from politics for a while and "did full-time spiritual path. I used to say I belonged to the trip-of-the-month club." Focusing on spirituality and meditation, she tried to "put myself together." Her marriage had broken up, many other marriages were breaking up, and some of her friends were having nervous breakdowns or even committing suicide. Yet even during this time of political retreat, politics was never completely absent from Barbara's thoughts. She tells a story to illustrate.

> I remember raising political issues at the Buddhist center where I was studying full-time one summer when they had nonunion lettuce. I was on kitchen duty making lunch. I said to the guy in charge—he was a more advanced Buddhist—I said, "This is a problem. This is nonunion lettuce." He said, "It's only a problem if you make it a problem." I paused for a very long time and said, "Well, I want to make it a problem." I brought it up in the whole room with the guru. . . . I did not get a very favorable response from people.

Barbara received a warmer reception for her views in another spiritual group she joined where she ran into a lot of SDS people who talked "movement-ese" to one another.

Barbara also became involved with the human potential movement and gestalt therapy and began working as a therapist in a collective. She was drawn to therapy from her experiences in consciousness-raising groups in the women's movement. In addition, Barbara felt a need to address the disintegration of her world. She says, "Everything was falling apart. I was falling apart, my friends were falling apart, my husband was falling apart. I wanted to fix it. . . . I was really interested in helping people like myself who wanted to live lives outside the mainstream to survive."

Looking back, Barbara says spiritual groups and therapy felt necessary, the only way to absorb the shocks of the 1960s, to be able to move on with life. She compares SDS veterans to veterans of Vietnam who had a difficult time integrating their war experiences into their lives.

> There was no way to integrate what happened to us . . . when your basic underlying assumptions about the world are shattered . . . over and over again. . . . Those of us who stayed . . . in that very stormy sea, I don't think anybody came out of it in good shape. Everybody needed five years . . . licking wounds and healing self. A lot of people didn't make it back. People are still damaged . . . to one degree or another. . . . I know of people who were hospitalized. I know of people who became psychotic or near psychotic. I know of people who for many years just didn't function very well. And I know of people who still don't function very well. . . . We called into question more and more . . . about life in our culture. . . . We tried to overthrow the biggest power on earth. . . . And

we used our very bodies to do it . . . what we ate, what we smoked, how we spent our time, our sex habits, everything. You don't do that and get away with it. You pay. That's why there should be . . . a monument to the dead and wounded from our side. Because I really . . . think Vietnam was also a civil war in this country. . . . There were heavy casualties on both sides.

Clearly the costs of activism for some SDS activists entailed not only harassment or arrests but psychological wounds as well, wounds that in some cases never healed.

A few activists emerged from the 1960s so scarred that they ended up withdrawing completely from politics. One SDS activist who paid a high personal toll for her experiences was Cindy Decker. Cindy felt very bruised from her final months in SDS. Cindy's collective of SDS activists, who were trying to organize tuna cannery workers in northern California, was wrenched apart by interpersonal problems. Cindy also was disturbed by the "cops and robbers" mentality of the movement at the end of the 1960s. In the early 1970s she tried working with Cesar Chavez organizing farmworkers but found that too demanding. Cindy's reaction to burnout was to disengage from politics. Cindy describes her life in the early 1970s: "I took acid about every three days for a real long time. David [her boyfriend] and I did incredible quantities of drugs. I just sort of fell away from being a political activist. It's not like I changed my politics. . . . My life just took a different . . . point of view."

Even though Cindy stopped being active, she continued to be enmeshed in a group of people who shared her beliefs and lived in a community surrounded by leftists. But she stopped going to demonstrations and spending her time on politics. She recalls, "I was totally burned out. It had been very costly in personal ways. It was true for a lot of people in the left. . . . We were just absolutely forging a frontier in interpersonal relationships, and there was a real schism there between the beliefs that we had been raised to observe and the way we were all behaving."

Cindy says being a pioneer of new lifestyles was both freeing and unsettling.

There weren't adult models for what we were doing. I wasn't getting married and having children and . . . living in a house and acquiring material possessions. . . . And that's all I was programmed to do was hitch up with some successful up-and-rising young [man]—preferably a military officer—and raise a handsome family. . . . It was real hard. . . . It was liberating but, any time you shed

something you're programmed to do, it's very stressful. All of us . . .
lived with a high degree of interpersonal stress. I tried to commit
suicide when I was twenty-six in a real serious way. . . . My life was
saved by my friends.

Stepping off the path had very real costs. Like many other leftists,
Cindy felt directionless, without guidance. She remembers her twenty-
fifth birthday as emblematic of the times. "I woke up on the down side
of an acid trip in a shack in Santa Monica . . . thinking, God, I am a quarter of a century old—where is my life going? I didn't have a vision of where
my life was going at all." After recovering from her despair, Cindy returned to school at UCLA and earned a master's degree in public health
in 1977.

Like Cindy, a few other SDS members also dealt with the aftermath
of the 1960s by retreating from politics. They retired, as Sale explains:
"Having put so much of themselves into politics, and with so much frustration to show for it now, many former SDSers went into what they half-
jokingly called 'retirement'—leading private lives, coming out for a march
or demonstration when it was called, but for the most part hanging back,
looking inward."[5]

Like Cindy, Aldyn McKean also withdrew from politics during the
1970s. Unlike Cindy, he retired rather than resigned, participating in sporadic political events over the course of the decade. Aldyn followed an
unusual path before growing disillusioned with politics. At the beginning of the 1970s Aldyn was still active in PL at Harvard as a "full-time
radical." In 1971 he was asked by leaders of PL to enlist in the army in
order to make contact with some people in South Vietnam who were
working inside the National Liberation Front and who shared PL's criticism of the North Vietnamese leadership. At the time Aldyn felt honored that he was chosen for this important job. After a few days mulling
it over and considering the risks, he decided he was willing to go. In retrospect Aldyn comments that he was chosen because "I was viewed as
reliable but not crucial and therefore, frankly, expendable."

Saying good-bye to an activist friend ("See you later, agitator," "In a
while, Sinophile"), Aldyn headed off to Vietnam. Aldyn found the army
was "closer to being in the real world than being in the Worker-Student
Alliance caucus of SDS in Cambridge, Massachusetts." Although he was
trained to be a door gunner on a helicopter, because of his education
Aldyn was placed in a job as a legal clerk and became familiar with the
Uniform Code of Military Justice. Aldyn used his knowledge of the pro-

cedures to organize the troops. For example, he organized the men to protest the practice restricting them to base rather than allowing them to go into town. Aldyn was careful, however, not to do anything that would get him thrown out of the army, thereby jeopardizing his mission. Eventually Aldyn ended up becoming part of an army rock band that, he says, "toured places too dangerous to send Bob Hope."

Meanwhile, Aldyn reported back by mail to his PL contacts to arrange for the National Liberation Front to contact him but became increasingly concerned when he never heard a word back from anyone in PL. His disillusionment with PL was gradual. Contributing to his disaffection, during this period Aldyn became aware of his desires for men. Knowing "it was probably best not to be openly gay," at this point he viewed himself as bisexual. Reflecting back on the time he spent in PL, Aldyn comments,

> To a certain extent I ended up adopting another identity that was created for me which was not wholly mine. It had certain advantages . . . [in] that it involved fighting imperialism and racism. It also did not allow me to express what I now consider to be my most deep personal feelings. . . . It was an unstated but nevertheless important part of the beliefs of that group that part of aligning with the working class was to be straight and heterosexual.[6]

Aldyn's recognition of his identity as a gay man clashed with his identity as a radical, as defined by PL. By the time Aldyn's tour of duty was over in 1972, he felt fed up with the left, particularly the "bureaucratic Leninist left." He no longer believed in the notion of the workers' revolution led by the vanguard party. Aldyn also felt he had missed out on "just being a long-haired hippie freak." Aldyn returned briefly to Cambridge and chose to stay with friends who had not been involved with SDS, friends who "smoked dope and lived in a commune and had long hair." He called up the PL leader, whom he had written throughout his time in Vietnam, to say he was back. Despite the fact that this man had never responded to Aldyn's letters the entire time he was gone, he merely replied, "Hey, it's great to hear from you. . . . Listen, we've got this leaflet that needs to be mimeographed." This ended Aldyn's involvement with PL.

Aldyn felt more accepted and welcomed in the counterculture.

> An influence on my pulling away from the left . . . [was] coming to terms with my own sexuality and supposedly being part of a movement and an organization that was about empowerment. In fact,

for me what that movement and that organization was, was very stultifying. . . . Interestingly enough, the people who were countercultural radicals . . . had no problem at all with my being gay . . . so for them it was not an issue.

Aldyn spent the rest of the 1970s moving: from California to New York, from playing in a rock band to studying anthropology and drama, from working on and off Broadway, to taking odd jobs and supporting himself in a street-singing duo. Although he was not involved with any political organization, Aldyn came out of "retirement" every now and then throughout the 1970s to attend antinuclear marches or gay rights demonstrations.

The few other activists who withdrew from politics during the 1970s redirected their politics into their work lives. In fact, many of those who felt battered and bruised by the 1960s ended up either returning to school or reorienting themselves toward careers. Dorothy Burlage replaced her passion for politics by a passion for work. By 1970 Dorothy felt completely disoriented, "a lost soul." She says, "It was over for me by the '70s. . . . I knew that I didn't want to be in a political movement again, that it was time to do something else with my life." Dorothy felt she had to leave politics in order to survive. "I had been around too much violence. . . . I just figured . . . if I kept it up, that I was getting more and more marginal, that the whole movement was making less and less sense. . . . I was losing my ability to keep a sense of balance and know what I was doing and why I was doing it . . . and [felt] that the best thing to do was to pull out." Not knowing what to do, Dorothy called a friend for advice. He suggested going to Harvard, so she entered a Ph.D. program there.

Although Dorothy describes herself as completely uninvolved with politics during the early 1970s, she in fact was active in the women's movement. After about a year and a half of political abstinence, Dorothy became involved in starting a women's counseling center. Yet Dorothy did not see her activities as political because they were so different from her earlier years of full-time organizing.

While Dorothy was determined not to be an activist, her politics did influence her work. In her studies she began examining the connection between economics and personality. That led her to studying families and, in particular, to understanding child development. Dorothy wrote her dissertation on the economics of divorce. This, she says, "brought me back to politics once more." After completing her Ph.D., Dorothy trained for two years at Children's Hospital. She fell in love with working with children and felt "like I found a home again." Recognizing that she was an "all-or-nothing person," and that she had given politics everything she had, Dorothy dedicated herself to providing better care for children. After so many years with activism being central to her identity, Dorothy redefined her priorities. Her values remained the same, but her identity shifted from politics to her career as a child psychologist.

Some activists who reoriented to careers discovered their activism provided them with perspectives and resources that helped their transition to the mainstream. Lynn Dykstra began the decade still active in Weatherman. In 1970 Lynn moved to Berkeley and continued her work as an activist. After about a year, a friend told her, "You know, politics is not all of life." Reflecting on this, Lynn says, "I had been living within this little political system of the Weathermen that tried to make everything be political and meaningful and . . . I found myself . . . becoming more and more isolated. . . . So I stopped being that radical and ended up moving back toward center a little bit and getting back in the mainstream."

After leaving Weatherman Lynn did not become active in any other organization, although she felt as if she was politically involved just by living in Berkeley amidst a community of people with shared views. "I became a Berkeley liberal person which, compared to the rest of the country, is still pretty far left." She continued to go to antiwar demonstrations and participated in a women's consciousness-raising group. Most of her energy, however, was spent thinking about who she was and what she wanted to do with her life. Calling this time a "real growth period," Lynn realized how her activism had transformed her. Whereas before she was seen as a "very quiet, mousy kind of person who just went along with the crowd," her years as an activist taught her to see herself differently, as someone who had important things to say. "So the person that I . . . felt more free to become was more active intellectually and socially. Women in my time period, even the women who were bright, were never encouraged to be intellectuals. I was able to . . . hang out with some men and a few women who . . . talked about important things in the world. I could . . . participate in that. So that was important."

During this time Lynn decided to enroll in premed classes. Her years as an activist allowed her to choose this path. She knew nothing about medical school and had no role models but medicine was a field that combined a lot of things she liked, such as science and helping people and offering a job with a lot of variety. She comments,

It was a transition that I was able to think about those things and decide rather than just float along. And that's a product of my having been politically active . . . to know that I had choices. Here I was fighting for lots of other people's freedom of choice and what came out of it is that I realized I did have choice and I could be empowered and I could do things myself. . . . So those were very good benefits.

Lynn also felt a fundamental connection between her political values and her choice of becoming a doctor. She viewed going to medical school as similar to being a radical in that she was devoting herself to making the world a better place.

In fact, the self-confidence and skills Lynn learned as an activist helped her even in getting into medical school. In the spring of 1973 after she applied, Lynn still had received no word of acceptance. She called the man who had interviewed her to find out what happened. He was shocked, informing her she had been at the top of the list. A few days later he called back to report that the dean of the college and the state legislature had made a deal that the incoming class would be no more than one-third female that year. Lynn was outraged, as was this man and the dean of admissions. Ultimately, Lynn was admitted and was told her job was to make sure women were never excluded again. The first year of medical school Lynn was elected to the admissions committee on her promise that sexual discrimination would be abolished. Lynn has carried the skills and knowledge she learned in SDS to improve conditions for women in medicine.

In short, while most leftists found ways to continue their politics during the 1970s, even those who "retired" brought their values and beliefs and applied the lessons they learned as activists to their work lives. Indirectly, they, too, found ways to continue to make social change.

## PATHWAYS OF YAF MEMBERS THROUGH THE 1970S

### Politics

Traditionalists' Political Paths   The majority of traditionalists also maintained their commitment to politics throughout the 1970s. Unlike leftists or libertarians, most traditionalists became integrated into mainstream politics. Using the skills and resources they acquired through their activism in YAF, as adults they worked for conservative causes within mainstream institutions. While SDS fell apart after the 1969 convention, YAF survived its own explosive 1969 convention with traditionalists in control of the organization. Thus, some activists continued their involvement with YAF during the 1970s. For example, Mitch Petry served as a national officer of YAF during the early 1970s. After finishing his term, Mitch decided "it was time to graduate to other things." He began work as a congressional aide, working first on the House of Representatives' side for six years, and then moving to the Senate. He gradually got involved in issues of long-term health care. In the late 1970s he served as chief legislative counsel to Senator Orrin Hatch.

Fran Griffin also remained active in YAF during the 1970s, first at the local level and then at the national level. After graduating from college in 1970, Fran got a job in the Illinois YAF office for about a year, being paid "next to nothing" for her work. In 1971 she started graduate school at the University of Chicago but still maintained her activism in YAF. In 1972, for instance, she was an active participant in the YAF campaign, Students Against McGovern. In the summer of that year she was also an intern for the conservative magazine *Human Events* in Washington.

In 1973 Fran was elected to serve on the national board of YAF. A year later she decided to run for the Illinois State Senate and received some financial support from YAF for her campaign. She lost the election. Meanwhile, she says, by 1975 much of the leadership of the national office turned against her. She was part of a minority coalition that was critical of the way things were being run in the organization, "the heavy-handedness of the national office" that was "too bureaucratic." As a result of this internal fighting, Fran was fired as chair of the Illinois YAF. Fran considered the conflict just part of "normal politics" and was not bitter when she left YAF.

Meantime, Fran continued her involvement with campus politics as well as with electoral campaigns. In 1976 one of Fran's YAF friends sent a letter to Congressman Tom Corcoran, recommending Fran for a job. She was immediately hired as a legislative correspondent and moved to Washington. Dissatisfied after a few months on the job, Fran began working as media director for the American Conservative Union (ACU), a prominent national lobbying organization founded in the aftermath of the Goldwater campaign. She enjoyed this position, coordinating publicity for various domestic and international issues. At the end of 1979 Fran was asked to be a field coordinator for Ronald Reagan's presidential campaign and worked in the Illinois, Michigan, and New Hampshire campaigns on behalf of Reagan. Like Fran, many other activists also transferred their energy and skills to ACU once they left YAF, serving on the ACU board or working for the organization. Don Devine, who also moved from YAF to ACU, comments that this was a common path for "the OAFs, the Old Americans for Freedom."[7]

Commitment to electoral politics also distinguishes traditionalists from leftists and libertarians. Traditionalists were much more likely to be active in electoral campaigns. After her involvement with YAF, Kitty Smith's primary political activity was electoral politics. Throughout the 1970s she worked on local and national campaigns, attended state and national Republican conventions, and served as a delegate to the state convention. In 1972 Kitty married Lauren Smith, a lawyer who was very active in YAF.[8] He got Kitty involved on the national level. When Lauren served as general counsel for Reagan in his 1976 campaign, Kitty also became involved. "I would go as a volunteer. Sometimes I'd be on the money table and sometimes . . . answer the phone and help out in every way. I'd bake lots of cookies and I'd make little hors d'oeuvres and bring them in and bake bread . . . and bring it in hot and have it on the receptionist's desk." In addition, Kitty also became involved with the New Right organization, the Conservative Caucus.

Whereas Kitty's involvement is more typical of traditional women's activities, volunteering and supporting organizations behind the scenes, other traditionalists, both male and female, took a more visible role. In fact, traditionalists were much more likely to run for elected office than were leftists or libertarians. David Keene, for example, ran for Wisconsin state senator in 1970. He won the primary but lost the election by about a thousand votes. The campaign against him compared Keene to Joseph McCarthy and depicted YAF as an "extremist" and "radical" organization.[9] After losing the election, Keene's YAF buddies, Pat Buchanan and Tom Huston, put him in touch with Vice President Spiro Agnew. Shortly after, Keene resigned his position as chair of YAF and came to Washington to work for Agnew as staff assistant for political affairs.

Overall, while five traditionalists ran for some type of elected office during the 1970s, only two libertarians and one SDS member ran for office. None of the activists were successful. In 1988, however, libertarian YAFer Dana Rohrabacher was elected to Congress (see chapter 9).

Libertarians' Political Paths    The majority of libertarians also maintained their political commitment through the 1970s, but not in mainstream organizations or through the Republican Party. Some activists became active in the Libertarian Party, which was formed in 1971, or in other libertarian organizations. Often activists moved from one libertarian organization to another. For example, after the 1969 YAF convention, Sheldon Richman continued to be active in the libertarian organization formed at the convention (see chapter 7). In 1972, through the Society for Individual Liberty, Sheldon got invited to a fund-raising dinner for Libertarian Party candidate John Hospers. Sheldon spent the day traveling with Hospers and soon after became involved with the party on the local level.

During his six years as a newspaper reporter, Sheldon also wrote several columns about libertarian candidates. But in 1977 the local paper that employed Sheldon could no longer afford his position and he was laid off. That year he went to his first national Libertarian Party convention and met people from the Cato Institute, a newly formed libertarian think tank. The following year Sheldon went to a summer seminar put on by Cato. He comments,

> That was an extremely influential week [for] me, particularly on the foreign policy side . . . because I was hearing lectures from [Leonard] Liggio and [Murray] Rothbard and Bill Evers. These people had this antimilitarism line as well as the reading material to explain it. . . . When I got out of that seminar I decided I didn't want to be a reporter any more because it was extremely frustrating to have to be an objective reporter . . . which means sitting there and never being able to offer any view. . . . I always covered government. I was covering the State House at that point. . . . It was very hard to have to treat all that very straight. . . . So I decided I wanted to do something in the movement.

Sheldon decided to find a job that embodied his political beliefs. In 1979 he was hired as research director for the Council for a Competitive Economy, a free market business group organized by the same people who started Cato, and moved to Washington. Sheldon says he "saw it as a chance . . . to get into the movement in a professional capacity." At the same time he became more active in the Libertarian Party and served on the platform committee for the 1979 convention in Los Angeles.

The blossoming of the libertarian movement offered opportunities for other activists as well. By the end of the 1960s libertarian SDSer Doug Knox had cofounded the New Left Project at Stanford, which attempted to keep the New Left together after the collapse of SDS. He also continued his involvement in antidraft work. By this point he identified as a decentralist and held a "pro-individalist, capitalist viewpoint." After completing his undergraduate degree, Doug entered graduate school in political science in 1974. At the same time he got a job at a conservative think tank collecting libertarian materials for its archives.

Meanwhile, Doug became active in the Libertarian Party and served on the national committee of the party from 1975 on. In 1977 Doug dropped out of graduate school to accept a position at *Inquiry,* a libertarian magazine. He says, "It was a serious attempt to continue this . . . cross-fertilization between individualistic, antigovernment or skeptical-of-imperial-ventures stuff on the left, and libertarian things." Other libertarian activists, like Sheldon and Doug, sustained their passion for politics throughout the decade within the multitude of libertarian organizations formed during the 1970s.

Some libertarians also continued participating in countercultural activities during the 1970s. Besides her involvement with women's issues (see below), Louise Lacey was also active with environmental issues and alternative lifestyles. In 1970 she became involved with Earth People's Park. Distinguishing it from People's Park, Louise explains,

> It started . . . when a convocation was called of representatives of families of friends. . . . There were tribes within the counterculture of friends and they called themselves families of friends. Many of them sent a representative to this gathering. . . . It was the first organizational meeting of an idea that had been born in a hot springs in New Mexico . . . among some people from the Hog Farm, some entertainment figures, and some notables of the counterculture.

The idea was to raise a million dollars in order to buy a big piece of land. They would deed the land to God so that it could not be sold again. Then they would create a political, social, and ecological example of the ideal society, of "anarchy in action." Louise began volunteering one day a week at the Earth People's Park office and tithed 10 percent of her salary to the organization. She remained involved with this project for two and a half years.

After Earth People's Park, Louise became involved in Tony Serra's campaign for mayor of San Francisco. Louise helped write Serra's platform. The first plank called for San Francisco to secede from the country and for California to become a free state. All personal and property taxes were to be abolished. San Francisco would become a haven for people fleeing drug enforcement laws and the draft, as well as a center for art and music. Serra's campaign slogan was Make the Streets Safe for Dancing.

Although Serra lost, he came in first among the alternative candidates.

Louise also lived communally and continued using drugs throughout the
1970s.

## Women Organizing Women

As with women on the left, many women from YAF also applied the
lessons and knowledge they learned through their activism to organize
other women. Traditionalists used their skills to form a movement aimed
at retaining women's traditional place in society. In contrast, libertarians joined in the effort to organize a feminist movement.

Traditionalist Women's Organizing   A number of traditionalist women
maintained their political activism during the 1970s by becoming involved
in the pro-family movement.[10] Like some women on the left, some traditionalist women say they truly found their voice in organizing other women.
Just as some SDS women describe their awakening to feminism, so some
traditionalist women describe their awakening to the dangers of feminism.
Jo Ann Gasper, for instance, says the International Women's Year (IWY)
conference held in Houston in 1977 led her to a political awakening.

> Intellectually, I knew there were liberals and conservatives, but it's
> different when you all of a sudden have that kind of eureka experi-
> ence and realize . . . that there were basically these two groups of
> people that had diametrically opposed political agendas and philoso-
> phies and world views. . . . [I] was appalled at the ideas that were
> being [voiced] from the other side. And came back [from IWY] and
> felt very much that if the women of America knew what was hap-
> pening, they would put down their brooms and go and defend their
> families. Because that was really what the onslaught was, was the
> real outright attack on the American family. . . . From my political
> philosophy days I knew that the family is really the basic unit of
> society. . . . If you destroy that family, then you destroy what's made
> America great.

Jo Ann found the entire IWY meeting offensive; she was disgusted by
the stacking of the deck during the election process and the games being
played. "The whole thing was just so contrary to everything that I had
been taught that was American. . . . Basically I was raped . . . it was just
that kind of brutal experience, philosophically, procedurally. This just
wasn't supposed to happen in America." In the aftermath of IWY, Jo
Ann started doing research on the ERA, abortion, and other issues. She

started a newsletter entitled *The Right Woman,* which monitored federal legislation and presented congressional news concerning women and the family. Shortly after she also began a newsletter that monitored the *Federal Register* for social issues. This sideline hobby soon took over Jo Ann's life. She quit her job as a business consultant and devoted herself to producing these two newsletters. Eventually, in the 1980s, Jo Ann went on to serve under President Reagan as deputy assistant secretary for population affairs at the Department of Health and Human Services.

Phyllis Schlafly played a critical role in raising the consciousness of other traditionalist women. After finishing college, Kathy Rothschild moved to Washington to work as the secretary for Dave Jones (former executive director of YAF) at the Charles Edison Youth Fund. Kathy stayed at the organization for several years, learning the ins and outs of direct mail fund-raising. When Dave left, Kathy took over the organization. Meanwhile, in 1972 Kathy read an article in *New Guard* written by Carol Dawson supporting the ERA. Kathy wrote a counter-article explaining why she opposed the ERA. In response, Phyllis Schlafly wrote to Kathy, congratulating her on the article. About three weeks later Schlafly called her, asking her to testify against ERA at the hearings of the Virginia legislature. Kathy remembers this important event.

> I said, "Yes, but I have never testified." "Don't worry, I'll write your testimony, we'll practice it, I'll tell you how to answer the questions." . . . Phyllis comes to town. She says, "Get ten of your most trusted women friends who are really smart. . . . We are going to teach them all about the ERA." Fine. Did that. . . . She gives the pitch. Everybody goes, "Okay, we understand. We knew we were against it and now we know why." We all marched ourselves down to Richmond and testified against ERA and we were overnight media . . . stars. . . . That was a big turning point in my political life . . . because in came Phyllis Schlafly.

Schlafly taught Kathy, as well as thousands of other women, not only the ins and outs of ERA, but also concrete skills and techniques of political organizing. Kathy began raising money for Virginia STOP ERA and became very involved in the campaign. Calling Schlafly "an incredible person," Kathy says,

> [Phyllis] really changed my life. Everything that I had learned before in politics was just added to by another layer of sophistication because Phyllis is a sophisticated politician. She is really sharp. . . .

Then I started going to her . . . Eagle Council meetings. . . . You
started out at breakfast at 7:30 or 8:00 and you went to meetings
and you learned, learned, learned. She would have speakers to educate us, not only about different parts of the ERA battle, but also
about . . . the media and how to act when you are on TV. . . . We
were really trained. She would bring the video cameras in. Video
was new then . . . nobody even knew what they were. . . . Phyllis
[is] the greatest teacher in the world.

The irony of Schlafly's role is that she functions as a great feminist
role model for women. She is an outspoken and effective leader who has
influenced and trained thousands of women. Her organization stands as
a prototype of how to motivate and educate women. Kathy remarks,

When you get into Phyllis's operation it's all women and we're
all . . . running for office, we're running campaigns, we're doing
fundraising, we're doing everything. . . . Through Eagle Forum and
STOP ERA I gained a lot of confidence in myself, my ability to do
things . . . in terms of competency to run, to administer an organization, a foundation to run a campaign. [I learned] that I could do
it just as well as any other man who was well equipped. It was the
qualifications that you had, not whether or not you happened to be
a man or a woman. . . . Phyllis is just . . . the greatest positive force
for . . . being a woman and being proud that you are a woman.

In 1975 Kathy left the Edison Fund to start her own public relations
firm. One of her main clients was Phyllis Schlafly, who hired her to travel
to key states where the ERA had not been ratified to train candidates on
organizing a campaign. Kathy found her YAF experiences invaluable.

[The people I met] had never been through YAF or Youth for Goldwater. They couldn't have organized their way out of a paper
sack. . . . They had been the mayor or they had owned the biggest
department store . . . and that is how they had gotten to be a state
senator or a state rep. They had never really run a campaign before. . . . I was just telling them all the things that I already had
learned through YAF.

Drawing on her YAF experiences, Kathy put together a training manual
and taught them how to write fund-raising letters and press releases and
how to raise money. She says, "They wanted the nitty-gritty. I'm thinking, They want what YAF did for us." She also trained candidates on

how to debate the ERA, directly transferring the skills and resources she learned from YAF.

Besides working with Schlafly, Kathy also knew New Right leader Paul Weyrich and served on the board of the Free Congress PAC that Weyrich organized. In 1977 Congressman Buz Lukens, an old friend Kathy knew from her YAF days, called to ask Kathy to take over as executive director of the American Legislative Exchange Council.[11] After consulting with Weyrich and Schlafly, Kathy accepted the job and stayed there from 1977 through 1985.

As can be seen, during the 1970s traditionalist women played key roles in taking charge of the pro-family movement. Through YAF they also had direct ties with leaders and organizations of the burgeoning New Right.

Libertarian Women's Organizing   Libertarian women also became active on women's issues during the 1970s, but not on the same side as traditionalists. All the libertarian women in this study supported feminism to one degree or another. Yet libertarian feminists depart from other feminists in opposing any dependence on government. They are against government sponsorship of abortion or child care and instead encourage self-reliance and self-sufficiency.[12]

The activities of Louise Lacey illustrate the principles of libertarian feminism. Since the 1960s everything Louise has done aimed at "making people more independent and making them feel a part of a larger whole." She wrote several books during the 1970s, one of which was published and became quite successful in the women's community. Entitled *Lunaception: A Feminine Odyssey into Fertility and Contraception,* the book emphasizes natural birth control. Louise explains, "It is fertility awareness based on self-knowledge. . . . What happens when you follow the discipline is that you find out that your body *is* in synch with the moon, and that probably that's an evolutionary pattern, that the light of the moon triggers ovulation." Congruous with her philosophy, Louise views this book as giving women independence and connecting them to other women. *Lunaception* became important in the natural family planning movement and was reprinted in French and German.

Louise also started a magazine called *Woman's Choice* during the 1970s. The byline of the magazine read, "An Intimate Monthly Journal of Feminine Expression." Each issue focused on a different topic such as success, depression, friends, or dreams. Louise saw the journal as a do-it-yourself consciousness-raising group. "It was the ultimate of self-help. . . . It would take an issue that was important and I would go out and . . . find people who [had] . . . given a lot of thought to the resolution of that concept. . . . I would get . . . a dozen experiences around that issue and print them all. . . . It was very powerful stuff."

Louise says the journal was a feminist publication in the "larger sense, not according to any particular creed." At the same time, Louise doesn't think of herself as a feminist because of the negative connotations of the term. She disagrees with aspects of the feminist political agenda.

> I don't agree with all kinds of things to do with legislative programs, or government-sponsored child care, or anything that requires the government to give rights . . . or money, which I don't think . . . we should be dependent on the government to give us. If we're dependent on them, and they take it away, we're stuck. I would work for an organization that solicited money for abortions for poor people, but I don't want the government paying for abortions for poor people because then they can take it away. . . . Why don't we just give the money to the women? I've never understood that.

True to libertarian feminist belief, Louise objects to dependence on others—whether it be government or individual men. Instead, Louise calls for complete self-determination and autonomy of women, a reliance on the self.

Another libertarian, Sharon Presley, helped form a libertarian feminist organization. In the mid-1970s Sharon met Toni Nathan at a Libertarian Party convention and together they formed the Association of Libertarian Feminists (ALF). Sharon recalls, "I'd certainly been aware of feminism. . . . I had not been involved in the women's movement, but was entirely sympathetic." Sharon served as the first national coordinator of ALF. ALF published position papers, including ones supporting ERA, abortion, and the decriminalization of prostitution. In addition, ALF organized a panel at every Libertarian Party convention.

One paper Sharon wrote, entitled "Libertarianism and Feminism," argues for a distinct libertarian feminist perspective.

> If a woman said to you, "I want to be free from the domination of men," but turned to a tyrannical husband not only for financial support but for decisions about her own personal and social life, you would undoubtedly consider her inconsistent. Yet that is what many feminists are doing on a political level. They say they want to be free of the domination of men but ask for favors and handouts from a government of men, for example, government day-care cen-

ters. They say they reject the authoritarian ways of thinking and acting that have characterized men throughout history but turn around and advocate the same old authoritarian methods that men have always used (compulsory taxation, more government controls, etc.).

This paper also states the purpose of ALF is "to encourage women to become economically self-sufficient and psychologically independent . . . oppose the abridgment of individual rights by any government on account of sex; work toward changing sexist attitudes and behavior exhibited by individuals; [and] provide a libertarian alternative to those aspects of the women's movement that tend to discourage independence and individuality."[13]

Other libertarian women used the knowledge and skills they learned in YAF to open avenues for women in the work world. Like some SDS women, libertarian Marilyn Bradley became fed up with politics and shifted her focus toward her career. Marilyn began moving away from traditional politics during the 1970s, in part because of the sexism she experienced on both the left and the right. Withdrawing from her previous political activities, she says, "I got fed up with the male egos involved . . . in the politics. It just seemed so meaningless." Meanwhile, Marilyn became more involved with therapy and the human potential movement. "I moved inward. . . . I decided that the key to changing the world was changing people's hearts and minds, starting with my own."

By this point Marilyn had become a feminist and got more involved in women's activities. While working on her master's degree, she served as a head resident for undergraduates. She turned her office into the women's center on campus, donating her feminist books to the center's shelves. She also began giving talks to sororities on women's liberation. After finishing her degree, Marilyn got a job as an administrative assistant at the university. Along with a handful of other women on campus, she helped organize a group called Women in Management, which met on a monthly basis and invited in speakers to discuss issues concerning women and work. By the mid-1970s Marilyn concentrated on building her career and breaking through the old boys' network. "I just decided . . . my career was going to be my thing. . . . I was going to be one of the first women to prove to those assholes. . . . I was professional and pleasant, but boy, was I determined. They weren't going to keep me down. I was going to kill to get ahead. Actually I didn't really kill, but boy, I worked hard."

Within a couple of years Marilyn had moved up to become associate director of one of the major offices at the university. When her boss took another position, it became clear that Marilyn was not going to be promoted to his position. She left and began working at a company nearby with one of her old leftist friends. By the 1980s the university lured Marilyn back to take over the directorship of her old office. Marilyn became the first woman (and youngest) director to hold this position. She directed a staff of ninety-three employees and managed a three-million-dollar budget. Marilyn had successfully pushed through the barriers restricting women's place. As with women in SDS, some libertarian women were using the lessons they learned as activists to push for change for women in the workplace.

## Work

**Traditionalists' Work Lives**    Traditionalists faced a smoother transition to adulthood and to their work lives than did leftists or libertarians. Like Mitch Petry, Fran Griffin, and Kathy Rothschild, many traditionalists found employment directly tied to their politics. YAF connections were especially important in obtaining such jobs. Connie Marshner, for example, got her first job through her ties to YAF. In 1971, during her senior year at college, Connie wrote to Dan Joy, the former editor of *New Guard,* to ask if he knew of any jobs in Washington. When he offered her a position, Connie's father accompanied her to Washington to meet him. Dan met with her father's approval and Connie was hired as Dan Joy's secretary. She followed Joy to Capitol Hill. Shortly after, when Walter Mondale's child development bill was working its way through Congress, Connie was given the task of analyzing the bill and writing up a rebuttal. This was Connie's introduction to social issues. She remained on Capitol Hill for the following fifteen years, eventually becoming one of the top leaders of the pro-family movement.

In sharp contrast to the left, traditionalists had no aversion to working within the system nor did they feel pressure from other activists to remain outside the mainstream. Many traditionalists launched their careers during the 1970s. Yet even those traditionalists who committed themselves wholeheartedly to their careers, maintained some involvement with the conservative movement. For Alan MacKay, much of the 1970s was devoted to his career as a lawyer and to family life with his seven daughters. Although Alan describes himself as not being very active during the 1970s, he actually continued his involvement in a number of ways.

After stepping down from being YAF chair in 1969, he served on the board of ACU until 1971. He also became active with Howard Phillips's New Right organization, the Conservative Caucus. For about ten years beginning in 1974 Alan served on the Conservative Caucus board and in 1976 he also served as state chair of the organization.

While leftists were protesting on the streets, dropping out of school, and stepping off professional career paths, traditionalists were building up their "career capital" by accumulating skills and experiences that were stepping stones for employment in mainstream institutions. While leftists applied the skills and resources they acquired during the 1960s toward other social movements, traditionalists used their skills in mainstream politics and in career development. Even when YAFers moved from one job to another during the 1970s, rarely were they unemployed and none lived on the margins. Few stepped far off "the track."

Although Emmy Lewis held a variety of jobs and moved around throughout the 1970s, mainly her work provided her with skills and resources that contributed to her career trajectory. After getting her bachelor's degree in 1968, Emmy moved to New York and got a job in advertising and public relations. She hated New York and, after two years, returned to Michigan where she first went to work for an international advertising agency as a copywriter and account executive; later she got a job as associate editor for a national magazine called *Snow*, the official publication of the U.S. Ski Association. After traveling around the world for six months, Emmy returned to politics in 1971 when she got involved in Nixon's presidential campaign. After the election, she visited Washington and met with conservatives she had known from her days with YAF, including Lee Edwards and Howard Phillips, then acting director of the Office of Economic Opportunity. Emmy was impressed by the idea of conservatives making changes in Washington. She briefly worked in Washington but returned to Michigan when she got married in 1972. From 1972 to 1974 Emmy served on the local Republican Committee in Ann Arbor and opened her own public relations and advertising business. One of her projects involved working as a consultant for New Right leader Richard Viguerie's direct mail company in Washington. She knew Richard from their days in the Goldwater campaign and YAF. Another employee at Viguerie's company, Steve Winchell, was also an old friend from YAF days. In 1974 when Winchell decided to start his own firm, he asked Emmy to join him. Emmy closed her business and moved to Washington to work with him on direct mail fund-raising and stayed there through the rest of the 1970s. She had stable employment, in various jobs, throughout the decade. Like other traditionalists, Emmy was busy building her career with work that was, for the most part, intimately connected to her politics. Unlike leftists, then, traditionalists were well integated into the mainstream, steadily employed, and committed to career trajectories throughout the 1970s.

**Libertarians' Work Lives**   Like traditionalists and leftists, a number of libertarians also found jobs that expressed their politics during the 1970s. Sharon Presley, for instance, actively sought work that represented her libertarian beliefs. After finishing her master's degree in psychology in 1972, Sharon joined another anarchist friend in New York and became co-proprietor of Laissez-Faire Books. Sharon viewed the bookstore as an extension of her beliefs.

> I considered [the bookstore] part of my political activism because we didn't open up a bookstore to make money. . . . Good thing, too, because we never did. . . . [It] was part of an educational process, to make these ideas more accessible to people and they in turn could take them on and do things with them. . . . We had anarchist books in the store as well as libertarian books.

Sharon remained at the bookstore until 1977 when she returned to school to get her Ph.D. in psychology.

Like leftists, libertarians also followed circuitous paths. Rather than focusing on careers, as many traditionalists did, libertarians were more likely to try on a variety of lifestyles and activities. Like other libertarians who were immersed in the counterculture, Rob Tyler wandered around during the 1970s and continued to be involved with the counterculture. After the libertarian purge at the 1969 YAF convention, Rob felt very bitter and spent the whole summer afterward smoking hashish and listening to Dylan records. During the early 1970s he organized libertarian meetings and conferences (see chapter 7) but soon got "burned out by organized politics." Although Rob registered with the Libertarian Party, it didn't interest him. He moved to Venice Beach and got involved with school, drugs, Rastafarianism, and reggae. At this point Rob retired from politics. He began graduate school in history, then decided to get a teaching credential. Disillusioned with teaching, he left this, too. Not knowing what to do, Rob drifted into law. "I somehow found myself going to law school because a friend of mine from elementary school sold me . . . a kilo or a pound [of marijuana] . . . and he told me he was going to law school at night. I said, 'Geez, what a concept. Going to law school at night?' Because I didn't know what to do."

While working for some attorneys, Rob started meeting Vietnamese and Cambodian clients who told him about their lives. They renewed his interest in politics.

> God, was I blown away by their stories! Something sparked me at the atrocities, the holocaust. I couldn't . . . comprehend what they had gone through. So I really realized that the left had utterly betrayed any decency or humanness they had. By supporting Hanoi they had supported the new regime of terror and holocaust on a much greater level than the right anticipated. . . . I began to be aware in '75 that something *horrible* had happened in Cambodia. . . . That sparked my interest again. So I got back involved and interested in political things.

Soon afterward Rob became involved in Ronald Reagan's presidential campaign.

Rob's partner in libertarian organizing, Dana Rohrabacher, also was enamored with the counterculture during the 1970s. His story is unusual, though, because of his shift in beliefs. Unlike the majority of libertarians, Dana became more conservative during the 1970s. After the 1969 YAF convention, Dana left behind the conservative movement and joined Rob in organizing libertarian conferences and meetings. Dana recalls,

> From '69 to about '71 or '72, my friends were basically new culture types. They were not conservatives at all. . . . Within about a six-month period, all of my ties to the conservative movement . . . were just severed. . . . I didn't have much in common with them any more. . . . I was a libertarian. I was more focusing on individual freedom and not focusing on defeating communism at the cost . . . of our liberty.

Once Dana finished school, he became "a free spirit," hitching around the country with his banjo. For about a year he gave libertarian speeches on campus, played his banjo, listened to rock-and-roll, and just had "a fun time." Dana wrote songs and played music as he traveled. The lyrics of his songs include the following:

> You can't legislate my morals,
> Or anything I do

I can have my pot, or have my girl
Because I'm not screwing you.

Another of Dana's lyrics went,

It's the politician's job to watch his flock
With FBI, IRS, with drug laws and no-knock
You must obey the laws, yeah, that's democracy
And all of this would pass away, if we had anarchy.[14]

Dana's life changed dramatically when he got married in 1971. He reflects on this period:

When I got married, I just decided, "Whoop, gotta be responsible now, I'm a married man." . . . Because I had the image of a father providing for his family. . . . By '72 I was basically working as a journalist and left politics pretty much behind me. . . . Certainly [left] the new culture aspect of it behind and had gotten out of libertarian activism. Just decided I was going to be a professional journalist.

Once he was a journalist, Dana viewed his time with the counterculture as a time of experimentation, a part of the growing-up process. He settled into a "pretty responsible life . . . earning a living and . . . [becoming] a good citizen. . . . I didn't all of a sudden become a staunch conservative . . . but I started being much more responsible in my life." Journalism fit Dana's interests in politics, ideas, and world affairs. His reporting did not go unnoticed. After four years working as a journalist for the *Orange County Register,* in 1976 Dana was hired by Lyn Nofzinger to be assistant press secretary for Ronald Reagan.

Dana's choice to work for Reagan represented a shift in his beliefs. He says,

Frankly, the reason I . . . started working for Ronald Reagan, [was because] . . . after three or four years of . . . evolving, I became more conservative again. . . . Also the world changed. . . . America changed in that time period, too. . . . The war in Vietnam ended, the Soviet Union went on an incredible military buildup and offensive. We were losing countries all over the place. And . . . when the war in Vietnam ended . . . the conservative movement . . . quit focusing on those things that were basically anti-freedom . . . [and] about social control. They started talking about economic issues again. . . . I can agree with . . . their free-market economics. . . . I went with Reagan because . . . I agreed with him the most. I am not now, nor ever will be, nor ever have been, a hired gun. I do not work for people [when] I think someone else is better. Life's too short for that. It does something to your soul.

Dana comments that the traditionalists who kicked him out of YAF in 1969 were all over Washington in the 1970s, but none of them got jobs in the Reagan campaign. "It must have been just incredible for these traditionalists, who had basically six years before kicked my fanny out of the conservative movement, to have had to turn around and see Dana Rohrabacher up there standing beside Reagan everywhere. They would *die* to have that same job." During the 1980s Dana successfully ran for Congress.

In sum, while traditionalists followed clear and steady routes through the 1970s, both politically and in terms of employment, libertarians more closely resembled leftists in following less certain and more experimental paths. A number of libertarians continued to identify with the counterculture and lived less conventional lives, questioning notions of traditional success and living on the margins. Yet by the end of the decade many libertarians had returned to graduate school. Overall, by the end of the 1970s 55 percent of all YAFers interviewed had either completed or were enrolled in graduate programs, the exact same proportion as SDS activists. Libertarians, however, were much more likely than traditionalists to have returned to graduate school. Eighty-five percent of libertarians either finished graduate degrees or were enrolled in such programs by the end of the 1970s, compared to 40 percent of traditionalists.[15]

### The Retreat from Politics

Most members of YAF did not look to the 1970s as a time to heal the self. Unlike SDS activists, they had suffered few costs for their activism and did not feel the need to recover from wounds suffered during the 1960s. Particularly for traditionalists, not only did YAF survive as their organization, but also the mid-1970s witnessed the ascendancy of conservative politics in the United States as conservative think tanks and organizations flourished, and conservative ideas and candidates gained in popularity.

Nevertheless, some traditionalists ended up withdrawing from politics. A few of the men put all their energies into their careers and participated only marginally in the political world. More commonly, traditionalist women left behind politics as they married and concentrated on their families and children. For example, Carol Dawson, who had worked full time in the Goldwater campaign, then for various senators and congressmen, President Nixon, and for the ACU as well, completely stopped her activities when her husband, Bob Bauman, the second national chair of YAF, was elected to the House of Representatives, a position he held from 1969 to 1980. During those years Carol devoted herself to being a political wife and raising four children.

The few libertarians who withdrew from politics did so because, like leftists, they felt politically burned out. They retreated as a result of the escalation of violence or the sectarianism of the times. By the end of the 1960s Gus DiZerega decided he had had his fill of organized politics. He comments, "I realized that if I was going to keep playing this game, I would have to become a lot more ruthless than I wanted to. I don't have a killer instinct. So I said, 'Okay, you've reached the end of the line with organized politics.'" Although he retreated from politics, Gus carried his beliefs into his work. While working as a newspaper columnist for the *Lawrence Journal World* in Kansas, Gus wrote a column entitled "On the Other Hand," which included ideas from both left and right.

After several years at this job, Gus's lottery number for the draft came up as sixty-nine ("the symbolism of that was quite appropriate: getting screwed by Uncle Sam!"). Gus moved to Berkeley to return to graduate school in political science and concentrate on his studies. He says,

I was gradually deciding that nobody's social theory impressed me as being particularly deep, that most kinds of analysis were deeply flawed, that that was why I wasn't being terribly pleased with what I saw organizations doing, and that I needed time to take stock, to sit, to think, to study. So it was about that time I finally became a scholar.

Meanwhile Gus supported himself by starting his own graphic arts business, selling hand-drawn cards on Telegraph Avenue in Berkeley. Gus remained politically inactive throughout the 1970s.

Although libertarians did not suffer costs for their activism to the same degree as did leftists, their involvement in the counterculture and their own radicalization led them to encounter unexpected twists and turns in their path to adulthood. For example, libertarian Marilyn Bradley discussed the tolls of the 1960s she witnessed during the early 1970s when a lot of her friends "were really going off the deep end, committing suicide, and stuff like that. . . . They were just doing all kinds of drugs and into all kinds of self-destructive behavior." No traditionalists mentioned similar predicaments.

Finally, like those in SDS, libertarians also stepped off the conventional path to adulthood in terms of lifestyle. A substantial number of both libertarians and SDS members remained single during the 1970s. Nearly half of SDS women remained single throughout the decade, while about one-third of SDS men did so. In addition, many SDSers cohabited and/or lived communally or collectively. Similarly, half of libertarian women remained single during the 1970s, while one-third of libertarian men did so. Meanwhile, in stark contrast, *none* of the traditionalist women and *only one* traditionalist man remained single throughout the 1970s. Further, while several libertarians lived communally or lived with a person outside marriage during the decade, none of the traditionalists adopted this lifestyle. Clearly, it was not just politics and ideology that divided traditionalists from other activists. Whether or not they married and how they chose to live also divided this generation.

## CONCLUSION

As we can see, for a number of reasons traditionalists traveled an easier road than did leftists or libertarians during the 1970s. For many leftists the 1970s was a period of recovery from the strains and conflicts of the 1960s, with SDS members feeling confused, dislocated, and even, in some cases, retreating from politics. Leftists and libertarians paid a toll for their radicalization, as they confronted difficult decisions about how to relate to mainstream America. They encountered dilemmas as they made their way into adult life and tried to balance their politics with work. Yet activists held true to their beliefs and the majority maintained their commitment to politics during this period of demobilization. Libertarians benefited from the growth of the libertarian movement; many found a place amidst the array of libertarian groups available during the 1970s.

Because traditionalists did not go through processes of radicalization, they did not take risks that jeopardized their careers or future success. Because they did not face the same costs for their activism in terms of arrests, expulsion from school, or jail sentences, they had less disruption in their lives. Nor did their ideological views hinder their advancement in careers, accumulation of wealth, or integration into mainstream politics. Therefore, they did not face a disjuncture between their lives as youths and as adults. Rather than experience the 1970s as a period of questioning, instability, or "licking the wounds and healing the self," traditionalists had a smooth path to adulthood. Absent from traditionalist accounts is the sense of confusion, alienation, doubts, and the psychological tolls that pervade leftist stories from the 1970s. In control of YAF, and with conservatives gaining power in the country, traditionalists acquired positions of political power during the 1980s and 1990s as the conservative wing of the 1960s generation ascended to power, forming an influential new movement called the New Right.

# CHAPTER NINE

# ADULT LIVES

What has happened to activists since the 1970s? Given the sense of exhilaration and efficacy leftists felt during the heady days of the 1960s, how did they fare as they faced the conservative tide of the late 1970s and 1980s? Did their beliefs change? And how did right-wing youth fare, having been ostracized during the 1960s and then seeing many of their dreams realized during the 1980s and 1990s with the elections of Presidents Reagan and Bush, the fall of communism, and the attacks on welfare? This chapter examines the pathways of leftists, libertarians, and traditionalists as they settled into adult lives and as they integrated the experiences of their youth into their adult identity. In particular, as activists have aged, concern over occupations, family, and personal relations have come to the forefront. Thus, part of the project of the 1980s and 1990s has been coming to terms with the place of politics for the long haul.[1]

## COMPETING IDENTITIES OF ADULT LIVES

Although politics has remained central to the identity of most SDS and YAF activists, the 1980s and 1990s have been times of pursuing other interests as well. Adulthood involves a shift in commitment from school to occupation, as well as a shift from affiliation solely with parents and peers, to building adult romantic and family relationships. These shifts involve the incorporation of new identities: as worker, spouse, and parent. Thus, identities vary over the life course and the salience of particular identities shifts as well. Identity with a profession or as a parent competes with, and oftentimes supersedes, identity as an activist. In short, the ability to sustain a master identity as an activist is typically limited in duration.[2]

## Work

For many people work is a primary aspect of identity. Through choice of occupation, individuals define themselves and find their place in the world. One of the main preoccupations for activists during the 1980s and 1990s has been finding work that is meaningful. Continuous with the 1970s, leftists and libertarians have followed a more circuitous path than traditionalists. Many libertarians and leftists remained both geographically and vocationally mobile throughout the past two decades. While a substantial number of these activists spent months or even years wandering between jobs and locations, unclear about their direction, none of the traditionalists followed similar paths.

Typical of the mobility of SDSers is Helen Garvy's story. After leaving jobs as a teacher and as a therapist, during the 1980s Helen moved to the country in northern California. Having lived cheaply for years on $100 to $200 a month, Helen used the extra money she earned to buy a piece of land. After helping another SDSer build a home for his aunt, Helen built a cabin for herself on her land. She then thought about what to do next in her life. During this time her father had open heart surgery. Helen decided to write a book examining the emotional aspects accompanying physical illness. While she was writing Helen also became involved in filmmaking. She went to Los Angeles to learn screenwriting. There she also learned the technical aspects of filmmaking, from writing to editing and production. At the time of the interview Helen had just finished her book. She was producing educational films, including ones on teenage pregnancy, birth control, and child abuse. Helen sees this work as continuous with her prior activities. "It's still changing the world and teaching people. Part of what you teach is confidence and how to look at things. It's all part of the same thing. . . . A lot of it is around empowerment and there's just a lot of ways to do that. I've never believed that there was one correct party line."

Another SDSer whose work followed a winding path is Barry Skolnick. Barry spent the entire 1970s in a Marxist-Leninist group, the October League. Half of that time Barry was organizing in factories; the other half he was in the leadership of the national organization. After the organization fell apart in 1979, Barry held a number of different jobs. He recalls, "I had some problems with the government trying to get me fired from different places. Just like my dad. . . . So I ended up driving a cab." After two years as a cab driver, Barry taught adult education classes and then worked as a journalist for a while. None of these jobs lasted long. At thirty-eight, Barry found himself out on the street, without a job, married, with one child, and another one on the way. He went to work in a company that manufactured truck parts. Soon he became their national sales manager, learning all about the truck and transportation industry. After eight years at that job Barry started his own company, importing and marketing for truck manufacturers. At the time of the interview he commented, "Now, ironically, [I'm] trying to develop joint ventures between American truck manufacturers and transportation companies and Soviet companies." Barry's career is atypical in that no other SDS activists have jobs in business. His wandering between various jobs, however, *is* typical.

Some SDS activists still feel restless, wanting to move on, even if they're unsure in what direction. Cathy Wilkerson comments (with a laugh), "I'm trying to figure out what I'm going to be when I grow up, how I'm going to earn a living." In 1980 Cathy emerged from the underground and turned herself in. After serving her time, she went to school at a community college in New York and got an associate's degree in engineering. At the time of the interview she was working as an aide to a radical lawyer and toying with the idea of graduate school. Subsequent to the interview Cathy became a math and science teacher working in a General Equivalency Diploma/job-training program in inner-city schools with young people who had dropped out.

Several other SDS activists commented that they are living "economically marginal" lives, a remark not mentioned by any traditionalists. Carl Oglesby, for example, is presently a freelance writer working on several book projects. He says, "I have a little better financial situation than I usually have because I had a very good lecture season last year. . . . But this year won't be that great. . . . Still in doubt, still in question, and I don't feel that I've settled anything." Whalen and Flacks's follow-up study of radical leftist activists in Santa Barbara found a similar struggle over vocation, a refusal to settle down or focus on material comfort. They found that not only did activists make less money than nonactivists, they followed experimental and tentative routes marked by fluidity.[3]

Although less common than with SDSers, some YAF libertarians also have drifted between jobs and locations. Some also keep their connection to the counterculture. During the 1980s Louise Lacey worked as a researcher on a drug treatment program study, was out of work for a while, then had a number of other jobs, including one for a chemical recycling company and another ghost writing. In 1987 Louise took a job in Silicon Valley writing software user manuals; she was still at this job at the time of the interview. Louise also makes an annual trip to the mountains to take LSD in order to place things in proper perspective.

Like some activists in SDS, some libertarians are also still trying to figure out their futures. At the time of the interview Gus DiZerega was working as a college professor teaching political science. He was uncertain whether he would remain in academia, given the limited job options for someone with his political beliefs. He said, "I supported myself for my dissertation research mostly as an artist, and if I'm not happy with what I have for next year, I'm bagging academia, going to do my writing on the side . . . maybe teach one course a year or something for fun . . . and live as an artist again." Gus has also become involved in shamanism and non-Western religion. As of 1997 Gus was still teaching American politics part-time and writing on environmental issues.

On the whole, libertarians have more stable job histories and more settled occupational lives than do SDSers. Traditionalists stand out from both libertarians and leftists in that none spent the last two decades wandering about, following circuitous routes. Rather, traditionalists typically moved from one political job to another, following a course that has brought many of them to positions of political prominence today. For example, Don Devine was a political science professor during the late 1970s but ran into trouble with the administration because of his political beliefs. When he was turned down for a promotion, he decided to leave. At the same time Ronald Reagan started his first term as president and appointed Don to be director of the Office of Personnel Management. Don was in charge of setting personnel policies for the two million civilians employed in the federal government. With the aim of restructuring government, Don oversaw a cut of one hundred thousand employees in nondefense employment in the first two years of his job. By Reagan's second term, Don had "stepped on so many feet . . . that I couldn't get reconfirmed the second time." After stepping down, Don set up Bob Dole's presidential campaign in 1984, served as his senior political consultant, and ran Dole's political action committee from 1985 to 1987. At the time of the interview, Don was working as an independent political campaign consultant.

Another traditionalist, Fran Griffin, worked for the ACU and on the Reagan campaign during the 1970s. In 1980 Fran began her own political consulting firm, Griffin Communications, "to service conservative, anti-Communist organizations."[4] Her company specializes in political public relations, handling all aspects of the press, writing releases, arranging press conferences and mailing lists and contacts with journalists. Her clients include the Heritage Foundation, the Conservative Caucus, Americans for a Free Afghanistan, *Human Events, Conservative Digest,* and conservative leaders such as Paul Weyrich, Richard Viguerie, and Phyllis Schlafly. Fran continues to run the business today.

In fact, Washington, D.C., is full of ex-YAFers. David Keene, who at the time of the interview was serving as chair of the American Conservative Union, GOP consultant, and adviser to Bob Dole, comments that he is surrounded by others who rose up through YAF.

> I could name fifty people in this town [from YAF]. . . . Most of the Reagan movement was part of that group. They were all kids who came up together, who still are friends and still work together. . . . We have a network of people. The original group all sits around and decries the fact that young people today aren't as smart as we were. . . . My closest friends were people that I met . . . through school and politics at that time, and then have brought each other all along since then.

YAF contacts have been critical for building the network of conservative organizations in Washington today.

Not only have traditionalists, libertarians, and leftists followed dissimilar paths. Their current occupations are markedly different. Overall, at the time of the interview, the SDS sample included seven professors, four therapists, four directors of social service agencies, three people working in nonprofit organizations (related to the environment, the homeless, and Central American policy), three lawyers, a judge, a journalist, a freelance writer, a filmmaker, a nurse, a surgeon, a public school teacher, and an owner of a counterculture health-foods restaurant. Other activists own a manufacturing company, do telemarketing consulting, are in graduate school, are unemployed, and one is a full-time homemaker. The majority, then, are concentrated in educational fields and social service occupations. Contrary to the media image that leftists have "sold out," abandoned their principles, and are busy making money, the majority of SDS activists have jobs that are consistent with their beliefs and values. The majority also continue to be politically active to one extent or another (see below). This finding is congruent with other follow-up studies of leftist activists of the 1960s.[5]

In terms of their occupational choices, once again libertarians are closer to leftists. Many libertarians presently have jobs related to education, including two professors, a high school teacher, a college vice president, a director of a nonprofit libertarian educational institute, and one activist who works in computer management at a university. Of the remaining libertarians in the sample, there are two lawyers, both of whom work in their own companies unrelated to politics; others include an engineer, a controller, a technical writer, a political consultant, and a congressman (Congressman Rohrabacher has become more traditionalist in recent years; see below).

In contrast to libertarians and leftists, many traditionalists currently are in positions with direct political affiliations; at the time of the interview seven owned or worked in political consulting firms aimed at fundraising, marketing, and campaigning for conservative candidates; two were editors of conservative journals; one was president of a nonprofit public policy organization focused on defense issues, and another was a high-level government appointee. The remaining traditionalists hold nonpolitical jobs including two businessmen, a managing editor of a major magazine, a vice president at a leading pharmaceutical company, a lawyer, an activist working in desktop publishing, and a woman who works at night in a lab. Interestingly, over half of the traditionalist women are full-time homemakers, a position only one SDS member and none of the libertarian women hold (see below).

In short, many traditionalists, particularly men, are seated in institutional positions of political power. These activists both helped usher in and benefited from the tide of conservatism that swept the country during the 1980s and 1990s. In contrast, the main base for leftists and libertarians has been colleges, universities, and other educational institutions. Their influence comes mainly through teaching and scholarly research, rather than through traditional political means.

## Political Identity and Jobs

As activists chose occupations, they confronted the issue of how to integrate politics into their adult lives. Some people resolved this dilemma by choosing work that embodied their political beliefs. As we've seen, many traditionalists have found jobs with direct political affiliations. Traditionalist Emmy Lewis now owns her own company, which specializes in direct marketing, membership development, and fund-raising. Her clients include the Republican National Committee, the Republican Senatorial Committee, the National Federation of Independent Business, and the National Right to Work Committee. She sees her job as a direct expression of her politics. She says, "When I get up before groups and talk about direct mail, I evangelize because it's the most important mass communications tool we conservatives have ever had." Clearly, Emmy's politics and her occupation are intertwined.

Similarly, some libertarians and leftists have also found jobs that directly express their politics. Since finishing her Ph.D., libertarian Sharon Presley has been a college professor. Now, she says, her forum for expressing her ideas is her classroom. Sharon's politics influence both her teaching and her research. Much of her research concerns issues of power, obedience, and resistance to authority. Sharon also raises these issues in her teaching. "I'm interested in why do people resist. . . . How can we encourage people to question unjust authority and not just to be sheep who go along with anything the government wants? . . . Ultimately, that has applicability for libertarian ideas." Sharon sees her work as contributing to a better climate for libertarianism by encouraging people to be more tolerant, more critical, more concerned with social issues, and more willing to resist authority. Subsequent to the interview, Sharon quit college teaching and started a nonprofit organization, Resources for Independent Thinking, which develops educational tools to increase critical thinking skills.

Some leftists as well have found careers that allow them to continue acting on their beliefs. Bernardine Dohrn, one of the leaders of Weatherman, has also found a way to live her politics. After being targeted by the FBI as one of the ten most wanted fugitives, Bernardine emerged from over a decade underground in 1980. She pleaded guilty to aggravated battery and jumping bail, was fined $1,500, and was placed on three years' probation. In 1982 Bernardine served seven months in jail for refusing to cooperate with a grand jury investigation of a Brink's robbery conducted by other radical activists. Although Bernardine passed the New York bar exam in 1984, in 1985 she was judged unfit for admission and therefore is unable to practice law.

Bernardine is now married to Bill Ayers, a fellow Weatherman leader. They are raising three boys (one is the son of Kathy Boudin, a 1960s radical who is still serving time for her role in the Brink's robbery). In 1991

Bernardine became the director of the Children and Family Justice Center at Northwestern University. As a legal advocate for children and families, Bernardine researches children's experiences in the legal system, works to improve Chicago's juvenile court system, and helps represent parents charged with child abuse or neglect, as well as children accused of delinquency. She sees her work in juvenile justice as a change in tactics, not substance: "It's a lens to see the whole world, all the issues of justice and equality and peace, all the issues I care about."[6] A new form of Bernardine's involvement was also evident during the 1996 Democratic convention. Bernardine and her husband, Bill, announced the start of a computer network, Democratics Online. The announcement read, "The progressive wing of the Democratic Party hasn't gone underground. We're on the Internet."[7]

Although many SDS activists have found a way to fuse their politics with their jobs, unlike traditionalists or libertarians, several leftists mention the ways their previous involvement has restricted options in their work lives. Like Barry Skolnick and Bernardine Dohrn, Vivian Rothstein has encountered difficulties in her work as a result of past political activities. In her previous job as a community relations officer, Vivian was promised a position as a department head, but the promotion was blocked because of her leftist affiliations. At the time of the interview Vivian was the director of the Ocean Park Community Center, an organization started by feminists, and the lead agency in Santa Monica working on poverty issues. The center operates four shelters: a battered women's shelter, one for homeless runaway kids, one for homeless adults, and another for homeless mentally ill women. Vivian is in charge of the organization, including fund-raising, budgeting, and all personnel matters. In this position as well she has run into difficulties. When the agency tried to get funding from the city, a landlord got up and protested. Vivian recalls,

[The landlord] said, "All you can say about the director of this agency is that she brings homeless people and coddles them . . . and she's been to Hanoi with Tom Hayden." Nobody knew that I'd been to Hanoi. I didn't really talk about it here because I was afraid there'd be situations where my credibility would be destroyed. . . . Now it's a point of pride, but for years I was afraid that . . . the word would get out and I would lose my job.

Despite such obstacles, Vivian loves her job and feels it is an extension of her beliefs. In particular, Vivian loves the combination of working on poverty and homelessness and trying to run the organization in a progressive way. She comments, "I feel more like I did in the movement working here than I have in the intervening years." Seeing political activism as her profession, Vivian is proud of her work. She says,

> It makes me feel really good to do work that I believe in. . . . So even though I can't figure out how to change things on a large scale any more, even on a small scale, it's what makes me feel good. . . . I don't think it's revolutionary . . . [but] I think it's important to do. . . . But it means that you can't want to make $75,000 a year and have a BMW. . . . I'm still trying to be a moral force in some way. That's kept me from feeling cynical.

Whereas some people have found occupations that embody their politics, others hold jobs that are entirely separate from their politics. These jobs are not a vehicle for the expression of politics, yet political values continue to shape these activists' work lives. SDSers are particularly likely to point out the ways in which politics informs their work, discussing how the skills and knowledge they acquired in the movement help them in their professional lives. Lynn Dykstra, who is now a surgeon, says her experiences in SDS taught her to fight for what she believes in at work. Saying she has been "branded a troublemaker," Lynn explains that her co-workers often appeal to her to speak out about problems they're too afraid to address. Lynn talks about how the knowledge she learned as an activist helps her in her present position.

> I don't think there's any way I could have been a surgeon without having gone through . . . some of the stuff I went through [in SDS]. . . . Surgery is a man's field. . . . You have to make decisions and you have to take responsibility for the things that you do. . . . Making decisions that . . . I was making when I was political . . . [and] taking those responsibilities allowed me to know that I could take responsibility for other things. . . . [Also] being a woman in medicine . . . you suddenly understand what it feels like to be black in the South . . . or an oppressed minority. . . . If I hadn't known about that stuff when I started medical school, I would have had . . . a lot of trouble trying to cope with the male-dominated system. . . . It was tough anyway, but at least I understood what was going on politically and knew that I didn't have to take it . . . [that] there were ways to change it. . . . If I hadn't gone through the political

things I went through . . . I wouldn't have the vocabulary or the
concepts to see it that way.

Lynn also sees a connection between her activism and her occupation because she tries to "help the world" through her work. In addition to saving lives, she brings her values to her relations with patients, spending
more time with patients than many of her male colleagues and generally
having a broader, more tolerant view of people.

Even Fred Faust, who now holds a position in a paper he once opposed, tries to bring his political values to his work. During the 1960s
Fred covered leftist politics for the student newspaper at Washington University. At the time he was critical of the mainstream city paper, the *St.
Louis Post Dispatch,* viewing it as too conservative, too much a part of
the establishment. During the 1970s Fred worked on an underground
paper, but when that folded in 1973, Fred started a typesetting business
that he ran for thirteen years. Today, ironically, he writes for the business page of the *Post Dispatch.* As he puts it, "My job now is to . . . cover
capitalism." Fred believes he is more sensitive to workers' problems because of his activism. One of the areas he covers is plant closings. Fred
reflects,

> In the past a lot of the business presses tended to automatically re-
> port everything from management's view and to even celebrate
> [plant closings] as a cost-cutting move. . . . I get particularly touched
> when I get calls from workers . . . saying, "Well, we're getting
> screwed." . . . Often there's not much I can do about it . . . but on
> the other hand, sometimes I can. . . . Some[times] . . . I can call the
> management and say, "This is what I've been told. Is it true?" So
> I try to pay more attention to asking questions . . . on what kind
> of notice was given, what's going to happen to the workers, those
> kinds of things. . . . I'd like to think that I'm approaching it with
> a little more sensitivity toward the people on the bottom than some
> might.

Although fewer YAF activists discuss the ways politics infuses their
work, several mention that YAF served as a training ground, teaching
them important lessons useful for their adult life and for their continued
involvement with politics. For instance, Allen Brandstater comments,

> Looking back on the young people I knew twenty years ago or
> more, today they are leaders. Three are assemblymen. One's a con-

gressman. Two or three of them are very successful lawyers. It was
a great training ground. I certainly learned more about leadership
and communication or persuasion or political management out of
YAF than I did out of any courses at USC or anything I learned in
high school. . . . You'll find this is a common thread among everyone involved in YAF . . . at least in its golden era, was the leadership that was taught.

Regardless of present occupation, the majority of activists on both
left and right have continued to be involved with politics during the 1980s
and 1990s. In addition to jobs that either directly or indirectly embody
their political values, activists participate in various political organizations. For SDS, involvement includes participation in organizations focused on Central America (human rights and health care), Physicians for
Social Responsibility, the National Lawyers Guild, AIDS education projects, ActUp, Harvard-Radcliffe Alumni Against Apartheid, marching in
pro-choice demonstrations, as well as participation in neighborhood organizations, public schools, and local electoral campaigns. Among libertarians, activists participate in pro-choice marches, are involved with
groups such as NOW, the Libertarian Party, the Society for Individual
Liberty, the Republican Party, and write columns and articles for journals. Many traditionalists, in addition to holding political positions, are
involved in electoral politics, particularly in various capacities of the local, state, and national levels of the Republican Party. In addition, traditionalist involvement includes the right-to-life movement, Eagle Forum,
Conservative Caucus, Republican Woman's Club, and columns and articles for newspapers and journals.

Although the majority of people remain active, there is a range in the
amount of involvement, from those who continue to be extremely committed to politics, to others who participate only occasionally. Several
SDS activists mentioned, for example, that although they do not belong
to any organizations, they continue to give money to liberal-left organizations such as the ACLU or Amnesty International. Further, some people
move in and out of their activism. For instance, YAFer Maggie Kohls
says her involvement has been sporadic. She reflects,

You get discouraged all the time. . . . It goes in cycles. . . . When I
joined YAF I was real excited, and then there was three years where
I didn't belong to anything. When I joined the [Libertarian] Party
I was real excited and I was real active for about six years. Then
I'd say from '82 to '88, '89 I didn't do anything. Now I'm active

again. I went to the conventions and I paid my dues but . . . you just get burned out . . . because it's all spare time. It's all unpaid. It's all, you know, three in the morning you're trying to stuff envelopes or something.

There are other factors besides burnout that explain this process of drifting in and out of politics. There are a number of reasons why people become less active politically. One main reason is commitment to careers.

### Careers and the Pulls away from Politics

As Maggie Kohls points out, for those who devote their unpaid time to activism, politics increasingly takes extra effort. In their youth time was plentiful and most people had few responsibilities, but now competing interests of work and family infringe on the time and energy needed for activism. For some people their work has taken on primary importance, surpassing their commitment to politics; their identity as professionals has replaced their primary identity as activists. For instance, as a top administrator at a liberal arts college, YAFer Marilyn Bradley's whole life is her career. She works until at least 7:30 each evening and also serves on boards and educational committees that frequently require her to travel on weekends. Marilyn comments,

> As immersed as I was in politics, I have been that immersed in professional life over the past ten years. . . . My priorities have shifted. . . . I took the same energy . . . [and] ability in leadership and I just plopped it into my profession. . . . I'm not involved politically. I would like to be, but I just don't have the time. I'm burning on all jets right now.

One day Marilyn hopes to be politically active again, but she doesn't see that happening any time soon. In addition to her career, she has a young son; her commitments to work and family fill up her life.

Similarly, SDSer Carol Christman's work has replaced politics. Carol withdrew from politics at the beginning of the 1980s when she "couldn't stand the splits any more." Remembering that time, she says, "I was in total existential crisis because really being a left activist was . . . my work. That was my life. . . . I didn't know what to do." Carol returned to graduate school, earned a Ph.D. in city and regional planning, and eventually moved to Boston with her husband, another SDS activist. At the time of the interview she was working as a social service administrator at an agency built by other leftists. Carol sets up worker assistance centers, primarily for dislocated women workers. She remarks, "I really have not done anything [political]. . . . For me now this job is like a political passion. . . . I love what I do. It's as close to being in the left . . . so for me it fulfills that need to be political. . . . There's a way in which I'm doing now a lot of the parts of what I loved then."

Carol seems to have reached a balance in finding a career that fulfills her, whereas others who have become engrossed in careers, particularly leftists, continue to be plagued by doubts about whether they are doing the right thing. For Michael Kazin the questions have to do with the conflicting pulls between career and politics as well with lifestyle. He says, "When we're worrying about how to pay for a new carpet upstairs, I still feel, and I hope I always will feel . . . 'What are we doing? We should be out there doing some kind of homeless work. . . . I should be working more with the labor movement, which is in deep trouble.'" Michael's life is consumed with his job as a college professor, writing and teaching, and being a father. He toys with the idea of quitting academia and becoming involved with a public interest group, but there is no organization compelling him to make this choice. He does integrate his beliefs into his teaching, but even there his doubts remain.

> My teaching is political . . . but it's not the same. That's where the guilt comes in. I like it too much. It's too easy a life. . . . I still have politics . . . [in] what I write. . . . But politics to me, coming out of the '60s, was not primarily an intellectual endeavor. . . . It was, you know, the struggle. It was trying to stop the war and align with radical blacks and it was being in the front lines.

SDSer Jim Shoch also continually wrestles with questions about the choices he's made. Jim spent the early 1980s working as the western regional coordinator for Democratic Socialists of America. Although the beginning years were exhilarating, it became increasingly difficult to keep the organization together. He recalls, "Either people were getting swamped by the work that they were doing, or they were having their first and second kid, or they were deciding they just could not make it on the margins and were going back to school, or were getting a bit disillusioned."

Meanwhile, Jim was sneaking off to the library, "reading like a crazy man." As he became convinced of the difficulties of creating socialism in America, he decided to return to school. He felt both "absolutely ex-

cited" as well as anxious about what graduate school meant for his identity as an activist. In 1986 Jim entered a Ph.D. program in political science at MIT. At the time of the interview he was still in school and the
questions were still there.

> I sometimes wonder where am I headed, what's the point of all
> this? . . . It is disorienting and . . . there are definitely moments
> when I think, I sure wish I could have found something else to do . . .
> that fits into a wider sense of how the left could regroup. . . . Maybe
> that's what I should have done. But I still to this day haven't re-
> motely come up with an idea of what that would have been.

As of 1998 Jim was employed as a political science professor.

In short, unlike libertarians or traditionalists, many leftists still feel
unsettled, a sense of dis-ease about the direction of their lives and
whether they are contributing to social change. The gap between their
youthful days standing outside the mainstream, leading their lives in a
critical fashion, versus their adult lives centered on work, family, or
material concerns such as buying new carpets, continues to pose questions that nag at them. As Dorothy Burlage comments, "Everybody that
I know . . . we all say the same thing. . . . We *still* don't feel comfortable that it's all right [to have a career]. . . . It's a feeling of not living
as meaningful a life as I did before, of not being as committed to my
ideals as I was before, feeling like I have to make a lot of compromises
to survive."

Besides commitment to careers, other leftists say the main obstacle to
their being politically active is the lack of a sustained movement or an
organization they feel compelled to join. Cathy Wilkerson says she would
immediately sign on to another organization if she found one worth joining. During the 1980s Cathy tried going to various meetings but again
felt alienated from the left. She remembers attending a meeting about El
Salvador where once again she felt mistreated.

> The organizers of the meeting didn't know who I was and I didn't
> tell them. And I got treated like a piece of shit just like I did as a
> woman in the '60s. . . . I got one-syllable answers to my questions
> and then they looked over my shoulder to see who else was more
> interesting in the room. Nothing had changed. Later on when the
> people that ran that meeting found out who I was, they fell all over
> themselves to talk with me. . . . It's very discouraging. . . . People

are in the Dark Ages on the left in terms of culture and values and relationships, how people treat each other. . . . So it's very hard to know how to relate to that.

Although another SDSer, Steve Kessler, presently is not attached to any one organization, he continues to go to meetings on various issues. Yet he, too, feels a vacuum with no movement to lead the way. Calling himself a "connoisseur of meetings . . . 'Oh, yes, that was a very good vintage,' or 'No, that was a poor vintage,'" Steve says that in the absence of a movement or party that gives clear direction, he feels isolated.

Ironically, while these SDS activists feel their reduced involvement is connected to the lack of a viable movement, traditionalist YAFer Alan MacKay says he is less motivated to be involved because of the very success of the conservative movement.

I'm much less involved than I used to be because in the '60s my feeling was, "If I don't do it, it won't get done." Today my feeling is there are a lot of people out there to do it and let them have a turn. If I were to feel that my personal participation was indispensable, it would be there . . . but the conservative tide in America has won and it is now establishment and I'm not. . . . When I find that everybody agrees with me, it's not fun any more. I lose interest.

A minority of people from both SDS and YAF have completely withdrawn from politics, no longer wanting to put time and energy into that part of their lives. People exit from politics for a variety of reasons. Traditionalist Bob Heisinger's work drew him out of politics, not lack of passion. As the Washington editor of a major national magazine, Bob feels it would be improper for him to engage in partisan politics. Other than contributing to campaigns of friends who are running for office, Bob has removed himself from the political world.

SDS activist Connie Brown has also withdrawn. She admits that she no longer has the same drive for politics that she did as a youth. She says,

I have a friend who works very hard in Brooklyn Parents for Peace trying to . . . make a nuclear-free harbor. I think that's great of her to do . . . but I just couldn't bear it. . . . I would hate to be in meetings and hate to write leaflets and would hate to send out envelopes. . . . I guess there isn't enough of [an incentive]. . . . Having a very busy life and a happy home is a great disincentive to political involvement.

The competing interests of work and family *are* great disincentives to activism, yet even among these people who have withdrawn from politics, most say they would "come out of retirement" if the right issue or cause came along. A core part of their identity remains tied to activism, dormant in their consciousness but available for future causes. For example, two libertarians—one from YAF and the other from SDS—both said the draft is an issue that would cause them to reenter politics. Another activist, SDSer Lynn Dykstra, says although her heart is no longer in politics, she sees a time in the future when she will return to activism. "I don't feel real strong political desires. I don't feel any need to make other people listen to my political views the way I used to. . . . [But] I think at some time in the rest of our lifetime something else is going to come up and . . . many of us will end up having to speak out as a group again and be very, very vocal. When that time comes, I'll know and I'll do it."

In short, despite the range of involvement from those who are relatively uninvolved to those who continue to be consumed by politics, for the vast majority of activists politics retains a central place in their identity. Most people continue to integrate politics into their life, in one way or another, and even those who are inactive can foresee a time in the future when they might reenter the political world. For most people, then, politics is not just a part of their youth but continues to define their adult lives and continues to pose important questions in their everyday world. But besides the competing world of work, families also beckon activists away from politics.

### Families

Besides establishing themselves in occupations, many activists in the 1980s and 1990s have invested in relationships. As they've aged, many activists have married, had children, bought homes, and settled down. The majority of both YAF and SDS activists married,[8] although traditionalists are much more likely to be married than leftists or libertarians. Overall, 80 percent of traditionalists, 58 percent of SDS activists, and 46 percent of libertarians were married at the time of the interview. Once again, libertarians and leftists are less likely to conform to conventional norms of adult life than are traditionalists.

Further, among libertarians and leftists, men are more than twice as likely to be married than women are.[9] Although divorce accounts for some of those living outside marriage,[10] 25 percent of libertarian women and 41 percent of SDS women have never married, in contrast to none of the traditionalist women. Given that activists were in their forties and fifties at the time of the interview, these never married women represent a marked departure from convention. Two of these never married women, both SDS activists, are lesbians; the remainder are women who have defied the expectation of marriage, voluntarily or not.[11]

Most of the women who have remained single say the situation is circumstantial, not intentional. SDSer Jane Adams says there were times in the past when she felt she needed a partner, but now she feels content. Jane has one teenage daughter; they both share a house with Jane's parents. Regarding marriage, Jane comments that "if it happens, that's nice, but I'm tired of looking." As she's gotten older, Jane knows more and more single women and she also finds the university environment where she teaches conducive to being single.

Even if being single is involuntary, several women who remain unmarried point out the benefits of remaining alone. Libertarian Louise Lacey recognizes the value of her independence. She never sat down and decided not to marry but says it has "furthered my ends" to remain single, that having children would have been a disaster for her mental health and for the things she wanted to accomplish.

One of the few women who says she consciously chose to remain single is libertarian Sharon Presley. Saying she never wanted to have children, Sharon is not a big fan of marriage. As an anarchist she doesn't believe the state has any business sanctioning personal relationships. Sharon also fears some of the psychological dimensions of marriage, such as "getting submerged or being perceived . . . as less of an independent entity." Sharon also enjoys living alone. She says, "Yeah, to have somebody that I care about and develop this deepening relationship over the years and all those romantic ideas? Yeah, that appeals to me. But marriage [imitates spitting], I wouldn't say absolutely that I would never do it, but it doesn't particularly grab me as something I feel I must do." Clearly, these women, all of whom identify with feminism, defy conventional norms and expectations both in their beliefs and in their lifestyles.

Besides the differences in the proportion of activists who are married, traditionalists also have more children than libertarians and leftists. Overall, the average number of children of traditionalist activists is 2.8, compared to 1.5 for leftists and 1.2 for libertarians. Further, about one-third of traditionalists have four or more children, compared to two SDS men, one libertarian man, and *none* of the leftist or libertarian women.

In short, libertarians and leftists have followed different paths from traditionalists not only in terms of careers and mobility, but also in terms of lifestyle and families. Both groups—and particularly the women in each of these groups—continue to lead less conventional lives. Final evidence of this difference is the fact that while four SDS activists identify as gay or lesbian, none of the YAF activists do so.[12] Flacks argues that decisions about whether to marry or how to spend one's leisure time are private, individual matters that, when socially patterned, take on public, historical meaning. Given the participation by libertarians and leftists in the counterculture, and their consequent differences in lifestyle from traditionalists, these configurations of individual lives represent a renegotiation of the terms and conditions of everyday life.[13] There have been unintended demographic consequences to the political commitments of this generation of activists.[14]

## The Pushes and Pulls of Families

Families act both to sustain commitment to politics and pull individuals away from activism. On the one hand, the vast majority of activists on both the left and the right chose partners with similar beliefs to their own, people who understood and supported their passion for politics.[15] In fact, many activists met their partner through their political activities. YAFer Anne Edwards, for instance, met her husband, Lee, through a letter to the editor of *New Guard,* YAF's monthly magazine. She says she could "no more marry out of my politics than out of my religion because it's a set of values."

Many other activists commented that they could not even imagine being involved with someone who did not share their political views. Traditionalist Kathy Rothschild says although her husband is not a "political animal like I am," he cares about the same things and holds similar views.

> I never dated Democrats. I never even dated liberals. Why waste time? Who wants to fight about politics at home? I could never understand how anybody could marry anybody [that different], because marriage is such a commitment of mind and heart. I love politics so much and I'm so vocal. When I watch the news, I stand there and I say, "You idiot! How could you say anything like that." . . . Because I'm just into it all the time. . . . So no man who is a liberal could stand me. It's not me standing him; it's him standing me.

Many others also comment that a marriage of people with opposing political views would be difficult, adding stresses and strains to married life. SDSer Michael Kazin is married to a woman seven years his junior, who entered high school at the end of the 1960s. Although she didn't share Michael's experiences, she does share his leftist values and beliefs. Michael says,

> I couldn't imagine . . . having a long-term relationship with somebody who I had major differences with about politics. Because politics is not just politics, it's philosophy. . . . She's a doctor and if [she] believed that national health insurance was a terrible thing . . . I would have a hard time living with someone like that. A hard time living with someone who thinks that black people are complaining too much about racism. . . . Also if she thought politics was unimportant . . . that would be tough. Relationships begin with sexual attraction, but obviously they don't last thirteen years if that's all there is.

Similarly, although SDSer Aldyn McKean wouldn't expect a man he's involved with to be an activist, he would need to share Aldyn's political values.

> The last two people that I've been involved with were members of ActUp. . . . It would be difficult for me to have a serious relationship with someone who did not basically support my politics. . . . There's no way that I could ever be involved with someone who was basically conservative and voted for Republicans. There are gay people who are like that, although somehow [laughs], I don't understand them.

A number of SDS members said that in addition to wanting partners with similar beliefs, they also need their friends to share their politics. In particular, the 1960s serve as a touchstone for many leftists. Some feel they can't be friends with someone who was uninvolved or had opposing views during the 1960s. Jeanne Friedman puts it this way:

> I can't make friends with people unless I can somehow locate them. . . . I have to know who they were and what they did in the '60s. I once dated this man and it was a pretty nice relationship . . . but the first few times we went out I kept on asking him what he was doing [during the 1960s]. Finally he said, "Is this some kind of litmus test?" I said, "It isn't that it's a litmus test. It's just that . . . I can't feel that I can get to know you unless I can place you." These

were watershed years in my life, and I can't *imagine* . . . somebody who was paying no attention whatsoever. . . . What would we have in common? . . . I have made friends who were both less and more active, but they all were impacted somehow, and approached it from the same point of view that I did. . . . But I can't . . . make friends with somebody who's on the other side. It cannot happen.

Other leftists as well say all their close friends still share their politics to one degree or another. For these activists their 1960s experiences are so intricately bound to their identity that they are critical to all their primary adult relationships. None of the traditionalists made parallel comments on friends with a similar 1960s background, but libertarian Louise Lacey does want friends who share her countercultural background, particularly the experience of taking hallucinogens.

I don't think I could get close to people today who didn't share some of my drug experience because so much of my spiritual development came out of that. . . . Unless you spent all your time on one acid trip fighting a bummer, everybody who took acid experiences this sense of oneness. . . . If you're an intelligent, sensitive person, you want to understand that, and you start pushing at the limits of your knowledge of what that means. So it means something about the way people communicate. It means something about the way I relate with that beautiful oak out there. It means something about what kind of food I put in my mouth and what I do with my newspaper when I'm done, and a hundred other things. So someone who hasn't . . . thought about those things because they didn't have that experience, I don't have a lot in common with.

On the one hand, these partners and friends with shared beliefs and experiences reinforce activists' values, sustaining their involvement in the political world. On the other hand, families can pull people away from politics. In particular, having children creates a shift in priorities. Parenthood becomes a central identity, absorbing time and energy. Both YAF and SDS activists discuss how their commitment to their children has become primary. SDSer Naomi Schapiro, a lesbian who now has two daughters whom she is raising with her partner, Kimi, comments,

I'm going to have to be less active certainly until the kids are a little older because I didn't have kids [in order] to go to meetings all the time. . . . [Also] I don't think I have quite as much energy as I did when I was twenty. . . . I'm also very committed to spending a lot of time with my kids. So it means that instead of writing a leaflet at ten at night, I'm scrubbing the bathroom because there wasn't any time to do it during the day, or preparing supper for the next day, or else just bed because I'm so tired.

Having children impedes activism not only because it limits a person's time for other things, but also because being a parent makes an individual more careful, less willing to take risks. SDSer Bernardine Dohrn puts it this way: "Having kids . . . throws you into a whole other way of seeing the world that in some ways is much richer and broader and multidimensional and something that you can relate to lots of people. [But] it also makes you slow down around taking risks and being able to make a whole set of decisions. . . . You have to come home that night and make dinner."

In addition, many activists have found that getting older and having children leads to a more settled life—involving house ownership or stable employment—and acts as a disincentive to political action. SDSer Michael Kazin says both his career as a professor of history and his family have taken him away from activism. At this stage of life, his priorities have shifted.

You know, having a house and a mortgage—it's banal, but it's true. Those things do have an impact [on political activity]. . . . And so does age. I like to have more than five hours' sleep a night. . . . I think more about planning for a few years down the line because . . . I don't have all the time in the world and there's things I want to get ready. And, if I were honest with myself, that's really more important right now than my politics.

Clearly, changes in the life cycle intervene in the expression of activism. Competing responsibilities for jobs, families, and children combined with a more settled lifestyle lessen the time and energy needed for the sustained political commitment of youthful idealism.

Whereas libertarians and leftists discuss this dilemma of finding time for politics amidst the balancing act of work and family, few traditionalists mention this dilemma. One possible reason for this difference is that traditionalists are more likely to be in marriages in which the women are full-time homemakers, alleviating the conflict between work and home. In fact, unlike libertarian and leftist women, many traditionalist women *have* become full-time homemakers. Once they began having children, these traditionalist women withdrew from both politics and paid employment. Over half of the traditionalist women in this study quit their jobs to stay home with their children, a lifestyle no libertarians and only one SDS woman chose. A few of these women work parttime out of their homes, but all feel their primary responsibility is to their families. These women don't face a time crunch between work, family, and politics. Rather they have set their families' needs above politics or career.

Traditionalist Connie Marshner offers the most dramatic transformation in priorities. By 1980 Connie had become one of the central figures of the pro-family movement, working with New Right leader Paul Weyrich at the Free Congress Foundation, and serving as a member of Library Court.[16] In 1984 Connie's life changed dramatically. Already having two sons, Connie was delighted when she gave birth to a daughter, Anna. But Anna was born with a heart condition and Connie and her husband, Bill, realized when Anna was only a couple of weeks old that her life was precarious. Connie devoted herself to being with her daughter every minute of the day. Connie recalls, "I . . . just loved her like I had never loved. . . . I had really tasted love for the first time." At six months of age, Anna died. Anna's death permanently changed Connie's view of the world.

> When I went back to work after Anna died, I realized how manipulative politics was. Everybody else has probably known that forever, but I had never seen that before. I saw that politics was . . . getting people to do what you wanted them to do. . . . All of a sudden I just didn't like it. . . . I wanted to be doing something that would change people's lives. And politics doesn't. It doesn't change their hearts. . . . So I began to get more and more disenchanted. . . . [Politics] was hollow.

Anna's death was the impetus for Connie to reprioritize her life. Connie realized she wanted to love wholeheartedly and with the devotion she had given her daughter, no longer taking any relationships for granted. Gradually Connie changed her life in order to spend more time with her family. First, she put her children in school in Washington near to her work and began leaving early to pick them up. She also tried working at home or part-time. Feeling this still wasn't enough, Connie began home schooling her children in the morning, which, she says, was "the most gratifying thing I ever did."[17] In the afternoons she continued working at home, editing the *Family Protection Report*. But she could no longer keep up with the Library Court meetings. Meanwhile, Connie's life still felt crowded; she continued to feel rushed and impatient. Finally, she de-

cided to quit her job. Connie now stays at home with her children. Looking back, she remarks about her days working full-time,

> Even though I was arguing against feminists and debating them and
> countering them legislatively . . . I was *living* like a feminist . . . in
> terms of putting my career first and farming my kids out . . . let-
> ting somebody else raise them. . . . I remember very clearly having
> the idea that, "Well, if I stay home and just raise the kids, I'd be
> wasting my time and my talents." I . . . got that from my mother . . .
> the idea that you're wasting yourself if you're serving somebody
> else. That's been very hard to let go of.

Connie's heart is no longer in politics. At the time of the interview
Connie had two more daughters and had completely withdrawn from
activism. Connie says there is a peacefulness to her life now, "like I have
finally found what I was looking for all those years." Every once in a while
Connie still does public speaking but says she never misses politics and
cannot see herself returning to the political world.[18]

Another traditionalist, Mary Fisk, has also forfeited politics to family. Now divorced from a YAF leader, Mary is committed to staying at
home with her eight-year-old son and her three-year-old adopted Korean daughter. She says politics is "low down on the list" of priorities.
Now that she's a single parent, spending time with her children is what
is most important. She is also active in her church. Politics, she says, is
"not a burning thing for me anymore." Like Connie, Mary says in retrospect she was trying to lead a liberated life that didn't work for her.

> When we were married . . . I had . . . everything the world says
> you're supposed to have. I had accepted the stereotypes of the fem-
> inists. And I felt betrayed. . . . I had the career. I was editor of a le-
> gal magazine. . . . I was going to Georgetown for my Ph.D. in phi-
> losophy. And I had this wonderfully upwardly mobile husband. But
> it wasn't enough. So that's when I started saying, "What do I re-
> ally want?" I want roots, I want a home, I want a family. That's
> what was important.

Mary worked until a week before her son was born. It never occurred
to her that she would want to stay home with him; she assumed she'd
be bored to death. She returned to work five weeks after he was born
but about six months later she realized that the highlight of her day was
coming home to her son. She comments, "I was so blinded by the stereo-
type that I had accepted that this was liberation. So I was growing into

my own definition of liberation. Not somebody else's." Mary now works part-time out of her house doing desktop publishing. She's involved with a group called Mothers At Home, a nonprofit organization that serves as an information source and support group for women who stay home with their children.

Connie and Mary seem to have permanently retired from politics, but other traditionalist women assume they'll return to activism once their children are older. When Kathy Rothschild married, she quit her job as director of the American Legislative Exchange Council and moved to Chicago with her husband. She now devotes herself to her daughters, Beth and Katie. Kathy admits she misses her job and politics but also knows she is doing what she wants and hopes to return to politics some day. "It would be untrue if I said I didn't miss politics, but I don't pine for it. I don't wake up every morning thinking, Gee, I wish I were there. . . . I imagine I will [return to politics]. Once it is in your blood, it is in your blood. . . . [But] my priorities now are my husband and my home and our children. . . . To do it right takes a lot of time."

Whether they balance the demands of work and home or concentrate on their children's needs, activists on both the left and the right have less time and energy for politics. In contrast to their days of youth, when activists were immersed in politics night and day, now competing interests pull them away from the political world—careers, families, involvement in churches and schools, and personal relationships. But even though they have less time available for politics, activists remain committed to their beliefs.

## CONTINUITY IN BELIEFS: THE PAST, THE PRESENT, AND THE FUTURE

### Political Values

Although there is a range in the amount of time activists currently allot to politics, from those who remain fully involved to those who have either temporarily or permanently withdrawn from the political world, there is a remarkable continuity in political values among activists. In organizational politics or away from it, the vast majority of people on both left and right have held true to their political beliefs. The sense of meaning they derive from these values and beliefs provides a continuity with their earlier selves. Thus, SDS activists continue to focus on social justice, egalitarianism, civil rights, and economic democracy. As John Brown Childs puts it, "We haven't given up our values. We're in different positions than we were in 1965. . . . I'm not twenty-four years old . . . but I still have essentially the same values. I'm against oppression; I'm against inequality; I'm for an egalitarian society. I think the rich get richer and the poor get poorer . . . and we should do something about it."

Many SDS activists say their core values have remained constant but their strategies have changed. A number of activists commented that they now focus on local or small-scale change rather than aiming for national or revolutionary change. The majority of SDS members today identify themselves as leftists, socialists, or democratic socialists. Two SDSers call themselves anarchists and two others say they are libertarians. By the 1990s few SDSers used the term "radical" in describing themselves.

Traditionalists in YAF also maintained their core values: support for free enterprise, the military, the traditional family; opposition to communism, abortion, gay rights, and welfare. Although two traditionalists expressed skepticism about U.S. involvement in the world, the majority of traditionalists believe in intervention. Lee Edwards explains,

> I'm not an isolationist; I never have been. . . . We have an interdependent world. Economically, politically, strategically we have to be concerned about what's happening around the world. We have to be involved in it. . . . Abraham Lincoln's line about the nation cannot be half slave and half free . . . can also be applied to the world. . . . There has to be reducing slavery wherever we can and increasing freedom wherever we can by a great variety of methods— Voice of America, National Endowment for Democracy, by military operations, stinger missiles . . . Contras.

Although the Communist world was crumbling at the time of the interview, Lee, along with other traditionalists, remains an ardent anti-Communist. He says,

> We believed then and we believe now that we are in a protracted conflict, political, economic, military, with the Soviet Union and its satellites, and no amount of Moscow propaganda about glasnost and perestroika can change that . . . it will all add up to smoke and mirrors unless and until . . . the Communist Party of the Soviet Union abandon permanently their Leninist dream of socializing the world. Then and only then will conservatives stop being anti-Communist.[19]

Like leftists and traditionalists, libertarians in YAF also remain committed to their core values: opposition to the draft and domestic statism;

support for individual liberty, private property, abortion, gay rights, and the decriminalization of drugs. Marilyn Bradley speaks of the values that have remained constant for her over the years: "I believe in individualism *and* the community. . . . I believe that the free-market system can work because people naturally will give if there's plenty. . . . I believe in community-based self-sufficiency and healthy competition. . . . And, fundamentally, I really believe in small communities. . . . I just think that mass anything is dehumanizing."

Revealing his continuing identity with the counterculture, Rob Tyler also speaks about the persistence of his values. "I still like the Grateful Dead. . . . Their principles are not too different than mine. They're pretty anarchist kind of guys, individual freedom and they like making money. Those are my values right there."

Yet in sharp contrast to traditionalists, libertarians are noninterventionists, believing that beyond free trade, the United States should not involve itself in foreign affairs. Dave Walter says unless there is an invasion army coming across Canada or Mexico, it is not our business to intervene.

> Anybody who favors intervention has to be prepared to say, "Not only do I favor intervening in the Middle East, but you can take my son and you can guarantee me that he will be in the front lines on the first attack." . . . It's always easy for old men to tell the young people they're going to go fight. There's a lot of good lines to those antiwar songs that made sense.

Clearly, the lines of ideological division between libertarians and traditionalists have not dissipated over the years.

In terms of identification, traditionalists continue to call themselves conservatives, traditionalists, and anticollectivists. Whereas the majority of libertarians label themselves libertarian, five call themselves anarchists, one calls himself a "Jeffersonian Democrat or a Burkean Anarchist," and two identify as conservative libertarians.

Although the majority of both left- and right-wing activists retained their core values, a few people on each side shifted beliefs. None renounced their former ideology to switch completely to the other side; still, a minority of activists moved in a different direction during the 1980s and 1990s. For instance, SDSer Barry Skolnick went through a modification of his beliefs, both as a result of political insight and due to a new perspective gained in the business world. During the 1970s when Barry was a Maoist, he traveled to China seven times. Although he was uncritical at the time, since then he's discovered his mistaken assumptions about socialism that, he says, enslaves rather than liberates people.

> I had so many people I knew [in China] who had gotten killed or sent off to the farms. . . . Then I knew a lot of the Cambodians who just got annihilated. . . . So I'm down on genocide and mass executions and gulags, reform through labor, and those kinds of things. But the political change was understanding why that happens . . . that it's not simply an aberration or Stalinism or some misapplied [theory]. But it has to do with the fact that Marxism presupposes a command economy and without the free market, you can't have democracy. You can't have political freedom. And vice versa. Without political freedom, you can't really have a free market.

Barry went through a gradual process of reevaluation. His work in manufacturing also led to a shift in his thinking. He now recognizes the need for a market system in order to feed people and make progress. He also says he now has a healthy respect for business, no longer viewing it negatively.

> I went through a tremendous transition. Talking to corporate people and finding out that they knew a lot of things . . . that they were not a bunch of dumb jerks . . . [or] money-grubbers. . . . There are a lot of great entrepreneurial people who are helping to bring progress to the world . . . doing revolutionary things in the areas of business, communications, transportation, agriculture. . . . We can learn a lot from people like that.

Despite these shifts in his thinking, Barry still sees himself as a leftist and is still politically active. He is involved in trying to reform Chicago politics and the public school system.

SDSer Carl Oglesby has also shifted his beliefs, becoming even more of a libertarian than he was during the 1960s. Although Carl describes himself as a "Bob Taft person," he votes Democrat. He says, "I'm a libertarian. . . . I'm not an anarchist, but I'm very distrustful of government. I don't like people to think of the government as the way to solve problems."

In his opposition to government involvement, Carl thinks affirmative action programs are problematic, the wrong way to reach economic equality. Similarly, rather than creating more welfare programs, Carl proposes building factories in ghettos and offering jobs to the unemployed.

Saying that "work is basic to the human spirit," he believes the aim of governmental action should be to provide opportunities for the economic productive life of all its citizens. At the time of the interview Carl had agreed to give a speech at an upcoming Libertarian Party convention.

Whereas Carl has grown more critical of welfare, a few libertarians have become more sympathetic to it. Marick Payton criticizes libertarians for placing liberty above all else, and particularly for ignoring issues of social equality. He's particularly disturbed by the libertarian rejection of welfare.

> [Libertarians] just don't try to address the issues of the inequality of circumstances people are born into. . . . [Libertarians argue that poor people] need to learn to appreciate the virtues of freedom and work hard and discipline themselves . . . and overcome the fact that they weren't raised in all of the circumstances that teach one how to thrive in that kind of environment. That's a grievous moral copout. I'm much more interested in what our society can do to truly provide all of its people a decent educational, nutritional, aspirational, moral shot at life.

Given his perspective, Marick has "more or less just joined the political mainstream as a reluctant Democrat."

Sharon Presley is another libertarian who feels increasingly concerned about issues of social justice. She comments,

> I see too many libertarians who are *obsessed* with economics. Well hey, fine, I believe all that stuff about laissez-faire and blah, blah, blah, but that's just part of the picture. If we as libertarians don't start being concerned with other kinds of issues of social justice, we're going to be left in the dust. So that has been something that's always upset me. . . . Social justice and individual liberty, that's the perspective from which I see all of this.

Sharon says there are many libertarians like herself who are compassionate and concerned about feminism, the poor, and health care, yet their voices are not often heard in the libertarian movement. Sharon sees common bonds with the left in these concerns. Feeling somewhat distant from libertarians who do not share her passion for social justice, she feels farthest apart from traditionalists. Sharon is particularly opposed to the social conservatives affiliated with the religious right who have gained power during the 1980s and 1990s.

Whereas a few libertarians have moved closer to the left in their concern for social justice, a couple of other libertarians have moved toward traditionalists. Congressman Dana Rohrabacher is the most visible libertarian who has become more conservative. In fact, he has been criticized by some libertarians for his position advocating tougher drug laws and for his alliance with Senator Jesse Helms in calling for cuts in the National Endowment for the Humanities' funding for the arts. Calling himself a conservative libertarian, Dana is now critical of the counterculture he once so wholeheartedly embraced.

> A lot of the "freedom" of the new culture at that time was just basically a total lack of responsibility. Basically you go to Woodstock and you listen to rock and roll music, but when you leave, the land's destroyed. . . . That was an ecological basket case for years after they left. They did not clean up their own mess. They were just a bunch of kids acting free and leaving a pigsty behind them.

The lyrics Dana wrote during the early 1970s, calling for the legalization of drugs and advocating anarchy, have been replaced by new lyrics. For instance, he wrote a song during the days of the Iran-Contra scandal, in defense of his friend Marine Corps Lieutenant Corporal Oliver North. Entitled "White House Blues," one stanza reads,

> I work at the White House, at NSC [National Security Council]
> Why is everybody pickin' on me?
> I just tried to help the Contras while on a Mideast cruise,
> And now I'm sitting in the White House, singing the White
>      House blues.[20]

Some traditionalists as well have shifted perspective. For example, a few traditionalists admit they feel much more compassionate about people on welfare than they did in the 1960s. Mary Fisk explains,

> When you're young, you have it all. I had it all. I was very smart, well educated, attractive. There were no limits to what I could do. . . . When you have everything, you have very little tolerance for people who don't have everything. . . . It's somehow their fault. If they can't support their families, well they should go get a job. . . . And then you grow. You get older and maybe you have a few failures or a few losses and you become vulnerable. . . . The conservative movement still . . . lacks compassion, still looks at people who are on welfare as somehow they deserve to be on welfare, because they don't really try.

Mary says she now accepts more role for government in addressing such social problems.

A substantial number of traditionalists also express regrets over their lack of support for civil rights during the 1960s. Several say they feel embarrassed or ashamed by their neglect to stand up for individual rights. Allen Brandstater says conservatives should have been in the forefront rather than being regressive about civil rights. "We should have been more involved or at least more sympathetic to the civil rights struggles. I'm not saying we all should have been devotees of Martin Luther King, but . . . if conservatives are believers in individual rights, we really missed the boat on that one. . . . I don't think we always lived the philosophy that we preached."[21] Recognizing the right's failure to support civil rights, a few traditionalists also said the Republican Party and the conservative movement should now be more inclusive and responsive to blacks.

In short, the majority of activists maintained their core values over the past three decades. None went through a reversal of ideology. However, for some activists their experiences as adults have changed their views on particular issues or shifted their perspectives.

### The Continuity of Self

According to Erikson, one of the major components of individual identity is a sense of continuity.[22] Our own uniqueness is grounded in this sense of personal continuity, a transcendent self that remains constant despite the varying changes encountered throughout the life course.[23] Although little empirical attention has been paid to the topic of self-perceived sameness and change, one of the few researchers who examines the issue, Handel, finds that most "ordinary" adults perceive stability of self, rather than a shifting sense of self, over time.[24]

Even though YAF and SDS activists' core values have remained constant over the past twenty years, some have had difficulty integrating their adult lives into the identity they adopted as youth. Toward the end of my interview I asked each activist, "What would the person you were in the 1960s say or think about what you've become and what you're doing today?" The majority of YAF activists, both traditionalist and libertarian, said their younger selves would be pleased with the people they are today. Most felt a consistency between their younger and older selves, saying that their lives as adults were fairly predictable. Traditionalist Alan MacKay reflects,

I'm comfortable with myself. I spend a lot of time thinking
about . . . my value system, what's important. I have a good job
which I enjoy, I have a good family, a happy marriage, seven good
kids, all of whom are decent, nice kids. . . . The country is doing
okay. It looks like . . . the conflict between communism and democracy is going to end in our favor, so that I don't have to worry
about my kids growing up under socialism or communism. . . . So
I think the young activist of twenty years ago looking at me today
would say, "You're fat and out of shape, but you haven't done all
that bad."

Libertarian Don Ernsberger also sees a continuity between his earlier
and current self. He says the 1960s Ernsberger wouldn't be surprised at
who he is today.

I'm a teacher. I've always wanted to be a teacher. Involved in a political side . . . that's the way I was then. I have been able to sit down
and be serious and talk about things and be affected by things. . . .
I also am a person who can just go out dancing, get drunk, and
have a good old time. So that's not surprising. I'm still pretty lib-
ertine sexually. . . . I still drink beer and eat munchies. I can't think
of very many things that would be a big surprise to my old self.

Only a small number of YAF activists felt a disjuncture between their
earlier and later selves. A few women, mainly traditionalists, said their
younger selves would be amazed by their success in careers. Having simply aspired to being wives and mothers, they would never have anticipated their professional accomplishments. For example, Jo Ann Gasper
says her younger self would never have predicted that she would get
phone calls from the president of the United States or serve in the top
administration of the government.

A few other YAFers felt their younger self would be judgmental of
who they've become, wishing they had accomplished more profession-
ally or believing they had become too cynical. In particular, a few libertarians saw a difference between who they were then and who they've
become today. Like many leftists, their radicalization during the 1960s
created a gap between their earlier self and their present self. For instance,
Rob Tyler said the question was hard to answer because it depended on
which 1960s self responded.

What point in the '60s? I mean the Goldwater period, the Reagan
period, the . . . Doors period, the antiwar period in '69? You know,

there's a lot of different notions there. I saw myself . . . in '65 being a politician. . . . So I would have been very surprised that he'd be a lawyer. . . . Law was never in my mind at all, never. . . . During the counterculture period . . . my big concern was what was I going to do at thirty. . . . My concern was extremely short-term. I'm down to the stems and seeds again. . . . I was in the be-here-now. . . . I wasn't very much future-oriented.

Libertarian Marick Payton also feels his earlier self would be critical of what he's doing today. Saying, "The person I was in the '60s would feel like I basically copped out into the pursuit of personal comfort and familial interests," Marick contrasts his lack of responsibilities during his youth with his present concerns that include "struggling to have a nice home in a nice community" and paying for private school for his daughter. He concludes, "I'm not very comfortable with the compromise I've made and continue to struggle with it and continue to have this sense that at some point, someday, I may feel I should radically change it."

In contrast to the consistency expressed among most YAF activists between their earlier and current lives, SDS activists were split in their response to this question. About one-quarter of SDS activists also report a continuity between their younger and older selves. These activists feel their earlier self would be pleased with who they are today: they are doing exactly what they expected to do as youth and feel no disjuncture with their changes over time.

Approximately one-quarter of SDS activists have a mixed response, saying their earlier selves would feel both positive and negative about the course they've taken. Vivian Rothstein, for instance, says her younger self would feel judgmental as well as proud of her life today.

I would think I was living a very middle-class life. I own a house and I have a color television, I have a VCR, I have a very . . . bourgeois lifestyle. And that I'd been living in a nuclear family for so many years; I never thought I would have been in such a traditional relationship. [But] I would feel good about working in poverty issues because that's really where I started. . . . So I would respect what I was doing.

Like libertarian Rob Tyler, some SDS activists had a hard time answering and explained, "It depends on which part of the 1960s you're looking at as to how my younger self would feel." Jeanne Friedman notes the difference of reaction between her early 1960s self and her later 1960s self.

God! Well . . . the early '6os person I was would think that I was
just fine now. The later '6os . . . person would think that I . . . had
sold out because . . . I'm making more money than I should. Although God knows I don't think that's true. And my son certainly
doesn't. . . . Not sold out in the sense of driving a BMW . . . but
even in the sense of having a nice house. The late '6os person might
think I should be living in the hills farming, eating organic food,
and doing drugs.

Yet in sharp contrast to YAF activists, close to half of all SDS activists
feel a disjuncture between their younger and older selves. The majority
say their younger selves would be judgmental and critical of who they've
become and what they're doing today. Like Jeanne, a number of people
comment that their earlier self would say they had "sold out," are now
too bourgeois, or would feel disappointed that they are not full-time activists. Bernardine Dohrn definitely feels her younger self would be critical: "I would think that I was too comfortable, put up with too many
compromises, not angry enough, not taking enough risks. . . . I was pretty
judgmental in those days." Unlike traditionalist women though, only one
SDS woman, Lynn Dykstra, who is now a surgeon, said her younger self
would be surprised at her professional success.

    Given the radicalization of *both* libertarians and leftists during the
1960s, we might expect more libertarians to feel a disjuncture between
their younger and older selves as activists settled down and focused on
work and families. One difference between libertarians and leftists, however, concerns their varying attitudes toward property rights and material wealth. For many SDS activists the upward mobility and desire for
material comfort of their adult lives are discordant with their earlier beliefs and lifestyle. Libertarians, on the other hand, do not regard wealth
or material comfort as a contradiction with their beliefs and, consequently,
do not face such a gap as they age and acquire greater wealth.

    Regardless of differences between YAF and SDS activists in the ease
with which they have accepted the changes in their lives, there was overwhelming consensus among all activists that they have become more tolerant with time. Many people contrast this to their earlier dogmatic self.
Several activists commented that the impulse toward intolerance or sectarianism is common during youth, and that as they matured, they were
able to accept differences of opinions and backgrounds. Both YAF and
SDS activists admit they are less preachy than in the past, less determined

to change someone else's mind. Traditionalist YAFer Jáime Ryskind says, "I'm more likely to see both sides of issues than I was when I was younger. . . . I was much more dogmatic when I was young, and I am less so as I've gotten older. . . . It's not so easy to say, 'Well, it's absolutely this way or absolutely this way.'"

Similarly, libertarian YAFer Dave Walter states, "I've mellowed and give people more the benefit of the doubt. You know, they don't agree with me, it's [probably] something in their life experience that allows them to see things differently. . . . So you mellow in that aspect, not as dogmatic as you were when you become a true believer."

Many activists also say they now see life and politics in a more complex way. They ask more questions and feel they have fewer answers than in the past. The world is less black and white. SDSer Cathy Wilkerson comments,

I have much more of an appreciation for life's complexities and the complexities of human nature. And [I'm] more at peace with that traditional aspect of the aging process. . . . Not more at peace to accept the status quo, but more at peace . . . that you can't get outraged from the moment that you wake up to the moment you go to sleep. You can only be outraged a third of the time . . . not 100 percent of the time [laughs].

Other activists as well say they now recognize the need for compromise and the importance of negotiation.

Accompanying this greater tolerance and understanding, many activists, particularly those in SDS, have also reconciled with their parents. The strained relations resulting from the politics of their youth are now past. A number of activists discuss the healing that has taken place. For some, making peace means agreeing never to discuss politics. Others have discovered a new respect for their parents as they have aged.

To summarize, there is a consistency over time in beliefs and values among activists on both the left and the right. Many people also feel a continuity of self between who they were in the 1960s and who they are today; although for those in SDS, there is a more complicated relationship between the past and the present. Because many leftists renounced materialism and rejected the mainstream, as they became adults and settled into occupations "within the system" or acquired material possessions, inevitably they faced a disjuncture between their earlier and current selves. Many felt their younger, dogmatic selves would judge harshly their present politics and lifestyle. Overwhelmingly, though, both SDS and YAF activists feel they are more tolerant and more open to compromise than they were as youth, now recognizing various shades of gray.

### Disillusionment and the Loss of Community

Given the rise of the New Right and the conservative ascendancy of the past two decades, we might expect leftists to be disillusioned, to feel a sense of weariness or pessimism about the political world. Certainly, given the changing configuration of American politics, YAF and SDS activists have faced divergent trajectories. Leftists came into their prime as youth, gaining a sense of power and influence during the 1960s and early 1970s. Yet as adults they faced a political world indifferent to their beliefs and witnessed a sustained backlash against many of their achievements. From the mid-1970s onward, the New Right successfully mobilized to elect Ronald Reagan to the presidency and to fill the legislature and the judiciary with its adherents. Further, the New Right has worked hard to reverse many liberal gains of the 1960s, with attacks on unions, affirmative action, welfare, feminism, and gay and lesbian rights. Meanwhile, outside the United States, the Communist world began to crumble, extinguishing the dream of socialism as a lived reality. The sense of possibility and idealism felt by leftists during the 1960s abruptly encountered a sobering reality.

YAFers, on the other hand, felt ostracized and marginal as youth in the 1960s. Committed to their ideals, they persevered even when campus after campus turned leftward during the late 1960s. Yet as they reached adulthood, they encountered a reversal of fortune. Having survived their minority status during the 1960s and early 1970s, they have helped bring many of their issues to prominence during the past two decades. The Reagan revolution marked the triumph of many of their values and beliefs. And, as we've seen, many traditionalists are in leadership positions and hold seats of institutional power today.[25]

Given these historical realities, we find with surprise that leftists are *less* disillusioned overall than are those on the right. Rather than disillusionment, the prevalent feeling expressed by leftists is a sense of loss of community.

**SDS and the Loss of Community**    Although a substantial portion of SDSers (39 percent) say they haven't felt disillusioned with politics over the past twenty years, among those who *do* report disillusion, the most common reason given is the failure of socialism. Some people felt disheartened learning about the atrocities in Cambodia or the totalitarianism in China, provoking a reassessment of their ideals of a Communist society. Sue Jhirad reflects,

> I don't have the same kind of faith in changing the world as I once did. . . . [One of the things] leading to cynicism is just looking at the international scene and seeing good movements turn into bad movements, or good ideals just lead to atrocities. . . . You find out that . . . genocide occurred in Cambodia. . . . That's humbling because that was going on at a time when we were . . . politically supporting them and didn't realize that it was happening.

Sue now feels disillusioned about the realities of communism. They have made her rethink her view of politics. She says, "Capitalism sucks, but communism hasn't done too well either!" Sue looks at the world and sees the continuing "impoverishment of the many and the enrichment of the few" so she has no illusions about capitalism, saying it's as bad as Marx predicted. But communism hasn't worked either. "The problem of communism is that no matter how great your ideals are, you're dealing with humans. And when you concentrate that kind of power and authority in small numbers of people's hands, the dictatorship of the proletariat always turns out to be the dictatorship of a certain number of people who . . . say what the proletariat position is. . . . That stinks."

Other SDSers also report a loss of illusions, as well as a sense of confusion, resulting from the collapse of communism during the 1980s and 1990s. Some people speak of having lost their political moorings, feeling adrift. Many feel there is no longer a model or blueprint for their ideal society or a viable means to build a socialist movement in the United States.

The second most common reason named by SDSers for feeling disillusioned is the conservative tide of the past two decades. In particular, the 1980 election of Ronald Reagan was "extremely dispiriting," as one activist put it. The rightward swing of American politics led to demoralization, as some activists felt sobered by the limits of their efforts toward social change. Jeanne Friedman comments,

> There's no question that the Reagan years put a damper on everything—it was hard to believe that so many people would go along with such garbage. . . . So in some sense it's been hard to look at the last ten years. . . . Not only have we not gone forward, but there's been all these setbacks. . . . I'm not disillusioned with what we

wanted. I'm disillusioned with how quickly things fell apart and with how well the Right was able to consolidate. In some sense the only disillusionment I have is that we were so naive, that with all our faults . . . we didn't realize how important we were . . . because look at what happened . . . just devastating.

Others, too, say they felt discouraged by the backlash against the gains of the 1960s, disheartened to see how the changes they fought so hard for were so easily undone.

Yet even among those SDSers who express a sense of discouragement, the majority persist in being politically active to one degree or another. Further, a substantial number of SDSers (39 percent) say they have *not* felt disillusioned. Calling herself an "incurable optimist," Bernardine Dohrn says, "It's not that I don't have days of being angry and discouraged, but not disillusioned at all. I feel just completely lucky to have been part of that generation and that experience. It's addictive. I want it again before I die." Bernardine stands firm in her beliefs. She views the fall of communism as posing new questions for the future about how to live in humane ways. She admits that without a real socialist model such questions become more difficult; yet even though the solutions are less obvious, her faith remains.

[It requires] the need for imagination and being able to dream, envision a different way of relating to each other and a different way of being. . . . It's hard to not be able to point to somewhere and say, "Well . . . like it is in Cuba in 1968. . . . Here's a country that eliminated starvation and illiteracy in three years because they reallocated resources." Not having that to point to makes it much harder. . . . [But] is all there is just stuff, malls, and VCR's? There's gotta be something better . . . but what it is and how you can picture it, how you can imagine a group of people trying to organize ourselves . . . that's the task . . . to build a movement again.

Rather than disillusionment, the predominant feeling expressed by many SDSers is a sense of loss of community.[26] Having lived their youth intimately bound to others of like mind, after years of sharing food, bed, politics, and friendship with other activists, many adult SDSers feel a sense of loss living the more conventional lives of isolated adults. Missing the sense of connection to a group of people, Jim Shoch finds that now his relations with others are "much more serial than they are fused." "People know people, but they don't know each other. So I have a lot of friends who my wife and I see socially, but . . . it's not communal. . . . It doesn't feel as good. . . . That community was forged in circumstances specific to the left . . . and I don't foresee it happening again. So there's a sadness there." Similarly, Bernardine Dohrn says that everyone she knows from the 1960s is in some permanent state of mourning about the loss of community.

Some people comment that the feeling of community was tied up with youth and that it cannot be re-created because now people are caught up with families, jobs, and other responsibilities and concerns. Yet many people have remained lifelong friends with other activists from that era. Although Dave Strauss says he feels a sense of loss, he also says the people he's closest to in his life are still people from that time. He comments, "Whenever we're with them, it's like coming home." For SDSers the bonds forged during the 1960s and early 1970s were vital and unique.

YAF and Disillusionment    Although the fall of communism and the rightward turn in American politics represents the realization of the dreams of many YAF activists, a vindication of their beliefs, surprisingly the majority report feeling disillusioned with politics at some point or another over the past twenty years. After their youthful idealism carried them through the 1960s, a variety of experiences led them to become discouraged. The most common reason discussed for becoming disillusioned, oddly enough, was the presidency of Ronald Reagan. Both libertarians and traditionalists became disenchanted with Reagan. Traditionalist Barbara Hollingsworth describes her shift in sentiment.

> I don't get disillusioned too easily, but toward the end of the Reagan years . . . because we were so euphoric when Reagan got in and . . . all of a sudden you realized that the election of this candidate was really not going to change the whole world the way you would like to see it. The things that you felt strongly about maybe [weren't] going to happen. . . . I felt disillusioned at that point, that . . . the whole system was not going to dismantle, the whole welfare system, the way the whole government operates, and the intrusiveness . . . is not going to disappear, in fact, was getting worse. So that was the major . . . disillusionment.

Others, too, felt disappointed when reality did not live up to their ideals and say they became disillusioned with the limited changes Reagan made or by his political appointments. Even Congressman Dana Rohrabacher, who worked for Reagan, admits he felt disenchanted with the limits of Reagan's agenda.

Libertarians also cite the Reagan years as disillusioning. Sheldon Richman says,

> I tend to be optimistic by nature [but], once in a while—especially these days, I have pessimistic moments. The contrast of what's going on in the Eastern world . . . ironically has made me depressed. Because it seems like so little is going on here. I kid that in ten years we may be defecting to Czechoslovakia. . . . The Reagan administration was a double disaster because not only did government grow, but [Reagan] associated all that with a libertarian rhetoric. A lot of people . . . wondered why libertarians didn't like Reagan. They would say, "He sounds like you and he's free enterprise, individual liberty." He could put on a good show . . . but in real terms there was no revolution in the libertarian direction. So I found that disillusioning.

For libertarian Louise Lacey, it was not so much Reagan that led to her disenchantment. Rather, echoing the view of many SDSers, Louise says she became disenchanted as the country became more and more conservative. "I have small disillusionments all the time. Mostly it's at the American public. It isn't at what our leaders do. I assume they're going to fuck up! But every time we have an election I think, How can people vote like that? . . . Why would you put Ronald Reagan [as president]? Why would you put George Bush? He used to run the CIA, for Christ's sake."

Other YAFers say they feel a general sense of cynicism with politics, having become disenchanted with political leaders they once held in high esteem or recognizing the power games and opportunism prevalent in the political world. For example, many cite Watergate and Richard Nixon as provoking their process of disillusionment.

In contrast to the substantial minority of SDSers who said they never felt disillusioned over the past twenty years, only three YAFers responded this way. All three of these activists are traditionalists. All feel pleased with the conservative turn of the country. As David Keene puts it, "There were times when we felt frustrated, but frankly we never had a sense that we were ever going to lose. Even when all that . . . stuff was happening in the late '60s . . . it was clear politically . . . that the Vietnam War and the activities of SDS were going to deliver the country to us. And that's what happened."

While many more YAF activists feel disillusioned than do SDS activists, only one YAF member, a libertarian, cited the loss of community as a central concern of the 1980s and 1990s. It's not clear whether other YAFers never felt the same sense of community during the 1960s and therefore did not experience the same sense of loss, or whether YAF activists still feel a deep sense of connection to others that has sustained them during the past two decades. The sole activist who shares the feeling of loss with the left is Marick Payton, one of the libertarians who shifted leftward in his beliefs. Marick laments the loss of shared values he felt during the 1960s, the feeling that people cared about "the right things." Rather than the sense that "the good life could be communally experienced" Marick says now the dominant ethic is a dog-eat-dog world, "intensely competitive and climbing and grasping and . . . consuming." Marick says he continually feels a "sense of paradise lost."

In short, although the historical changes of the past two decades, particularly the downfall of communism and the rightward shift in American politics, have had a sobering effect and even led to disillusionment for some activists in SDS, the most poignant loss felt by many leftists is the absence of community. Many people long for the time in their youth when they were part of a larger whole, bound together in a movement for social change, united through their ideals and action.

No longing for a lost community troubles YAF activists. Rather, many feel disillusioned as the realities of the conservative changes of the 1980s and 1990s have not lived up to the ideals of their youth. While they applaud the fall of communism, many have felt disappointed by the world of realpolitik, by opportunism, and by the limited changes achieved. For them, ironically, America's rightward turn has been accompanied by a loss of idealism.

## Full Circle: Children of the 1960s Generation

One final way the experiences of the 1960s continue to affect activists' lives is in the ways they are raising their children. Politics influences the beliefs and values they are instilling in their offspring, as well as the hopes they have for their children's future. We arrive, then, full circle as activists on the left and the right, like their parents before them, pass on their world to the next generation.

For traditionalists, instilling a general set of moral values in their offspring is of utmost importance. These values are rooted in religious beliefs. Several traditionalists discuss the need to teach spiritual values, faith, and the importance of being good. Others say they want their children to "be able to love and serve their fellow man" or "have a spirit of caring and kindness toward other people." Mitch Petry believes moral lessons are more important to teach his son than political lessons. "The moral views are [important] . . . the work ethic, basic views of looking at the world, of not being selfish and helping others, and your basic moral outlook. . . . To me the political identification is more fleeting."

Traditionalist Anne Edwards says she and her husband, Lee, have tried not to be self-righteous in raising their two daughters and have tried to explain things to them both intellectually and spiritually. "We're as used to talking religion as we are talking politics. We talk tolerance." Because of these "dangerous times," Anne also felt the need to guide her daughters and started talking to them at a very young age about promiscuity, drugs, and alcoholism.

In sharp contrast to traditionalists, libertarians are raising their children to be skeptical of religion. They are most interested in teaching their youth about liberty and faith in the individual. For example, both Sheldon Richman and his wife are atheists. Sheldon has thought a lot about how to bring up his three children without religion. He relates the issue to other questions he hopes to raise.

> They're going to learn versions of history that I don't agree with about the wars and other things. . . . I'm not sure quite what to do because it could put undue pressure on them to be taught that what their teachers are telling them [is wrong]. I don't want to do it in a raucous or aggressive way. . . . I want to try to do it in a constructive way. . . . The same thing with religion. I don't want them going around the neighborhood telling kids they're stupid for believing in God. On the other hand, I don't want to teach them relativism. . . . "Well, it's true for them, but not for us," because I don't believe that. . . . I want them to know that I think we're right and I think my position can be demonstrated. But that doesn't mean you have to make a nuisance of yourself.

Similarly, libertarian Don Ernsberger believes religion is a "sort of laziness; that if you're religious . . . that essentially what you're doing is you're saying, 'I don't want to deal with this.' So religion comes in and takes care of it for you." Don tries to raise his children not to be lazy in this way, although he's not "real preachy" about it. For these libertarians, teaching critical thinking and a skepticism about dogma is essential.

Among SDS activists, parents strive to instill values of egalitarianism in their children. Teaching them about racial and gender equality is especially important.[27] Jane Adams recalls her efforts to instill feminist values in her daughter, Dawn. Throughout Dawn's childhood, Jane criticized children's books and advertisements she viewed as sexist. Jane recalls,

Dawn used to get really angry at me about it because . . . I'd be this running criticism of ads and cartoons and shows and whatnot. Now she does it. She's a real feminist. . . . If it hadn't been for the '60s, I know I wouldn't have been sensitized to that stuff. . . . It took that change of consciousness. . . . I [feel] like we've gotten over those . . . hurdles that the culture sets up . . . to become racist and to accept gender stereotypes. . . . I've worked very hard to impart those kinds of values.

Many other SDS activists talk about raising their children to be nonsexist, giving dolls to their sons and teaching them to cook, or teaching their daughters to be strong and self-confident. Cindy Decker tries to provide an environment where her daughter "feels like an equal human being instead of a servant." Cindy feels it is important that her daughter knows she is "something besides beautiful. I don't want her just to be an object." While Cindy worries about her daughter, Bernardine Dohrn worries about raising her sons. She says, "The issue of raising boys has been something . . . I wrestle with a lot. You know, who are they and how do they have values and how do they be[come] whole people . . . and want whole people as their friends."

Besides feminism, SDS activists also teach their children about racial equality. Judy Baker has raised her two sons to "be interdependent with a broad group of people, rich people and poor people, and people of all colors." She and her husband chose to bring up their children in an integrated neighborhood in Boston. Several other SDS activists made this same choice, believing it was important to send their kids to integrated schools. Sue Jhirad explains,

We've talked to [our children] about sexism and racism. They've also had lives where at least a good portion of their growing up they were living in working-class neighborhoods. . . . My daughter's grown up in Medford; most of her friends are working-class Catholic. That's been good for her. And she was in a daycare which was mainly black. . . . I deliberately put her there because I honestly don't think what you tell your kids to think makes that much sense. It's more what they actually live. . . . If you put them in life experiences where they have contact with black kids and working-class kids, then they don't develop those kind of snobby, prejudiced attitudes.

Most YAF and SDS activists are also bringing up their children in a politicized household, much like the ones in which they themselves were raised. Dinner conversations often revolve around politics. Politics is "in the air" in homes of traditionalists, libertarians, and leftists. Traditionalist Kathy Rothschild comments,

> When you have children, it changes your perspective. . . . That's the full circle. My parents wanted to share their lifestyle, their religious philosophy, their political philosophy with their children and I want to do the same thing. That starts at home when they are little. Beth [her daughter] knows everything. She could say, "Dukakis is a turkey" when she was two. . . . I would like to see my kids involved. . . . I would like them to be aware of the world around them.

Similarly, libertarian SDSer Doug Knox says politics is also integral to his family. In order to expose his children to libertarian ideas, Doug seeks out children's book with libertarian themes. Political ideas also are discussed often. Doug says, "The milieu of our family is political."

Not only are politics discussed at home. A number of activists on the left and the right also mention bringing their children with them to political meetings, conferences, and demonstrations. When Dave Walter's children were small, they would accompany their parents to demonstrations, their strollers displaying signs of protest. Because of Dave's involvement with the Libertarian Party, his kids have also met several of the party's presidential candidates, who have stayed at their home. They have even accompanied Dave to a few Libertarian Party conventions.

When libertarian Don Ernsberger and his wife attended a pro-choice demonstration in Washington, Don told his seventeen-year-old daughter about the protest and invited her along. He was delighted when she decided to go. His eight-year-old son also accompanied them to the demonstration. Similarly, SDSer Judy Baker invited her two sons along to demonstrate in Washington in support of abortion rights.

The sons of SDSers Bernardine Dohrn and Bill Ayers have accompanied their parents to many demonstrations and political meetings. Politics runs deep in their lives. Their oldest son, Zayd Osceola, was named in honor of Zayd Shakur, a Black Panther killed in a shoot-out with police, and Osceola, the Seminole chief who sheltered runaway slaves. Their middle son, Malik Cochise, was named after Malcolm X (El-Hajj Malik El-Shabazz) and the nineteenth-century Apache chief who fought settlers encroaching on tribal land. Every summer the children are sent to a leftist camp where they stay in bunks named after Harriet Tubman and Eugene Debs and study subjects like South Africa and the campaign against nuclear power.[28] Commenting, "They're very political kids," Bernardine tells a funny story about her children's view of their parents' politics:

[One day] . . . as we're driving along [one of the kids says], "Poppy, tell us the story of when you burned your credit card." [Bill responds,] "I'm radical, but I'm not that radical! It's easy to burn a draft card. Nobody burns credit cards!" [laughs] So they have these funny fractured versions of [our history]. . . . What can they possibly imagine about what it means to be underground? . . . Malik will say, "I was born underground." I don't know what he pictures when he says that.

Not all children so willingly participate in political events. SDSer Jeanne Friedman says her teenage son was reluctant to go with her to demonstrations. "When he was little, we went to lots of demonstrations together, but he hasn't done that in a while. When there was this last antiwar demonstration, he didn't come. He said, 'Oh, do I have to go?' Sometimes I say, 'Yes, you have to go. There are things that you must do if you have any integrity at all.' We try and talk about it."

SDSer Naomi Schapiro worries that if she is *too* politically active, it may eventually turn her two young daughters away from politics. "I don't want to go to so many meetings that they hate the idea of politics because it's all their mother ever did. . . . We do take them to demonstrations, but not very often. We take them down to the gay pride demonstration every year and we take them to some [other] demonstrations."

Given the years these activists have spent in politics, the centrality of politics to their own identity, and the passion they still feel for creating social change, it is not surprising that the majority of people on both the left and the right hope their children will carry on in their tradition. Most would be pleased if their offspring shared both their politics and their activism. Speaking of his hopes for his children, SDSer Michael Kazin says, "I'd like them to [share my politics]. I'd like them to improve on them. . . . Because I don't think . . . given what's happened, that people who think like me have all the answers. . . . I hope they're both interested in politics. . . . I'd like to feel there's continuity there."

Libertarian Maggie Kohls also wants her daughters to care about her politics. "I want them to be libertarians. We always had people in high school whose parents . . . never discussed politics in front of them because they didn't want to influence them. If you believe in something, why wouldn't you want to influence somebody? No matter what it is." When Maggie's two grown daughters both voted Republican she was satisfied that at least they didn't vote Democrat.

At the very least, most parents hope their children will be politically conscious and informed about the world around them. Thinking about her children, SDSer Bernardine Dohrn says, "I want them to care about the world. . . . I want them to be active in pursuit of their values and socially engaged, and with a sense that they can affect the world, can make a difference."

While many parents hope their children will follow in their footsteps, some activists feel reluctant to push their children toward politics, feeling it is important to let their children make their own choices and follow their own path. Traditionalist Alan MacKay and his wife are acutely aware of allowing their seven daughters to form their own opinions. Alan says,

> What we have done with our kids is to encourage them to be very independent and have their own free choice. . . . We've leaned over very far—perhaps too far—in the direction of letting them form their own value judgments. . . . We were very, very anxious not to impose our value system on the kids with regard to anything—religion or politics or anything else, preferring for them to learn, ask questions if they wanted to. . . . I would have objected strenuously if anybody tried to impose values on me when I was a kid. We thought as a matter of their own freedom, they had the right to their own opinions.

A few people say they are not at all concerned about whether their children are even political. Traditionalist Jo Ann Gasper says, "I really haven't thought about [my ambitions for my children]. I want our children to be healthy and well-rounded people." Echoing this, SDSer Vivian Rothstein says she wouldn't feel disappointed if either of her two kids were uninterested in politics. "I don't see myself as raising little activists. I feel like it's going to be real important to cherish whatever they do, whatever it is."

Despite these few parents who are unconcerned about whether their children will become politically involved, many activists say their children's apathy or disinterest in politics would be disappointing. Equally disturbing to some would be their children ending up on the opposite side of the political fence. Traditionalist women were particularly likely to say they would find it deeply troublesome if their children ended up becoming leftists or even Democrats. For example, Mary Fisk said she'd be disappointed if her kids turned out liberal.

> It is a philosophical orientation . . . the perception of the human being is so different. The liberal view is an arrogant one: there's an elite that knows best what's best for the masses. I don't want them to have that kind of approach to people. I want them to treat people like individuals. . . . So it's not that they would be for or against a political issue. . . . It's a fundamental approach to reality. So that's why I would be disappointed if they were liberal.

Among those SDSers who said they'd be upset if their children ended up having opposing beliefs, Cindy Decker said she would be "extremely offended" if her children became right-wing Republicans, but she would be even "more aghast" if her daughter turned out being subservient to men.

Only a few activists said they wouldn't care at all if their children ended up on the "opposite side." Asked whether she would be upset if her children ended up becoming Democrats or liberals, traditionalist Dawne Winter said, "You love your children. . . . You love them no matter what. . . . If they were really committed and . . . thought about the issues and were not just knee-jerk, I [would have] a great deal of respect for them." Traditionalist Mitch Petry even sees the benefits of his children holding opposing beliefs. He says it might be a healthy thing, given the many aspects of the Republican Party that he finds discouraging.

What *will* become of these daughters and sons of 1960s activists? At the time of the interview, the children of activists ranged from ten months to thirty-one years old. From the political leanings evidenced by these children to date, parents who are concerned that their offspring may defect to the other side have little to worry about. Not all the grown children of activists are politically involved, but the majority share the values of their parents. Most *are* indeed following in their parents' footsteps in terms of their beliefs.

Further, just as many YAF and SDS activists first became politically conscious growing up with parents who were committed and involved, so there are signs that a number of the children of these activists are also compelled by politics and seem to be heading in that direction.

The grown children of traditionalists tend to have conservative beliefs and values. Some are already involved in political organizations.

Mike Thompson's son was the head of College Republicans at Emory University and was elected state chair of the Georgia College Republicans. His daughter worked in Tennessee as a volunteer in Governor Don Lundquist's campaign in 1994 and then worked in the governor's administration. Lynn Bouchey's daughter aspires to be the first woman president; his son has worked for the Republican National Committee. All of Don Devine's children are Republicans or conservative to one degree or another. His two eldest are not involved in politics, but his third child, a daughter, was active in Young Republicans at the University of Maryland and his youngest son, who holds the most conservative views, is the one most interested in politics.

Similarly, several libertarians see libertarian leanings evident in their children. Dave Walter says his daughter was apolitical until she got her first paycheck and noticed how much came out in taxes. She finally understood what her father had been talking about for years. Dave's son adopted atheism on his own and eagerly followed the developments in East Germany and the fall of the Berlin wall. Dave sees signs of dawning activism.

Like those on the right, children of SDS activists also seem to share their parents' values and beliefs, regardless of whether or not they're politically active. Several people mentioned, for example, that their sons or daughters are feminists. Sue Jhirad's son, Rod, shares his parents' values. Sue describes him as "antiwar and antiracism and for women's rights." A couple of SDS activists also have grown children who are active in women's organizations or the gay rights movement. Some are political in other ways. For instance, one of Carl and Beth Oglesby's grown children works producing antiracist videos.

Some of the political journeys of these children of the 1960s generation are also strikingly parallel to the paths traveled by their parents. At the age of ten, libertarian Don Ernsberger's daughter decided she didn't believe in any religion. Although Don and his wife are atheists, they wanted their daughter to experience religion and make up her own mind. Like her father before her, after years of attending Sunday school, she simply decided to give up all religion.

Traditionalist Kitty Smith's son may represent a new generation of young conservative activists. At the age of eight he discovered Young Americans for Freedom. Kitty recalls,

Adam found Young Americans for Freedom by himself. I took him to some meeting. . . . He really didn't have any place else to go and

I didn't have a baby-sitter so I brought him along. He was all dressed up and had his blazer on and he was talking to some people. Afterward he said, "Have you heard of this organization called Young Americans for Freedom?" He said, "I don't know if I'm old enough, but I think that it's the right thing for me to be involved with."

Kitty's other son also enjoys politics and has named their cat Reagan.

Meanwhile, on the other side of the political divide, SDSer Sue Jhirad's daughter, Cathy, is already very outspoken. Sue tells a story that illustrates Cathy's views. Cathy was walking down the street one day with two friends who were Italian Catholic. They passed a black guy sitting on the street. After they passed, one friend muttered, "That nigger." Sue says Cathy went berserk:

She actually shoved this little girl, which is something she's never done. She said, "That's the worst thing you could say. That's horrible. . . . It's totally insulting. It's totally prejudiced." . . . She just flipped out. . . . The little girl got very upset. I later talked to Cathy and said, "Maybe that's not the best way to deal with it. . . . I'm really glad you stood up . . . but you shouldn't have shoved her. You should explain to her." . . . So we had a discussion. . . . She told me later what she said to this little girl. . . . "My mother was arrested in the South fighting for black people's rights and by your doing that, you make a joke out of everything that she did." I was really moved by this because I might have mentioned to her once that I was arrested in the South . . . but it really had an impact on her and it really made her think.

Cathy also has gotten into big arguments with her Catholic girlfriends about abortion. Clearly, she is carrying on the traditions of her parents.

Even some of the conflicts between parents and children are reminiscent of earlier battles activists experienced in their youth. SDSer Jeanne Friedman says she and her son often battle over the length of his hair. "I always want him to have his hair longer than he's willing to have. When he was younger, we'd go into Supercuts and have nearly screaming fights. He'd tell the person, 'Take it off,' and I'd say, 'Don't you *dare* cut off that kid's hair.' When he got older, he stopped letting me go with him . . . because it was always embarrassing."

Like their parents, these children of the 1960s generation are being exposed to politics and having experiences that are proving formative to their beliefs. Just like their parents before them, these youth are learning to articulate ideas, to stand up for themselves, to speak out, and to work toward social change. As activists of the 1960s have become parents, they have come full circle. As they teach their children lessons from their own lives, as they guide them with their own deeply held values and beliefs, who knows what more will sprout from the seeds of the 1960s? Perhaps once again history will intersect with biography. Perhaps the children of these impassioned activists from the 1960s will foment changes—of one kind or another—in the twenty-first century. Just as their parents are historically linked into a continuing dialogue with others of their generation, inextricably bound through their experiences with activists of varied political hues, perhaps the children of traditionalists, libertarians, and leftists will cross paths in the future to continue their parents' conversations in new ways.

## CONCLUSION

What comes through loud and clear in the stories of activists of the 1960s is the continuity in their lives, the varying means by which they remain true to their core values. Politics has survived the transitions to adulthood. Contrary to media images of sold-out leftists now on Wall Street, or *The Big Chill* portrayal of former activists who have grown cynical and apathetic, the majority of activists on both left and right continue to be politically active in one way or another. The transformative effects of activism continue to shape the daily lives, choices, and pathways of traditionalists, libertarians, and leftists. However, while traditionalists have found it easy to move from their early political involvement into adult careers, the radicalization of libertarians and leftists, and their critical stance outside the mainstream, continues to pose dilemmas for them as adults. Libertarians and leftists also lead less conventional lives than traditionalists in terms of geographic and job mobility, marriage, and children.

Although the salience of politics to the identity of both left- and right-wing activists persists through the 1990s, there are now competing identities as parents and professionals. As activists have aged and found meaningful work, become parents, bought homes, and settled down, activism is no longer the master identity of their youth. At this stage of the life cycle responsibilities of work and home absorb the time and energy of activists. Many former members of SDS and YAF have found jobs through which to channel their political commitment; others carry the values and lessons they learned during the 1960s to their present careers.

Ironically, although the 1980s and 1990s witnessed the triumph of conservatism and many traditionalists hold seats of political power today, many YAFers have felt disillusioned over the past twenty years as the Reagan revolution failed to meet their expectations, and as they faced the world of realpolitik. Rather than disillusionment, SDSers in contrast feel a deep sense of lost community as they no longer experience the communal bonds of the 1960s in their adult lives.

One final way that activists carry on their values and continue to shape the future of their country is through their children. As parents these activists of the left and the right, like their parents before them, are socializing their children to be vocal and concerned about the world, instilling in them their beliefs and values in order to create social change. The enduring impact of the generation of the 1960s will no doubt also be seen through this next generation as they, too, step out into the political world.

# CONCLUSION

We shall not cease from exploration
And the end of all our exploring
Will be to arrive where we started
And know the place for the first time.
—T. S. Eliot, "Little Gidding"

The generation of the 1960s is indeed a generation divided. Yet activists of the 1960s are also inevitably bound together through their shared histories. Representing fundamentally different—and even opposing— worldviews, activists share a passion for politics. Both YAF and SDS members were raised by conscious and involved parents in homes in which politics was a part of everyday life. As they reached adolescence these women and men were motivated to put their beliefs into action. Coming together with other like-minded individuals, each wing of the 1960s generation was "sucked into the vortex of social change"[1] during the dramatic historical and political events of the 1960s.

In Karl Mannheim's terms, YAF and SDS represent two polar forms of response to historical events they experienced in common. As each wing attempted to master their common destiny, they learned to interpret their world in terms of each other. In Mannheim's words, "Together they constitute an 'actual' generation precisely because they are oriented toward each other, even though only in the sense of fighting one another."[2] Yet as the 1960s progressed the divisions within this generation became more complex. Once active, these youth went through further transformations. We have seen the importance of social interaction in the development of ideology as well as in sustaining commitment to the movement. Whereas families, teachers, and community leaders were critical to the formation of political consciousness during childhood, peers became increasingly important once activists were involved. Peers in SDS and YAF acted both to solidify and push forward political beliefs and action. In addition, for libertarians and leftists, peers were vital to the process of radicalization. Frustrated by the slowness of change, disillusioned by government complicity, and horrified by repression and police brutality, peers shared experiences and endless discussions. They were fundamental to shifts in activists' beliefs and tactics. Yet peers also served as a force of constraint, leading to pressure, guilt, and, for some activists, even a world of total politics in which group expectations overwhelmed all other interests, in which politics reigned supreme above all else.

Increasingly, there were also marked divisions *within* SDS and YAF—over ideology, the Vietnam War, over the counterculture and drugs, and over feminism. Through the course of the 1960s these divisions became increasingly important until they tore both organizations apart at the end of the decade. As these internal divisions played themselves out, sectors of the left and the right converged over common beliefs and action. The countercultural New Left overlapped with the libertarian right and discovered common ground in antiwar protest and hostility toward the state, and in the use of drugs. Further, issues of gender separated members of each organization as women from both groups began forming a movement in their own interests.

This unique intersect of the left and the right speaks to the peculiarities of American political ideology in which suspicion of authority, opposition to government, and the ideals of individual freedom, decentralization, and community control are core values for segments of both left and right. Expanding Mannheim's notion of antagonistic generation-units, then, the 1960s case indicates antagonisms *within* each wing that provided an opening for a distinct new generational configuration. Although the libertarians' hopes for a unification of the libertarian Right and the decentralist New Left during the early 1970s did not last, the ideological divisions within YAF did allow the blossoming of the libertarian movement, a vibrant movement that continues to attract adherents both from the left and the right.

As SDS activists carried the voice of the generation during the 1960s, its other wing, the New Right, rose to prominence in the 1970s and 1980s. Exemplifying "the wave-like rhythm of change of the *Zeitgeist*" Mannheim discusses—first one polar tendency, and then another rises—so did the politics of the 1960s forge the way for the politics of the 1970s and 1980s. As activists reached adulthood, as they settled into occupations, their paths diverged. The main institutional bases of leftists and libertarians are social service agencies, nonprofit organizations, and educational institutions. Meanwhile, traditionalists have gained power through their base in the political world—as consultants, advisers, and as part of the "Reagan revolution." Their experiences in YAF offered them a training ground and a social network that were critical to their positions of power today. As former YAF chair Alan MacKay puts it, the 1960s was "a necessary period of trial for a conservative movement to go through in order to achieve a higher call." Alan recalls the advice he gave to young conservatives when he stepped down from YAF in the late 1960s.

> One of the things I said was "You young conservative leaders have to be prepared to become the government of the United States." In 1968–69 that was nonsense, pie in the sky, but I believed it . . . and I was right. And today those people are in Congress, the Senate, the state houses, and so on. I really challenged them to stop criticizing . . . and be prepared to run the government. "Think about what you will do when you are in charge. Stop thinking of yourself as an outsider." And we went through that period of fire and trial and being a minority and being humiliated and looked down on and ridiculed and so . . . in the '70s and certainly in the '80s, [we] have become the government of the United States, have dominated the government, and will continue to do so for the rest of the century.

Indeed the late 1970s and 1980s witnessed the triumph of YAF as YAF members and the philosophy of the organization swept Washington and captured the spirit of the times. YAF's stamp is as indelibly marked on the 1980s and 1990s as SDS's signature is on the 1960s.

Finally, there is a sense in which this generation stands divided from other generations. Having come of age during the tumultuous years of the 1960s, its members are forever intertwined through the profound experiences they shared. Having lived through exhilarating, frustrating, and terrifying times, they are bound together in common conversation, inextricably linked through their shared fate. SDS activist Bernardine Dohrn speaks to this sense of mutuality:

> [The 1960s is] an incredibly common frame of reference. . . . The older that I get, there's a common frame of reference with people our age. . . . There's something about that generation of us. So that even [when] I worked . . . in a big law firm for a woman who is exactly my age who is a lawyer . . . [who] had worked in the U.S. Attorney's office prosecuting draft resisters and [who is] a right-wing

Republican, we hit it off instantly, the moment we met. . . . Partly because there were only five women in my law school class, and I knew there were only five women in hers, and I knew how old she was right away. And we knew so much about each other . . . that we became friends. And she came and testified at my bar hearing for me. It's kind of bizarre, but I think that that's another slice of it, that's crossed political lines, that's . . . a committed generation.

In this case common experiences of gender along with a shared passion for politics created a bond, a sense of common destiny, that superseded ideology to form a base for friendship.

The transformations activists went through as a result of their participation not only creates bonds among YAF or SDS members but also inevitably links activists across ideology. They share not only a location based on age but lived through "a feast of powerful experiences," as one activist put it. These experiences were fundamental to their definition of self and acted to bind individuals together across ideology. Bernardine Dohrn speaks of being "completely stamped [by the 1960s] the way the Depression generation was stamped." Similarly, YAFer Anne Edwards says the 1960s "framed my entire life." Every one of these activists was irreversibly changed by the decade of the 1960s.

Above all, what is clear is that for members of both YAF and SDS participation in the social movements of the 1960s was a transformative experience, offering a realization of self, a way to affirm identity.[3] This identity became a core part of the self that survived beyond the 1960s. Although activists have faced competing identities connected to work and family during the 1980s and 1990s, the coherence of values and self gives their lives a sense of order. Although many YAF members have felt disillusioned as the realities of the 1980s did not match their youthful ideals, and although many SDS members continue to feel a loss of a sense of community, across the political spectrum there is a continuity in identity and meaning that signifies the enduring impact of political commitment.

# ARCHIVES AND PRIMARY SOURCES

From the Hoover Archives, Stanford University

Eric C. Bellquist Papers
Patrick Dowd Papers
Joseph Dumbacher Papers
Carl Gershman Papers
Hardin Jones Papers
Marvin Liebman Papers
New Left Collection
Frank L. Price Collection
Henry Regnery Papers

From the Young Americans for Freedom National Office—miscellaneous organizational materials (correspondence, pamphlets, documents)

From the Institute for Humane Studies—miscellaneous materials

Additional primary materials were also provided by a number of activists in this study.

**On Microfilm**

Students for a Democratic Society Papers, 1958–1970. Glen Rock, New Jersey: Microfilming Corporation of America

**Periodicals**

*Left and Right*
*The Libertarian*
*The Libertarian Forum*
*New Guard*
*New Left Notes*
*SDS Bulletin*

# NAMES AND DATES OF INTERVIEWS

## SDS MEMBERS

Jane Adams: September 17, 1990
Judy Baker: July 25, 1989
Connie Brown: November 19, 1990
Dorothy Burlage: July 23, 1989
John Brown Childs: December 17, 1990, and September, 23, 1991
Andrea Cousins: July 25, 1989
Norm Daniels: July 27, 1989
Bernardine Dohrn: September 12, 1990
Rory Ellinger: September 18, 1990
Fred Faust: September 19, 1990
Jeanne Friedman: October 27, 1990
Helen Garvy: October 23, 1990
Barbara Haber: December 6, 1990
Phil Hutchings: October 24, 1990
Mike James: September 13, 1990
Sue Jhirad: July 26, 1989
Michael Kazin: July 19, 1989, and May 2, 1991
Steve Kessler: November 10, 1990
Terry Koch: November 9, 1990, and August 5, 1991
John Maher: April 24, 1991
Aldyn McKean: November 28, 1989

Beth Oglesby: November 19, 1990
Carl Oglesby: July 24, 1989
Bob Ross: July 27, 1989
Vivian Rothstein: February 9, 1990
Naomi Schapiro: October 27, 1990
Jim Shoch: July 28, 1989
Dave Strauss: September 16, 1990
Cathy Wilkerson: March 6, 1990

## Pseudonyms

Derek Barron: June 7, 1991
Carol Christman: November 19, 1990
Cindy Decker: October 31, 1990
Lynn Dykstra: November 10, 1990
Steve Goldstein: July 22, 1989
Doug Knox: October 29, 1990
Barry Skolnick: September 14, 1990

## YAF MEMBERS

Helen Blackwell: March 21, 1990
Lynn Bouchey: March 22, 1990
Allen Brandstater: February 6, 1990
Carol Dawson: July 7, 1989, and April 29, 1991
Don Devine: March 12, 1990
Gus DiZerega: January 19, 1990
Anne Edwards: July 10, 1989
Lee Edwards: July 11, 1989
Don Ernsberger: November 19, 1989
Mary Fisk: April 30, 1991
Jo Ann Gasper: March 19, 1990
Fran Griffin: March 19, 1990
Barbara Hollingsworth: April 30, 1991
Harvey Hukari: December 7, 1990
Dave Jones: July 11, 1989
David Keene: July 20, 1989
Maggie Kohls: September 15, 1990
Louise Lacey: December 8, 1990, and December 19, 1990
Emmy Lewis: March 13, 1990

Alan MacKay: July 26, 1989, and September 20, 1991
Connie Marshner: May 2, 1991, and September 30, 1991
Jay Parker: July 13, 1989
Marick Payton: January 30, 1990
Sharon Presley: February 7, 1990
Sheldon Richman: March 20, 1990
Dana Rohrabacher: March 15, 1990
Kathy Rothschild: September 13, 1990
Jáime Ryskind: March 14, 1990
Dave Schumacher: September 1, 1989, and September 7, 1989
Kitty Smith: March 21, 1990
Scott Stanley: July 12, 1989
Mike Thompson: July 20, 1989
Dave Walter: November 20, 1989
Dawne Winter: March 14, 1990

### Pseudonyms

Marilyn Bradley: August 15, 1991
Bob Heisinger: July 17, 1989
Mitch Petry: March 13, 1990
Rob Tyler: February 6, 1990

# THE SHARON STATEMENT
(adopted in conference at Sharon, Connecticut,
September 9–11, 1960)

In this time of moral and political crisis, it is the responsibility of the youth of America to affirm certain eternal truths.

WE, as young conservatives believe:

THAT foremost among the transcendent values is the individual's use of his God-given free will, whence derives his right to be free from the restrictions of arbitrary force;

THAT liberty is indivisible, and that political freedom cannot long exist without economic freedom;

THAT the purposes of government are to protect these freedoms through the preservation of internal order, the provision of national defense, and the administration of justice;

THAT when government ventures beyond these rightful functions, it accumulates power which tends to diminish order and liberty;

THAT the Constitution of the United States is the best arrangement yet devised for empowering government to fulfill its proper role, while restraining it from the concentration and abuse of power;

THAT the genius of the Constitution—the division of powers—is summed up in the clause which reserves primacy to the several states, or to the people, in those spheres not specifically delegated to the Federal Government;

THAT the market economy, allocating resources by the free play of supply and demand, is the single economic system compatible with the requirements of personal freedom and constitutional government, and that it is at the same time the most productive supplier of human needs;

THAT when government interferes with the work of the market economy, it tends to reduce the moral and physical strength of the nation; that when it takes from one man to bestow on another, it diminishes the incentive of the first, the integrity of the second, and the moral autonomy of both;

THAT we will be free only so long as the national sovereignty of the United States is secure; that history shows periods of freedom are rare, and can exist only when free citizens concertedly defend their rights against all enemies;

THAT the forces of international Communism are, at present, the greatest single threat to these liberties;

THAT the United States should stress victory over, rather than coexistence with, this menace; and

THAT American foreign policy must be judged by this criterion: does it serve the just interests of the United States?

# NOTES

## INTRODUCTION

1. Lee Edwards, "Flag-Waving in the Flag-Burning '60s," *New Guard* 26, no. 1 (winter/spring 1989): 14.

2. Pat Korten, quoted in Bernard Weinraub, "Unrest Spurs Growth of Conservative Student Groups," *New York Times,* October 12, 1969.

3. Clancy Sigal quotes YAFer Steve Wiley as saying that up to 90 percent of U.S. conservative groups are currently staffed by YAF alumni and that many Reagan appointees also came out of YAF. See Clancy Sigal, "Doing the Right Thing," *Los Angeles Times Magazine,* April 29, 1990, 28. Also see James C. Roberts, *The Conservative Decade: Emerging Leaders of the 1980s* (Westport, Conn.: Arlington House, 1980); and John A. Andrew III, *The Other Side of the Sixties: Young Americans for Freedom and the Rise of Conservative Politics* (New Brunswick, N.J.: Rutgers University Press, 1997).

4. The best source on the history of SDS is Kirkpatrick Sale, *SDS* (New York: Vintage Books, 1973). The only book that details the origin and early years of YAF is Andrew, *Other Side of the Sixties;* as of this writing no source fully documents YAF's history during the 1960s.

5. Karl Mannheim, "The Problem of Generations," in *Essays on the Sociology of Knowledge,* ed. Paul Kecskemeti (London: Routledge and Kegan Paul, 1952), 291.

6. See Rebecca E. Klatch, *Women of the New Right* (Philadelphia: Temple University Press, 1987).

7. Glen Elder, "Age Differentiation and the Life Course," *Annual Review of Sociology* 1 (1975): 165–190.

8. Bernice L. Neugarten and Gunhild O. Hagestad, "Age and the Life Course,"

in *Handbook of Aging and the Social Sciences,* ed. Robert Binstock and Ethel Shanas (New York: Van Nostrand Reinhold, 1976), 35–55.

9. Erik Erikson, *Identity: Youth and Crisis* (New York: W. W. Norton, 1968).

10. See Richard G. Braungart, "Youth and Social Movements," in *Adolescence in the Life Cycle: Psychological Change and Social Context,* ed. Sigmund Dragastin and Glen Elder (New York: John Wiley, 1975), 255–289. Also see Kenneth Keniston, "Psychological Development and Historical Change," *Journal of Interdisciplinary History* 2 (1971): 329–345.

11. Norman B. Ryder, "The Cohort as a Concept in the Study of Social Change," *American Sociological Review* 30 (1965): 43–61.

12. Richard Flacks, *Youth and Social Change* (Chicago: Markham Publishing, 1971).

13. On post-materialist values, see Ronald Inglehart, "Post-Materialism in an Environment of Insecurity," *American Political Science Review* 75 (1981): 880–900. On growing up in the nuclear age, see Margaret Mead, *Culture and Commitment: A Study of the Generation Gap* (Garden City, N.Y.: Doubleday, 1970); also see T. Allen Lambert, "Generations and Change: Toward a Theory of Generations as a Force in Historical Process," *Youth and Society* 4 (1972): 21–46. On youth culture, see Flacks, *Youth and Social Change.*

14. There are a few scattered articles on youth of the left and right. Two of the few analysts who study both the left and right are Richard and Margaret Braungart. See, for example, Richard G. Braungart and Margaret M. Braungart, "Reference Group, Social Judgment, and Student Politics," *Adolescence* 53, no. 14 (spring 1979): 135–157; Margaret M. Braungart and Richard G. Braungart, "The Life-Course Development of Left- and Right-Wing Youth Activist Leaders from the 1960s," paper presented at the 199th Annual Scientific Meeting of the International Society of Political Psychology, Secaucus, N.J. (July 1–5, 1988); and Braungart, "Youth and Social Movements."

Even among more recent reassessments of the 1960s, virtually all of the attention is focused on the left. See, for example, Wini Breines, *Community Organization in the New Left, 1962–1968: The Great Refusal* (New York: Praeger, 1982); Todd Gitlin, *The Sixties: Years of Hope, Days of Rage* (New York: Bantam, 1987); James Miller, *Democracy Is in the Streets: From Port Huron to the Siege of Chicago* (New York: Simon and Schuster, 1987). Although Whalen and Flacks do not include student activists on the right, their follow-up study of left-wing activists compares with a subsample of students involved in sororities and fraternities; see Jack Whalen and Richard Flacks, *Beyond the Barricades: The Sixties Generation Grows Up* (Philadelphia: Temple University Press, 1989). To my knowledge the only book that focuses on the right during the 1960s is Andrew, *Other Side of the Sixties.* Since Andrew's thorough historical examination of the rise and early development of YAF stops in 1964, it never traces the internal conflicts and the overlaps between left and right during the mid to late 1960s.

15. In part the bias toward studying left-wing movements reflects the fact that the field of social movements blossomed during the late 1970s and 1980s when many former activists from the New Left began studying movements sympathetic with their own ideology. Unfortunately, the fact that right-wing move-

ments are understudied not only yields a dearth of empirical data on the right but also results in theory-building based exclusively on "progressive" movements.

16. Marvin Rintala, "Generations, Political," in *Encyclopedia of the Social Sciences*, ed. David Sills (New York: Macmillan, 1968), 6: 94.

17. Gregory Stone, quoted in Andrew J. Weigert, J. Smith Teitge, and Dennis W. Teitge, *Society and Identity: Toward a Sociological Psychology* (Cambridge: Cambridge University Press, 1986), 14.

18. Tamotsu Shibutani, *Society and Personality: An Interactionist Approach to Social Psychology* (New Brunswick, N.J.: Transaction Books, 1987), chap. 8.

19. Erikson, *Identity*, 21.

20. Scott A. Hunt, Robert D. Benford, and David A. Snow, "Identity Fields: Framing Processes and the Social Construction of Movement Identities," in *New Social Movements: From Ideology to Identity*, ed. Enrique Larana, Hank Johnston, and Joseph R. Gusfield (Philadelphia: Temple University Press, 1994), 185–208.

21. On new social movements see, for example, Alberto Melucci, "The Process of Collective Identity," in *Social Movements and Culture*, ed. Hank Johnston and Bert Klandermans (Minneapolis: University of Minnesota Press, 1995), 41–63; Alberto Melucci, "A Strange Kind of Newness: What's 'New' in New Social Movements?" in *New Social Movements: From Ideology to Identity*, ed. Enrique Larana, Hank Johnston, and Joseph R. Gusfield (Philadelphia: Temple University Press, 1994), 101–130; Jean Cohen, "Strategy or Identity: New Theoretical Paradigms and Contemporary Social Movements," *Social Research* 52, no. 4 (winter 1985): 663–716.

22. Collective identity is also a term laden with ambiguity. For varying definitions of collective identity see, for example, three studies in Aldon D. Morris and Carol McClurg Mueller, eds., *Frontiers in Social Movement Theory* (New Haven: Yale University Press): Debra Friedman and Doug McAdam, "Collective Identity and Activism," 156–173; William A. Gamson, "The Social Psychology of Collective Action," 53–76; and Verta Taylor and Nancy E. Whittier, "Collective Identity in Social Movement Communities: Lesbian Feminist Mobilization," 104–129. See also Melucci, "Process of Collective Identity."

23. See William A. Gamson, "Constructing Social Protest," in *Social Movements and Culture*, ed. Hank Johnston and Bert Klandermans (Minneapolis: University of Minnesota Press, 1995).

24. Peter L. Berger and Thomas Luckmann, *The Social Construction of Reality: A Treatise in the Sociology of Knowledge* (New York: Anchor Books, 1967), 173.

25. Anselm Strauss, *Mirrors and Masks: The Search for Identity* (Glencoe, Ill.: Free Press, 1959), 100.

26. See, for example, Jo Freeman, *The Politics of Women's Liberation* (New York: Longman, 1975); and Sara Evans, *Personal Politics: The Roots of Women's Liberation in the Civil Rights Movement and the New Left* (New York: Alfred A. Knopf, 1979).

27. The paucity of studies on female activists was one of the main reasons for my previous study on contemporary right-wing politics. See Klatch, *Women of the New Right*.

28. In addition, I conducted interviews with numerous other activists involved on the left and right who did not figure in the final sample, though their interviews informed the study.

29. In SDS the sample includes twenty-four rank-and-file members and twelve people who were part of the national leadership and/or were at the Port Huron conference, six of whom were women. The YAF sample consists of twenty-three rank-and-file members and fifteen who held national office and/or were at the founding Sharon conference of YAF, two of whom were women. Among the rank-and-file activists some were leaders or founders of local chapters.

30. This division between early and late activists was particularly important for SDS, given previous findings of differences in background between early and late activists (see Milton Mankoff and Richard Flacks, "The Changing Social Base of the American Student Movement," *Annals of the American Academy of Political and Social Science* 395 [May 1971]: 54–67). My SDS sample includes eighteen early activists (ten women and eight men), and eighteen later activists (seven women and eleven men).

31. Among the traditionalists, twelve are men and thirteen are women. Among the libertarians, nine are men and four are women. The small proportion of female libertarians reflects the reality, according to both women and men interviewed, that a much lower proportion of libertarians were female during the 1960s. In general, women on the right tended to be traditionalists. For a report on the percentage of YAFers who were libertarian, see "Young Americans for Freedom: A Philosophical and Political Profile," *New Guard* 10, no. 1 (January 1970): 21–22.

32. See, for example, Miller, *Democracy Is in the Streets;* Whalen and Flacks, *Beyond the Barricades;* and Doug McAdam, *Freedom Summer* (New York: Oxford University Press, 1988). For a review of the problems of using life histories in studying social movements, see Donatella Della Porta, "Life Histories in the Analysis of Social Movement Activists," in *Studying Collective Action,* ed. Mario Diani and Ron Eyerman (London: Sage Publications, 1992), 168–193.

33. David Thelen, "Memory and American History," *Journal of American History* 75, no. 4 (March 1989): 1121.

34. See John Bodnar, "Power and Memory in Oral History: Workers and Managers at Studebaker," *Journal of American History* 75, no. 4 (March 1989): 1201–1221.

35. Diana Gittins, quoted in Molly Andrews, *Lifetimes of Commitment: Aging, Politics, Psychology* (Cambridge: Cambridge University Press, 1991), 64.

36. Andrews, *Lifetimes of Commitment,* 65.

37. Tamara Hareven, "The Search for Generational Memory: Tribal Rites in Industrial Society," *Daedalus* (fall 1978): 137–149.

38. See, for example Joan Acker, Kate Barry, and Joke Esseveld, "Objectivity and Truth: Problems in Doing Feminist Research," *Women's Studies International Forum* 6, no. 4 (1983): 423–435; two chapters in Sandra Harding, ed., *Feminism and Methodology* (Bloomington: Indiana University Press, 1987): Sandra Harding, "Introduction: Is There a Feminist Method?," 1–14; and Dorothy Smith, "Women's Perspective as a Radical Critique of Sociology," 84–96.

## CHAPTER ONE: THE NEW AGE

1. The Intercollegiate Studies Institute (ISI) was founded in 1953 to combat campus socialists. By 1961 ISI listed 21,000 members. See *Time*, February 10, 1961, 34.

2. Caddy was state chair of the D.C. college Young Republicans; Franke was the editor of *The Individualist*, an ISI newsletter, as well as the *Campus Republican*, an official publication of the national college Young Republicans. For further discussion of the political involvement of Caddy and Franke prior to the formation of YAF, see John A. Andrew III, *The Other Side of the Sixties: Young Americans for Freedom and the Rise of Conservative Politics* (New Brunswick, N.J.: Rutgers University Press, 1997), 66–69.

3. Author's interview with Scott Stanley, July 12, 1989. Also see M. Stanton Evans, *Revolt on the Campus* (Chicago: Henry Regnery, 1961), for discussion of the origins of YAF and Andrew, *Other Side of the Sixties*, chap. 3.

4. For discussion of the background of Al Haber, see James Miller, *Democracy Is in the Streets: From Port Huron to the Siege of Chicago* (New York: Simon and Schuster, 1987), 22–40.

5. In 1905 a group of students and young professionals formed the Intercollegiate Socialist Society. The leaders of this organization included Jack London, Upton Sinclair, Clarence Darrow, and Senator Paul Douglas. A radical student group, ISS rallied across campuses in support of the American socialist movement and against imperialism and fascism. By 1913 ISS had chapters on 64 campuses. In 1917 ISS changed its name to the League for Industrial Democracy but retained its student members. By 1925 LID had 2,000 student members; a youth affiliate, Students of the League for Industrial Democracy, formed. SLID reached a peak of over 120 campus chapters during the 1920s as it distributed literature, organized aid for striking workers and the unemployed, fought against ROTC, and set up student strikes for peace. In 1935 SLID merged with the Communist-dominated National Student League to form the American Student Union, organized to oppose fascism in Europe. In 1939 the ASU fell apart over the Hitler-Stalin pact. SLID did not reorganize until 1946. By 1960 only three chapters remained—at Columbia, Yale, and Michigan—and at most a few hundred members. See Todd Gitlin, *The Sixties: Years of Hope, Days of Rage* (New York: Bantam Books, 1987), 110; Tom Hayden, *Reunion: A Memoir* (New York: Random House, 1988), 29–30; C. Clark Kissinger, "Introduction to SDS," n.d., in Students for a Democratic Society Papers, 1958–1970 (hereafter SDS Papers), reel 37 (4B: 195); and Miller, *Democracy Is in the Streets*, 28–30.

6. See Kirkpatrick Sale, *SDS* (New York: Vintage Books, 1973), 16–17.

7. Michael Harrington was a member of LID and the elder stateman of the Young People's Socialist League, a youth group that grew out of the Socialist Party of the Old Left. SNCC was one of the main civil rights organizations of the time.

8. See Miller, *Democracy Is in the Streets*, 38–39; and Sale, *SDS*, 26–27.

9. See Sale, *SDS*, 31–34, for full discussion of this incident.

10. Sale, *SDS*, 35.

11. Marvin Liebman Papers, box 108, Hoover Archives, Stanford University (hereafter Liebman Papers).

12. See quote from M. Stanton Evans in "The YAF Story," reprinted in *New Guard* 10, no. 1 (January 1970): 16.

13. M. Stanton Evans, "Recollections on the Sharon Statement," *New Guard* 10, no. 7 (September 1970): 9.

14. Although the issue of Birchers never came up at Sharon, it proved to be a source of tension throughout the 1960s. In 1965 YAF president Tom Huston purged the Birch faction from YAF. See confidential report from Randall Teague to national board of directors, November 24, 1969, in Patrick Dowd Papers, box 2, file YAF National Board: Minutes of meetings, 1970, Hoover Archives, Stanford University. Also see William Dunphy, "The YAF's Are Coming," *The Commonweal*, April 14, 1961, 74–76.

15. Directory of College Conservative Clubs, Spring, 1961, Young Americans for Freedom, Henry Regnery Papers, box 80, Hoover Archives, Stanford University.

16. Liebman Papers.

17. At the time of the Port Huron conference, SDS had 800 dues-paying members (at one dollar a year), with 2,000 scattered activists on its mailing lists. See Sale, *SDS*, 46.

18. For extensive discussion of the events and experiences during the Port Huron convention, see Gitlin, *The Sixties*, 111–126; Hayden, *Reunion*, 84–102; Miller, *Democracy Is in the Streets*, chap. 6; and Sale, *SDS*, 47–59.

19. Interestingly, James Miller reports that before drafting the Port Huron Statement, Hayden read all the titles on the SDS recommended reading list including the Declaration of Independence, the 1960 Democratic Party platform, the early manuscripts of Karl Marx, Daniel Bell, John Dewey, Dostoyevsky, Castro, and the *Sharon Statement* (emphasis mine). See Miller, *Democracy Is in the Streets*, 78.

20. The Port Huron Statement has been reprinted in many places. A full version of the document appears in the appendix of Miller, *Democracy Is in the Streets*, 329–374.

21. The term "participatory democracy" was first used by one of Hayden's teachers at the University of Michigan, Arnold Kaufman (Miller, *Democracy Is in the Streets*, 94). Miller includes an extensive discussion of the multiple meanings of the term as used by activists in SDS, and the particular ambiguity of Hayden's interpretation. Miller argues that in 1962 participatory democracy represented the ideal of "democracy of individual participation," by 1964 it meant rule by consensus, and in 1965 it was seen as a radical alternative to representative institutions. Because the term remained open to interpretation, it was able to unite people with different interests linked by a common political quest (142–148).

22. In fact, Tom Hayden wrote his graduate thesis on Mills. For discussion of the influence of Mills on Hayden as well as on other New Leftists, see Hayden, *Reunion*, 77–81, and Miller, *Democracy Is in the Streets*, 79–91.

23. See Miller, *Democracy Is in the Streets*, 119.

24. For further discussion of this dispute see Gitlin, *The Sixties*, 112; Hayden, *Reunion*, 90; and Miller, *Democracy Is in the Streets*, 116.

25. An interesting discussion of this difference between the two groups is found in Todd Gitlin, "Student Political Action, 1960–1963: The View of a Participant," September 1963, SDS Papers, reel 37 (4B: 115). Noting that unlike the left, YAF retained a close association with adult conservatives, Gitlin argues that the link allowed conservative leaders to bring uninitiated students into the real world of conservative politics. For further discussion of the evolving conflict between SDS and LID see Gitlin, *The Sixties*, 116–126; Hayden, *Reunion*, 91–93; and Miller, *Democracy Is in the Streets*, 127–135.

26. See Hayden, *Reunion*, 94–95.

27. Sale, *SDS*, 55–57.

28. Sale, *SDS*, 57.

29. Sale, *SDS*, 48–49.

30. Hayden, *Reunion*, 102.

31. Hayden, *Reunion*, 98.

32. Gitlin, *The Sixties*, 102, 107.

33. Robert Moffit, "Reflections on the Sharon Statement," *New Guard*, October 1970, 22.

34. Gitlin, *The Sixties*, 122.

35. Gitlin, "Student Political Action."

36. Hayden, *Reunion*, 98.

37. Miller, *Democracy Is in the Streets*, 122. Miller reports that the printed version of this remark (written by Tom Hayden) was omitted from the final draft of the statement owing to objection from socialists in the group.

38. Author's interview with Stan Evans, May 24, 1988.

39. Tom Hayden, "Student Social Action," March 1962, SDS Papers, reel 37 (4B: 160).

40. Roger Leed, "The Hollow Men," *The Activist* 2, no. 3 (spring 1962): 15.

41. Usher F. Ward, "The Young Americans for Freedom and the New Conservatism," n.d., SDS Papers, reel 39 (4B: 409). Also see Gitlin, "Student Political Action."

## CHAPTER TWO: BACKGROUNDS

1. Karl Mannheim, "The Problem of Generations," in *Essays on the Sociology of Knowledge*, ed. Paul Kecskemeti (London: Routledge and Kegan Paul, 1952), 298.

2. Kirkpatrick Sale argues the social base of SDS shifted during the mid- to late 1960s; in contrast to early activists, later SDSers tended to be from outside the East and tended to be non-Jewish, nonurban, from a nonprofessional class, and often without a family tradition of activism; see Kirkpatrick Sale, *SDS* (New York: Vintage Books, 1973), 204. Also see Milton Mankoff and Richard Flacks, "The Changing Social Base of the American Student Movement," *Annals of the American Academy of Political and Social Science* 395 (May 1971): 67 n 16.

3. See, for example, Richard G. Braungart, "SDS and YAF: A Comparison of Two Student Radical Groups in the Mid-1960s," paper presented at the 61st

annual meeting of the American Sociological Association, August–September 1966, Miami Beach, Florida.

4. SDS women in my study have the highest proportion (53 percent) of mothers employed during their childhood or preteenage years, followed by SDS men (39 percent of mothers employed), YAF men (33 percent), and finally, YAF women (25 percent). Except for male YAFers' mothers, at least 50 percent of all activists' mothers were employed in professional or technical jobs. However, this occupational category includes a diverse range of jobs that masks the reality that most women are actually employed in the "female sector." Half of the mothers in this category are, for example, either nurses, elementary schoolteachers, or librarians. Only a minority of mothers work in nontraditional professions, e.g., lawyer, engineer, or college professor. The second biggest job category in which mothers are employed is clerical jobs, with the remainder divided between service, blue-collar, and private household jobs.

5. These categories only reflect the background of the activists, not their present affiliation. Also, the categories do not reflect religiosity; for instance, many of the Jewish activists in SDS were raised in secular homes and did not regularly participate in religious ceremonies (see chapter discussion of religious upbringing). These differences in religious background are consistent with prior research. See Richard G. Braungart, "Status Politics and Student Politics: An Analysis of Left- and Right-Wing Student Activists," paper presented at the 1970 Annual Research Institute of the District of Columbia Sociological Society, College Park, Maryland; and Richard G. Braungart, "Youth and Social Movements," in *Adolescence in the Life Cycle: Psychological Change and Social Context,* ed. Sigmund Dragastin and Glen Elder (New York: John Wiley, 1975), 255–289.

6. Although a serious attempt was made to further diversify the sample, repeated efforts to locate other minority activists were unsuccessful. In fact, the small proportion of minorities in this study reflects the reality that many minority youth active during this period were involved on the left, primarily in organizations focused on the civil rights of their own ethnic group.

7. This difference in ethnic background between right- and left-wing activists corresponds with previous research. See, for example, Braungart, "SDS and YAF."

8. See, for example, James Donovan and Morton Shaevitz, "Student Political Activists: A Typology," *Youth and Society* 4, no. 4 (June 1973): 379–411; Braungart, "SDS and YAF"; and Braungart, "Status Politics and Student Politics," 195–209.

9. Lewis and Kraut also find a significant relationship between parents' dedication to and interest in political issues and student activism. They conclude that parents of activists across the ideological spectrum foster social consciousness and provide a model of activism by bringing political and social concerns into daily family living; see Steven H. Lewis and Robert E. Kraut, "Correlates of Student Political Activism and Ideology," *Journal of Social Issues* 28, no. 4 (1972): 131–149.

10. Contrary to Sale (*SDS;* see note 2 above), activists in this sample who joined SDS early in the 1960s were just as likely to be red-diaper babies as those joining from 1965 through 1968.

11. The monthly YAF magazine *New Guard* conducted a study of its readership in 1966 and found 54 percent were "incubated conservatives," i.e., those affected by parental conservatism as opposed to 46 percent who were "converted conservatives." See *New Guard* 6, no. 9 (September 1966): 11.

12. See, for example, Donovan and Shaevitz, "Student Political Activists"; M. Kent Jennings and Richard Niemi, "Continuity and Change in Political Orientations: A Longitudinal Study of Two Generations," *American Political Science Review* 69 (1975): 1316–1355; and James L. Wood and Wing-Cheung Ng, "Socialization and Student Activism: Examination of a Relationship," *Research in Social Movements, Conflicts and Change* 3 (1980): 21–43.

13. Richard Flacks, "The Liberated Generation: An Exploration of the Roots of Student Protest," *Journal of Social Issues* 23, no. 3 (1967): 68.

14. Of these four activists, two were Catholic, one was raised as a Baptist, and the other one grew up in an Orthodox Jewish home.

15. The activists identify religion as important even if they are no longer religiously oriented.

16. Peter L. Berger and Thomas Luckmann, *The Social Construction of Reality: A Treatise in the Sociology of Knowledge* (New York: Anchor Books, 1967), 131.

## CHAPTER THREE: THE MAKING OF AN ACTIVIST

1. See, for example, Jo Freeman, *The Politics of Women's Liberation* (New York: Longman, 1975); and Doug McAdam, *Freedom Summer* (New York: Oxford University Press, 1988).

2. The Christian Anti-Communist Crusade, organized and led by Dr. Fred Schwarz from his Long Beach, California, headquarters, was an Old Right organization prominent in the 1960s. Through television and radio, tape-recorded lectures, and mailings, Schwarz warned of the imminent Communist takeover of the world. In the mid-1960s he also led the crusade against the civil rights movement, charging it was dominated and led by a worldwide Communist revolutionary movement.

3. SDS set up ERAP projects in the ghettos of a dozen cities beginning in the fall of 1962 to help improve the conditions of life for the poor through direct action and community unions.

4. Several YAF members mentioned one of the few actions YAF took in support of civil rights: at the 1962 YAF convention held in Fort Lauderdale, Florida, when the executive director of YAF discovered the convention hotel was segregated, he threatened to cancel YAF's participation unless all delegates could register. All did register but, ironically, much of the convention's discussion centered on opposing the proposed civil rights bill.

5. Lee Edwards, "Flag-Waving in the Flag-Burning '60s," *New Guard* 26, no. 1 (winter/spring 1989): 14–23.

6. One YAFer in this sample, Alan MacKay, actually worked in the black ghetto of Roxbury during 1967 trying to match people seeking jobs with businesses in the private sector.

For an interesting discussion of Jay Parker's opposition to collectivism and the need for black capitalism see Jay Parker, "Reflections of a Black Conservative," *New Guard* 9, no. 5 (May 1969): 3–6.

7. George Wallace's 1968 presidential campaign created divisions within YAF. The editors of YAF's monthly magazine, *New Guard,* refused to accept advertisements from the Youth for Wallace organization. This action prompted thousands of southern YAF members to quit and form the National Youth Alliance. Subsequently, a YAF resolution was passed that condemned the NYA for being racist. See *YAF in the News* 2, no. 6 (March 1970), in Patrick Dowd Papers, box 3, file Newsletters, Hoover Archives, Stanford University (hereafter *YAF in the News,* date, Dowd Papers).

Similarly, in 1970 members of YAF led a boycott against Georgia governor Lester Maddox for his racist views. See *YAF in the News* 2, no. 10 (July 1970); and *YAF in the News* 2, no. 11 (August 1970), both in Dowd Papers.

8. David Keene, quoted in David S. Broder, *Changing of the Guard: Power and Leadership in America* (New York: Penguin Books, 1980), 175.

9. Edwards, "Flag-Waving."

10. Lee Edwards quoted in James C. Roberts, *The Conservative Decade: Emerging Leaders of the 1980s* (Westport, Conn.: Arlington House, 1980), 26.

11. Jim Williams, "Goldwaterism: Its Origin and Impact," 1964; and Jim Williams, "Goldwaterism and How It Grew," *SDS Bulletin* 3, no. 1 (September 1964): 1, 20–24 (both in SDS Papers, reel 39 [4B: 425 and 426]).

12. Richard Flacks, "Taking Goldwater Seriously," 1964, SDS Papers, reel 36 (4B: 93).

13. Al Haber and Barbara Haber, "Taking Johnson Seriously: A Response to Richard Flacks," 1964, SDS Papers, reel 37 (4B: 137).

14. Also, whereas only four activists on the left actually organized the SDS chapter they became involved with, one-third of activists on the right were responsible for organizing the YAF chapter they joined. Half of the YAFers who initiated chapters were female.

15. ISI was originally called the Intercollegiate Society of Individualists when it was founded in 1953 by Frank Chodorov, with William F. Buckley Jr. serving as the first president. In 1960 Buckley proposed changing the name of the organization, but the change was not official until 1966. For further discussion of this change see George H. Nash, *The Conservative Intellectual Movement in America since 1945* (New York: Basic Books, 1976), 389–390 n 90.

16. See, for example, McAdam, *Freedom Summer;* Freeman, *Politics of Women's Liberation;* David A. Snow, Louis A. Zurcher Jr., and Sheldon Ekland-Olson, "Social Networks and Social Movements: A Microstructural Approach to Differential Recruitment," *American Sociological Review* 45 (October 1980): 787–801; Bert Klandermans and Dirk Oegema, "Potentials, Networks, Motivations and Barriers: Steps towards Participation in Social Movements," in *Social Movements: Perspective and Issues,* ed. Steven M. Buechler and F. Kurt Cylke Jr. (Mountain View, Calif.: Mayfield Publishing, 1997).

17. See, for example, Lewis S. Feuer, *The Conflict of Generations: The Character and Significance of Student Movements* (New York: Basic Books, 1969);

and Stanley Rothman, Anne H. Bedlington, Phillip Isenberg, and Robert Schnitzer, "Ethnic Variations in Student Radicalism: Some New Perspectives," in *Radicalism in the Contemporary Age: Sources of Contemporary Radicalism,* ed. S. Bialer (Boulder, Colo.: Westview Press, 1977), 151–211.

18. See Doug McAdam, *Political Process and the Development of Black Insurgency* (Chicago: University of Chicago Press, 1982).

19. Hank Johnston, Enrique Larana, and Joseph R. Gusfield, "Identities, Grievances, and New Social Movements," in *New Social Movements: From Ideology to Identity,* ed. Enrique Larana, Hank Johnston, and Joseph R. Gusfield (Philadelphia: Temple University Press, 1994), 13.

20. Erik Erikson, *Identity: Youth and Crisis* (New York: W. W. Norton, 1968).

## CHAPTER FOUR: TRADITIONALISTS, ANARCHISTS, AND RADICALS

1. Kenneth Burke, quoted in Anselm Strauss, *Mirrors and Masks: The Search for Identity* (San Francisco: Sociology Press, 1969), 40. I draw on Strauss's discussion of the meaning of commitment in this section.

2. See chapter 3, note 3.

3. See Scott A. Hunt, Robert D. Benford, and David A. Snow, "Identity Fields: Framing Processes and the Social Construction of Movement Identities," in *New Social Movements: From Ideology to Identity,* ed. Enrique Larana, Hank Johnston, and Joseph R. Gusfield (Philadelphia: Temple University Press, 1994), 190.

4. Frank Meyer was a proponent of fusion between traditionalists and libertarians. For discussion of Meyer's philosophy and influence, see George H. Nash, *The Conservative Intellectual Movement in America since 1945* (New York: Basic Books, 1976).

5. Peter L. Berger and Thomas Luckmann, *The Social Construction of Reality: A Treatise in the Sociology of Knowledge* (New York: Anchor Books, 1967), 150–153.

6. Kenneth Keniston, *Young Radicals: Notes on Committed Youth* (New York: Harcourt, Brace and World, 1968), 144.

7. See Strauss, *Mirrors and Masks,* 100.

8. Bert Klandermans, "The Social Construction of Protest and Multiorganizational Fields," in *Frontiers in Social Movement Theory,* ed. Aldon D.Morris and Carol McClurg Mueller (New Haven: Yale University Press, 1992), 91–92.

9. Whalen and Flacks find police brutality to be a radicalizing factor for non-activist members of fraternities and sororities; see Jack Whalen and Richard Flacks, *Beyond the Barricades: The Sixties Generation Grows Up* (Philadelphia: Temple University Press, 1989), chap. 2. Wood and Ng also find the presence of police and the use of force drew liberal or moderate students to protest at the University of California, Berkeley; see James L. Wood and Wing-Cheung Ng, "Socialization and Student Activism: Examination of a Relationship," *Research in Social Movements, Conflicts and Change* 3 (1980): 21–43.

10. Transcript from *Making Sense of the Sixties,* no. 4, "In a Dark Time," shown January 22, 1991, on the Public Broadcasting System.

11. Todd Gitlin, *The Whole World Is Watching: Mass Media in the Making and Unmaking of the New Left* (Berkeley: University of California Press, 1980), 234.

12. Initially the Free Speech Movement at UC-Berkeley involved a united front of groups on both the left and right. In 1963 when the university administration banned the distribution of literature of all kinds from the entrance to campus, leftist groups like the Young People's Socialist League joined with College Young Republicans and Students Active Against Totalitarianism, a John Birch Society youth group, to protest the ban. By September 1964 the movement became affiliated solely with left-wing protest. I am indebted to John Mc-Claughry, a member of the College Young Republicans, for this information (personal correspondence).

13. The economist Murray Rothbard, an isolationist libertarian of the "older" generation, was an influential figure to many libertarians in the 1960s and 1970s. During the 1960s Rothbard, along with Karl Hess, led the radical libertarian anarchist revolt on the right, inspiring many antiestablishment followers among the younger generation. See, for example, Nash, *Conservative Intellectual Movement*, 313–318.

14. Doug McAdam, "Recruitment to High-Risk Activism: The Case of Freedom Summer," *American Journal of Sociology* 92, no. 1 (July 1986): 64–90.

15. A good source on surveillance of SDS that contains confidential memos of the FBI is the Frank L. Price Collection, box 26, Hoover Archives, Stanford University. These files show that from 1968 through 1970 J. Edgar Hoover targeted SDS, calling it the "militant core of New Left extremism."

16. I do not suggest that traditionalists were free from the personal costs of activism. Many faced ostracism and harassment by other students, as discussed previously.

17. See Steven H. Lewis and Robert E. Kraut, "Correlates of Student Political Activism and Ideology," *Journal of Social Issues* 28, no. 4 (1972): 131–149. Also see Riley Dunlap, "Radical and Conservative Student Activists: A Comparison of Family Backgrounds," *Pacific Sociological Review* 13 (1970): 171–181.

18. See William A. Gamson, "The Social Psychology of Collective Action," in *Frontiers in Social Movement Theory*, ed. Aldon D. Morris and Carol McClurg Mueller (New Haven: Yale University Press, 1992), 53–76.

19. Klandermans, "Social Construction of Protest," 83.

20. Gary Alan Fine, "Public Narration and Group Culture: Discerning Discourse in Social Movements," in *Social Movements and Culture*, ed. Hank Johnston and Bert Klandermans (Minneapolis: University of Minnesota Press, 1995), 127–143.

21. Andrew J. Weigert, J. Smith Teitge, and Dennis W. Teitge, *Society and Identity: Toward a Sociological Psychology* (Cambridge: Cambridge University Press, 1986), 63.

22. Verta Taylor and Nancy E. Whittier, "Collective Identity in Social Movement Communities: Lesbian Feminist Mobilization," in *Frontiers in Social Movement Theory*, ed. Aldon D. Morris and Carol McClurg Mueller (New Haven: Yale University Press, 1992), 113.

## CHAPTER FIVE: THE COUNTERCULTURE

1. The first use of the term "counterculture" was by an academic, Theodore Roszak, in his book *The Making of a Counterculture: Reflections on the Technocratic Society and Its Youthful Opposition* (Garden City, N.Y.: Anchor Books, 1969). The phrase is identified primarily with the white New Left. Other forms of counterculture, particularly incorporating elements of cultural nationalism, were aspects of black and Chicano political activism.

2. For discussion of the values embodied in the counterculture see Lauren Langman, Richard L. Block, and Ineke Cunningham, "Countercultural Values at a Catholic University," *Social Problems* 20, no. 4 (spring 1973): 521–533; D. Lawrence Wieder and Don H. Zimmerman, "Generational Experience and the Development of Freak Culture," *Journal of Social Issues* 30, no. 2 (1974): 137–161; and Jack Whalen and Richard Flacks, *Beyond the Barricades: The Sixties Generation Grows Up* (Philadelphia: Temple University Press, 1989), 11–13.

3. Whalen and Flacks, *Beyond the Barricades*, 2, 11.

4. Richard Flacks, *Making History: The American Left and the American Mind* (New York: Columbia University Press, 1988), 176.

5. Morris Dickstein, *Gates of Eden: American Culture in the Sixties* (New York: Penguin Books, 1989), chap. 7. Flacks argues rock music of the latter part of the decade expressed apocalyptic visions, hostility toward industrial society and encroaching technology, paranoia about official authority, antagonism toward conventional morality, and an affinity with non-Western spiritual traditions (Flacks, *Making History*, 183).

6. Greil Marcus, transcript from *Making Sense of the Sixties*, no. 3, "Breaking Boundaries, Testing Limits," shown on PBS January 22, 1991.

7. Langman et al. found widespread diffusion of countercultural values even among students at a conservative Jesuit university in the days following the killings at Kent State, May 4–14, 1970. See Langman et al., "Countercultural Values at a Catholic University."

8. See Flacks, *Making History*, for discussion of the history of cultural radicalism in social movements of the left.

9. See this argument in regard to postwar Britain in John Clarke, Stuart Hall, Tony Jefferson, and Brian Roberts, "Subcultures, Cultures and Class," in *Resistance through Rituals: Youth Subcultures in Post-War Britain*, ed. Stuart Hall and Tony Jefferson (London: Hutchinson, 1976), 9–74. Also see D. Lawrence Wieder and Don H. Zimmerman, "Generational Experience and the Development of Freak Culture," *Journal of Social Issues* 30, no. 2 (1974): 137–161.

10. Carl Oglesby became active in SDS at the end of 1964. In many ways he bridges the worlds of the early and later activists. Because he was thirty at the time he became active and first entered the group through friendships with the old guard, he had allegiances with older activists. Yet he was seen as a part of the new generation of activists and held populist and libertarian views that were closer to the younger group of activists.

11. See Todd Gitlin, *The Whole World Is Watching: Mass Media in the Making and Unmaking of the New Left* (Berkeley: University of California Press, 1980), chap. 4.

12. Kirkpatrick Sale, *SDS* (New York: Vintage Books, 1973), 664. From this point on SDS membership continued to escalate. By October 1966 SDS claimed 25,000 members and 265 chapters and by June 1968 membership was estimated to be anywhere between 40,000 and 100,000 with 350 chapters.

13. Gitlin, *Whole World Is Watching*, 130. Although there are no significant differences in demographic background between early and late activists in the present study, Kirkpatrick Sale argues the social base of SDS shifted during the mid- to late 1960s. In contrast to early activists, later SDSers were from outside the East, primarily from the Midwest and Southwest, and tended to be non-Jewish, nonurban, from a nonprofessional class, and often without a family tradition of political involvement (see Sale, *SDS*, 204). For further discussion of the changes pre- and post-1965 see Robert J. Ross, "Generational Change and Primary Groups in a Social Movement," in *Social Movements of the Sixties and Seventies*, ed. Jo Freeman (New York: Longman, 1983), 177–189.

14. Gitlin, *Whole World Is Watching*, 130–131. For further discussion of the anarchist tendencies within Prairie Power, written by a former national secretary of SDS, see Greg Calvert, *Democracy from the Heart: Spiritual Values, Decentralism, and Democratic Idealism in the Movement of the 1960s* (Eugene, Oreg.: Communitas Press, 1991).

15. On Prairie Power see Sale, *SDS*, 281.

16. McRobbie and Garber argue that stereotypical images of women pervaded hippie culture, e.g., the Earth Mother with baby at breast or the gentle, lyrical image of Joni Mitchell. See Angela McRobbie and Jenny Garber, "Girls and Subcultures," in *Resistance through Rituals: Youth Subcultures in Post-War Britain*, ed. Stuart Hall and Tony Jefferson (London: Hutchinson, 1976), 209–222. For further discussion of whether or not the counterculture "liberated" women see Alice Echols, *Daring to Be Bad: Radical Feminism in America 1967–1975* (Minneapolis: University of Minnesota Press, 1989), 42–43.

17. Gitlin also refers to this incident and claims that others in the national office believed marijuana was legally defensible but was a distraction and an indefensible "tactical stupidity" (Gitlin, *Whole World Is Watching*, 131 n).

18. Breines argues that the "prefigurative politics" of the New Left in itself provided new ways of being: through its own practices the movement tried to create and sustain relationships and political forms that prefigured and embodied the desired society. For instance, the New Left sought to create a community of direct, total, and personal relationships as well as communitarian counterinstitutions. See Wini Breines, *Community and Organization in the New Left, 1962–1968: The Great Refusal* (New York: Praeger, 1982).

19. Judy Smith, quoted in "The Twentieth Reunion of the Harvard-Radcliffe Strike: April 7–8, 1989" (Harvard-Radcliffe Strike Reunion Committee, 1989), 23.

20. As we'll see in chapter 7, sectarian differences toward the counterculture was one of the dividing lines at the 1969 SDS convention. In opposition to PL, the Weatherman faction tended to embrace the counterculture. Yet in the present study the numbers were split between Weatherman activists who identified with the counterculture and those who had mixed opinions.

21. Sale, *SDS*, 64.

22. Sale, *SDS*, 263–264.

23. See, for example, "Drugs: Enslaver—Not Liberator!," New Left Collection, box 62, Hoover Archives, Stanford University (hereafter New Left Collection, box [, file]).

24. "NC Supports Panthers," *New Left Notes* 4 (April 1969), in Carl Gershman Papers, box 11, file 7, Hoover Archives, Stanford University.

25. "Nixon's Unsilent Supporters," *Time*, November 21, 1969.

26. Although early and later libertarian YAF activists were equally open to the counterculture, the older generation of libertarians (outside YAF) took a firm stance against the counterculture. Murray Rothbard, for example, called the counterculture "that blight of blatant irrationality that hit the yonger generation and the intellectual world like a veritable plague." He viewed the counterculture as being hostile to reason, logic, science, technology, and progress while exalting immediate and momentary sensory awareness, advocating "dropout-ism," and upholding an image of the poverty-stricken back-to-nature noble savage. Rothbard advised, "We must eradicate the counterculture before it destroys the world" (see "The New Left, RIP," *The Libertarian Forum* 2, no. 6 [March 1970]: 2–3). Like the early SDSers, Rothbard also feared that the "cultural revolution" would alienate the middle class (see his "Ultra-Leftism," *The Libertarian Forum* 1, no. 16 [November 1969]: 2).

27. Harvey H. Hukari Jr., "Review: Odyssey 69: Freedom on a Bike?" *New Guard* 9, no. 8 (October 1969): 23–24.

28. This comment was taken from a local college paper published by YAF. See Doris Pfeiffer and Scott Harris, "Where Is America?" *The Davis Arena*, November 3, 1969.

29. David Brudnoy, "Re-Review: Hot Pornool Porn—and Propaganda," *New Guard* 9, no. 1 (January 1970): 31–32.

30. James D. Hartwell, letter to the editor, *New Guard* 9, no. 10 (December 1969).

31. Paul Willis, "The Cultural Meaning of Drug Use," in *Resistance through Rituals: Youth Subcultures in Post-War Britain*, ed. Stuart Hall and Tony Jefferson (London: Hutchinson, 1976), 106–118.

32. Wieder and Zimmerman, "Generational Experience and the Development of Freak Culture."

33. Quote from Jay Stevens, author of *Storming Heaven: LSD and the American Dream* (New York: Harper and Row, 1987), in transcript of *Making Sense of the Sixties*, no. 3, "Breaking Boundaries, Testing Limits" shown on PBS January 22, 1991.

34. Milton Mankoff and Richard Flacks, "The Changing Social Base of the American Student Movement," *Annals of the American Academy of Political and Social Science* 395 (May 1971): 54–67.

35. Gitlin, *The Sixties*, 218.

36. Rod Manis, quoted in Alan Rinzler, ed., *Manifesto: Addressed to the President of the U.S. from the Youth of America* (New York: Macmillan, 1970), 117–118.

## CHAPTER SIX: THE WOMAN QUESTION

1. Specifically, 71 percent of SDS women's fathers and 57 percent of YAF women's fathers have a college or graduate degree, 94 percent of SDS women's fathers and 80 percent of YAF women's fathers worked in higher-level white-collar jobs, and only 6 percent of SDS women's fathers and 7 percent of YAF women's fathers worked in blue-collar jobs.

2. Of the SDS women's mothers, 35 percent have at least a college degree compared to 38 percent of YAF women's mothers; none of the YAF mothers have a graduate degree.

3. For discussion of the occupations of activists' mothers, see chapter 2, note 4.

4. For discussion of women and World War II see William H. Chafe, *The American Woman: Her Changing Social, Economic, and Political Roles, 1920–1970* (New York: Oxford University Press, 1972). For discussion of women's roles during the 1950s, see Wini Breines, *Young, White, and Miserable: Growing Up Female in the Fifties* (Boston: Beacon Press, 1992).

5. See two works by Kathleen Gerson, *Hard Choices: How Women Decide about Work, Career, and Motherhood* (Berkeley: University of California Press, 1985) and *No Man's Land: Men's Changing Commitments to Family and Work* (New York: Basic Books, 1993).

6. See "YAF State Chairmen: March 1, 1966," in Patrick Dowd Papers, box 2, file YAF National Board: Memoranda, circulars, and printed matter, Hoover Archives, Stanford University (hereafter Dowd Papers YAF board memos). Similarly, a list of the California State Board of Directors of YAF as of July 11, 1969, shows eighteen men, one woman; see Patrick Dowd Papers, box 1, file YAF/California state chapter: Memoranda and circulars, Hoover Archives, Stanford University (hereafter Dowd Papers, YAF/Calif. memos).

7. Jane Adams served as national secretary in 1965–66 and Bernardine Dohrn served as interorganizational secretary in 1968–69. See Kirkpatrick Sale, *SDS* (New York: Vintage Books, 1973), 663–664. In addition, Helen Garvy served as assistant national secretary in 1963–64.

8. Sara Evans, *Personal Politics: The Roots of Women's Liberation in the Civil Rights Movement and the New Left* (New York: Alfred A. Knopf, 1979), 112. Evans argues that from the beginning SDS was based on a competitive intellectual style dominated by men (108–110) and that the skills most valued promoted male leaders (112).

9. For discussion of SDS see Evans, *Personal Politics*, 110–111. For YAF this conclusion is based on an extensive literature review of YAF materials.

10. Frinde Maher, letter to the editor, *New Left Notes* 4, no. 6 (February 1969): 2.

11. Evans, *Personal Politics*, 192.

12. "Miss YAF, April 1968," *New Guard* 8, no. 4 (April 1968).

13. "YAF Sessions," in *YAF 1968 Convention Program*, New Left Collection, box 42, file YAF.

14. See, for example, "Notes from the YAF Rally," *National Review*, March 27, 1962, 190–191.

15. See, for example, Marlene Dixon, "The Restless Eagles: Women's Liberation 1969," in *The New Women: a MOTIVE Anthology of Women's Liber-*

*ation,* ed. J. Cooke, Charlotte Bunch-Weeks, and Robin Morgan (Indianapolis: Bobbs Merrill, 1970), 32–43; Cynthia Fuchs Epstein, "Ten Years Later: Perspectives on the Women's Movement," *Dissent* (spring 1975): 169–176; Evans, *Personal Politics;* Judith Hole and Ellen Levine, *Rebirth of Feminism* (New York: Quadrangle Books, 1971).

16. Sexism within the New Left has been well documented. See, for example, Evans, *Personal Politics;* Jo Freeman, *The Politics of Women's Liberation* (New York: Longman, 1975); Robin Morgan, ed., *Sisterhood Is Powerful: An Anthology of Writings from the Women's Liberation Movement* (New York: Vintage Books, 1970); and Alice Echols, *Daring to Be Bad: Radical Feminism in America, 1967–1975* (Minneapolis: University of Minnesota Press, 1989).

17. Evans, *Personal Politics,* 115 and 166.

18. Evans, *Personal Politics,* 152.

19. Marge Piercy, "The Grand Coolie Damn," in *Sisterhood Is Powerful: An Anthology of Writings from the Women's Liberation Movement,* ed. Robin Morgan (New York: Vintage Books, 1970), 473.

20. Doug McAdam finds similar views among female SNCC volunteers. In his words, "While [these volunteers] clearly experienced subtle and not so subtle forms of sexism, they too feel the whole issue has been blown out of proportion. If SNCC failed, in gender terms, to live up to the full implications of its rhetoric, it still was far more egalitarian in its practices than American society in general" (Doug McAdam, personal correspondence, March 7, 1991).

21. See, for example, Lois Hoffman, "The Effects on Children of Maternal and Paternal Employment," in *Families and Work,* ed. Naomi Gerstel and Harriet Engel Gross (Philadelphia: Temple University Press, 1987), 362–395.

22. Nancy Whittier calls such intragenerational differences within the women's movement "micro-cohorts." See Nancy E. Whittier, *Feminist Generations: The Persistence of the Radical Women's Movement* (Philadelphia: Temple University Press, 1995).

23. For discussion of changes within SDS, see chapter 5.

24. Evans, *Personal Politics,* 113.

25. Evans, *Personal Politics,* 161–162. Also see Echols, *Daring to Be Bad,* 33.

26. Evans, *Personal Politics,* 167. In general the present findings indicate that Evans overstates the role of early SDS women in founding feminism's second wave during the late 1960s (and underestimates the role of later activists).

27. Mary King and Casey Hayden, "A Kind of Memo from Casey Hayden and Mary King to a Number of Other Women in the Peace and Freedom Movements," in *Freedom Song: A Personal Story of the 1960s Civil Rights Movement* (New York: William Morrow, 1987), appendix 3.

28. For further discussion of this see Evans, *Personal Politics,* chap. 7.

29. David A. Snow and Robert D. Benford, "Master Frames and Cycles of Protest," in *Frontiers in Social Movement Theory,* ed. Aldon D. Morris and Carol McClurg Mueller (New Haven: Yale University Press, 1992), 137.

30. See Doug McAdam, "Culture and Social Movements," in *New Social Movements: From Ideology to Identity,* ed. Enrique Larana, Hank Johnston, and Joseph R. Gusfield (Philadelphia: Temple University Press, 1994), 36–57.

31. See Evans, *Personal Politics,* 175.

## CHAPTER SEVEN: PARADISE LOST

1. See Peter L. Berger and Thomas Luckmann, *The Social Construction of Reality: A Treatise in the Sociology of Knowledge* (New York: Anchor Books, 1967), 157.

2. The Communist exclusion clause was removed from the SDS constitution at the national SDS convention in 1965.

3. See Kirkpatrick Sale, *SDS* (New York: Vintage Books, 1973), 333, for further discussion of PL's programs.

4. For further discussion see Sale, *SDS,* 397, 508–509, 533–534.

5. Sale, *SDS,* 456; also see 263–264.

6. Greg Calvert, quoted in Todd Gitlin, *The Sixties: Years of Hope, Days of Rage* (New York: Bantam Books, 1987), 383.

7. The text of a resolution proposed by Mike Klonsky, entitled "Toward a Revolutionary Youth Movement," originally appeared in the December 23, 1968, issue of *New Left Notes.*

8. See Sale, *SDS,* 509–510.

9. Sale, *SDS,* 559.

10. See Alice Echols, *Daring to Be Bad: Radical Feminism in America, 1967–1975* (Minneapolis: University of Minnesota Press, 1989); and Sara Evans, *Personal Politics: The Roots of Women's Liberation in the Civil Rights Movement and the New Left* (New York: Alfred A. Knopf, 1979).

11. See Echols, *Daring to Be Bad,* 44.

12. Eventually some of the women in this group formed two other entities, Off Our Backs and Furies.

13. The Revolutionary Union was a Maoist sect originally called the Bay Area Revolutionary Union. Eventually RU split into the Revolutionary Communist Party (which took the traditional Marxist line that class was primary) and Venceremos (which saw racial minorities as a distinct agent of change).

14. Echols, *Daring to Be Bad,* 132–133.

15. Sale, *SDS,* 536–537.

16. Jack Whalen and Richard Flacks, *Beyond the Barricades: The Sixties Generation Grows Up* (Philadelphia: Temple University Press, 1989), 72–74.

17. Berger and Luckmann, *Social Construction of Reality,* 145.

18. Berger and Luckmann, *Social Construction of Reality,* 159.

19. For further discussion of the insularity of those in Weatherman, see Sale, *SDS,* 584 and 624–625.

20. See Sale, *SDS,* 563–579; Gitlin, *The Sixties,* chap. 17; and Echols, *Daring to Be Bad,* 120–134.

21. Mike Klonsky, then national secretary, reported that the SDS bid for a 1969 convention site was turned down by at least thirty-seven colleges and universities and at least twenty-five meeting halls, parks, and camps. Klonsky claimed the FBI and Justice Department threatened college administrators with character assassination and loss of federal education funds if they allowed the convention on their campus. See "Radical Students Pick Chicago as Convention Site," *San Diego Union,* June 12, 1969, A-6. By 1969 the national image of SDS promoted by the media was of an extremist organization determined to overthrow

the U.S. government. See Todd Gitlin, *The Whole World Is Watching: Mass Media in the Making and Unmaking of the New Left* (Berkeley: University of California Press, 1980).

22. See Echols, *Daring to Be Bad,* 122–123.

23. See Jack A. Smith, "SDS Ousts PLP," *Guardian,* June 28, 1969, 1–3, 11.

24. Sale, *SDS,* 573.

25. Gitlin, *The Sixties,* 387–388.

26. Sale, *SDS,* 574–579.

27. Richard Flacks, "Making History vs. Making Life: Dilemmas of an American Left," *Working Papers* 2, no. 2 (summer 1972): 68.

28. See Mike Klonsky, Noel Ignatin, Marilyn Katz, Sue Eanet, and Les Coleman, "Revolutionary Youth Movement II" in "Debate Within SDS: RYM-II vs. Weatherman," 1969, SDS Papers, reel 38 (4B: 280).

29. See Sale, *SDS,* 587, for discussion of other incidents of violence between PL and Weatherman.

30. Lee Edwards, "The Other Sixties: A Flag-Waver's Memoir," *Policy Review,* fall 1988, 64.

31. Ron Kimberling, "Vietnam: A Libertarian View," *The Forty-Niner* (student newspaper published at Cal State, Long Beach), October 15, 1969.

32. A statement issued jointly by Stokely Carmichael, the chairman of SNCC, and Carl Oglesby, then president of SDS, could as easily have come from the libertarian right. It read: "We are opposed to a system under which a group of men can compel another man who has had no voice in their decision to renounce his liberty and risk his life-blood for a cause which is not his. . . . In a supposedly 'free society' conscription is a form of legalized enslavement of the worst kind." See "SNCC/SDS Joint Draft Statement" read before House Committee on Armed Services, *New Left Notes* 1, no. 25 (July 8, 1966).

33. See, for example, "The Movement Grows," *The Libertarian* 1, no. 5 (June 1969): 1–2.

34. Bill Steel, quoted in Lowell Ponte, "The Libertarian Link," *Penthouse,* November 1970, 72.

35. The case of Don Meinshausen illustrates the radical shift some libertarians made, to view government as the main enemy. Meinshausen became active in YAF at Essex County College in Newark in September 1968. Working for the House Internal Security Committee (formerly HUAC), he infiltrated SDS to spy on the left and find connections between SDS and the Communist Party. He became an SDS organizer and grew close to people in the Anarchist Caucus of SDS. He was also influenced by conversations with Karl Hess and was getting more and more into drugs. The day before he was supposed to testify on his activities as a paid infiltrator of SDS, Meinshausen drafted a statement condemning the committee, Congress, and the U.S. government: "During my membership in SDS I learned of a much more dangerous organization which has seized and destroyed more lives and property than SDS ever could—I am speaking about the U.S. government." He said he hoped to persuade delegates at the national YAF convention not to fight SDS but to join it in fighting the government. See Donald Meinshausen, "Statement by Donald Meinshausen," read before the House Internal Security Committee, August 6, 1969; I am indebted to Don Meinshausen for

giving me a copy of this statement. Also see "Informer on SDS Vexes House Unit," *New York Times,* August 16, 1969, 52; and "The Changeling: Interview with Don Meinshausen," in *Decade of Crisis: America in the Sixties,* ed. Andrew Kopkind and James Ridgeway (New York: World Publishing, 1968), 269–278.

36. Quoted in J. M. Cobb, "Young Authoritarians for Freedom," *The Libertarian Connection,* February 1970. Also see William F. Buckley Jr., "Conservatism Revisited," *New Guard* 10, no. 7 (September 1970): 14.

37. Karl Hess, "The Death of Politics," *Playboy,* March 1969, 185.

38. "State of the Student, State of the University: Corporate Liberalism on Campus," from SDS chapter at Indiana University, SDS Papers, n.d. Also see Greg Calvert, *Democracy from the Heart: Spiritual Values, Decentralism, and Democratic Idealism in the Movement of the 1960s* (Eugene, Oreg.: Communitas Press, 1991).

39. David Friedman, quoted in Alan Rinzler, ed., *Manifesto: Addressed to the President of the U.S. from the Youth of America* (New York: Macmillan, 1970), 52. David Friedman wrote a regular column from a libertarian perspective ("The Radical") in *New Guard* and founded the Harvard Society of Individualists.

40. Sale also mentions ex-YAFers who ended up joining SDS by 1967 (Sale, *SDS,* 352).

41. Gus DiZerega, "Opening to the Right," *New Left Notes* 2, no. 10: 6–8.

42. Carl Oglesby and Richard Shaull, *Containment and Change: Two Dissenting Views of American Foreign Policy* (New York: Macmillan, 1967).

43. Author's personal correspondence with Carl Oglesby, May 19, 1989.

44. Oglesby and Shaull, *Containment and Change,* 166–167.

45. Carl Oglesby, "Notes on a Decade Ready for the Dustbin," *Liberation,* August–September 1969, 5–19.

46. Phillip Abbott Luce quoted in George Fox, "Counter-Revolution," *Playboy,* n.d., 179; reprinted in *YAF in the News* (March 1970), in Dowd Papers. Luce is the only activist I found who crossed over from SDS to YAF. He was a leading figure in Progressive Labor in SDS until January 1965. During that time he was indicted by the government for leading illegal student trips to Cuba; later he was acquitted. At the end of a long process of reevaluating his goals and beliefs he became a leader within YAF, both speaking and writing about the dangers of the left. In the early 1970s he wrote a newsletter, "The Pink Sheet on the New Left," to inform members of Congress, law enforcement officers, and others about leftist activities. See Frank L. Price Collection, box 15, Hoover Archives, Stanford University; and Phillip Abbott Luce, "Against the Wall: On Leaving the Left Behind," *New Guard* 9, no. 8 (October 1969): 13–15.

47. Ron Docksai, quoted in "Free Campus News Service Release," October 2, 1970.

48. Flyer entitled "The Blue Button: Support Peace on Campus," n.d., Dowd Papers, YAF/Calif. memos.

49. "YAF Plans Campaign on Campus Violence," *Morning Register* (Santa Ana, Calif.), n.d. See *YAF in the News: A News Summary of YAF* 2, no. 10 (July 1970), Dowd Papers, YAF board memos.

50. See "YAF and The Right Scene," *New Guard* 10, no. 6 (summer 1970): 30–33; "YAF Students to Sue Colleges That Close," *Boston Herald-Traveler,* n.d., in Patrick Dowd Papers, box 3, Hoover Archives, Stanford University; and Annual Report 1970 in "From the National Chairman: YAF's Rendezvous with Destiny: 1970–71," Dowd Papers, YAF board memos.

51. "SDS: Foreign Agent?" *YAF in the News* 2, no. 7 (April 1970), Dowd Papers.

52. See Bernard Weinraub, "Unrest Spurs Growth of Conservative Student Groups," *New York Times,* October 12, 1969; "Trial of Three Set for January 6," *Baltimore Morning Sun,* n.d., in *Maryland YAF in the News* 1, no. 2; "Fight Erupts at University of Maryland SDS Rally," *Maryland YAF in the News* 1, no. 2; and Kenneth Reich, "Conservatives Strike Back on US Campuses," *Los Angeles Times,* March 2, 1969.

53. Memo from Pat Dowd to California YAF chapter chairmen, March 12, 1969, Dowd Papers, YAF/Calif. memos.

54. Quoted in Ponte, "Libertarian Link," 72.

55. Letter from Pat Dowd entitled "A Nation-Wide Mailing to Leaders of YAF," n.d., Dowd Papers, YAF/Calif. memos.

56. Letter from Donald Ernsberger to Mrs. Marquita Maytag, August 1, 1969, Patrick Dowd Papers, box 1, file Letters received, 1968–69, Hoover Archives, Stanford University (hereafter Dowd Papers, letters received, date).

57. See Jerome Tuccille, "Report from St. Louis: The Revolution Comes to YAF," *The Libertarian Forum* 1, no. 12 (September 1969): 3; and Jerry W. Venters, "Young Americans Remain in Traditionalist Grip," *St. Louis Post Dispatch,* September 2, 1969.

58. Tuccille, "Report from St. Louis," 3; and Cobb, "Young Authoritarians for Freedom."

59. Murray Rothbard, "Listen, YAF," *The Libertarian Forum* 1, no. 10 (August 1969): 2.

60. Jerome Tuccille, *Radical Libertarianism: A Right-Wing Alternative* (New York: Bobbs-Merrill, 1970), 101–102.

61. "Young Conservatives Hear Buckley Speech," *St. Louis Post Dispatch,* August 29, 1969.

62. Tuccille, *Radical Libertarianism,* 103.

63. Cobb, "Young Authoritarians for Freedom."

64. See Cobb, "Young Authoritarians for Freedom"; Venters, "Young Americans Remain in Traditionalist Grip"; and Tuccille, "Report from St. Louis."

65. Flyer from "Libertarian Caucus," n.d., Dowd Papers, YAF/Calif. memos.

66. Venters, "Young Americans Remain in Traditionalist Grip."

67. "Use 'Economic Muscle,' Conservatives Are Told," *St. Louis Post Dispatch,* August 30, 1969.

68. Tuccille, *Radical Libertarianism,* 106; also see Cobb, "Young Authoritarians for Freedom."

69. Jerome Tuccille, *It Usually Begins with Ayn Rand* (San Francisco: Cobden Press, 1971), 104.

70. Cobb, "Young Authoritarians for Freedom."

71. Cobb, "Young Authoritarians for Freedom."

72. Tuccille, "Report from St. Louis."

73. Tuccille, *Radical Libertarianism,* 107–109.

74. Minutes of the national board of directors meeting, St. Louis, August 31, 1969, Patrick Dowd Papers, box 2, file YAF National Board: Printed matter and reports, Hoover Archives, Stanford University (hereafter Dowd Papers, YAF board reports).

75. Resolution submitted by C. William George, New Jersey YAF vice chair and introduced by Ron Docksai, national secretary, n.d., Dowd Papers, YAF board memos.

76. Minutes from YAF board meeting, Washington, D.C., October 3–5, 1969.

77. "California Libertarian Report: Post-Convention issue no. 1," ed. Bill Steel and Ron Kimberling, n.d., Dowd Papers, YAF board reports.

78. Memo from Randall Teague to national board of directors, October 24, 1969, Dowd Papers, YAF board reports.

79. Letter from Patrick Dowd to Wayne Thorburn, October 23, 1969, Patrick Dowd Papers, box 1, file Letters sent, 1969–70, Hoover Archives, Stanford University (hereafter Dowd Papers, letters sent, date).

80. Letter from Berl Hubbell to Patrick Dowd, October 31, 1969, Dowd Papers, letters received, 1969–70.

81. Ponte, "Libertarian Link."

82. James E. Bylin, "Rightists for Liberty (or Maybe Anarchy)," *Wall Street Journal,* April 28, 1970; and Ponte, "Libertarian Link," 72.

83. "Stanford Conservatives Break with National Organization," November 6, 1969, Dowd Papers, YAF board memos.

84. James McNabb Jr., "Stanford YAF Goes Up in Smoke; Free Campus Movement Born," *Palo Alto (Calif.) Times,* n.d., Dowd Papers, YAF board memos.

85. Flyer distributed by the Radical Libertarian Alliance, n.d., New Left Collection, box 39, file Libertarian.

86. "Fire and Sandstone: The Last Radical Guide to Stanford," prepared by Stanford Radical Caucus and the New Left Project, n.d., 43, New Left Collection, box 37, file SDS-Stanford.

87. Letter from Patrick Dowd to David Keene, December 6, 1969, Dowd Papers, letters sent, 1969–70; and *YAF in the News* 2, no. 4 (December 1969), Dowd Papers.

88. Marin Walker, "Looking for a New Utopia," *Manchester Guardian Weekly,* March 27, 1971.

89. Letter from Patrick Dowd to David Keene, December 6, 1969, Dowd Papers, letters sent, 1969–70.

90. Confidential memo from Randall Teague to national board of directors, September 19, 1969, Dowd Papers, YAF board reports.

91. SIL merged with the Society for Rational Individualism, a Randian group headed by Jarret Wollstein in Maryland.

92. John F. Morrison, "Son of Old Right," *Philadelphia Magazine,* 1970, 112.

93. Murray Rothbard, "SDS—Two Views. II: Continue the Struggle," *The Libertarian Forum* 1, no. 8 (July 1969): 3.

94. Earl Francis was a "heroic individualist martyr to the U.S. government." The government refused to recognize his homesteading claim to a gold mine and ordered him off the land and his house blown up. Francis complied, blowing himself up too. See "The Movement Grows," *The Libertarian* 1, no. 5 (June 1969): 1–2.

95. See Gus DiZerega, "Opening to the Right," *New Left Notes* 2, no. 10: 8.

96. Phone conversation with Carl Oglesby, May 14, 1990.

97. Ponte, "Libertarian Link," 72–73.

98. Dana Rohrabacher, quoted in "Split on the Right Wing of Young Republicans," *Eastside Sun,* October 23, 1969, Dowd Papers, YAF board memos.

99. Ed Royce went on to serve as a member of Congress from California.

100. Ponte, "Libertarian Link," 25–27.

101. "YAF and the Right Scene," *New Guard* 10, no. 8 (October 1970): 32–33; and C. S. Horn, "YAF 10: Reunion in Sharon," *National Review,* October 6, 1970.

102. M. Stanton Evans, "YAF at Twenty: The Conservative Mainstream," *National Review,* October 31, 1970, 1326.

103. William A. Gamson, "The Social Psychology of Collective Action," in *Frontiers in Social Movement Theory,* ed. Aldon D. Morris and Carol McClurg Mueller (New Haven: Yale University Press, 1992), 64–65.

104. Max Heirich, "Change of Heart: A Test of Some Widely Held Theories about Religious Conversion," *American Journal of Sociology* 83, no. 3 (November 1977): 653–680.

105. David A. Snow, E. Burke Rochford Jr., Steven K. Worden, and Robert D. Benford, "Frame Alignment Processes, Micromobilization, and Movement Participation," in *Social Movements: Perspectives and Issues,* ed. Steven M. Buechler and F. Kurt Cylke (Mountain View, Calif.: Mayfield Publishing, 1997), 221.

## CHAPTER EIGHT: PICKING UP THE PIECES

1. See Alice Echols, *Daring to Be Bad: Radical Feminism in America: 1967–1975* (Minneapolis: University of Minnesota Press, 1989).

2. During the late 1960s some SDS members recognized the dilemma activists faced as they grew older and had to make decisions about their work lives. In July 1967 some older activists organized a Radicals in the Professions conference in Ann Arbor to address vocations for radicals. In November they began printing a monthly publication, entitled "Radicals in the Professions Newsletter," with the intent "to attempt to provide post-student radicals with a forum for exchange of information and ideas about the whole question of lifelong Movement work." See "Radical Education Project," February 1969, in Frank L. Price Collection, box 18, folder SDS, Hoover Archives, Stanford University. Also see "Radicals in the Professions," reprinted from *Our Generation* (October 1967), Hardin Jones Papers, box 31, file SDS 1965–1968, Hoover Archives, Stanford University; and Barbara Haber and Al Haber, "Getting By with a Little Help from Our Friends," 1967, SDS Papers, reel 37 (4B: 132).

3. Of these SDSers, 71 percent of the women and 42 percent of the men had established or were headed toward professional careers.

4. Carl Oglesby, transcript from *Making Sense of the Sixties,* no. 5, "Picking Up the Pieces," shown on PBS, January 23, 1991.

5. Kirkpatrick Sale, *SDS* (New York: Vintage Books, 1973), 622–623.

6. Aldyn McKean, "The Twentieth Reunion of the Harvard-Radcliffe Strike: April 7–8, 1989" (Harvard-Radcliffe Strike Reunion Committee, 1989), 38.

7. For further discussion of ties between ACU and YAF, see John A. Andrew III, *The Other Side of the Sixties: Young Americans for Freedom and the Rise of Conservative Politics* (New Brunswick, N.J.: Rutgers University Press, 1997), 213–214.

8. Lauren Smith also served as one of the defense attorneys for Richard Nixon.

9. See "McKenna's Gold Comes from the Mud," *New Guard* 10, no. 1 (January 1970): 6–9.

10. I use the term "pro-family," which its adherents chose to describe their movement. Those opposed to the movement call it the "anti-feminist" movement or associate it with the religious right.

11. The American Legislative Exchange Council was founded in 1973 to help "elected representatives throughout the nation share ideas and legislative proposals in all areas of public policy" and serve as a "forum for the exchange of sound, imaginative ideas. These are ideas for reducing and controlling the bureaucracy, lowering the tax burden and safeguarding precious individual liberties" (American Legislative Exchange Council, "1981 Annual Report," 4).

12. For further discussion of the similarities and differences between libertarian feminism and other feminists, see Rebecca E. Klatch, *Women of the New Right* (Philadelphia: Temple University Press, 1987).

13. Sharon Presley, "Libertarianism and Feminism," Association of Libertarian Feminists; reprinted from the May 2, 1974, "Opinion" in *Majority Report* (personal copy donated by Sharon Presley).

14. Robert W. Stewart, "Rohrabacher's 'Wild' '60s Songs Surface," *Los Angeles Times,* September 26, 1992. After reviewing old lyrics of Rohrabacher's songs, Stewart comments that the choice of targets—the police, military, and politicians—seem ironic, given Rohrabacher's image as a right-wing congressman who strongly supported the Gulf War, drug testing of congressional staffers, and tough crime statutes.

15. In contrast to SDS, men were much more likely than women to go on to graduate school. By the end of the decade *all* of the libertarian men had enrolled or completed their graduate degrees, as had 58 percent of traditionalist men, 50 percent of libertarian women, and only 23 percent of traditionalist women.

## CHAPTER NINE: ADULT LIVES

1. In addition to the formal interviews, from time to time I received further information on activists' lives through phone conversations and correspondence. A substantial number of activists reviewed the manuscript pages before publication and added new information during 1997–1998.

2. I have drawn here upon ideas from Viktor Gecas and Jeylan T. Mortimer,

"Stability and Change in the Self-Concept from Adolescence to Adulthood," in *Self and Identity: Perspectives across the Lifespan*, ed. Terry Honess and Krysia Yardley (London: Routledge and Kegan Paul, 1987), 265–286; and Andrew J. Weigert, J. Smith Teitge, and Dennis W. Teitge, *Society and Identity: Toward a Sociological Psychology* (Cambridge: Cambridge University Press, 1986).

3. Jack Whalen and Richard Flacks, *Beyond the Barricades: The Sixties Generation Grows Up* (Philadelphia: Temple University Press, 1989), 264.

4. Fran Griffin, "Press Strategy Memo from Griffin Communications," n.d.

5. See, for example, Whalen and Flacks, *Beyond the Barricades*; N. J. Demerath, Gerald Marwell, and Michael Aiken, *Dynamics of Idealism: White Activists in a Black Movement* (San Francisco: Jossey-Bass, 1971); James Max Fendrich and Kenneth Lovoy, "Back to the Future: Adult Political Behavior of Former Student Activists," *American Sociological Review* 53 (1988): 780–784; James Max Fendrich and Robert W. Turner, "The Transition from Student to Adult Politics," *Social Forces* 67 (1989): 1049–1057; Dean Hoge and Teresa Ankney, "Occupations and Attitudes of Former Student Activists 10 Years Later," *Journal of Youth and Adolescence* 11 (1982): 355–371; M. Kent Jennings, "Residues of a Movement: The Aging of the American Protest Generation" *American Political Science Review* 81 (1987): 367–382; Doug McAdam, *Freedom Summer* (New York: Oxford University Press, 1988); Doug McAdam, "The Biographical Consequences of Activism," *American Sociological Review* 54 (1989): 744–760; Alberta J. Nassi and Stephen I. Abramowitz, "Transition or Transformation? Personal and Political Development of Former Berkeley Free Speech Movement Activists," *Journal of Youth and Adolescence* 8 (1979): 21–35; Stephen I. Abramowitz and Alberta J. Nassi, "Keeping the Faith: Psychological Correlates of Activism Persistence into Middle Adulthood," *Journal of Youth and Adolescence* 10 (1981): 507–523.

6. Bernardine Dohrn, quoted in Susan Chira, "Same Passion, New Tactics: At Home with Bernardine Dohrn," *New York Times*, November 18, 1993.

7. John Kifner, "28-Year-Old Snapshots Are Still Vivid, and Violent," *New York Times*, August 26, 1996.

8. This category includes people who are on second or even third marriages.

9. Specifically, 79 percent of SDS men are married compared to only 35 percent of SDS women; similarly, 56 percent of libertarian men are married compared to 25 percent of libertarian women.

10. At the time of the interviews 50 percent of libertarian women, 24 percent of SDS women, and 23 percent of traditionalist women were currently divorced as compared to 33 percent of libertarian men, 17 percent of traditionalist men, and 10 percent of SDS men. Yet if we include in the number of people who were "ever divorced" those who subsequently remarried, the gap between libertarians and traditionalists closes. Overall, 46 percent of libertarians had divorced compared to 40 percent of traditionalists and 26 percent of SDS members. In short, traditionalists' belief in the sanctity of marriage vows does not make them more likely to remain in first marriages than other activists.

11. Doug McAdam found a similar "marital gap" among women and men who participated in Freedom Summer. He argues that white women volunteers in the civil rights movement remained more radical politically than their male

counterparts, contributing to their marginality. See McAdam, *Freedom Summer,* 220–223.

12. Other YAF activists have come out as gay in the past number of years including the first chairman of YAF, former congressman Bob Bauman; Doug Caddy, another influential early YAFer; Arizona congressman Jim Kolbe; and one of the older generation of conservative leaders who helped found YAF, Marvin Liebman. To date I know of no acknowledged lesbian YAF members. While traditionalists generally reject homosexuality and libertarians advocate gay rights, all these gay YAF activists are traditionalists and none of the libertarian activists I interviewed or met identified themselves as gay.

13. See Richard Flacks, *Making History: The American Left and the American Mind* (New York: Columbia University Press, 1988), chap. 3.

14. For further discussion of the demographic consequences of activism see Doug McAdam, "Social Movements as a Force for Demographic Change," in *How Movements Matter,* ed. Marco Giugni, Doug McAdam, and Charles Tilly (Minneapolis: University of Minnesota Press, 1998).

15. The only activist in the study who married "across organizations" was SDSer Doug Knox, whose wife was involved in Young Republicans and worked in the national office of YAF during college; both became libertarians. Subsequent to the interview, the couple separated.

16. Library Court was initiated by Paul Weyrich in 1977 to form a "pro-family coalition." Meetings were held bimonthly to discuss tactics, with more than twenty national organizations participating. See Allen Hunter, "In the Wings: New Right Ideology and Organization," *Radical America* 15 (spring 1981): 119–120. For further discussion of Connie Marshner's role as leader of the pro-family movement see Rebecca E. Klatch, *Women of the New Right* (Philadelphia: Temple University Press, 1987).

17. Two other traditionalist women are home schooling their children as well. Home schooling is embraced by the pro-family movement *and* by a segment of the countercultural New Left. See, for example, Mitchell Stevens, "Neo-Institutionalism and Social Movement Research: Hierarchy and Autonomy in the Home Education Movements," unpublished paper.

18. The other most recognized national leader of the pro-family movement in this sample, Jo Ann Gasper, quit her job in the Department of Education once her fifth child was born. She, too, realized that family had to come before her career.

19. Lee Edwards, "Flag-Waving in the Flag-Burning '60s," *New Guard* 26, no. 1 (winter/spring 1989): 23.

20. Robert W. Stewart, "Rohrabacher's 'Wild' '60s Songs Surface," *Los Angeles Times,* September 26, 1992.

21. Also see Edwards, "Flag-Waving in the Flag-Burning '60s."

22. Erik Erikson, *Identity: Youth and Crisis* (New York: W. W. Norton, 1968).

23. See Gecas and Mortimer, "Stability and Change in the Self-Concept."

24. Amos Handel, "Perceived Change of Self among Adults: A Conspectus," in *Self and Identity: Perspectives across the Lifespan,* ed. Terry Honess and Krysia Yardley (London: Routledge and Kegan Paul, 1987), 320–337. Noting that individuals who perceive themselves as having radically changed had in fact en-

countered a higher number of critical experiences in the past, e.g., changes in marital partner, jobs, etc., Handel concludes that a life history's factual nature and its subjective interpretation are both significant in self-perceived change.

25. For further discussion of former YAFers in top government and political posts, see John A. Andrew III, *The Other Side of the Sixties: Young Americans for Freedom and the Rise of Conservative Politics* (New Brunswick, N.J.: Rutgers University Press, 1997), 217–220.

26. For further discussion of the sense of dislocation felt by participants in the civil rights, student, and feminist movements, see McAdam, *Freedom Summer,* chap. 6; Whalen and Flacks, *Beyond the Barricades,* chap. 4; and Nancy E. Whittier, *Feminist Generations: The Persistence of the Radical Women's Movement* (Philadelphia: Temple University Press, 1995), chap. 3.

27. Among the few studies about the children of 1960s activists on either the left or the right, one finds that white women civil rights activists raise their children with humanistic attitudes. See Rhoda Lois Blumberg, "White Mothers as Civil Rights Activists: The Interweave of Family and Movement Roles," in *Women and Social Protest,* ed. Guida West and Rhoda Lois Blumberg (New York: Oxford University Press, 1990), 177–178.

28. See Chira, "Same Passion, New Tactics."


## CONCLUSION

1. Karl Mannheim, "The Problem of Generations," in *Essays on the Sociology of Knowledge,* ed. Paul Kecskemeti (London: Routledge and Kegan Paul, 1952), 303.

2. Mannheim, "Problem of Generations," 307.

3. For further discussion of social movement participation as a realization of the self see William A. Gamson, "The Social Psychology of Collective Action," in *Frontiers in Social Movement Theory,* ed. Aldon D. Morris and Carol McClurg Mueller (New Haven: Yale University Press, 1992), 56.

# INDEX